Disassembling Code
IDA Pro and SoftICE

DISASSEMBLING
CODE
IDA Pro and SoftICE

alist

VLAD PIROGOV

A-LIST, LLC
295 East Swedesford Rd.
PMB #285
Wayne, PA 19087
702-977-5377 (FAX)
mail@alistpublishing.com
http://www.alistpublishing.com

This book is printed on acid-free paper.

Disassembling Code IDA Pro and SoftICE

By Vlad Pirogov

ISBN 1931769516

Printed in the United States of America

06 07 7 6 5 4 3 2 1

A-LIST, LLC, titles are available for site license or bulk purchase by institutions, user groups, corporations, etc.

Book Editor: Julie Laing

Contents

Preface

Modifying somebody else's code is unethical and even may be illegal. Long ago, when MS-DOS was the prevailing operating system, I wrote a small resident printer driver. At that time, the problem of localizing code or reencoding printers was urgent. One year later, I located my driver in use by some other company. This driver was installed by a Mister X. However, Mister X didn't limit himself to installing the driver. That person also modified the copyright information, specifying that the driver's author was himself. I do not feel angry about that occasion anymore, although a feeling of resentment still remains. Thus, I understand very well the feelings of software developers whose programs have been illegally reverse-engineered and modified.

However, ignoring reality is not the right behavior. To efficiently protect their programs, developers must know the cracker's toolset. Furthermore, in addition to negative effects, attacks on protection systems, worms, and computer viruses have some positive effect, because their existence makes software developers pay more attention to security and develop protection mechanisms more carefully. To a certain extent, attacks on software and computer systems play the role of stimulators for the software's "immune system," although indisputably on a large scale they can result in a virus epidemic harming many users or even ruining their computer systems. This book provides some examples of reverse engineering and of patching executable code. Note that all of these examples are intended for educational purposes only.

There are other reasons for investigating executable code. Understanding the internal mechanisms of executable code operation, and the way in which individual structures of high-level programming languages are converted into Assembly commands, is important for writing more efficient and highly-optimized programs. Often, low-level debugging is required for understanding the causes of random errors that occur at run time. Finally, every professional programmer must be curious and willing to understand how his or her programs operate. Isn't it interesting to discover how the source code of a program written in C++ or Delphi is transformed after it is processed with a compiler? Thus, all examples provided in this book are aimed at achieving positive goals and in no case at performing illegal actions.

When planning this book, I didn't intend to write an official textbook (although such textbooks are few and the time has come for them to be written). Rather, I tried to provide materials that I have accumulated during my long years of professional activity. In the future, I hope to write a textbook on the basis of this book. I'll do this with pleasure.

This book pays the most attention to such powerful tools of executable code investigation as the IDA Pro disassembler and the SoftIce debugger. These tools are characterized by practically unlimited capabilities, and hopefully you'll add them to your armory.

This book contains lots of reference materials. This is possibly a typical programming style that manifests itself in attempts to write a universal, all-sufficient program (which, by the way, remains an unattainable dream). I support the opinion that only few books do not force the reader to undertake, every ten pages, a long search in other books and on the Internet.

When writing this book, I oriented it toward operating systems from the Windows NT/2000/XP/2003 family. Nevertheless, lots of materials provided here will be applicable for the Windows 9x operating systems, although I didn't test my materials on this platform.

Most examples considered in this book relate to the C++ programming language and the Microsoft Visual C++ compiler, although there are some examples related to Borland C++ 5.0. The Pascal language and the Delphi compiler are paid less attention. You might ask why I use such a limitation. The answer is that I chose the classical language and the most powerful and popular compiler.

Target Audience

This book is not intended for readers who have no programming experience. If you program in some high-level programming language but are not acquainted with Assembly, you'll need to consult some book dedicated to Assembly programming from time to time. Most examples provided here are written in C++, so programmers should not encounter any difficulties understanding these examples.

I hope that this book will be useful to everyone interested in the internal mechanisms of program operation and willing to understand how high-level programming language constructs are converted to machine commands. In other words, this book is intended for all IT professionals interested in code investigation and the secrets of programming.

Acknowledgments

I would like to express my thanks to Igor Shishigin, who offered me the opportunity to write this book. I enjoyed working on it and hope that it will be useful to you.

Chapter 1:

INTRODUCTION TO DISASSEMBLING

The *assembler* and the *disassembler* are two sides of the same coin. The assembler converts the source code of the program written in Assembly language into the binary code, and the disassembler converts the binary module into a sequence of Assembly commands. Thus, for analysis of the disassembled code it is necessary to know machine commands, their binary format, and their Assembly representation. Also, it is important to understand the structure of data representation in computer memory, as well as to know the structure of programs written for the Windows operating system. All of these topics will be covered in this chapter.

1.1. Representing Information in Computer Memory

The main goal of this section is to describe how numeric data are stored in computer memory.

1.1.1. Investigating the Memory

Consider a simple program written in the C programming language (Listing 1.1).

NOTE

All C programs will be compiled using the Microsoft Visual C++ compiler (which is supplied as part of Visual Studio .NET 2003). In my opinion, this is the best C++ compiler available. Special cases will be mentioned individually.

The program in Listing 1.1 must output the contents of the memory area, starting from the block that stores the variable value. This memory area, sent to any device, is called the *dump*. The program outputs to the screen the memory area that stores variables.

Listing 1.1. A simple program that outputs the memory dump

```
#include <stdio.h>
#include <windows.h>
int k = 0x1667;
BYTE   *b = (BYTE*)&k;
void main()
{
        int j = 0;
        printf("\n%p    ", b);
        for(int i = 0; i < 400; i++)
        {
                printf("%02x   ", *(b++));
                if(++j == 16&&i<398)
                {
                        printf("\n");
                        j = 0;
                        printf("%p    ", b);
                };
        };
        printf("\n");
};
```

Compile the program, then start command-line session and run it. The console screen would display a table made up of hexadecimal (hex) numbers (Fig. 1.1).

Judging by the memory pattern, it contains data in addition to the value of the k variable, which is 0x1667 (the least significant byte of the word has the smallest address). What are these data? How is it possible to understand these tables of hex numbers? I will begin by covering issues that advanced users might consider elementary — namely, with representation of numbers in computer memory. Most readers that have mastered these concepts can skip *Sections 1.1.2* and *1.1.3*.

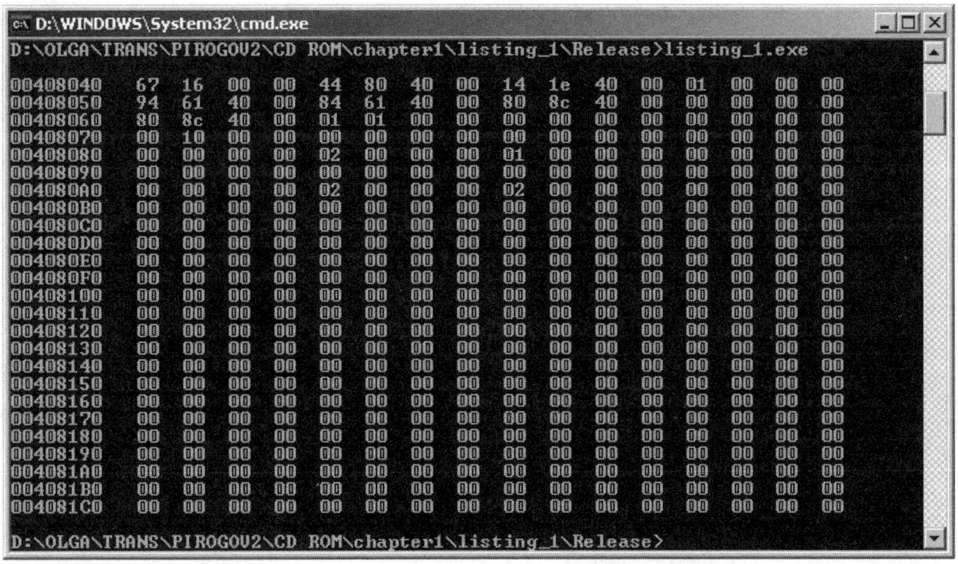

Fig. 1.1. Memory dump displayed by the program presented in Listing 1.1

1.1.2. Scales of Notation

Decimal Notation

Most individuals have known the decimal scale of notation from childhood. It is natural and traditional. Binary notation is not as natural for humans, but it is natural for computers. Computer memory is made up of elements that can be in one of two possible states. One of the states is conventionally designated as zero, and the alternative state is one. As a result, all information in memory is written as binary numbers, or sequences of ones and zeros. In addition, computer memory is divided into blocks, each block containing eight items. These blocks are called memory cells or *bytes*. A single digit in binary notation is called a *bit* (bit stands for binary digit). Thus, each memory cell is made up of eight binary digits, or 8 bits.

Recall that decimal system numbers are base 10 numbers. This means that every decimal system number can be represented as a sum of the powers of ten, where the number positions serve as coefficients. Consider the following example:

$$4567 = 4 \times 10^3 + 5 \times 10^2 + 6 \times 10^1 + 7 \times 10^0$$

In other words, every digit's contribution depends on the position that it takes. The position of the digit depends on the ordinal number counted from right to left, starting from zero. Such numeral systems are also called positional numeral systems.

Binary Notation

Binary notation is also a positional numeral system. Thus, any binary number can be represented in the form of a sum of the powers of two, for example:

$$11101001 = 1 \times 2^7 + 1 \times 2^6 + 1 \times 2^5 + 0 \times 2^4 + 1 \times 2^3 + 0 \times 2^2 + 0 \times 2^1 + 1 \times 2^0$$

This method of writing binary numbers is actually the method of converting it to another numeral system. For example, if you carry out these actions in decimal system notation, you'll obtain 233.

Converting a decimal system number into the binary representation is somewhat more difficult. This can be done according to the following algorithm:

1. Divide the given number by two and take the remainder as the next most significant bit.
2. If the result is greater than one, return to step 1.
3. The binary number is composed of the last result of division (the most significant bit) and all remainders from the division.

For instance, consider conversion of the number 350 to binary notation:

$$
\begin{array}{r}
350\ \underline{|2} \\
\underline{350}\ 175\ \underline{|2} \\
0\ \underline{174}\ 87\ \underline{|2} \\
1\ \underline{86}\ 43\ \underline{|2} \\
1\ \underline{42}\ 21\ \underline{|2} \\
1\ \underline{20}\ 10\ \underline{|2} \\
1\ \underline{10}\ 5\ \underline{|2} \\
0\ \underline{4}\ 2\ \underline{|2} \\
1\ \underline{2}\ 1 \\
0
\end{array}
$$

As the result of the preceding computations, it is obtained that the binary representation of the decimal system number 350 is 101011110.

To ensure that numbers in different notations can be adequately distinguished in Assembly programs, a single-character B suffix is used for designating binary numbers. For decimal system numbers, the D suffix is used, which can be omitted. For hex numbers, the H suffix is used. For example: 10000B, 345H, 100, etc.

By analogy with decimal fractions, it is possible to consider binary fractions. For example, the binary number 1001.1101 can be represented as follows:

$$1 \times 2^3 + 0 \times 2^2 + 0 \times 2^1 + 1 \times 2^0 + 1 \times (1/2^1) + 1 \times (1/2^2) + 0 \times (1/2^3) + 1 \times (1/2^4)$$

A binary fraction can also be converted into decimal notation by simply using arithmetic operations. For example, to convert the number 1001.1101 into a decimal number, it is necessary to carry out all operations specified in the binary number representation. As a result, you'll obtain the following number in decimal notation: 9.8125.

Decimal fractions are also easily converted into binary notation. The integer and fractional parts of the number are converted separately. The algorithm for converting the whole part of the number was already covered. The fractional part is converted as follows:

1. Multiply the fractional part by two (the system base).
2. In the resulting number, separate the integer part (this will be either zero or one). This will be the first digit after the decimal point in the binary numeral system.
3. If the fractional part of the resulting number is not zero, return to step 1; otherwise, terminate computation. It is possible to specify the computation's precision — in other words, the number of digits after the decimal point — and terminate computations when this precision is achieved.

Now, consider a practical example of converting the decimal system number into the binary representation. Assume that it is necessary to convert 105.406 into binary notation. The algorithm of converting the integer part of the number has already been considered. Thus, 105 in binary representation equals 1101001. To convert the fractional part, use the algorithm just considered. The sequence of computations is presented here. Note that in this example it was necessary to stop the computation when a precision of nine characters after the decimal point was reached.

$$0.406 \times 2 \qquad 0 \times (1/2^1)$$
$$0.812 \times 2 \qquad 1 \times (1/2^2)$$
$$0.624 \times 2 \qquad 1 \times (1/2^3)$$
$$0.248 \times 2 \qquad 0 \times (1/2^4)$$
$$0.496 \times 2 \qquad 0 \times (1/2^5)$$
$$0.992 \times 2 \qquad 1 \times (1/2^6)$$
$$0.984 \times 2 \qquad 1 \times (1/2^7)$$
$$0.968 \times 2 \qquad 1 \times (1/2^8)$$
$$0.936 \times 2 \qquad 1 \times (1/2^9)$$

As a result of this computation, you'll find out the following:

$$105.406 \approx 1101001.011001111$$

Thus, converting decimal system numbers into the binary notation, in which they are stored in the computer memory, is an additional factor of precision loss.

Hexadecimal Numeral System

The hex numeral system is more compact than the decimal numeral system. Numbers in hex numeral systems are easily converted into the binary system, and vice versa. Finally, the hex numeral system corresponds to the computer memory's architecture considerably better than any other notation. Sixteen hex digits are used for designating numbers: 0, 1, 2, 3, 4, 5, 6, 7, 8, 9, A, B, C, D, E, and F. The method of converting numbers from a decimal to a hex system, and vice versa, is similar to the method described in the previous section; the only difference is that in this case the system base is 16 instead of 2. Hopefully, you will easily derive the required algorithms on your own.

Consider the method of converting numbers from hex system into the binary system, and vice versa. The main principle here is exceedingly simple: Four digits of a binary number, a *quaternion*, correspond to one digit of a hex number, and vice versa. Fig. 1.2 demonstrates the conversion of the 10101101 binary number to a hex number.

Fig. 1.3 illustrates backward conversion of the hex number 14A into a binary format.

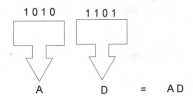

Fig. 1.2. Converting a binary number to a hex number

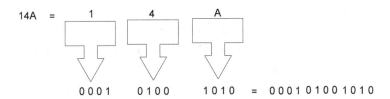

Fig. 1.3. Converting a hex number to a binary number

As already mentioned, the hex numeral system, out of all numeral systems, best maps to the computer memory's architecture. The computer memory is easily divided into cells containing 8 bits each. However, 8 bits corresponds to two hex digits. For example, 1345H will take two memory cells, the least significant cell (according to the convention) will contain 45H, and the most significant cell will store 13H.

The conversion of fractions from the hex numeral system to the binary numeral system, and vice versa, is easy; you do this in the same way as for integer numbers. The fractional part, like the integer part, is converted according to the following principle: One hex digit corresponds to four binary digits. Consider the binary number 101.10001 and convert it into hex notation. According to this rule, the result will be as follows: $101 \geq 0101 \geq 5$. Furthermore, the fractional part can be represented as follows: $10001 \geq 10001000 \geq 88$ (note that in fractional part, all quartets of digits are counted from left to right). As a result, the 101.10001 binary number corresponds to 5.88 in hex notation. As in the integer part, conversion of the fractional part is reduced to dividing the binary digits into quaternions and padding incomplete quaternions with zeros (from left to right).

1.1.3. Representing Numbers in Computer Memory

Unsigned Integer Numbers

The principle of representing unsigned integer numbers in computer memory is trivial:

1. The number must be converted to the binary numeral system.
2. It is necessary to determine the memory size required to store that number. As already mentioned, the most convenient way of doing this is to convert the number into hex notation, after which the amount of memory required for storing this number will be immediately clear. According to convention, memory is allocated by single memory cells (bytes), double cells (words), and quadruple cells (4 bytes, or a double word). Assembly language provides special directives for reserving memory for storing numeric constants and variables:

- `Name1 DB value 1 ; Reserve 1 byte`
- `Name2 DW value 2 ; Reserve 2 bytes`
- `Name3 DD value 3 ; Reserve 4 bytes`
- `Name4 DQ value 4 ; Reserve 8 bytes`
- `Name5 DT value 5 ; Reserve 10 bytes`

When dealing with variables, which usually will be the case, it is necessary to determine the range, within which the variable value would change, and reserve the memory for storing this variable on the basis of the obtained information. Because contemporary Intel processors are oriented toward operations over 32-bit numbers, the best approach for the moment is to orient them toward variables of the same dimensions.

Consider the fragment of some C program, shown in Listing 1.2.

Listing 1.2. A fragment of a program written in C

```
BYTE e = 0xab;

WORD c = 0x1234;

DWORD b = 0x34567890;

__int64 a = 0x6178569812324572;
```

This fragment defines four variables: the e 1-byte variable, the c 2-byte variable, the b 4-byte variable,[i] and the a 8-byte variable. Using the program presented in Listing 1.1, output the memory area where these variables are stored. You'll obtain the following sequence of bytes:

ab 00 00 00 34 12 00 00 90 78 56 34 00 00 00 00 72 45 32 12 98 56 78 61

Consider this sequence of bytes carefully. You should find all of the variables without difficulties. The most important conclusions that can be drawn by studying this sequence of bytes are as follows.

☐ As you should recall, in Listing 1.1 the memory contents were displayed from the lower (least significant) to the higher (most significant) address. Thus, the least significant bytes of all numbers (variables) take the least significant addresses of the word. The least significant word in a double word, in turn, takes the smaller address. Finally, in a 64-bit variable, the least significant double word must take the smaller address. This issue is important for analysis of the binary code. Later, you'll be able to identify variables in one glance at the memory region.

☐ As you can see, all variables require a memory size that is a multiple of a 4-byte value. After each initialized variable, the compiler inserts a special directive for alignment by a 32-bit boundary (Align 4). However, the situation is not that simple, and alignment might be different with a different order of variables. This topic will be covered in more detail in *Section 3.1.1*.

Examples

Thus, a 16-bit number, such as A890H, will be stored in memory as the following sequence of bytes: 90 A8. A 32-bit number, such as 67896512H, will be stored as 12 65 89 67. Finally, a 64-bit number, F5C68990D1327650H, for example, will be stored as 50 76 32 D1 90 89 C6 F5.

Signed Numbers

Because the memory contains only binary digits, it would be logical to dedicate a separate bit for storing the number sign. For example, if you have one memory

---

[i] BYTE is simply unsigned char, WORD is unsigned short int, and DWORD is unsigned int. Definitions of these data types can be found, for example, in the windows.h file.

cell, you'll be able to use arithmetic operations over the numbers ranging from −127 to +127 (11111111 to 01111111). This approach won't be too bad; however, it would be necessary to introduce separate addition operations for signed and unsigned numbers. There is an alternative method of introducing signed numbers. In the algorithm of building such numbers, a certain number is known to be positive and a number with the inverse sign is easily found: $a + (-a) \equiv 0$.

When working with a set of single-byte numbers, it is natural to consider that 1 equals the 00000001 binary number. By solving the equation $00000001 + x = 00000000$, you'll obtain a result that at first glance seems paradoxical: $x = 11111111$. In other words, using this alternative approach, −1 must be considered equal to 11111111 (255 in the decimal system equivalent and FF in hex). Now, it is time to elaborate on this theory. Obviously, $-1 - (1) = -2$. Therefore, according to this theory, −2 must be equal to 11111110 and 00000010 must represent +2. Check whether these figures correspond to the previously described theory, and you'll see that 11111110+00000010 = 00000000. Thus, the self-evident identity is true: $+2 + (-2) = 0$. This means that the chosen approach is consistent and the process can be continued (Table 1.1).

Table 1.1. Signed single-byte numbers

Positive number	Binary representation	Negative number	Binary representation
+0	00000000	−0	00000000
+1	00000001	−1	11111111
+2	00000010	−2	11111110
+3	00000011	−3	11111101
+4	00000100	−4	11111100
+5	00000101	−5	11111011
...	. . .	...	. . .
+120	01111000	−120	10001000
+121	01111001	−121	10000111
+122	01111010	−122	10000110

continues

Table 1.1 Continued

Positive number	Binary representation	Negative number	Binary representation
+123	01111011	−123	10000101
+124	01111100	−124	10000100
+125	01111101	−125	10000011
+126	01111110	−126	10000010
+127	01111111	−127	10000001
+128	Doesn't exist within the limits of 1 byte	−128	10000000

Consider Table 1.1 more carefully. What was the result of elaborating this theory? The signed numbers can range from −128 to +127.

Thus, a single-byte number can be interpreted both as a signed and as an unsigned number. According to the first approach (signed), 11111111 will equal −1; with unsigned numbers, it will equal 255. Thus, everything depends on the chosen interpretation. The most interesting fact is that addition and subtraction are carried out according to the same method for both signed and unsigned numbers. Therefore, the processor has only one command for each operation: ADD and SUB. When executing a specific operation. There might be overflow or carry to the nonexistent bit;[i] however, this topic deserves separate consideration. This problem could be solved by reserving one or more memory cells. All of these considerations can be easily extended to 2- and 4-byte numbers. Thus, the maximum unsigned 16-bit number equals 65,535, and signed numbers belong to the range from −32,768 to +32,767.

Another interesting issue relates to the most significant bit. As you can see, this bit can be used to determine the sign. However, this bit is not entirely isolated and participates with the other bits in forming the number value.

Having the skills to navigate signed and unsigned numbers is important for an investigator of software code. For example, having encountered commands such as cmp eax, 0FFFFFFFEh, it is necessary to bear in mind that this might be the cmp eax, -2 command.

---

[i] It can be easily proven that simultaneously representation of signed and unsigned numbers is possible because the number size is limited by 1 or more bytes.

Consider the sequence of variables shown in Listing 1.3.

Listing 1.3. A sequence of different variables

```
signed char e = -2;
short int c = -3;
int b = -4;
__int64 a = -5;
```

As you can see, all variables shown in this listing are signed variables with negative values. When displaying the memory block containing these variables, the following sequence of bytes will be obtained:

```
FE 00 00 00 FD FF 00 00 FC FF FF FF 00 00 00 00 FB FF FF FF FF FF FF FF
```

Thus, the value of an 8-bit variable set to −2 in computer memory is represented as FEh, the value of a 16-bit variable set to −3 is represented by the FFFDh sequence, and the value of a 32-bit variable set to −4 is represented as FFFFFFFCh. Finally, a negative 64-bit variable set to −5 is represented as follows: FFFFFFFFFFFFFFFBh. Recall that when representing a 64-bit variable, the 4 least significant bytes must be located at an address smaller than the most significant bytes.

Real Numbers

To use real numbers in commands of the Intel processor (the arithmetic coprocessor[i]), they must be represented in computer memory in the *normalized form*. In general, the normalized form of a number appears as follows:

$$A = (NS) \times M \times N^q$$

Here, *NS* designates the number sign; *M* stands for *mantissa*, which usually meets the <1 condition; *N* is the base of the numeral system; and *q* is the exponent, which might be positive or negative. Numbers represented this way are often called *floating-point numbers*. Consider a practical example of a floating-point number. Try to represent 5.75 in the normalized form. First, it is necessary to convert

---

[i] Starting with Intel 486, the arithmetic coprocessor is an integral, built-in part of the microprocessor.

this number into the binary notation. This task is trivial: 5 in binary notation will be represented as `1001`, and 0.75 equals (1/2) + (1/4). In other words, $5.75 = 1001.11\,B$. Furthermore, $1001.11\,B = 1.00111 \times 2^3$. Thus, the normalized number will comprise the following components: $NS = +1$, $M = 1.00111$, $N = 2$, and $q = 3$. Note that when using such a representation, the first number of the mantissa always equals one; consequently, it is possible to do without storing it. Intel format is based on this possibility. In addition, it is necessary to bear in mind that the q exponent is stored in the memory in the form of a sum with a certain number, to ensure that it is always positive. The Intel processor can work with the following three types of real numbers:

❑ *Short real number* — For storing a short real number, 32 bits are allocated. Bits 0–22 are reserved for the mantissa. Bits 23–30 are intended for storing the q exponent added to the number 127. The last bit, bit 31, is intended for storing the number sign (if this bit is set to one, then the number is negative; otherwise, the number is positive).

❑ *Long real number* — Here, 64 bits are allocated for storing such a number. Bits 0–51 are reserved for storing the mantissa. Bits 52–62 are intended for storing the q exponent added to 1024. The last bit, bit 63, determines the number sign (if this bit is set to one, then the number is negative; otherwise, the number is positive).

❑ *Extended real number* — For storing such numbers, 80 bits are allocated. Bits 0–63 are intended for storing the mantissa. Bits 64–78 store the q exponent added to 16,383. The last bit, bit 79, is intended for storing the number sign (if this bit is set to one, then the number is negative; otherwise, the number is positive).

Consider a practical example illustrating representation of a floating-point number in the memory. Assume that the following variable is declared in some program written in C:

```
float a = -80.5;
```

The `float` type corresponds to the short real number. This means that its memory representation will take 32 bits. Now, try to view the memory using the standard approach. Here are 4 bytes that represent the previously mentioned number:

```
00  00  a1  c2
```

To make this representation easily understandable, convert it into the binary representation:

```
00000000 00000000 10100001 11000010
```

To make this representation more understandable, rewrite it starting from the most significant byte to emphasize the mantissa, exponent, and sign:

```
11000010 10100001 00000000 00000000
```

Now, separate the mantissa. Recall that 23 bits are allocated for storing it. Thus, the following binary number will be obtained: 0100001. Note that mantissa bits are counted starting from the most significant one (in this case, this is bit 22). The trailing zeros are discarded because the whole mantissa is located to the right of the decimal point. However, the obtained number doesn't represent the mantissa exactly. As already mentioned, the first number of the mantissa is always equal to one; consequently, there is no need to store it. Thus, when using Intel representation, this one should be restored. Therefore, the following number will represent the mantissa: 1.0100001B. The sign of the whole number is negative because bit 31 is set to one. As relates to the exponent, it must be obtained from the 10000101B binary number. In decimal system representation, this will equal 133. To obtain the exponent for a short real number, subtract 127 from this value; the result will be 6. Thus, to obtain a real fractional number from the mantissa, the decimal point must be shifted six positions to the right. The result will be 1010000.1B. In hex notation, this is 50.8H; if you convert this number to decimal notation, the result will be 80.5.

To have hands-on practice, consider the following sequence of bytes:

```
00  80  FB  42
```

Try to prove that this sequence of bytes corresponds to the representation of 125.75.

On the basis of the material in this section, it is possible to conclude that if real numbers are used in a program, they might become approximate before any actions are carried out over them. This is because all real numbers must be normalized before they can be written into the memory.

Binary-Coded Decimals

Binary-coded decimal (BCD) notation is a special method of representing decimal numbers in computer memory. In this case, each of the digits of an unsigned decimal number is represented as the 4-bit binary equivalents (nibbles). The Intel processor supports two types of such numbers: packed and unpacked.

❑ Every digit of a packed number is encoded by a nibble (4 bits, or half a byte). In this case, the 4 most significant bits contain the most significant digit. Thus, a byte can contain a number ranging from 0 to 99. For example, 56 will be represented as `01010110B`.

❑ Each digit of an unpacked number is encoded by a single byte. In this case, only the 4 least significant bits store digits and the 4 most significant bits must contain zeros. Thus, 1 byte can contain a number from 0 to 9.

BCDs are rarely used in programming nowadays; therefore, I won't consider this topic further.

1.2. Intel Pentium Processor Commands and Registers

This section is dedicated to the overview of the Intel Pentium commands and registers. This material is useful if you will be investigating executable code. The information provided here will be helpful not only for beginners but also for experienced users. It can be used as a reference that is always handy.

1.2.1. Pentium Microprocessor Registers

The Pentium microprocessor comprises general-purpose registers, the flags register, segment registers, control registers, system address registers, and debug registers. The `EIP` register, which also is known as the instruction pointer, deserves special mention. It always contains the address of the executable command relative to the start of the segment. This register cannot be accessed directly; however, lots of commands change its contents indirectly — for example, the commands that pass control.

General-Purpose Registers

The list of general-purpose registers includes the following:

❑ EAX = (16 + AX = (AH + AL))
❑ EBX = (16 + BX = (BH + BL)).

- ❑ ECX = (16 + CX = (CH + CL))
- ❑ EDX = (16 + DX = (DH + DL))
- ❑ ESI = (16 + SI)
- ❑ EDI = (16 + DI)
- ❑ EBP = (16 + BP)
- ❑ ESP = (16 + SP)

The EAX, EBX, EDX, and ECX registers are called working registers. Note that of all these registers have subregisters. For example, the first 16 bits of the EAX register are designated as AX. The least significant byte, AX, is in turn designated as AL, and the most significant bit is AH. The EDI and ESI registers are called index registers. They play a special role in index operations. The EBP register is usually employed for addressing parameters and local variables in the stack. The ESP register is the stack pointer that is automatically modified by PUSH, POP, RET, and CALL; however, it is rarely used explicitly. The ESI, EDI, ESP, and EBP registers also have subregisters. For example, the first 16 bits of the EDI register are designated as DI.

Flags Register

The flags register contains 32 bits. The bit values used by this register are as follows:

- ❑ Bit 0, carry flag (CF) — This bit is set to one if in the course of addition or multiplication there was a carry from the most significant bit or if a bit was borrowed in the course of subtraction.
- ❑ Bit 1 — One.
- ❑ Bit 2, parity flag (PF) — This bit is set to one if the least significant byte of the result contains an even number of ones; otherwise, this bit is set to zero.
- ❑ Bit 3 — Zero.
- ❑ Bit 4, auxiliary carry flag (AF) — This bit is set to one if there was a number was carried (or borrowed) from the third bit into bit 4.
- ❑ Bit 5 — Zero.
- ❑ Bit 6, zero flag (ZF) — This bit is set to one if the result of the operation is zero; otherwise, this bit is set to zero.
- ❑ Bit 7, sign flag (SF) — This bit equals the most significant bit of the result of the previous operation.
- ❑ Bit 8, trap flag (TF) — Setting this flag to one results in INT 3 being called after each command. This flag is used by debuggers in real mode.

❑ Bit 9, interrupt flag (IF) — Resetting this flag to zero results in the microprocessor ceasing to accept interrupts from external devices.

❑ Bit 10, direction flag (DF) — This flag is taken into account in string operations. If the flag is set to one, the address is automatically decremented in string operations.

❑ Bit 11, overflow flag (OF) — This bit is set to one if the result of the operation over a signed number has exceeded the allowed limits.

❑ Bits 12 and 13, input/output privilege level (IOPL) — These bits define the privilege level required to allow the code to execute input/output commands and other privileged commands.

❑ Bit 14, nested task flag (NT).

❑ Bit 15 — Zero.

❑ Bit 16, resume flag (RF) — This flag is used with the debug breakpoint registers.

❑ Bit 17, virtual mode flag (VM)— In protected mode, this flag enables the virtual 8086 mode.

❑ Bit 18, alignment control flag (AC) — If this flag is set to one, exception 17 is thrown if an unaligned operand is accessed.

❑ Bit 19, virtual function of the IF flag (VIF) — This flag works in the protected mode.

❑ Bit 20, virtual interrupt pending flag (VIP).

❑ Bit 21, identification command availability flag.

❑ Bits 22–31 — Must be zero.

Segment Registers

Segment registers include CS, the code segment; DS, the data segment; SS, the stack segment; and ES, GS, and FS, auxiliary registers. All segment registers are 16-bit registers. Segment registers are intended to participate in forming the memory address either directly or using selectors that point to a certain structure (in descriptors table) that determines the segment, in which the address being formed is located.

Control Registers

The list of control registers includes the following:

❑ The CR0 register:

   ● Bit 0, protection enabled flag (PE) — Switches the processor to protected mode.

- Bit 1, monitor coprocessor flag (MP) — Causes exception 7 with each WAIT command.
- Bit 2, coprocessor emulation (EM) — Causes exception 7 with each coprocessor command.
- Bit 3, task switching flag (TS) — Determines whether or not the given coprocessor context relates to the current task. It causes exception 7 when executing the next coprocessor command.
- Bit 4, extension type — Indicates support for coprocessor instructions (ET).
- Bit 5, numeric error (NE) — Enables native mechanisms for reporting coprocessor errors.
- Bits 6–15, reserved.
- Bit 16, write protect (WP) — Enables write protection at the supervisor privilege level.
- Bit 17, reserved.
- Bit 18, alignment mask (AM) — Enables automatic alignment checking.
- Bits 19–28, reserved.
- Bit 29, not write-through (NW) — Disables write-through for writes that hit the cache or invalidation cycles.
- Bit 30, cache disable (CD) — Prevents the cache from filling.
- Bit 31, paging (PG) — Enables paging when set to one.

❑ The CR1 register is reserved for future use.

❑ The CR2 register stores the 32-bit linear address, at which the last page fault occurred.

❑ In the CR3 register, the 20 most significant bits store the physical base address of the page directory table. Other bits are as follows:

- Bit 3, page level write transparent (PWT) — Controls the write-through or write-back page caching policy.
- Bit 4, page-level cache disable (PCD) — Controls caching of the current page directory.

❑ The CR4 register:

- Bit 0, virtual 8086 mode extensions (VME) — Enables interrupt- and exception-handling extensions in virtual 8086 mode when set to one.
- Bit 1, protected-mode virtual interrupts (PVI) — Enables hardware support for a virtual interrupt flag (VIF) in protected mode when set to one.

- Bit 2, time stamp disable (TSD) — Restricts the execution of the RDTSC instruction to procedures running at privilege level 0.
- Bit 3, debugging extensions (DE) — Enables breakpoints on accessing input/output ports.
- Bit 4, page size extensions (PSE) — Enables 4-MB pages when set to one.
- Bit 5, physical address extension (PAE) — Enables the paging mechanism to reference at least 36-bit physical addresses when set to one.
- Bit 6, machine-check enable (MCE) — Enables the machine-check exception when set to one.
- Bit 7, page global enable (PGE) — Enables the global page feature when set to one.
- Bit 8, performance-monitoring counter enable (PCE) — Enables execution of the RDPMC instruction for programs or procedures running at any protection level when set to one.
- Bit 9, operating system support for FXSAVE and FXRSTOR instructions (OSFXSR) — Enables the FXSAVE and FXRSTOR instructions to save and restore the contents of the XMM and MXCSR registers, along with the contents of the x87 floating-point unit (FPU) and MMX registers, when set to one.

System Address Registers

These registers are used in the protected mode of Intel processors. The Windows operating system also operates in this mode.

- ❑ GDTR — This is a 6-byte register containing the linear address of the global descriptor table (GDT).
- ❑ IDTR — This is a 6-byte register containing the 32-bit linear address of the interrupt descriptor table.
- ❑ LDTR — This is a 10-byte register containing the 16-bit selector (index) for GDT and an 8-byte descriptor.
- ❑ TR — This is a 10-byte register containing the 16-bit selector for GDT and the entire 8-byte descriptor from GDT, describing the task state segment (TSS) of the current task. TSS is a segment of special format that contains all required information about the given task, and a special field that ensures task interactions and intercommunications.

Debug Registers

- ❑ DR0–DR3 — These registers store the 32-bit linear addresses of the breakpoints. The operating mechanism of these registers is as follows: Any address formed by a program is compared with the addresses stored in the debug registers. If a match is encountered, the processor generates the debug exception (INT 1).

❒ DR6 (equivalent to DR4) — This register reflects the checkpoint status. Bits of this register are set according to the debug conditions that have caused the debug exception. Significant bits of this register are as follows:

- Bit 0, breakpoint condition detected (B0) — If this bit is set to zero, this indicates that the last exception has occurred when the breakpoint determined in DR0 was reached.
- Bit 1 — This bit is similar to B0 but in relation to the DR1 register.
- Bit 2 — This bit is similar to B0 but in relation to the DR2 register.
- Bit 3 — This bit is similar to B0 but in relation to the DR3 register.
- Bit 13, debug register access detected (BD) — Protects debug registers.
- Bit 14, single step (BS) — If this bit is set to one, the exception was generated because the trap flag (bit 8 in flags register) is set to one.
- Bit 15, task switch (BT) — If the value of this bit is one, the exception was caused by switching to the task with the trap bit set.

❒ DR7 (equivalent to DR5) — This bit controls the breakpoints setting. In this register, for each of the debug registers (DR0–DR3) there are fields that determine the conditions, for which it is necessary to generate interrupts. The first four pairs of bits (8 bits) of this register, a pair per register, indicate whether the corresponding register would define a breakpoint for the local task (in which case the first bit must be set to one) or for all tasks running in the system (in which case the second bit of the pair must be set to one). Bits 16–31 define the type of access, for which the interrupt will be activated (when fetching a command or reading or writing to or from the memory) and specify the data size:

- Bits 16–17, 20–21, 24–25, and 28–29 define the type of access as follows: 00 by a command, 01 for writing, 11 for reading and writing, and 10 for not used.
- Bits 18–19, 22–23, 26–27, and 30–31 define the size of the operand as follows: 00 for byte, 01 for 2 bytes, 11 for 4 bytes, and 10 for "not used."

1.2.2. Main Instruction Set

The main instruction set includes all commands of the microprocessor, except for the coprocessor instructions and MMX instructions.

The designations adopted for presenting materials in subsequent tables are as follows:

❑ dest and src — Destination operand and source operand

❑ m — Operand located in memory

❑ r — Operand that is a processor register

❑ r8, r16, and r32 — 8-, 16-, and 32-bit processor registers, respectively

❑ mm — 64-bit MMX register

❑ m32 and m64 — 32-bit and 64-bit operands, respectively, located in memory

❑ ir32 — Normal processor registers

❑ imm — Immediate operand (constant), 1 byte in size

Table 1.2. Data exchange commands

Command	Description
MOV dest, src	Load data to or from the register, memory, or immediate operand. For example: MOV AX, 10; MOV EBX, ESI; MOV AL, BYTE PTR MEM; and MOV DWORD PTR MEM, 10000H.
XCHG r/m, r	Exchange data between registers or between a register and the memory. The command for exchanging data between memory cells is not provided in the Intel processor instruction set.
BSWAP reg32	Swap bytes from the least significant–most significant order into the most significant–least significant order. Bits 7–0 exchange positions with bits 31–24, and bits 15–8 exchange positions with bits 23–16. This command was introduced in the Intel 486 processor.
MOVSXB r, r/m	Extend a byte to a word or double word with duplication of the sign bit and load it into the destination. For example: MOVSXB AX, BL and MOVSXB EAX, BYTE PTR MEM. The command was introduced in the Intel 386 processor.
MOVSXW r, r/m	Load the source word, extended to a double word with duplication of the sign bit, into the destination. For example: MOVSXW EAX, WORD PTR MEM. This command was introduced in the Intel 386 processor.
MOVZXB r, r/m	Load the source byte extended to a word or double word with duplication of the zero bit into the destination. For example: MOVSXB AX, BL and MOVSXB EAX, BYTE PTR MEM. This command was introduced in the Intel 386 processor.

continues

Table 1.2 Continued

Command	Description
MOVZXW r, r/m	Load the source word extended to a double word with duplication of the zero bit into the destination. For example: MOVZXW EAX, WORD PTR MEM. This command was introduced in the Intel 386 processor.
XLAT	Load a byte from the table in the data segment, the starting point of which is pointed by EBX (BX) into AL. The initial value of AL plays the role of the offset.
LEA r, m	Load the effective address, for example:
	LEA EAX, MEM;
	LEA EAX, [EBX]
	This command is featured by certain "magic" properties that allow efficient arithmetic. For example, the LEA EAX, [EAX*8] command multiplies the contents of EAX by 8, and the LEA EAX, [EAX][EAX*4] command multiplies the contents of EAX by 5. The LEA ECX, [EAX][ESI+5] command is equivalent to the following three commands:
	MOV ECX, EAX
	ADD ECX, ESI
	ADD ECX, 5
	Note that the LEA command allows multiplying only by 2, 4, and 8; therefore, if it is necessary to use a different multiplier, multiplication must be combined with addition.
LDS r, m	Load the DS:reg pair from memory. In this case, the word (or double word) is first, and DS contains the next word.
LES r, m	Similar to the previous command but in relation to the ES:reg pair.
LFS r, m	Similar to the previous command but in relation to FS:reg.
LGS r, m	Similar to the previous command but in relation to GS:reg.
LSS r, m	Similar to the previous command but in relation to SS:reg.

continues

Table 1.2 Continued

Command	Description
Conditional settings of the first bit of the byte: SETcc r/m	Check the cc condition. If this condition has been met, then the first bit of the byte is set to one; otherwise, this bit is set to zero. Conditions are similar to the ones used in conditional jumps (JE, JC). For example: SETE AL. This command was introduced in the Intel 386 processor. All variants of this command are as follows:
	SETA/SETNBE — Set if greater.
	SETAE/SETNB — Set if greater or equal.
	SETB/SETNAE — Set if smaller.
	SETBE/SETNA — Set if smaller.
	SETC — Set if there is a carry.
	SETE/SETZ — Set if zero.
	SETG/SETNLE — Set if greater.
	SETGE/SETNL — Set if greater or equal.
	SETL/SETNGE — Set if smaller.
	SETLE/SETNG — Set if smaller or equal.
	SETNC — Set if there is no carry.
	SETNE/SETNZ — Set if smaller or equal.
	SETNO — Set if there is no overflow.
	SETNP/SETPO — Set if there is no parity.
	SETNS — Set if there is no sign.
	SETO — Set if there is overflow.
	SETP/SETPE — Set if there is parity.
	SETS — Set if there is a sign.
LAHF	Load flags into AH (obsolete).
SAHF	Save AH into the flags register (obsolete).

continues

Table 1.2 Continued

Command	Description
Conditional movings: CMOVX dest, src	CMOVA/CMOVNBE — Move if greater.
	CMOVAE/CMOVNB — Move if greater or equal.
	CMOVB/CMOVNAE — Move if smaller.
	CMOVBE/CMOVNA — Move if smaller.
	CMOVC — Move if there is carry.
	CMOVE/CMOVZ — Move if zero.
	CMOVG/CMOVNLE — Move if greater.
	CMOVGE/CMOVNL — Move if greater or equal.
	CMOVL/CMOVNGE — Move if smaller.
	CMOVLE/CMOVNG — Move if greater or equal.
	CMOVNC — Move if there is no carry.
	CMOVNE/CMOVNZ — Move if smaller or equal.
	CMOVNO — Move if there is no overflow.
	CMOVNP/CMOVPO — Move if there is no parity.
	CMOVNS — Move if there is no sign.
	CMOVO — Move if there is no overflow.
	CMOVP/CMOVPE — Move if there is parity.
	CMOVS — Move if there is a sign.

Table 1.3. Input/output commands

Command	Description
IN AL(AX, EAX), Port IN AL(AX, EAX), DX	Load from the input/output port into the accumulator. The port is addressed directly through the DX register.
OUT port, AL (AX, EAX) OUT DX, AL (AX, EAX)	Output into the input/output port. The port is addressed directly through the DX register.

continues

Table 1.3 Continued

Command	Description
[REP] INSB [REP] INSW [REP] INSD	Output the data from the port addressed by the DX register into the following memory cell: ES:[EDI/DI]. After input of a byte, word, or double word, EDI/DI is corrected by 1, 2, or 4. If the REP prefix is present, the process continues until the contents of CX equal zero.
[REP] OUTSB [REP] OUTSW [REP] OUTSD	Output the data from the DS:[ESI/SI] memory cell into the output port, the address of which is stored in the DX register. After output of a byte, word, or double word, the ESI/SI pointer is corrected by 1, 2, or 4.

Table 1.4. Instructions for operations over the stack

Command	Description
PUSH r/m	Load a word or double word into the stack. Because the stack becomes unaligned by the double word boundary if a word is loaded into it, it is recommended to push double words into the stack anyway.
PUSH const	Load an immediate 32-bit operand into the stack.
PUSHA	Load the EAX, EBX, ECX, EDX, ESI, EDI, EBP, and ESP registers into the stack. This command was introduced in the Intel 386 processor.
POP r/m	Retrieve a word or double word from the stack.
POPA	Retrieve the data from the stack into the EAX, EBX, ECX, EDX, ESI, EDI, EBP, and ESP registers. The command was introduced in the Intel 386 processor.
PUSHF	Load the flags register into the stack.
POPF	Retrieve the flags register from the stack.

Table 1.5. Instructions for integer arithmetic

Command	Description
ADD dest, src	Add two operands. The first operand can be a register or memory cell, and the second operand can be a register, memory cell, or constant. If both operands are memory cells, this operation is impossible.

continues

Table 1.5 Continued

Command	Description
XADD dest, src	Exchange operands and then carry out the ADD operation. This command was introduced in the Intel 486 processor.
ADC dest, src	Add with the account of the carry flag; the carry flag is added to the least significant bit.
INC r/m	Increment the operand.
SUB dest, src	Subtract one operand from another operand. All other features are similar to the addition (the ADD command).
SBB dest, src	Subtract with the account of the carry bit. The carry bit (flag) is subtracted from the least significant bit.
DEC r/m	Decrement the operand.
CMP r/m, r/m	Compare (subtracts the operands without changing their values).
CMPXCHG r, m, a	Compare and exchange. This command accepts three operands (register—operand—source, memory cell—operand—destination, or accumulator; in other words, AL, AX or EAX). If the values in the destination operand and accumulator are equal, then the destination operand is replaced with the source operand, and initial value of the destination operand is loaded into the accumulator. This command was introduced in the Intel 486 processor.
CMPXCHG8B r, m, a	Compare and exchange 8 bytes. The command was introduced in the Intel Pentium processor. It compares the number stored in the EDX:EAX pair of registers with the 8-byte number in memory.
NEG r/m	Invert the operand sign.
AAA	ASCII adjust after addition. This command adjusts the result of addition as set by the American Standard Code for Information Interchange (ASCII) (binary addition of two unpacked BCDs). The AAA instruction must follow an ADD instruction that adds (binary addition) two unpacked BCDs and stores a byte result in the AL register. The AAA instruction then adjusts the contents of the AL register so that they contain the correct one-digit, unpacked BCD result.
	If the addition produces a decimal carry, the AH register is incremented by one and the AL register is incremented by six (binary addition).
	For example, assume that AX contains the 9H number. In this case, executing the ADD AL, 8/AAA pair of commands results in AX containing 0107H, in other words, the 17 ASCII number.

continues

Table 1.5 Continued

Command	Description
AAS	ASCII adjust after subtraction. This operation adjusts the result of the subtraction of two unpacked BCDs to create an unpacked BCD result.[i]
	If the subtraction produces a decimal carry, the AH register is decremented by one and the AL register is decremented by six (binary addition).

	Consider the following example:
	`MOV AX, 205H ; Load the 25 ASCII number.`
	`SUB AL, 8   ; Binary subtraction`
	`AAS`

	As a result, AX will contain the 0107H code, in other words, unpacked BCD 17.
AAM	ASCII adjust after multiplication. This instruction adjusts the result of the multiplication of two unpacked BCDs to create a pair of unpacked (base 10) BCDs. For this command, it is assumed that the AX register contains the result of binary multiplication of two decimal system digits (ranging from 0 to 81). After completion of this operation, the AX register will contain a 2-byte product in ASCII format. It is assumed that the least significant digit is contained in AL and the most significant digit is contained in AH. The AAM instruction is only useful when it follows an MUL instruction that multiplies (binary multiplication) two unpacked BCDs and stores a word result in the AX register. The AAM instruction then adjusts the contents of the AX register so that they contain the correct two-digit, unpacked (base 10) BCD result.
AAD	ASCII adjust *before* division. This command adjusts two unpacked BCDs (the least significant digit in the AL register and the most significant digit in the AH register) so that a division operation performed on the result will yield a correct unpacked BCD. The AAD instruction is only useful when it precedes a DIV instruction that divides (binary division) the adjusted value in the AX register by an unpacked BCD. The AAD instruction sets the value in the AL register to (AL + (10*AH)) and then clears the AH register to 00H. The value in the AX register then equals the binary equivalent of the original unpacked, two-digit (base 10) number in registers AH and AL.

continues

---

[i] Recall that ASCII numbers assume one digit is used per byte and BCD numbers assume that one digit is used per nibble (4 bits). In other words, the AX register can contain either a two-digit ASCII number or a four-digit BCD number.

Table 1.5 Continued

Command	Description
DAA	Decimal adjust AL after addition. This operation adjusts the sum of two packed BCDs to create a packed BCD result and is only useful when it follows an ADD instruction that adds (binary addition) a pair of two-digit, packed BCDs and stores a byte result in the AL register. The DAA instruction then adjusts the contents of the AL register so that they contain the correct two-digit, packed BCD result.
DAS	Decimal adjust after subtraction. This instruction adjusts the result of the subtraction of two packed BCDs to create a packed BCD result and is only useful when it follows a SUB instruction that subtracts (binary subtraction) a single two-digit, packed BCD from another and stores a byte result in the AL register. The DAS instruction then adjusts the contents of the AL register so that they contain the correct two-digit, packed BCD result.
MUL r/m	Multiply AL(AX, EAX) by an unsigned integer number. The result will be contained in AX, DX:AX, EDX:EAX.
IMUL r/m	Perform signed multiplication (similar to MUL). All operands are considered signed. This instruction has three forms, depending on the number of operands. The one-operand form is identical to that used by the MUL instruction. The two-operand form is follows: IMUL r, src and r <- r*src. The three-operand form of this instruction is as follows: IMUL dst, src, imm and dst <- src*imm.
DIV r/m (src)	Perform unsigned division. This operation is similar to unsigned multiplication. It divides the accumulator and its extension (AH:AL, DX:AX, EDX:EAX) by the divisor src. The quotient is then placed into the accumulator, and the remainder is saved in the accumulator extension.
IDIV r/m	Performs signed division. This is similar to unsigned division.
CBW	Convert a byte to a word (CBW). This instruction doubles the size of the operand through sign extension. It extends the byte (AL) into a word and copies the sign bit in the source operand into every bit in the AH register.
CWD	Convert a word to a double word. This instruction doubles the size of the source operand (AX) into the double word (DX:AX) and copies the sign bit (bit 15) of the word in the AX register into every bit of the DX register.

continues

Table 1.5 Continued

Command	Description
CWDE	Convert a word to a double word. This instruction doubles the source operand (AX) through sign extension. This is similar to CWD but uses EAX as the destination.
CDQ	Convert a double word (EAX) to a quadword (EDX:EAX).

Table 1.6. Logical operations

Command	Description
AND dest, src	Logical AND operation. This resets to zero every bit of dest, provided that the corresponding bit of src is zero.
TEST dest, src	Similar to AND but does not change dest. This operation is used for checking whether there are nonzero bits.
OR dest, src	Logical OR. This sets to one all bits in dest, for which the corresponding bits in src are not zero.
XOR dest, src	Exclusive OR. Each bit of the result is one if the corresponding bits of the two operands are different; each bit is zero if the corresponding bits of the operands are the same.
NOT dest	Inverts the values of all bits.

Table 1.7. Shift operations

Command	Description
RCL/RCR dest, src	Rotate through carry left and rotate through carry right. These commands cyclically shift all bits of the source operand to the left or right, including the carry flag, into rotation. Src may be either CL or the immediate operand.
ROL/ROR dest, src	Rotate left and rotate right. These commands are similar to RCL/RCR but use CF differently. CF doesn't participate in the cyclic shift, and its original value is not a part of the result. But CF receives a copy of the bit shifted from one end to the other.
SAL/SAR dest, src	Shift arithmetically left or right. In the right shift, the most significant bit is duplicated. In the left shift, the least significant bit is filled with zero. The "popped out" bit is loaded into CF.

continues

Table 1.7 Continued

Command	Description
SHL/SHR dest, src	Shift logically left or right. A logical shift right is different from SAR in that the most significant bit is also filled with zero.
SHLD/SHRD dest, src, count	Three-operand commands for left and right shifts. The first operand, as usual, can be either a register or a memory cell. The second operand must be a general-purpose register, and the third operand is either CL or the immediate operand. The essence of this operation is that dest and src are first joined and then shifted by the number of bits specified by count. The result is then placed into dest.

Table 1.8. String operations

Command	Description
REP	Repeat the string operation until ECX is reset to zero. There are several variations with this prefix, such as REPZ (REPE) for repeat until zero (ZF = 1) and REPNZ (REPNE) for repeat as long as zero.
MOVS dest, src	Move a byte, word, or double word from the chain addressed by DS:[ESI] into the dest chain addressed by ES[EDI]. The EDI and ESI registers are automatically corrected according to the value of the direction flag (DF). This command has the following variants: MOVSB (byte) for moving by single bytes, MOVSW (word) for moving by words, and MOVSD (double word) for moving by 4-byte blocks. Dest and src do not need to be specified explicitly.
LODS src	Load a string. This is the command for loading a string into an accumulator. The following variants of the command are available: LODSB, LODSW, and LODSD. When executing this command, a byte, word, or double word is loaded into AL, AX, or EAX, respectively. The ESI register is automatically changed by one, depending on the state of DF. The REP prefix is not used.
STOS dest	An inverse of LODS. In other words, this command passes a byte, word, or double word from an accumulator into the string and automatically corrects EDI.
SCAS dest	Scan a string. It subtracts a string element, dst, from the contents of an accumulator (AL, AX, EAX) and modifies flags. The REPNE prefix allows the required element within the string to be found.

continues

Table 1.8 Continued

Command	Description
CMPS dest, src	Compare strings. This command subtracts a byte, word, or double word of the dst string from the corresponding element of the src string. Flags are modified depending on the subtraction result. The EDI and ESI registers are automatically shifted to the next element. If the REPE prefix is used, the command continues comparison until the end of the string is reached or as long as elements are equal. If the REPNE prefix is used, the command continues comparison until the end of the string is reached or until elements are equal.

Table 1.9. Commands for operations over flags

Command	Description
CLC	Clear the carry flag in the EFLAGS register.
CMC	Complement the carry flag. This inverts CF.
STC	Set CF in the EFLAGS register.
CLD	Clear the direction flag. This resets DF to zero.
STD	Set DF in the EFLAGS register.
CLI	Clear the interrupt flag. This disables maskable hardware interrupts.
STI	Set the interrupt flag. This enables maskable hardware interrupts.
CTS	Reset the task switching flag.

Table 1.10. Control flow commands

Command	Description
JMP target	There are five forms of this command, differing by the distance of the destination and the current address and by the method of specifying the target address. When working in Windows, jumps within the limits of a 32-bit segment are mainly used (NEAR). The target address can be specified directly (by a label) or indirectly; in other words, this value can be stored in the memory cell or register (JMP [EAX]).

continues

Table 1.10 Continued

Command	Description
JMP target	Another type of jump — a short jump — takes only 2 bytes. The range of the offset within which the jump takes place, is 128–127. The use of such jumps is limited.
	An intersegment jump can appear as follows: JMP FWORD PTR L, where L is the pointer to the structure containing a 48-bit address, started with the 32-bit offset address and followed by a 16-bit selector (segment, call gateway, task state segment). Also, the following variant of intersegment jump is possible: JMP FWORD ES:[EDI].
Conditional jumps	JA/JNBE — Jump if above, jump if not below or equal.
	JAE/JNB — Jump if above or equal, jump if not below.
	JB/JNAE — Jump if below, jump if not above.
	JBE/JNA — Jump if below or equal, jump if not above.
	JC — Jump if there is a carry.
	JE/JZ — Jump if equal, jump if zero.
	JG/JNLE — Jump if greater, jump if not less or equal.
	JGE/JNL — Jump if greater or equal, jump if not less.
	JL/JNGE — Jump if less, jump if not greater or equal.
	JLE/JNG — Jump if less or equal, jump if not greater.
	JNC — Jump if there is no carry.
	JNE/JNZ — Jump if not equal, jump if not zero.
	JNO — Jump if there is no overflow.
	JNP/JPO — Jump if there is no parity, jump if the parity is odd.
	JNS — Jump if there is no sign.
	JO — Jump if there is overflow.
	JP/JPE — Jump if there is parity, jump if the parity is even.
	JS — Jump if there is a sign.
	JCXZ — Jump if CX equals zero.
	JECXZ — Jump if ECX equals zero.
	In the flat memory model, conditional jump commands carry out jumps within a 32-bit register.

continues

Table 1.10 Continued

Command	Description
Loop control; all commands of this group decrement the contents of the ECX register	LOOP — Perform a loop operation if ECX content does not equal zero. LOOPE (LOOPZ) — Perform a loop operation if the contents of ECX do not equal zero and ZF equals one. LOOPNE (LOOPNZ) — Perform a loop operation if the contents of ECX do not equal zero and ZF equals zero.
CALL target	Pass control to procedure (label) and saves the address that follows the CALL command into the stack. In the flat memory model, the return address is a 32-bit offset. An intersegment call requires both the selector and the offset to be pushed into the stack (in other words, a 48-bit value, where 16 bits are for the selector and 32 bits are for the offset).
RET [N]	Return from the procedure. An optional parameter, N, assumes that the command also automatically clears the stack (frees N bytes). There are several variants of the command that assembler chooses automatically, depending on the procedure type (NEAR or FAR). However, it is also possible to explicitly specify the return type (RETN or RETF). In the flat memory model, RETN with a 4-byte return address is used by default.

Table 1.11. Commands for supporting high-level programming languages

Command	Description
ENTER par1, par2	Prepare the stack when entering a procedure. The par1 parameter shows the number of bytes for local variables within a procedure, and par2 specifies the nesting level of the procedure. When par2 equals zero, nesting is not allowed (this situation arises when programming in C language).
LEAVE	Exit a high-level procedure. This restores the original stack contents after executing the ENTER command.
BOUND r16, m16 or BOUND REG32, MEM32	Check the array index against the bounds. It is assumed that the register contains the current address of the array and that the second operand defines 2 words or 2 double words in the memory. The first argument is considered the minimum index value, and the second argument is the maximum index value. If the current index goes beyond these limits, then the INT 5 command is generated. These commands are used for control if the index falls within the specified range, which is important for debugging purposes.

Table 1.12. Interrupt commands

Command	Description
INT n	Call to the interrupt procedure. This is a 2-byte command. The contents of the flags register are pushed into the stack, followed by the fully qualified return address. In addition, the trap flag (TF) is reset. After this, an indirect jump through the *n*th element of the interrupt descriptor table is carried out to the interrupt handler. The 1-byte INT 3 command is named the debug exception handler and is actively used in debuggers.
INTO	Similar to the INT 4 command, provided that overflow flag equals one. If OF equals zero, the command doesn't carry out any actions.
IRET	Interrupt return. This command retrieves the return address and flags register from the stack and returns from the interrupt. The privilege level bit will be modified only if the current privilege level equals zero.

Table 1.13. Processor synchronization commands

Command	Description
HLT	Halt. This program stops instruction execution and switches the processor to the halt state. Processor can be switched to resume operation by an external interrupt.
LOCK	Assert LOCK# signal prefix. This is a bus locking prefix. It forces the processor to form the LOCK# signal for the time of execution of the command that follows the prefix. In a multiprocessor system, this signal blocks requests to the bus from other processors.
NOP	No operation.
WAIT (FWAIT)	Synchronize with the coprocessor. Most coprocessor commands handle this command automatically.

Table 1.14. Commands for processing chains of bits (introduced in the Intel 386 processor)

Command	Description
BSF(BSR) dest, src	Bit scan forward and bit scan reverse. Here, Dest is a 16-bit or a 32-bit register. Src is a register or a memory cell. When the BSF command is executed, the src operand is scanned starting from least significant bits. The BSR command scans starting from the most significant bits. The number of the first encountered bit set to one is placed into the dest register, and the zero flag is reset to zero. If src contains zero, then ZF equals one, and the contents of dest are undefined.
BT dest, src	Bit test. This selects the bit in the bit string specified by src at the bit position specified by dest and stores its value in the carry flag.
BTC dest, src	Bit test and complement. This selects the bit in the bit string specified by src at the bit position specified by dest, stores the bit value in CF, and complements the bit value in the bit string.
BTR dest, src	Bit test and reset. This selects the bit in the bit string specified by src at the bit position specified by dest, stores the bit value in CF, and resets the bit value in the bit string to zero.
BTS dest, src	Bit test and set. This selects the bit in the bit string specified by src at the bit position specified by dest, stores the bit value in CF, and sets the bit value in the bit string to one.

Table 1.15. Protection control commands

Command	Description
LGDT src	Load the value in the source operand into GDTR. Src is a 6-byte value (memory location).
SGDT dest	Store GDTR in the memory.
LIDT src	Load the value from the source operand into IDTR.
SIDT dest	Store IDTR in the memory.
LLDT src	Load the local descriptor table register (LDTR). This loads the source operand (16 bits) into the segment selector field of LDTR.

continues

Table 1.15 Continued

Command	Description
SLDT dest	Store LDTR. This stores the segment selector from LDTR in the destination operand. The destination operand can be a general-purpose register or a memory location (16 bits).
LMSW src	Load the machine status word (MSW). This loads the source operand into MSW, bits 0–15 of register CR0. The source operand can be a 16-bit general-purpose register or a memory location.
SMSW dest	Store MSW. This saves MSW into a register or memory location (16 bits).
LTR src	Load the task register (TR). This loads the source operand into the segment selector field of TR. The source operand (a general-purpose register or a memory location) contains a segment selector that points to a task state segment.
STR dest	Store TR. This stores the segment selector from TR in the destination operand. The destination operand can be a general-purpose register or a memory location (16 bits).
LAR dest, src	Load access rights byte. This loads the access rights from the segment descriptor specified by the second operand (src) into the first operand (dest) and sets ZF in the flags register.
LSL dest, src	Load segment limit. This loads the unscrambled segment limit from the segment descriptor specified with the second operand (source operand) into the first operand (destination operand) and sets ZF in the EFLAGS register. The source operand (which can be a register or a memory location) contains the segment selector for the segment descriptor being accessed. The destination operand is a general-purpose register.
ARPL r/m, r	Adjust RPL field of the segment selector. This compares RPL fields of two segment selectors, and if the RPL field of the destination operand is less than the RPL field of the source operand, ZF is set to one and the RPL field of the destination operand is increased to match that of the source operand.
VERR seg	Verify a segment for reading. This sets ZF to one if the task is allowed to read in the SEG segment.
VERW seg	Verify a segment for writing. This sets ZF to one if the task is allowed to write into the SEG segment.

Table 1.16. Commands for exchanging data with control registers

Command	Description
MOV CRn, src	Load src into the CRn control register.
MOV dest, CRn	Read from the CRn control register.
MOV DRn, src	Load src into the DRn debug register.
MOV dest, DRn	Read from the DRn debug register.
MOV TRn, src	Load src into the TRn test register.
MOV dest, TRn	Read from the TRn test register.
RDTSC	Read the timestamp counter. The TSC value is stored into the EDX:EAX pair of registers.

Table 1.17. Commands for identifying and controlling architecture

Command	Description
CPUID	CPU identification. This returns the processor identification information. It depends on the contents of the EAX register.
	If EAX=0, the processor returns the string of characters containing information about the manufacturer into the EBX, EDX, and ECX registers. For example, AMD processors return the AuthenticAMD string and Intel processors return the GenuineIntel string.
	If EAX=1, the identification code is returned in the least significant word of the EAX register.
	If EAX=2, processor configuration parameters are returned in the EAX, EBX, ECX, and EDX registers.
RDMSR r/m	Read from model-specific register (MSR) into ECX.
RDPMC	Read performance-monitoring counters. This places the value of one of the two programmable performance monitoring counters into the EDX:EAX pair of registers. The choice of the counter depends on the contents of the ECX register.
WRMSR r/m	Write to the MSR. This writes the ECX contents into the MSR.
SYSENTER	Fast system call.
SYSEXIT	Exit from the system call.

Table 1.18. Caching control commands

Command	Description
INVD	Invalidate internal caches. This invalidates (flushes) the processor's internal caches and issues a special-function bus cycle that directs external caches to flush themselves. Data held in internal caches is not written back to main memory.
WBINVD	Write back and invalidate caches. This writes all modified cache lines and invalidates the caches.
INVLPG r/m	Invalidate TLB entry. This invalidates (flushes) the translation lookaside buffer (TLB) entry specified with the source.

1.2.3. Arithmetic Coprocessor Commands

In this section, I'll cover the main issues related to the operation of the arithmetic coprocessor.

Before the release of the Intel 80486 processor, coprocessors were supplied separately. Nowadays, the coprocessor is a built-in and integral part of the processor.

Structure and Operation

The arithmetic coprocessor operates over its own set of commands and over its own set of registers. However, command prefetching is carried out by the processor.

The arithmetic coprocessor carries out operations over the following data types: word (16 bits), short integer (32 bits), long word (64 bits), packed BCD (80 bits), short real number (32 bits), long real number (64 bits), and extended real number (80 bits). Formats, in which real numbers are stored, were considered in *Section 1.1*. In addition to normal numbers, some coprocessor operations might result in special cases.

Special Cases

The special cases that might occur as a result of coprocessor operations are as follows:

- ❐ Positive zero — All bits are set to zero.
- ❐ Negative zero — The sign bit equals one.
- ❐ Positive infinity — The sign bit is set to zero, all bits of the mantissa are set to zero, and all bits of the exponent are set to one.

- ❏ Negative infinity — The sign bit is set to one, all bits of the mantissa are set to zero, and all bits of the exponent are set to one.
- ❏ Denormalized numbers — All bits of the exponent are set to zero.
- ❏ Indefinite numbers — The sign bit is set to one, all bits of the exponent are set to one, the first bit of the mantissa is set to one (for an 80-bit number, the first 2 bits of the mantissa are set to one), and the other bits are zeros.
- ❏ Signaling NaNs[i] (SNaNs) — All bits of the exponent are set to one, the first bit of the mantissa is zero (for an 80-bit number, the first 2 bits are one and zero), and there are ones among the other bits.
- ❏ Quiet NaNs (QNaNs) — All bits of the exponent are set to one, the first bit of the mantissa is zero (for an 80-bit number, the first 2 bits of the mantissa are ones), and there are ones among the other bits of the mantissa.
- ❏ Unsupported numbers do not correspond to standard numbers and are not described as special cases.

When the coprocessor executes an operation, the processor waits for this operation to complete. In other words, before each coprocessor command, the assembler automatically generates the command that checks whether the coprocessor is busy. If the coprocessor is busy, the processor is switched to the waiting state. Sometimes programmers need to manually insert the WAIT command after the coprocessor command.

Data Registers

The coprocessor has eight 80-bit data registers that represent a stack structure. These registers are also called the coprocessor stack. The registers are named R0–R7; however, they cannot be accessed directly. Each register can take any position in the stack. The names of the relative stack registers are ST(0)–ST(7).

There is also the status register (or the status word, SW), the flags of which allow you to assess the result of the completed operation. The control register (or the control word, CW) contains the bits that influence the result of execution of the coprocessor commands.

---

[i] NaN stands for "not a number." NaNs are nonnumbers; they are not part of the real number set. The encoding space for NaNs in floating-point format is beyond the ends of the real number line. This space includes any value with the maximum allowable biased exponent and a nonzero fraction (the sign bit is ignored for NaNs).

The tags register (or the tag word, TW) is made up of 16 bits describing the contents of the coprocessor registers — 2 bits per data register. The tag reflects the contents of the data register. Here are the tag values: 00 for a real nonzero number, 01 for true zero, 10 for special numbers, and 11 for no data.

In addition to the previously-listed register, the coprocessor has the FIP and FDP registers. The FIP register contains the address of the last executed command, except for FINIT, FCLEX, FLDCW, FSTCW, FSTSW, FSTSWAX, FSTENV, FLDENV, FSAVE, FRSTOR, and FWAIT. The FDP register contains the address of the command operand, except for the preceding commands.

When carrying out computations using a coprocessor command, the most important role is delegated to exceptions, also called special cases. A typical exception is division by zero. Exception bits are stored in the status register. Exceptions must be taken into account to obtain correct results.

Exceptions

The list of exceptions is as follows:

- Incorrect result (rounding)
- Invalid operation
- Division by zero
- Underflow (tiny result)
- Overflow (too large result)
- Denormalized operand

The Status Word

The coprocessor status word reflects its overall state. It includes the following bits:

- Bit 0, invalid operation exception (IE) flag
- Bit 1, denormalized operation exception (DE) flag
- Bit 2, division by zero exception (ZE) flag
- Bit 3, overflow exception (OE) flag
- Bit 4, underflow exception (UE) flag
- Bit 5, inexact result (precision) exception (PE) flag
- Bit 6, stack fault exception (SF) flag
- Bit 7, exception summary (ES) flag

❒ Bits 8, 9, 10, and 14, condition flags (C0, C1, C2, and C3)

❒ Bits 11–13, number (0–7) specifying which register is the top of the stack

❒ Bit 15, FPU busy flag — Matches ES

The Control Word

The control word of the arithmetic coprocessor determines one of several available methods of processing numeric data. Bits of the control word (CW) are as follows:

❒ Bit 0, invalid operation mask (IM)

❒ Bit 1, denormalized operand mask (DM)

❒ Bit 2, division by zero mask (ZM)

❒ Bit 3, overflow mask (OM)

❒ Bit 4, underflow mask (UM)

❒ Bit 5, inexact result (precision) mask (PM)

❒ Bits 6 and 7, reserved

❒ Bits 8 and 9, precision control (PC)

❒ Bits 10 and 11, rounding control (RC)

❒ Bit 12, infinity control (IC)

❒ Bits 13–15, reserved

The following are possible causes of exceptions:

❒ Stack fault. The result is an indefinite number.

❒ Operation over an unsupported number. The result is an indefinite number.

❒ Operation over an SNaN. The result is a QNaN.

❒ Comparison of a number with QNaN or SNaN. The result is C0 = C2 = C3 = 1.

❒ Addition of infinities (the same sign) or subtraction of infinities (different signs). The result is an indefinite number.

❒ Multiplication of infinity by zero. The result is an indefinite number.

❒ Division of infinity by infinity or division of zero by zero. The result is an indefinite number.

❒ FPREM and FPREM1 commands if the divisor is zero or if the dividend equals infinity. The result is an indefinite number, and C2 = 0.

❒ Trigonometric operations over infinity. The result is an indefinite number, and C2 = 0.

❑ Root or logarithm operations if the argument is negative. The result is an indefinite number.

❑ FBSTP command if the source register is empty, contains a QNaN or SNaN, contains infinity, or is more than 18 decimal characters in length. The result is an indefinite number.

❑ FXCH if one of the operands is empty. The result is an indefinite number.

Coprocessor Commands

Tables 1.19–1.23 provide a complete list of the FPU commands and a brief description of the operations they carry out.

Table 1.19. Data exchange commands

Command	Description
FLD src	Load a real number into ST(0) (stack top) from the memory location. In this case, ST(0)->ST(1). The memory location might be 32 bits, 64 bits, or 80 bits. The FLD ST(0) command duplicates the stack top.
FILD src	Load an integer number from the memory into ST(0). In this case, ST(0)->ST(1). The memory area can be 16 bits, 32 bits, or 64 bits.
FBLD src	Load a BCD into ST(0) from an 80-bit memory area.
FLDZ	Load 0 into ST(0).
FLD1	Load 1 into ST(0).
FLDPI	Load PI into ST(0).
FLDL2T	Load LOG2(10) into ST(0).
FLDTL2E	Load LOG2(e) into ST(0).
FLDLG2	Load LG(2) into ST(0).
FLDLN2	Load LN(2) into ST(0).
FST dest	Write a real number from ST(0) into the memory. The memory area might be 32 bits, 64 bits, or 80 bits.
FSTP dest	Write a real number from ST(0) into the memory. The memory area might be 32 bits, 64 bits, or 80 bits. In this case, the stack top is popped from the stack.

continues

Table 1.19 Continued

Command	Description
FBST dest	Write a BCD into the memory. The memory area is 80 bits.
FBSTP dest	Write a BCD into the memory. The memory area is 80 bits. In this case, the stack top is popped from the stack.
FXCH st(i)	Exchange the values of the stack top and the i register. If the operand is not specified, then ST(0) and ST(1) are exchanged.
FCMOVc dest, src	Move conventional data. This command copies ST(i) (src) into ST(0) (dest). There are the following forms of this command:

- FCMOVE — Copy if equal ($ZF = 1$)

- FCMOVNE — Copy if not equal ($ZF = 0$)

- FCMOVB — Copy if below ($CF = 1$)

- FCMOVBE — Copy if below or equal ($CF = 1$ or $ZF = 1$)

- FCMOVNB — Copy if not below ($CF = 0$)

- FCMOVNBE — Copy if not below or equal ($CF = 0$ or $ZF = 1$)

- FCMOVU — Copy if unordered (incomparable) ($PF = 1$)

- FCMOVNU — Copy if not unordered (comparable) ($PF = 0$)

Table 1.20. Data comparison commands

Command	Description
FCOM	Compare two real numbers, ST(0) and ST(1). Flags are set the same way as for the subtraction operation: ST(0) – ST(1).
	In this command and further on (up to the FCOMI command), the C0, C2, and C3 flags are set as follows:
	ST(0) > src C0 = 0, C2 = 0, C3 = 0
	ST(0) < src C0 = 1, C2 = 0, C3 = 0
	ST(0) = src C0 = 0, C2 = 0, C3 = 1
	If operands are unordered (cannot be compared), then C0 = C2 = C3 = 1.
FCOM src	Compare ST(0) with the operand contained in the memory. The operand might be 32 bits or 64 bits.

continues

Table 1.20 Continued

Command	Description
FCOMP src	Compare the real number in ST(0) with the operand in memory. The ST(0) is popped from the stack. The operand might be a register or memory area.
FCOMPP	Compare ST(0) and ST(1). Two registers are popped from the stack.
FICOM src	Compare an integer number in ST(0) with the operand. The operand might be either 16 bits or 32 bits.
FICOMP src	Compare an integer number in ST(0) with the operand. The operand might be a 16-bit or 32-bit memory area or a register. In the course of this operation, ST(0) is popped from the stack.
FTST	Test whether ST(0) equals zero.
FUCOM ST(i)	Make an unordered comparison of ST(0) with ST(i).
FUCOMP ST(i)	Make an unordered comparison of ST(0) with ST(i). In the course of this operation, the stack is popped.
FUCOMPP ST(i)	Make an unordered comparison of ST(0) with ST(i). In the course of this operation, the stack is popped twice.
FCOMI src	Compare and set flags. The four commands (FXAM) have the following influence on the bits of the flags register: ST(0) > src ZF = 0, PF = 0, CF = 0 ST(0) < src ZF = 0, PF = 0, CF = 1 ST(0) = src ZF = 1, PF = 0, CF = 0 If the operands are unordered, then all three flags are set to one.
FCOMIP src	Compare, set bits, and pop.
FUCOMI src	Make an unordered comparison and set flags.
FUCOMIP src	Make an unordered comparison, set flags, and pop.
FXAM	Analyze the contents of the stack top. The result is stored into bits C3, C2, and C0 as follows: 000 — Unsupported format 001 — NaN 010 — Normalized number 011 — Infinity 100 — Zero 101 — Blank operand 110 — Denormalized number

Table 1.21. Arithmetic commands

Command	Description
FADD src	Add the floating point number:
FADD ST(i), ST	ST(0) <- ST(0) + src, where src is a 32-bit or 64-bit number ST(i) <- ST(i) + ST(0)
FADDP ST(i), ST	Add the floating point number: ST(i) <- ST(i) + ST(0). In the course of this operation, the stack is popped.
FIADD src	Add the integer number: ST(0) <- ST(0) + src, where src is a 16-bit or 32-bit number.
FSUB src	Subtract the floating point number:
FSUB ST(i), ST	ST(0) <- ST(0) – src, where src is a 32-bit or 64-bit number ST(i) <- ST(i) – ST(0)
FSUBP ST(i), ST	Subtract the floating point number: ST(i) <- ST(i) – ST(0). When carrying out this operation, the stack is popped.
FSUBR ST(i), ST	Subtract the floating point number reverse: ST(0) <- ST(i) – ST(0).
FSUBRP ST(i), ST	Subtract the floating point reverse and pop ST(0) <- ST(i) – ST(0). When carrying out this operation, the stack is popped.
FISUB src	Subtract integer numbers: ST(0) <- ST(0) – src, where src is a 16-bit or 32-bit number.
FISUBR src	Subtract integer numbers and pop ST(0) <- ST(0) – src, where src is a 16-bit or 32-bit number. When carrying out this operation, the stack is popped.
FMUL	Multiply the floating point number:
FMUL ST(i)	The first case: ST(0) <- ST(0)*ST(1)
FMUL ST(i), ST	The second case: ST(0) <- ST(i)*ST(0)
	The third case: ST(i) <- ST(i)*ST(0)
FMULP ST(i), ST(0)	Multiply the floating point and pop ST(i) <- ST(i)*ST(0). When carrying out this operation, the stack is popped.
FIMUL src	Multiply ST(0) by an integer number: ST(0) <- ST(0)*src. The operand might be a 16-bit or 32-bit number.
FDIV	ST(0) <- ST(0)/ST(1)
FDIV ST(i)	ST(0) <- ST(0)/ST(i) ST(i) <- ST(0)/ST(i)
FDIV ST(i), SY	

continues

Table 1.21 Continued

Command	Description
FDIVP ST(i), ST	Divide the floating point numbers and pop: ST(i) <- ST(0)/ST(i). When carrying out this operation, the stack is popped.
FIDIV src	Divide integer numbers: ST(0) <- ST(i)/src. The divisor might be a 16-bit or a 32-bit number.
FDIVR ST(i), ST	Divide the floating point numbers: ST(0) <- ST(i)/ST(0).
FDIVRP ST(i), ST	Divide the floating point numbers reverse and pop: ST(0) <- ST(i)/ST(0). When carrying out this operation, the stack is popped.
FIDIVR src	Divide integer numbers reverse: ST(0) <- src/ST(0).
FSQRT	Extract the square root from ST(0) and store back.
FSCALE	Scale by a power of two: ST(0) <- ST(0)*2^ST(1).
FXTRACT	Extract the exponent and mantissa from the number ST(0). The exponent will be stored in ST(0), and the mantissa will be in ST(1).
FPREM	Find the remainder from the division: ST(0) <- ST(0)MOD(ST(1)).
FPREM1	Find the remainder from the division according to the IEEE standard.
FRNDINT	Round to the nearest integer number stored in ST(0): ST(0) <- int(ST(0)).
FABS	Find the absolute value: ST(0) <- ABS(ST(0)).
FCSH	Invert the sign: ST(0) <- (-ST(0)).

Table 1.22. Transcendental functions

Command	Description
FCOS	Compute the cosine: ST(0)<-COS(ST(0)). The contents of ST(0) are interpreted as an angle measured in radians.
FPTAN	Compute the partial tangent. The contents of ST(0) are interpreted as an angle in radians. The tangent value is returned to the place of the argument, then the value of one is pushed into the stack.

continues

Table 1.22 Continued

Command	Description
FPATAN	Compute the arctangent. The following function is computed: `Arctg(ST(1)/ST(0))` After the computation, the stack is popped and the result goes to the top of the stack.
FSIN	Compute the cosine: `ST(0) <- SIN(ST(0))`. The contents of `ST(0)` are interpreted as an angle in radians.
FSINCOS	Compute sine and cosine: `ST(0) <- SIN(ST(0))` and `ST(1) <- COS(ST(0))`.
F2XM1	Compute $2^X - 1$: `ST(0) <- 2^ST(0) - 1`.
FYL2X	Compute `Y*LOG2(X)`: `ST(0) = Y, ST(1) = X`. When this function is executed, the stack is popped and the result is pushed into the stack top.
FYL2XP1	Compute `Y*LOG2(X)`: `ST(0) = Y, ST(1) = X`. When this function is executed, the stack is popped and the result is pushed into the stack top.

Table 1.23. Coprocessor control commands

Command	Description
FINIT	Initialize the coprocessor.
FNINIT	Initialize the coprocessor without waiting.
FSTSW AX	Write the status word into `AX` (`SW -> AX`).
FSTSW dest	Write the status word into `dest` (16 bits).
FNSTSW dest	Save the status word into `dest` (16 bits).
FLDCW src	Load the control word (16 bits) from `dest`.
FSTCW dest	Save the control word into `dest`.
FCLEX	Clear FPU exception flags after checking for error conditions.
FNCLEX	Clear FPU exception flags without checking for error conditions.
FSTENV dest	Store the FPU environment (`SW`, `CW`, `TAGW`, `FIP`, `FDP`) in the memory after checking for error conditions.

continues

Table 1.23 Continued

Command	Description
FNSTENV dest	Store the FPU environment (SW, CW, TAGW, FIP, FDP) in the memory without checking for error conditions.
FLDENV src	Load the FPU environment from the memory.
FSAVE dest	Save the FPU state (SW, CW, TAGW, FIP, FDP) in the memory after checking for error conditions.
FNSAVE dest	Save the FPU state (SW, CW, TAGW, FIP, FDP) in the memory without checking for error conditions.
FRSTOR src	Restore the FPU state.
FINCSTP	Increment the FPU register's stack pointer.
FDECSTP	Decrement the FPU register's stack pointer.
FFREE ST(i)	Free the FPU register. Label ST(i) as free.
FNOP	FPU has no operation.
WAIT (FWAIT)	Instruct the processor to wait for FPU to complete the current operation.

1.2.4. MMX Extension

MMX Architecture

The MMX extension is mainly oriented toward use in multimedia applications. The main idea of MMX consists of simultaneous processing of several data elements per instruction. The MMX extension was introduced in the Pentium P54C modification of the Intel Pentium processor and is present in all later modifications of this processor.

The MMX extension uses new types of packed data: packet bytes (8 bytes), packed words (4 words), packed double words (2 double words), and quadwords. As you can see, these are 64-bit numbers. The MMX extension includes eight general-purpose registers (designated as MM0–MM7). The size of these registers is 64 bits. Physically, these registers are used by the least significant bits of the FPU data registers (R0–R7). MMX commands "spoil" the status register and the tags register. Therefore, combined use of MMX commands and coprocessor commands might cause certain difficulties. In other words, before you use MMX commands, you'll have to save the coprocessor context, which can considerably slow the operation of your program. Also, it is important to note that MMX commands operate directly of coprocessor registers, not over the pointers to the stack elements.

MMX Instructions

MMX instructions are briefly outlined in Tables 1.24 and 1.25.

Table 1.24. MMX extension commands

Command	Description
EMMS	Clear the registers stack. This sets all bits of the tags word to one.
MOVD mm, m32/ir32	Move the data into the 32 least significant bits of an MMX register and fill the most significant bits with zeros.
MOVD m32/ir32, mm	Move the data from the 32 least significant bits of an MMX register.
MOVQ mm, mm/m64	Move the data into an MMX register.
MOVQ mm/m64, mm	Move the data from an MMX register.
PACKSSDW mm, mm/m64	Pack double words into words with signed saturation. This command packs, with signed saturation, 2 double words in mm and 2 double words in mm/m64 into 4 double words in mm. In other words, this command copies 2 double words from mm into the 2 least significant words of mm and 2 double words from mm/m64 into the 2 most significant words. If the value of some double word happens to be greater than 32,767 or less than –32,768, then 32,767 and –32,768, respectively, will be written into the double words.
PACKSSWB mm, mm/m64	Pack words into bytes with signed saturation. This command packs, with signed saturation, 4 words in mm and 4 words in mm/m64 into 8 bytes in mm. In other words, 4 words from mm are converted into the 4 least significant bytes of mm, and 4 words from mm/m64 are converted into the 4 most significant bytes. If the value of some word happens to be greater than 127 or less than –128, then 127 and –128, respectively, will be placed into the bytes.
PACKUSWB mm, mm/m64	Pack and saturate 4 signed words from the destination operand (first operand) and 4 signed words from the source operand (second operand) into 8 unsigned bytes in the destination operand. If the signed value of a word is beyond the range of an unsigned byte (that is, greater than 255 or less than 0), the saturated byte value of 255 or 0, respectively, is stored in the destination.

continues

Table 1.24 Continued

Command	Description
PADDB mm, mm/m64 PADDW mm, mm/m64 PADDD mm, mm/m64	Add the individual data elements (bytes, words, or double words) of the source operand (second operand) to the individual data elements of the destination operand (first operand). If the result of an individual addition exceeds the range for the specified data type (overflows), the result is wrapped around it, meaning that the result is truncated so that only the lower (least significant) bits of the result are returned (that is, the carry is ignored).
PADDSB mm, mm/m64 PADDSW mm, mm/m64	Add packed bytes (words) with sign saturation.
PADDUSB mm, mm/m64 PADDUSW mm, mm/m64	Add packed bytes (words) with unsigned saturation.
PAND mm, mm/m64	Perform the logical AND operation.
PANDN mm, mm/m64	Perform the logical AND NOT operation. This performs a bitwise logical NOT on the quadword destination operand (first operand). Then, the instruction performs a bitwise logical AND operation on the inverted destination operand and the quadword source operand (second operand). Each bit of the result of the AND operation is set to one if the corresponding bits of the source and inverted destination bits are one; otherwise, it is set to zero. The result is stored in the destination operand location.
PCMPEQB mm, mm/m64 PCMPEQD mm, mm/m64 PCMPEQW mm, mm/m64	Packed compare for equal. This compares the individual data elements (bytes, words, or double words) in the destination operand (first operand) to the corresponding data elements in the source operand (second operand). If two data elements are equal, the corresponding data element in the destination operand is set to all ones (true); otherwise, it is set to all zeros (false). The destination operand must be an MMX register; the source operand may be either an MMX register or a 64-bit memory location.
PCMPGTB mm, mm/m64 PCMPGTD mm, mm/m64 PCMPGTW mm, mm/m64	Packed compare for greater than. This compares the individual signed data elements (bytes, words, or double words) in the destination operand (first operand) to the corresponding signed data elements in the source operand (second operand). If a data element in the destination operand is greater than its corresponding data element in the source operand, the data element in the destination operand is set to all ones (true); otherwise, it is set to all zeros (false). The destination operand must be an MMX register; the source operand may be either an MMX register or a 64-bit memory location.

continues

Table 1.24 Continued

Command	Description
PMADDWD mm, mm/m64	Packed multiply and add. This multiplies the individual signed words of the destination operand by the corresponding signed words of the source operand, producing 4 signed, double word results. The 2 double word results from the multiplication of the high-order words are added together and stored in the upper double word of the destination operand; the 2 double word results from the multiplication of the low-order words are added together and stored in the lower double word of the destination operand. The destination operand must be an MMX register; the source operand may be either an MMX register or a 64-bit memory location.
PMULHW mm, mm/m64	Packed multiply higher. This multiplies the 4 signed words of the source operand (second operand) by the 4 signed words of the destination operand (first operand), producing 4 signed, double word, intermediate results. The high-order word of each intermediate result is then written to its corresponding word location in the destination operand. The destination operand must be an MMX register; the source operand may be either an MMX register or a 64-bit memory location.
PMULLW mm, mm/m64	Packed multiply low. This multiplies the 4 signed or unsigned words of the source operand (second operand) with the 4 signed or unsigned words of the destination operand (first operand), producing four double word, intermediate results. The low-order word of each intermediate result is then written to its corresponding word location in the destination operand. The destination operand must be an MMX register; the source operand may be either an MMX register or a 64-bit memory location.
POR mm, mm/m64	Bitwise logical OR.
PSHIMD mm, imm PSHIMQ mm, imm PSHIMW mm, imm	PSHIMD represents the PSLLD, PSRAD, and PSRLD instructions with the immediate operand (a counter). PSHIMQ represents the PSLLQ and PSRLQ instructions with the immediate operand (a counter). PSHIMW represents the PSLLW, PSRAW, and PSRLW instructions.
PSLLD mm, mm/m64 PSLLQ mm, mm/m64 PSLLW mm, mm/m64	Packed shift left logical. This shifts the bits in the data elements (words, double words, or a quadword) in the destination operand (first operand) to the left by the number of bits specified in the unsigned count operand (second operand). The result of the shift operation is written to the destination operand. As the bits in the data elements are shifted left, the empty low-order bits are cleared (set to zero). If the value specified by the count operand is greater than 15 (for words), 31 (for double words), or 63 (for a quadword), then the destination operand is set to all zeros.

continues

Table 1.24 Continued

Command	Description
PSRAD mm, mm/m64 PSRAW mm, mm/m64	Packed shift right arithmetic. This shifts the bits in the data elements (words or double words) in the destination operand (first operand) to the right by the amount of bits specified in the unsigned count operand (second operand). The result of the shift operation is written to the destination operand. The empty high-order bits of each element are filled with the initial value of the sign bit of the data element. If the value specified by the count operand is greater than 15 (for words) or 31 (for double words), each destination data element is filled with the initial value of the sign bit of the element.
PSRLD mm, mm/m64 PSRLQ mm, mm/m64 PSRLW mm, mm/m64	Packed shift right logical. This shifts the bits in the data elements (words, double words, or quadwords) in the destination operand (first operand) to the right by the number of bits specified in the unsigned count operand (second operand). The result of the shift operation is written to the destination operand. As the bits in the data elements are shifted right, the empty high-order bits are cleared (set to zero). If the value specified by the count operand is greater than 15 (for words), 31 (for double words), or 63 (for a quadword), then the destination operand is set to all zeros.
PSUBB mm, mm/m64 PSUBW mm, mm/m64 PSUBD mm, mm/m64	Packed subtract. This subtracts the individual data elements (bytes, words, or double words) of the source operand (second operand) from the individual data elements of the destination operand (first operand). If the result of the subtraction exceeds the range for the specified data type (overflows), the result is wrapped around. This means that the result is truncated so that only the lower (least significant) bits of the result are returned (that is, the carry is ignored).
PSUBSB mm, mm/m64 PSUBSW mm, mm/m64	Packed subtract with saturation. This subtracts the individual signed data elements (bytes or words) of the source operand (second operand) from the individual signed data elements of the destination operand (first operand). If the result of the subtraction exceeds the range for the specified data type, the result is saturated. The destination operand must be an MMX register; the source operand can be either an MMX register or a quadword memory location.
PSUBUSB mm, mm/m64 PSUBUSW mm, mm/m64	Packed subtract unsigned with saturation. This subtracts the individual unsigned data elements (bytes or words) of the source operand (second operand) from the individual unsigned data elements of the destination operand (first operand). If the result of the individual subtraction exceeds the range for the specified unsigned data type, the result is saturated (the minimal number — zero — is used as the result).

continues

Table 1.24 Continued

Command	Description
PUNPCKHBW mm, mm/m64	Interleave the 4 high-order bytes of the source operand and the 4 high-order bytes of the destination operand and write them to the destination operand.
PUNPCKHWD mm, mm/m64	Interleave the 2 high-order words of the source operand and the 2 high-order words of the destination operand and write them to the destination operand.
PUNPCKHDQ mm, mm/m64	Interleave the high-order double word of the source operand and the high-order double word of the destination operand and write them to the destination operand.
PUNPCKLBW mm, mm/m64	Unpack the low-order bytes of the source operands and interleave them with the low-order bytes of the destination operand.
PUNPCKLWD mm, mm/m64	Unpack the low-order words of the source operand and interleave them with the low-order words of the destination operand.
PUNPCKLDQ mm, mm/m64	Unpack the low-order double words of the source operand and interleave them with the low-order double words of the destination operand.
PXOR mm,mm/m64	Exclusive OR.

New MMX Instructions

With the release of the Pentium 4 processor, previously-listed instructions of the MMX group have gained access to 128-bit registers (xmm). Table 1.25 lists new MMX instructions.

Table 1.25. New MMX commands

Command	Description
PADDQ xmm, xmm/m128	Add 128-bit operands.
PSUBQ xmm, xmm/m128	Subtract 128-bit operands.
PMULUDQ xmm, xmm/m128	Multiply 64-bit operands. The result must not exceed 128 bits.
PSLLDQ xmm, imm	Shift left logical the double quadword. This shifts the contents of the source operand to the left by the amount of bytes specified by an immediate operand (imm × 8 bits).

continues

Table 1.25 Continued

Command	Description
PSRLDQ xmm, imm	Shift right logical the double quadword. This shifts the contents of the source operand to the right by the amount of bytes specified by an immediate operand (imm × 8 bits).
PSHUFHW xmm, xmm/m128, imm	Shuffle the packed high words. This instruction shuffles the word integers packed into the high quadword of the source operand and stores the shuffled result in the high quadword of the destination operand. An 8-bit immediate operand specifies the shuffle order.
PSHUFLW xmm, xmm/m128, imm	Shuffle the packed low words. The PSHUFLW instruction copies words from the low quadword of the source operand (second operand) and inserts them in the low quadword of the destination operand (first operand) at word locations selected with the order operand (third operand).
PSHUFD xmm, xmm/m128, imm	Shuffle the packed double words. This copies double words from source operand (second operand) and inserts them into the destination operand (first operand) at the locations selected with the order operand (third operand).
PUNPCKHQDQ xmm, xmm/m128	Unpack the high quadwords. This instruction interleaves the high quadword of the source operand and the high quadword of the destination operand and writes them to the destination register.
PUNPCKLQDQ xmm, xmm/m128	Unpack the low quadwords. This instruction interleaves the low quadwords of the source operand and the low quadwords of the destination operand and writes them to the destination register.
MOVDQ2Q mm, xmm	Move the quadword integer from an XMM to an MMX register. This instruction moves the low quadword integer from an XMM source register to an MMX destination register.
MOVQ2DQ xmm, mm	Copy the content of the mm register into the least significant half of xmm. The MOVQ2DQ (move quadword integer from an XMM to an MMX register) instruction moves the quadword integer from an MMX source register to an XMM destination register.
MOVNTDQ m128, xmm	Store the double quadword using a nontemporal hint. This instruction stores packed. The address must be aligned to a 16-byte boundary.
MOVDQA xmm, xmm/m128 MOVDQA xmm/m128, xmm	Move the aligned double quadword. The MOVDQA instruction transfers a double quadword operand from memory to an XMM register, or vice versa. Alternatively, it transfers it between XMM registers. The memory address must be aligned to a 16-byte boundary.

continues

Table 1.25 Continued

Command	Description
MOVDQU xmm, xmm/m128 MOVDQU xmm/m128, xmm	Move the unaligned double quadword. This instruction per-forms the same operations as the MOVDQA instruction, except that 16-byte alignment of a memory address is not required.
MOVMSKPD r32, xmm	Extract the sign mask from two packed, double-precision, floating-point values. This copies the values of sign bits (63 and 127) into bits 0 and 1 of the r32 register. Other bits are cleared.
MASKMOVDQU xmm, xmm	Store selected bytes from the source operand (first operand) into a 128-bit memory location. The mask operand (second operand) selects, which bytes from the source operand are written to memory. The source and mask operands are XMM registers. The location of the first byte of the memory location is specified by DI/EDI and DS registers. The memory location does not need to be aligned on a natural boundary. (The size of the store address depends on the address-size attribute.)

1.3. Specific Features of Windows Programming

This section is a brief introduction to Windows programming. It doesn't pretend to play the role of a learning course; that would require a separate book. I only want to remind you about the main principles of Windows programming, which hope-fully will be useful when analyzing executable modules.

1.3.1. General Concepts

Windows programming is based on the use of *application program interface* (API) functions. Using API functions, an application can communicate directly with the Windows operating system. Applications built on the basis of such interactions are more tightly integrated into the operating system and, consequently, have more powerful capabilities in comparison to other programs. Sometimes, API functions are called *system calls*. However, this designation is not particularly correct. System calls (in UNIX, for example) are calls to system procedures stored in the operating system kernel. The operating system provides a range of such procedures to simplify resource management for application programs. API functions are an additional interface layer between system procedures and application programs. When calling an API function, you do not know whether it would be executed entirely by the code of the dynamic link library (DLL) loaded into your address space or it would use some procedures stored in the kernel. The Windows operating system is changing and evolving, newer versions are released, but API remains without changes (although new functions might be added to it). Thus, it becomes possible to achieve full compatibility with programs written using only the basic set of API functions.

API functions are supported by using DLLs stored in the system directory (windows\system32). Linking of these libraries is ensured by the compiler (so-called late implicit binding). The total number of API functions is enormous; it exceeds 3,000. Most intensely used are API functions located in the following four DLLs:

❏ Kernel32.dll — This library stores the main system control and management functions (including functions for controlling memory, applications, resources, and files).

❏ User32.dll — This library contains various functions of the user interface (including the ones for processing window messages, timers, and menus).

❏ Gdi32.dll — This is the graphics device interface (GDI) library, containing lots of graphics window functions.

❏ Comctl32.dll — This library contains functions that service various controls. In particular, this library is responsible for the new control style (Windows XP interface style).

If the API function accepts a pointer to string as one of the input arguments, then such a function has two versions: the one with the A prefix for ANSI strings, and one with the W prefix for the Unicode strings. For example, there are two versions for the MessageBox API function: MessageBoxA and MessageBoxW. In high-level programming languages, such as C++, it is necessary to initially determine, with which strings the program operates. Therefore, the compiler automatically selects an appropriate version of the function. When writing a program in Assembly, it is necessary to explicitly specify, which version of a specific function should be used.

There are two main types of application programs under Windows: *console* applications and *graphical user interface* (GUI) applications. A specific feature of a console application is that when executing such an application, the system creates a text window, called the console, for this application (or, as a variant, the application inherits the console from the parent process). GUI applications work with graphical windows that can contain graphics and various controls, such as buttons, edit fields, and list boxes. GUI applications are also called *graphical* or *windowing* applications. Windows can run other types of applications — services and drivers, which are also known as system applications. In addition, Windows can run applications in Posix and OS/2 subsystems, although with limited possibilities. These types of applications will not be covered in detail in this book.

Usually, Windows programs are written using library functions (C/C++) or library classes (in Delphi, they are called components). In this case, interaction with the operating system is hidden under the layer of libraries. As a result, the analysis of the executable code becomes more complicated because it becomes necessary to determine, which library function or class is in use. This can be achieved by analyzing the library code to determine, which API functions are called, and to understand the aim of these calls. These are not trivial tasks. The goal of this section is to explain the general structure of a Windows program to enable you to understand approaches to analysis of API calls.

In essence, all differences between console and GUI applications consist of the Subsystem flag stored in the portable executable (PE) header (see *Section 1.5*). This flag is set when linking an application. The following command-line options should be chosen when linking applications using link.exe: /SUBSYSTEM:WINDOWS for GUI applications and /SUBSYSTEM:CONSOLE for console applications. Accordingly, when working with high-level programming languages, the compiler must provide options that allow you to choose between console and GUI applications. At the same time, console and GUI applications are equal in access rights to the operating system resources. Any console application can create graphical windows and work with them, and any GUI application, in turn, can work with console windows.

1.3.2. Console Applications

Console applications are compact, both in compiled form and in source code form. The console itself deserves special attention. As you presumably know, a console is a text-mode window. Interaction between a console application and such a window is reduced to the following:

❑ If a console application is started by another console program, then a child program by default inherits the console of the parent program.

❑ If the parent program has no console, the system creates a new one for the newly-started application.

❑ A console application can have only one console.

❑ A console program can create a new console using the `AllocConsole` API function, provided that it gets rid of the existing console.

One reason the console appeared in the Windows operating system, which initially was oriented toward graphics applications, was the necessity of running older applications written for MS-DOS. As you may recall, MS-DOS was initially oriented toward working with text strings. When running such a program, Windows automatically allocates a console for it and automatically redirects to the console all its input and output.

The classical structure of the console application can be called a batch structure (Listing 1.4). The program consists of the sequence of the actions that need to be executed. For example, the program might open some file, carry out some actions, and then close the file and terminate operation.

Listing 1.4.[i] A typical console application

```
#include <windows.h>
char *s = "Example of console program.\n\0";
char buf[100];
DWORD d;
void main()
{
// Free the console if it has been inherited.
        FreeConsole();
// Create a new console.
        AllocConsole();
// Obtain the output handle for console output.
        HANDLE ho = GetStdHandle(STD_OUTPUT_HANDLE);
// Obtain the handle for console input.
        HANDLE hi = GetStdHandle(STD_INPUT_HANDLE);
```

---

[i] All C++ programs in this book were developed in the Visual Studio .NET environment unless stated otherwise.

```
// Output a string to the console.
        WriteConsole(ho, s, lstrlen(s), &d, NULL);
// Use the ReadConsole function for viewing the console screen.
        ReadConsole(hi, (void*)buf, 100, &d, NULL);
// Close the handles.
        CloseHandle(ho);
        CloseHandle(hi);
// Free the console.
        FreeConsole();
}
```

Listing 1.4 shows an example of a typical console application that outputs a string to the text screen. A specific feature of this program is that it creates its own console, no matter whether it was started from a console or otherwise. The sequence of FreeConsole()/AllocConsole() function calls frees the existing program console and creates a new one. Nothing happens to the inherited console; the program simply gains the possibility of creating its own console. If you remove the FreeConsole function in the beginning of this program and start it from the console application, then no new console would be created. The program will redirect all of its output to the existing console, despite the presence of the AllocConsole() function.

The program in Listing 1.4 is based on API functions. Even the lstrlen function used for obtaining the string length is actually an API function. Now, consider how IDA Pro[i] recognizes the executable code (Listing 1.5).

Listing 1.5. The disassembled listing of the executable code

```
.text:00401000 _main   proc near             ; CODE XREF: start + 16E↓p
.text:00401000         push    ebx
.text:00401001         mov     ebx, ds:FreeConsole
.text:00401007         push    esi
.text:00401008         push    edi
.text:00401009         call    ebx                      ; FreeConsole
.text:0040100B         call    ds:AllocConsole
```

---

[i] The IDA Pro 4.7 disassembler will be used for listings throughout this book.

```
.text:00401011  mov     edi, ds:GetStdHandle
.text:00401017  push    0FFFFFFF5h                  ; nStdHandle
.text:00401019  call    edi                         ; GetStdHandle
.text:0040101B  push    0FFFFFFF6h                  ; nStdHandle
.text:0040101D  mov     esi, eax
.text:0040101F  call    edi                         ; GetStdHandle
.text:00401021  push    0                           ; lpReserved
.text:00401023  mov     edi, eax
.text:00401025  mov     eax, lpString
.text:0040102A  push    offset NumberOfCharsWritten ; lpNumberOfCharsWritten
.text:0040102F  push    eax                         ; lpString
.text:00401030  call    ds:lstrlenA
.text:00401036  mov     ecx, lpString
.text:0040103C  push    eax                  ; nNumberOfCharsToWrite
.text:0040103D  push    ecx                         ; lpBuffer
.text:0040103E  push    esi                         ; hConsoleOutput
.text:0040103F  call    ds:WriteConsoleA
.text:00401045  push    0                           ; lpReserved
.text:00401047  push    offset NumberOfCharsWritten ; lpNumberOfCharsRead
.text:0040104C  push    64h                  ; nNumberOfCharsToRead
.text:0040104E  push    offset unk_4072C8           ; lpBuffer
.text:00401053  push    edi                         ; hConsoleInput
.text:00401054  call    ds:ReadConsoleA
.text:0040105A  push    esi                         ; hObject
.text:0040105B  mov     esi, ds:CloseHandle
.text:00401061  call    esi                         ; CloseHandle
.text:00401063  push    edi                         ; hObject
.text:00401064  call    esi                         ; CloseHandle
.text:00401066  call    ebx                         ; FreeConsole
.text:00401068  pop     edi
```

```
.text:00401069          pop     esi
.text:0040106A          xor     eax, eax
.text:0040106C          pop     ebx
.text:0040106D          retn
.text:0040106D _main    endp
```

Even at the first glance of an inexperienced user, it becomes immediately clear that the IDA Pro disassembler has solved the problem of disassembling executable code excellently. Nevertheless, in this chapter I am not going to describe disassembled listings; the next and further chapters will concentrate on this problem. For the moment, I would only like to draw your attention to how the programs written using only API functions produce a transparent and clearly understandable executable code.

When speaking about programs similar to the one shown in Listing 1.4, most programmers use C++ library functions instead of API functions. Listing 1.6 represents such a program.

Listing 1.6. An example of a console application using C++ library functions instead of API functions

```
#include <stdio.h>
char *s = "Example of console program.\n\0";
char buf[100];
void main()
{
        puts(s);
        gets(buf);
}
```

It is necessary to mention that the program in Listing 1.6 doesn't create a new console of its own but uses the console provided by the operating system. In general, however, its features and behavior are the same as the ones of the program shown in Listing 1.4. For working with the console, this program uses the puts and gets functions. The most interesting feature here is that the IDA Pro disassembler easily disassembles standard C++. Looking deeper into the code of the puts function, for example, you can easily notice that execution of this function is finally reduced to execution of the `WriteFile` API function, which in this case is equivalent to the `WriteConsole` function. However, application developers often use nonstandard libraries, the functions of which cannot be easily recognized and whose goals are not immediately clear. In particular, this happens if you attempt to disassemble a program written in Delphi. For example, in the Delphi environment execution of the `write` console operator requires you to call two library procedures, the intention and goals of which cannot be recognized by IDA Pro.

The linear (or, in other words, batch) structure of a console program is simple enough. Although the operations as such might be complex, their sequential order considerably simplifies code investigation. However, if you want to write a program that would tightly interact with the user, you'll have to process keyboard and mouse events. In this case, the program structure would become considerably more complicated. You'll have to introduce a function for processing the main console events and a loop for processing keyboard and mouse events. Listing 1.7 shows an approximate design of such a program.

Listing 1.7. An example of a console program that interacts with the user

```
#include <windows.h>

BOOL WINAPI handler(DWORD);
void inputcons();
void print(char *);

HANDLE h1, h2;
char *s1  = "Error input!\n";
char s2[35];
char *s4  = "CTRL+C\n";
char *s5  = "CTRL+BREAK\n";
char *s6  = "CLOSE\n";
char *s7  = "LOGOFF\n";
char *s8  = "SHUTDOWN\n";
char *s9  = "CTRL\n";
char *s10 = "ALT\n";
char *s11 = "SHIFT\n";
```

```c
char *s12 = "\n";
char *s13 = "Code %d \n";
char *s14 = "CAPSLOCK \n";
char *s15 = "NUMLOCK \n";
char *s16 = "SCROLLOCK \n";
char *s17 = "Enhanced key (virtual code) %d \n";
char *s18 = "Function key (virtual code) %d \n";
char *s19 = "Left mouse button\n";
char *s20 = "Right mouse button\n";
char *s21 = "Double click\n";
char *s22 = "Wheel was rolled\n";
char *s23 = "Character '%c' \n";
char *s24 = "Location of cursor x=%d y=%d\n";

void main()
{
// Console initialization
        FreeConsole();
        AllocConsole();
// Obtain the output handle.
        h1 = GetStdHandle(STD_OUTPUT_HANDLE);
// Obtain the input handle.
        h2 = GetStdHandle(STD_INPUT_HANDLE);
// Set the events handler.
        SetConsoleCtrlHandler(handler, TRUE);
// Call the function with the message-processing loop.
        inputcons();
// Delete the handler.
        SetConsoleCtrlHandler(handler, FALSE);
// Close the handles.
        CloseHandle(h1); CloseHandle(h2);
// Free the console.
        FreeConsole();
// Exit the program.
        ExitProcess(0);
```

```
};


// Events handler
BOOL WINAPI handler(DWORD ct)


{
// Is this a <CTRL>+<C> event?
        if(ct == CTRL_C_EVENT) print(s4);
// Is this a <CTRL>+<BREAK> event?
        if(ct == CTRL_BREAK_EVENT) print(s5);
// Is it necessary to close the console?
        if(ct == CTRL_CLOSE_EVENT)
        {
                print(s6);
                Sleep(2000);
                ExitProcess(0);
        };
// Is it necessary to terminate the session?
        if(ct == CTRL_LOGOFF_EVENT)
        {
                print(s7);
                Sleep(2000);
                ExitProcess(0);
        };
// Is it necessary to terminate the operation?
        if(ct == CTRL_SHUTDOWN_EVENT)
        {
                print(s8);
                Sleep(2000);
                ExitProcess(0);
        };
        return TRUE;
};


// The function containing the console's message-processing loop
```

```
void inputcons()
{
        DWORD n;
        INPUT_RECORD ir;
        while(ReadConsoleInput(h2, &ir, 1, &n))
        {
// Process mouse events.
                if(ir.EventType == MOUSE_EVENT)
                {
// Double-click.
                        if(ir.Event.MouseEvent.dwEventFlags == DOUBLE_CLICK)
                                print(s21);
// Move the mouse cursor over the console.
                        if(ir.Event.MouseEvent.dwEventFlags == MOUSE_MOVED)
                        {
                wsprintf(s2, s24, ir.Event.MouseEvent.dwMousePosition.X,
                        ir.Event.MouseEvent.dwMousePosition.Y);
                                print(s2);
                        };
// Mouse wheel
                        if(ir.Event.MouseEvent.dwEventFlags == MOUSE_WHEELED)
                                print(s22);
// Left mouse button
if(ir.Event.MouseEvent.dwButtonState == FROM_LEFT_1ST_BUTTON_PRESSED)
                print(s19);
// Right mouse button
if(ir.Event.MouseEvent.dwButtonState == RIGHTMOST_BUTTON_PRESSED)
                print(s20);
                };
                if(ir.EventType == KEY_EVENT)
                {
                        if(ir.Event.KeyEvent.bKeyDown != 1)continue;
```

```
// Extended keyboard

if(ir.Event.KeyEvent.dwControlKeyState == ENHANCED_KEY)
                        {

wsprintf(s2, s17, ir.Event.KeyEvent.wVirtualKeyCode);
                                print(s2);
                        };
// Is this the <CAPS LOCK> key?

if(ir.Event.KeyEvent.dwControlKeyState == CAPSLOCK_ON)
                                print(s14);
// Is this the left <ALT> key?

if(ir.Event.KeyEvent.dwControlKeyState == LEFT_ALT_PRESSED)
                                print(s10);
// Is this the right <ALT> key?

if(ir.Event.KeyEvent.dwControlKeyState == RIGHT_ALT_PRESSED)
                                print(s10);
// Is this the left <CTRL> key?

if(ir.Event.KeyEvent.dwControlKeyState == LEFT_CTRL_PRESSED)
                                print(s9);
// Is this the right <CTRL> key?

if(ir.Event.KeyEvent.dwControlKeyState == RIGHT_CTRL_PRESSED)
                                print(s9);
// Is this the <SHIFT> key?

if(ir.Event.KeyEvent.dwControlKeyState == SHIFT_PRESSED)
                                print(s11);
// Is this the <NUM LOCK> key?

if(ir.Event.KeyEvent.dwControlKeyState == NUMLOCK_ON)
                                print(s15);
// Is this the <SCROLL LOCK> key?

if(ir.Event.KeyEvent.dwControlKeyState == SCROLLLOCK_ON)
```

```
                                print(s16);
// Handler for normal keys
                        if(ir.Event.KeyEvent.uChar.AsciiChar >= 32)
                        {

wsprintf(s2, s23, ir.Event.KeyEvent.uChar.AsciiChar);
                                print(s2);
                        } else
                        {
                                if(ir.Event.KeyEvent.uChar.AsciiChar > 0)
                                {
// Keys with codes >0 but <32 are processed here.

wsprintf(s2, s13, ir.Event.KeyEvent.uChar.AsciiChar);
                                        print(s2);
                                } else
                                {
// These keys are called functional keys.

wsprintf(s2, s18, ir.Event.KeyEvent.wVirtualKeyCode);
                                        print(s2);
                                };
                        };
                };
        };
// Error message
        print(s1);
        Sleep(5000);
};


// Console output function
void print(char *s)
{
        DWORD n;
        WriteConsole(h1, s, lstrlen(s), &n, NULL);
};
```

I won't describe this program in detail because I expect that you are an experienced programmer. If you are interested in programming console applications, I recommend that you read my book about Windows programming [3].

When analyzing the program presented in Listing 1.7, it is possible to discover an interesting detail: The handler function is not called explicitly. Its address is specified in the SetConsoleCtrlHandler API function. Naturally, the only method of accessing this important fragment of the program is to analyze the call to the SetConsoleCtrlHandler function to obtain its address. The IDA Pro disassembler behaves in exactly this way. Consider the program fragment shown in Listing 1.8.

Listing 1.8. IDA Pro analyzes the SetConsoleCtrlHandler call to obtain the address of the handler function

```
.text:00401453    mov     edi, ds:SetConsoleCtrlHandler
.text:00401459    push    1                 ; Add
.text:0040145B    push    offset loc_401000 ; HandlerRoutine
.text:00401460    mov     hConsoleInput, eax
.text:00401465    call    edi               ; SetConsoleCtrlHandler
```

The disassembler not only correctly recognizes the call to SetConsoleCtrlHandler but also correctly interprets both parameters of this function. Do not become confused by the mov hConsoleInput, eax command; it has no relation to the ConsoleCtrlHandler call. On the contrary, it relates to the previous call — GetStdHandle. This is the cost of optimization.

NOTE

It should be admitted that contemporary compilers can optimize the code much better than professional programmers in Assembly. A programmer is always bound to observe various conventions, such as programming style and code readability. These conventions do not matter for the compiler. Various methods of optimization will be covered later in this book.

Recall the previously described fragment. Because of the SetConsoleCtrlHandler function, the disassembler correctly determines the beginning of the handler function, which allows correct disassembling of this function.

Pay attention to the inputcons function. Principally, it doesn't contain anything unusual. The calls to the ReadConsoleInput function in the loop allow you to detect events that cannot be traced by the `handler` function. This loop could be called the message-processing loop of a console application. Such loops are more typical of windowing applications; however, for console applications this approach is also permitted. Naturally, there is a considerable difference between the two methods of message processing. Each application can have only one console window; therefore, there is no need to determine, to which window an individual message relates. A GUI application can have several windows but only one message loop (see *Section 1.3.3*). Under these circumstances, each message is marked by the handle of the window, for which that message is intended. At this point, some difficulties might arise, which will be explained in the next section.

1.3.3. Windowing Applications

Windowing applications, also known as GUI applications, are based on event-driven mechanisms. In other words, the main part of the code of such applications is concentrated in specialized functions, which, similar to the `handler` function from the previous section, are called by the system at a specific event. In addition, for this type of application, the presence of the message-processing loop is typical. The message-processing loop is used to redirect each newly-arrived message to the appropriate `handler` function (Listing 1.9).

Listing 1.9. A typical GUI application

```
#include <windows.h>

LRESULT CALLBACK WndProc(HWND, UINT, WPARAM, LPARAM);

int APIENTRY WinMain(HINSTANCE hInstance,
                     HINSTANCE hPrevInstance,
                     LPSTR     lpCmdLine,
                     int       nCmdShow)
{
       char cname[] = "Class";
       char title[] = "A simple Windows application";
       MSG msg;

       // The structure for window class registration
```

```
WNDCLASS wc;
wc.style          = 0;
wc.lpfnWndProc    = (WNDPROC)WndProc;
wc.cbClsExtra     = 0;
wc.cbWndExtra     = 0;
wc.hInstance      = hInstance;
wc.hIcon          = LoadIcon(hInstance, (LPCTSTR)IDI_APPLICATION);
wc.hCursor        = LoadCursor(NULL, IDC_ARROW);
wc.hbrBackground  = (HBRUSH)(COLOR_WINDOW + 1);
wc.lpszMenuName   = 0;
wc.lpszClassName  =cname;

// Register the class.
if(!RegisterClass(&wc)) return 0;

// Create the window.
HWND  hWnd = CreateWindow(
        cname,                    // Class
        title,                    // Header
        WS_OVERLAPPEDWINDOW,      // Window style
        0,                        // X coordinate
        0,                        // Y coordinate
        500,                      // Window width
        300,                      // Window height
        NULL,                     // Handle of the parent window
        NULL,                     // Menu handle
        hInstance,                // Application identifier
        NULL);                    // Pointer to the structure sent
                                  // by the WM_CREATE message
// Check whether the window has been created.
if (!hWnd) return 0;

// Display the new window.
ShowWindow(hWnd, nCmdShow);

// Update the window contents.
```

```
        UpdateWindow(hWnd);

        // Message-processing loop
        while (GetMessage(&msg, NULL, 0, 0))
        {

        // Translate the virtual key codes to ASCII codes.
                TranslateMessage(&msg);

        // Redirect the message to the window procedure.
                DispatchMessage(&msg);
        }

        return 0;
};

// Window procedure
LRESULT CALLBACK WndProc(HWND hWnd,
UINT message,
WPARAM wParam,
LPARAM lParam)
{
        switch(message)
        {

// Message sent when creating the window
        case WM_CREATE:
                break;

// Message sent when destroying the window
        case WM_DESTROY:

// Message sent when exiting the message-processing loop
                PostQuitMessage(0);
                break;
```

```
// Message sent when redrawing the window contents
        case WM_PAINT:
                break;

// Return unprocessed messages.
                default:
        return DefWindowProc(hWnd, message, wParam, lParam);
        }
        return 0;
}
```

Listing 1.9 demonstrates a minimal GUI application characterized by all minimal functional capabilities of a Windows application. In general, Windows applications are built on the basis of the main window. All remaining windows "orbit" the main window like planets of the solar system around the sun. Thus, it is easy to distinguish the three main components of such an application:

❏ Definition and registration of the window class, to which the main window should belong
❏ Message-processing loop, the main task of which is "catching" the messages arriving to the application and redirecting them to the required window function (not just the main window function)
❏ The main window function and, possibly, functions of other windows

Being aware of such relationship patterns, it is possible to purposefully search for individual elements of a GUI application.

`DispatchMessage` is the main API function in the message-processing loop. This function redirects the newly-arrived messages to the given window function. The message structure appears as shown in Listing 1.10.

Listing 1.10. The message structure

```
typedef struct {
    HWND hwnd;
    UINT message;
    WPARAM wParam;
```

```
    LPARAM lParam;
    DWORD time;
    POINT pt;
} MSG
```

In the preceding listing, you will find the following:

- ❑ hwnd — The handle of the window, to which the current message is addressed.
- ❑ message — The code of the current message.
- ❑ wParam — An optional parameter containing supplementary information.
- ❑ lParam — An optional parameter containing supplementary information.
- ❑ time — The time, at which the message was sent.
- ❑ pt — The mouse cursor coordinate at the time the message was sent. The least significant word designates the X coordinate, and the most significant word designates the Y coordinate.

The hwnd value defines the window, to which the message must be sent. For each window — to be more precise, for each window class — there is a special message-processing function (see Listing 1.9). The system knows this, and the message arrives where necessary. Users, however, do not know this. By the way, the main part of the program code is either concentrated within such functions or is called from them. How is it possible to solve this problem? To solve it (at least, to begin solving it correctly), recall that most window functions must be registered. The function and the window class are registered. For example, consider Listing 1.9: The address of the message-processing function is loaded into the lpfnWndProc field. In other words, having looked at the disassembled application code, you'll learn the function address. For example, consider a fragment of the disassembled listing produced by the IDA Pro disassembler (Listing 1.11).

Listing 1.11. A fragment of a disassembled GUI application code produced by IDA Pro

```
.text:00401077  mov [esp + 80h + WndClass.lpfnWndProc], offset loc_401000
```

Here, loc_401000 determines the window function address. The program understands the RegisterClass function and the structure that this function accepts as an argument. Listing 1.12 shows a fragment obtained using the W32Dasm v. 10 disassembler, which also has a good reputation.

Listing 1.12. A disassembled fragment obtained using the W32Dasm v. 10 disassembler

```
:00401077 C744241800104000          mov [esp+18], 00401000
:0040107F 896C241C                   mov dword ptr [esp+1C], ebp
:00401083 896C2420                   mov dword ptr [esp+20], ebp
:00401087 89742424                   mov dword ptr [esp+24], esi


* Reference To: USER32.LoadIconA, Ord:01BDh
                                     |
:0040108B FF15C4504000               Call dword ptr [004050C4]
:00401091 68007F0000                 push 00007F00
:00401096 55                         push ebp
:00401097 89442428                   mov dword ptr [esp+28], eax


* Reference To: USER32.LoadCursorA, Ord:01B9h
                                     |
:0040109B FF15C8504000               Call dword ptr [004050C8]
:004010A1 89442424                   mov dword ptr [esp+24], eax
:004010A5 8D44240C                   lea eax, dword ptr [esp+0C]
:004010A9 8D542450                   lea edx, dword ptr [esp+50]
:004010AD 50                         push eax
:004010AE C744242C06000000           mov [esp+2C], 00000006
:004010B6 896C2430                   mov dword ptr [esp+30], ebp
:004010BA 89542434                   mov dword ptr [esp+34], edx


* Reference To: USER32.RegisterClassA, Ord:0216h
                                    |
:004010BE FF15CC504000              Call dword ptr [004050CC]
:004010C4 6685C0                    test ax, ax
```

Having carefully considered the listing produced by W32Dasm, you should immediately conclude that it is considerably less informative than the one generated by IDA Pro. Nevertheless, in most cases, it correctly determines API functions. Thus, it is easy to find the `RegisterClass` function. Then, by the other functions preceding `RegisterClass`, it is possible to conclude that the `mov [esp + 18], 00401000` command assigns the value of the window function address to the `lpfnWndProc` field. Thus, having detected the window function, an investigator can analyze its text and then find an individual fragment that carries out the specific action.

The window function is intended for processing messages delivered to it. There are lots of messages informing the window function about various events that occur to the window or some of its controls. Finally, it is possible to send custom, user-defined messages to the window function. For this purpose, there is a special `WM_USER` constant, and all messages defined programmatically must be greater than or equal to this constant. By the text of the window function, it is possible to determine the reaction of the program to a specific event and thus to understand the working mechanism of the specific GUI application.

The problem, however, is that the window function doesn't relate to a specific window: It relates to the entire class of windows. When the application is based on API programming, one function can correspond to one window. However, this is rarely the case. Processing messages intended for different windows doesn't require considerable effort, because every message contains a window descriptor (handle). However, this results in certain difficulties when analyzing executable code, because in the course of static code analysis it is difficult to determine, for which window the message processed by the current code fragment is intended. At this point, debuggers are helpful; they can help set breakpoints to the code of the window function or, as with the SoftIce debugger, even to a specific message from a specific window.

Naturally, the message-processing loop plays an extremely important role in every GUI program. Having located it in the disassembled code, you'd be able to locate the program fragment that precedes the loop — in other words, determine where in the program the main window is created and where the main window class is registered. To search for the message-processing loop, use such API functions as `GetMessage`, `PeekMessage`, `TranslateMessage`, and `DispatcheMessage`, as well as the `IsDialogMessage` function.

1.3.4. Applications Based on Dialogs

Listing 1.13 presents an example of an application, in which the main window is a modal dialog (Fig. 1.4).

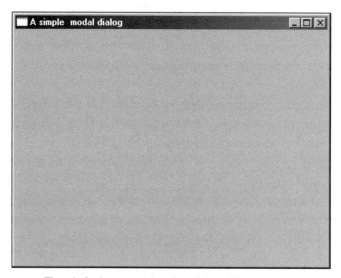

Fig. 1.4. An example of a dialog (Listing 1.13)

Listing 1.13. An example application that uses a modal dialog

```
// Resource identifiers
// Definitions of style constants
#define WS_VISIBLE          0x010000000L
#define WS_SYSMENU          0x00080000L
#define WS_MINIMIZEBOX      0x00020000L
#define WS_MAXIMIZEBOX      0x00010000L


// Modal dialog definition
DIALOG DIALOGEX 10, 10, 150, 100
STYLE  WS_VISIBLE | WS_SYSMENU | WS_MINIMIZEBOX |WS_MAXIMIZEBOX
CAPTION "Modal dialog"
FONT 12, "Arial"
{
```

```
}

// Program module
#include <windows.h>

int DWndProc(HWND, UINT, WPARAM, LPARAM);

__stdcall WinMain(HINSTANCE hInstance,
    HINSTANCE hPrevInstance,
    LPSTR lpCmdLine,
    int nCmdShow
)
{
// Create a modal dialog.
DialogBoxParam(hInstance, "DIALOG", NULL, (DLGPROC)DWndProc, 0);

// Close the application.
ExitProcess(0);
};

// Message-handling function of the modal dialog
int DWndProc(HWND hwndDlg, UINT uMsg, WPARAM wParam, LPARAM lParam)
        {
                switch(uMsg)
        {
// Message that arrives when the dialog is created
        case WM_INITDIALOG:
                break;
// Message that arrives in case of an attempt at closing the window
        case WM_CLOSE:
        EndDialog(hwndDlg, 0);
        return TRUE;
```

```
// Message from window controls
      case WM_COMMAND:
              break;
      };

              return FALSE;
      };
```

In contrast to normal windows, modal dialogs are characterized by the following features:

❏ Modal dialogs are created on the basis of a template stored in program resources or created in the memory. In the example from Listing 1.13, the modal dialog is created on the basis of the template stored in the resources file.

❏ Modal dialogs are created using the `DialogBoxParam` function. The fourth parameter of this function specifies the address of the function that processes window messages. The `DialogBoxParam` function doesn't return control until the `EndDialog` function is called.

❏ The message-processing function of a dialog is similar to the message-processing function of a normal window. If the function receives the message and processes that message itself, it returns `TRUE`; otherwise, it returns `FALSE`. As relates to messages, the main difference is that the `WM_INITDIALOG` message comes to the dialog instead of the `WM_CREATE` message that comes to a normal window.

❏ In contrast to a normal window, the dialog has no message-processing loop. To be more precise, there is one, but the operating system creates it and processes and redirects the message. Thus, you can encounter applications that have no obvious message-processing loops.

❏ Important issues of working with modal dialogs are the processing of the `WM_CLOSE` message and the call to the `EndDialog` function, which removes the modal dialog from the memory.

By the way, the window called by the `MessageBox` API function is a typical example of a modal dialog box. In this case, the system not only processes the message but also creates the window template and organizes the window message function.

NOTE In the resources file (see Listing 1.13), window style constants are defined explicitly. However, this is not necessary. You can simply insert the following line of code: #include windows.h>. Alternatively, you can use the Resource Wizard of the Visual Studio .NET product, after which you needn't worry about the contents of the resources file.

Again, consider how IDA Pro disassembled this file (Listing 11.14). The DialogBoxParam function helps you find the dialog's message-processing function.

Listing 1.14. The disassembled code of the fragment shown in Listing 1.13

```
.text:00401000 ; BOOL __stdcall DialogFunc(HWND, UINT, WPARAM, LPARAM)
.text:00401000 DialogFunc  proc near ; DATA XREF: WinMain(x, x, x, x) + 6↓o
.text:00401000
.text:00401000              hDlg  = dword ptr  4
.text:00401000              arg_4 = dword ptr  8
.text:00401000
.text:00401000              cmp   [esp+arg_4], 10h
.text:00401005              jnz   short loc_401014
.text:00401007              mov   eax, [esp + hDlg]
.text:0040100B              push  0          ; nResult
.text:0040100D              push  eax        ; hDlg
.text:0040100E              call  ds:EndDialog
.text:00401014
.text:00401014 loc_401014:                   ; CODE XREF: DialogFunc + 5↑j
.text:00401014              xor   eax, eax
.text:00401016              retn
.text:00401016 DialogFunc  endp
.text:00401016
.text:00401016 ; ----------------------------------------------------------
.text:00401017              align 10h
.text:00401020
.text:00401020 ; ------- S U B R O U T I N E ----------------------------
.text:00401020
.text:00401020
```

```
.text:00401020 ; __stdcall WinMain(x,x,x,x)
.text:00401020 _WinMain@16  proc near         ; CODE XREF: start + 186↑p
.text:00401020
.text:00401020 hInstance      = dword ptr  4
.text:00401020
.text:00401020               mov     eax, [esp + hInstance]
.text:00401024               push    0                     ; dwInitParam
.text:00401026               push    offset DialogFunc   ; lpDialogFunc
.text:0040102B               push    0                     ; hWndParent
.text:0040102D               push    offset TemplateName ; lpTemplateName
.text:00401032               push    eax                   ; hInstance
.text:00401033               call    ds:DialogBoxParamA  ; Create a modal
.text:00401033                                 ; dialog box from a dialog box.
.text:00401033                                         ; Template resource
.text:00401039                 push    0                     ; uExitCode
.text:0040103B                 call    ds:ExitProcess
.text:00401041                 int     3           ; Trap to debugger.
.text:00401041 _WinMain@16     endp
```

Finally, it is necessary to mention another type of window: nonmodal dialogs. Windows of this type require an explicit message-processing loop. Listing 1.15 provides an example of an application, in which a nonmodal dialog plays the role of the main window.

Listing 1.15. An example application, in which a nonmodal dialog plays the role of the main window

```
// Resources file
// Resource identifiers
// Definitions of style constants
#define WS_VISIBLE          0x010000000L
#define WS_SYSMENU          0x00080000L
#define WS_MINIMIZEBOX      0x00020000L
#define WS_MAXIMIZEBOX      0x00010000L
```

```
// Definition of the nonmodal dialog
DIALOG DIALOGEX 10, 10, 150, 100
STYLE  WS_VISIBLE | WS_SYSMENU | WS_MINIMIZEBOX |WS_MAXIMIZEBOX
CAPTION "Nonmodal dialog"
FONT 12, "Arial"
{
}

// Program module
#include <windows.h>
MSG msg;

int DWndProc(HWND, UINT, WPARAM, LPARAM);

__stdcall WinMain(HINSTANCE hInstance,
    HINSTANCE hPrevInstance,
    LPSTR lpCmdLine,
    int nCmdShow)

{
// Nonmodal dialog
    HWND hdlg = CreateDialog(hInstance, "DIALOG", NULL, (DLGPROC)DWndProc);
// Message-processing loop
        while (GetMessage(&msg, NULL, 0, 0))
        {
                IsDialogMessage(hdlg, &msg);
        }
// Close the application.
        ExitProcess(0);
};

// Window function of the nonmodal dialog
int DWndProc(HWND hwndDlg, UINT uMsg, WPARAM wParam, LPARAM lParam)
        {
        switch(uMsg)
        {
```

```
// Message coming when the dialog is created
        case WM_INITDIALOG:
                break;
// Message coming in an attempt at closing the dialog
        case WM_DESTROY:
                PostQuitMessage(0);
                break;
        case WM_CLOSE:
                DestroyWindow(hwndDlg);
                return TRUE;
// Message from window controls
        case WM_COMMAND:
                break;
        };


                return FALSE;
        };
```

As you can see from Listing 1.15, the program is similar to a normal windowing application. However, there still are some specific features:

❑ The most obvious feature is that there is no window class registration block.

❑ The message-processing loop is slightly modified. Instead of the normal TranslateMessage and DispatchMessage functions, the IsDialogMessage function is used. The use of the latter relates to the problem with using the <Tab> key for switching among the window controls. The IsDialogMessage function is used to ensure that everything is working correctly in the nonmodal dialog. In general, when an application contains both normal windows and nonmodal dialogs, the message-processing loop might appear as shown in Listing 1.16.

Listing 1.16. Message-processing loop of an application containing normal windows and nonmodal dialogs

```
while (GetMessage(&msg, NULL, 0, 0))
{
if(!IsDialogMessage(hw, &msg))
```

```
        {
                TranslateMessage(&msg);
                DispatchMessage(&msg);
        }
}
```

Here, `hw` is the nonmodal dialog handle. However, the `IsDialogMessage` function can also be used for a normal window.

A certain difference in processing of the window closing event (clicking the **Close** button in the top right corner) also attracts attention. A normal window is actually closed by the system and, accordingly, the `WM_DESTROY` message is delivered to the window function, which is processed to exit the message-processing loop (`PostQuitMessage`). The nonmodal window is not closed automatically; therefore, it is necessary to process the `WM_CLOSE` message and then close the window using the `DestroyWindow` function. There are no secrets here. The `DefWindowProc` function processes the `WM_CLOSE` message and implicitly calls the `DestroyWindow` function.

1.4. Command Format of the Intel Microprocessor

1.4.1. General Considerations

When you consider the list of Intel Pentium microprocessor, you might ask, how are these commands stored in computer memory? And what is the difference, for example, between `MOV EAX, EBX` and `MOV EAX, EDI` commands? The goal of this section is to demonstrate some regular patterns of encoding Intel processor commands. If you become interested in analysis of the command format, this will help you considerably when investigating executable code.

Fig. 1.5 shows the memory area, in which the program code is located. This dump was created using the OllyDbg debugger, which will be covered later in this chapter. To decrypt this sequence of bytes and turn it into machine commands (to be more precise, into Assembly commands), it is necessary to know the formats of these commands. For the moment, I'll concentrate your attention on this topic.

Address	Hex dump
00401000	55 8B EC 53 C7 05 D0 86 40 00 32 00 00 00 C7 05
00401010	C4 86 40 00 58 02 00 00 C7 05 C8 86 40 00 BC 02
00401020	00 00 A1 D0 86 40 00 3B 05 C4 86 40 00 8D 1D 53
00401030	10 40 00 89 1D CC 86 40 00 77 05 A1 C4 86 40 00
00401040	3B 05 C8 86 40 00 76 06 FF 25 CC 86 40 00 A1 C8
00401050	86 40 00 A3 C0 86 40 00 A1 C0 86 40 00 50 68 FC
00401060	60 40 00 E8 06 00 00 00 83 C4 08 5B 5D C3 53 56
00401070	57 BE 70 80 40 00 56 E8 0F 02 00 00 8B F8 8D 44
00401080	24 18 50 FF 74 24 18 56 E8 50 03 00 00 56 57 8B
00401090	D8 E8 7D 02 00 00 83 C4 18 5F 5E 8B C3 5B C3 83
004010A0	3D DC 86 40 00 02 74 05 E8 F6 0E 00 00 FF 74 24
004010B0	04 E8 76 0D 00 00 68 FF 00 00 00 FF 15 40 80 40
004010C0	00 59 59 C3 6A 18 68 00 61 40 00 E8 14 17 00 00
004010D0	BF 94 00 00 00 8B C7 E8 64 18 00 00 89 65 E8 8B
004010E0	F4 89 3E 56 FF 15 08 60 40 00 8B 4E 10 89 0D F8
004010F0	86 40 00 8B 46 04 A3 04 87 40 00 8B 56 08 89 15

Fig. 1.5. Dump of the program code

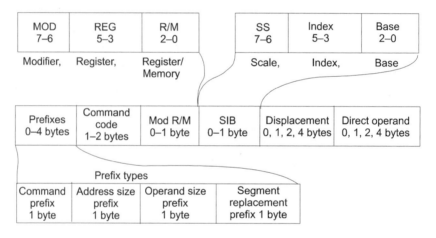

Fig. 1.6. The Intel processor command format

First, it is necessary to point out that the command length might range from 1 byte to 10 bytes or even more. Fig. 1.6 shows the general format of the Intel processor command. As you can see, the command structure might be complex. Fortunately, however, it is possible to understand its structure, because the processor correctly interprets the command code and executes it. With luck, your intention of understanding it will not be a hopeless job.

To begin with, consider prefixes. As you can see, prefixes are optional. It would be logical to assume that all prefixes shown in Fig. 1.6 must have strictly defined codes to ensure that the prefix and the command code cannot be confused in the course of decryption. There are four types of prefixes:

❑ The command prefix can take the following values:
  - F3H — The repeat prefix REPE/REPZ
  - F2H — The repeat prefix REPNE/REPNZ
  - F0H — The bus blocking prefix LOCK
❑ The address size (size replacement) prefix takes the 67H value.
❑ The operand size (size replacement) prefix takes the 66H value.
❑ Segment replacement prefixes take the following values:
  - 2EH — For the CS register
  - 36H — For the SS register
  - 3EH — For the DS register
  - 26H — For the ES register
  - 64H — For the FS register
  - 65H — For the GS register

It is important to mention that no more than two prefixes of the same type can be encountered within the same command. An attempt at writing such a command would cause a processor error.

Thus, knowing prefix codes, it is possible to tell with certainty, from which component the command begins: from the code or from the prefix. Note that this is the case only if you know for sure, from which address the command being studied starts. Otherwise, disassembling will start from the middle of the command, and the resulting Assembly code won't correspond to the reality.

1.4.2. Command Code

Now, consider the code of the processor command. The code provided in Listing 1.17 presents a small and easy fragment of an Assembly program.

Listing 1.17. A small Assembly program for studying formats of the Intel processor commands

```
PUSH        EAX
PUSH        EBX
PUSH        ECX
```

```
POP        ECX
POP        EBX
POP        EAX
RET
```

As you can see, the contents of three registers, each register in turn, are stored in the stack. Then the values saved in the stack are popped into the same registers. After completion of these commands, the program exits the procedure. Thus, if you consider the memory area, in which these commands are stored, you'll notice the following sequence of bytes:

50 53 51 59 5B 58 C3

The first idea that comes to mind is that each of the preceding commands requires 1 byte. You can see typical 8-bit commands. For example, C3H is nothing but the code of the RET (to be more precise, the RETN) command. The first 6 bytes, however, are the most interesting. First, consider PUSH commands. Here are binary equivalents of these commands: 01010000B (PUSH EAX), 01010011B (PUSH EBX), and 01010001B (PUSH ECX). Note that these commands differ only in their least significant bytes. Consequently, the following conclusion is self-evident: The command as such is encrypted in the command code; in other words, it specifies, which action and which register are subject to the given operation. To confirm this assumption, consider binary codes of the following three POP commands: 01011001B (POP ECX), 01011011B (POP EBX), and 01011000B (POP EAX). The situation becomes clearer. For instance, compare binary representations of the PUSH EBX and POP EBX commands. Note that the first 2 bits are matching. In essence, however, the first 2 bits are also matching for other pairs of commands, such as PUSH EAX/POP EAX and PUSH ECX/POP ECX. To be precise, the first 3 bits are matching. On the other hand, for all PUSH commands, the first 5 bits are matching (01010B). Accordingly, the situation is the same for all POP commands (01011B). The regular pattern just discovered is not a random one. Actually, not only operations but also registers are encrypted in the code of the PUSH reg and POP reg commands. Register codes are universal. They can be encountered not only in the command code but also in the Mod R/M field. This issue will be covered later in this chapter.

For the moment, consider the codes of 32-bit working registers:

❏ EAX — 000B	❏ EBX — 011B	❏ ECX — 001B	❏ EDX — 010B
❏ EDI — 111B	❏ ESI — 110B	❏ ESP — 100B	❏ EBP — 101B

At first glance, everything is straightforward, because a regular pattern has been discovered. However, the situation is not that simple. There are also 16-bit registers, as well as 8-bit registers. But the most disappointing issue is that the codes of the PUSH and POP operations dealing with registers other than the previously-listed working registers or even memory cells that play the role of operands, are different. All of these issues will be covered in due order.

Note that PUSH and POP commands are not applicable to 8-bit registers. Thus, problems with addressing 8-bit registers do not arise in relation to PUSH and POP commands. However, there are also 16-bit registers. It might seem surprising, but 16-bit registers are encoded in the same way as 32-bit registers. For example, the AX register has the 110B code. And what about commands that push data into the stack where 16-bit registers can be encountered? The answer is straightforward: The operand size replacement prefix preceding the command code is used, in other words, 66H. Thus, for example, the PUSH AX command will be represented by 2 bytes: 66 50. A command such as POP EAX will be represented by the following sequence: 66 58. Having encountered this prefix, the processor is informed that within the current command it is necessary to replace a 32-bit operand with a 16-bit one. This allows you to draw the following conclusion: Using 32-bit registers is more efficient than using 16-bit registers.

Unfortunately, the regular patterns related to the codes of the registers in the POP and PUSH commands are limited to this rule. Here are the codes of these commands applicable to the segment registers:

❏ PUSH CS — 0EH	❏ PUSH FS — 0FA0H	❏ POP ES — 07H
❏ PUSH DS — 1EH	❏ PUSH GS — 0FA8H	❏ POP FS — 0FA1H
❏ PUSH SS — 16H	❏ POP DS — 1FH	❏ POP GS — 0FA9H
❏ PUSH ES — 06H	❏ POP SS — 17H	

The only pattern that can be discovered here is that the codes of the pairs of commands (such as PUSH DS/POP DS) differ by one. Also, it is necessary to note that these commands for segment registers FS and GS have 2-byte codes. Because these registers were introduced in newer models of the Intel family of processors, there were no 1-byte codes for them. In general, processor developers are always constrained in their choice of possible solutions; therefore, you shouldn't expect overall regularity in those solutions.

Continuing the investigation process, it is logical to find an answer to the following question: Are the command bytes used anywhere besides at designating the command and the register codes?

Consider conditional jump commands. First, it is necessary to find out how the near jumps (in other words, jumps within 256 bytes) are encoded. Consider a small fragment of an Assembly program (Listing 1.18). Note that although this example has no practical meaning, it allows you to detect certain interesting patterns.

Listing 1.18. A fragment of the Assembly program intended for studying the jump instructions format

```
        JZ    _LAB
        JNZ  _LAB
        JB    _LAB
        JNB  _LAB
        JG    _LAB
        JNG  _LAB
_LAB:
```

Viewing this code with the debugger, you'll see the following sequence of bytes:

```
74 0A 75 08 72 06 73 04 7F 02 7E 00
```

Clearly, every command takes 2 bytes, and the second byte defines the address, to which the jump will take place, provided that appropriate condition is carried out. As you can easily see after considering carefully the codes of the first and the last commands, this is simply displacement (see Fig. 1.6) from the end of the command. Thus, everything is clear — at least for the moment.

Now, consider the first bytes of the command more carefully. The general pattern is as follows:

❏ JZ — 01110100B   ❏ JB — 01110010B   ❏ JG — 01111111B
❏ JNZ — 01110101B   ❏ JNB — 01110011B   ❏ JNG — 01111110B

The conclusion is self-evident: The code of the conditional jump operation is simply 70H, and the 4 least significant bits define the condition. At the same time, it is obvious that the least significant bit defines inversion: For JZ, this bit is zero, for JNZ this bit is one, etc. At the same time, some rules of intuitive logic are observed: *equal to zero* corresponds to the zero value of this bit, and *greater than* means that this bit is set to one. Bits 1–3 define the condition as such. Because 3 bits allow eight different conditions to be specified, it is possible to combine Table 1.10 and the newly-obtained results to compose Table 1.26.

Table 1.26. Conditional jumps codes

Command	Code
JB/JNAE/JC	001
JBE/JNA	011
JE/JZ	010
JL/JNGE	110
JLE/JNG	111
JO	000
JP/JPE	101
JS	100

A natural question might arise: What about conditional jumps, for which the offset in a 32-bit segment plays the role of the address? To investigate this issue, modify the code fragment presented in Listing 1.18. The modified version is in Listing 1.19.

Listing 1.19. Investigating conditional jump codes when the offset in a 32-bit segment acts as the address

```
        JZ   _LAB
        JNZ _LAB
        JB   _LAB
        JNB _LAB
        JG   _LAB
        JNG _LAB
        DB    1000H DUP(0)
_LAB:
```

By inserting a data block after the JNB command, you will force the assembler to generate jumps with the 32-bit offset. The result will appear as shown in Listing 1.20.

Listing 1.20. The dump of the code presented in Listing 1.19

```
OF 84 1E  10 00 00
OF 85 18  10 00 00
OF 82 12  10 00 00
OF 83 0C  10 00 00
OF 8F 06  10 00 00
OF 8E 00  10 00 00
```

In the preceding listing, the result is presented as a table, where each row corresponds to its associated command. As you can see, now the command code is made up of 2 bytes. The first byte of each row is always 0FH. The structure of the second byte has been already considered. The operation code is 80H, and it is followed by the condition code and inversion bit. As relates to the address, it looks strange at first. Well, the address (to be more precise, the offset), is simply a normal 32-bit number, for which the standard principle must be used: The most significant byte in the word must have the higher address, and the most significant word must have the higher address. Thus, the result 1E 10 00 00 is nothing but 00 00 10 1E, and this is the exact distance in bytes between the JNZ _LAB command and the RET command. The situation is the same for other conditional jump commands.

1.4.3. The MOD R/M Byte

Consider a seemingly easy operation: MOV EAX, EBX. Its code is made up of 2 bytes: 8B C3. Because there are lots of variants for sending data between registers, it would be logical to assume that both registers are encoded here: EAX and EBX. Also, it would be logical to assume that the first byte is the opcode and the registers are encoded in the second byte. Thus, C3 in binary representation is 11000011. To make a comparative analysis, consider the MOV EBX, EAX command. The code of this command is 8B D8. By the way, this confirms the assumption that the first byte contains the opcode. However, D8H corresponds to 11011000B. Compare this byte to the binary representation of C3. Naturally, these bytes differ from each other by the following bit triplets: 000B and 011B. These are the previously-mentioned codes of the EAX and EBX register. Great! The code of the MOV command operating over two 32-bit registers has been practically clarified. You have encountered the MOD R/M byte, the structure of which will now be considered in more detail (see Fig. 1.6).

The MOD R/M byte has the following three fields (see Fig. 1.6):

❐ The MOD field — Along with the R/M field, this field forms 32 possible values: 8 registers and 24 indexing modes. In the example provided earlier, this field had the value 11 and specified that the R/M field would represent the register code.

❐ The REG/Code field — This field designates either the register code or the additional 3 bits of the operation code.

❐ The R/M field — This field can designate the register as the location of the operand or encode the addressing mode, along with the MOD field.

A reasonable question can arise: What would the difference be between the MOV EAX, EBX and the MOV AX, BX operations? You have probably guessed this already. The latter command will start with the prefix — the additional 66H byte mentioned previously.

And what about MOV commands where 8-bit registers are encountered? Because the developers were short of 3-bit codes, it would be logical to assume that the code of the command would change. This assumption proves true. For example, the MOV BL, AL command would be encoded by 2 bytes: 8A D8. Note that there are eight 8-bit registers; consequently, they also can be encoded using the same 3 bits:

❐ AL — 000B   ❐ CL — 001B   ❐ AH — 100B   ❐ CH — 101B

❐ BL — 011B   ❐ DL — 010B   ❐ BH — 111B   ❐ DH — 110B

Now, you'll easily notice that the D8H byte corresponds to the BL and AL registers. By the way, it is possible to guess that the MOV command, where there is one register and one immediate operand, must do without the MOD R/M byte. In this case, it is necessary to encode only one operand. For example, the code of the MOV EBX, 1234H command will be equivalent to BB 34120000, and the MOV ECX, 1234H command will correspond to B9 34120000. Try to investigate this issue on your own. As can be easily seen, the command code corresponds to B8H, and the first 3 bits define the register, into which the immediate operand will be saved. However, you'll be surprised when you consider the MOV EAX, 1234H command. The command code will be B8 34120000. This way, the developers have taken into account that the command for moving data into the EAX register (accumulator) will be carried out more often than the command for copying data into other registers. Thus, they made this command shorter.

Consider the fragment in Listing 1.21.

Listing 1.21. A test program for studying the format of MOV commands

```
MOV EAX, DATA1
MOV EBX, DATA1
MOV ECX, DATA1
MOV EDX, DATA1
MOV EDI, DATA1
MOV ESI, DATA1
```

Here, DATA1 is some 32-bit variable. Having disassembled this fragment, you'll obtain the result in Listing 1.22.

Listing 1.22. The disassembled listing of the program shown in Listing 1.21

```
A1    00104000
8B1D 00104000
8B0D 00104000
8B15 00104000
8B3D 00104000
8B35 00104000
```

As can be easily noticed, the EAX register also differs from the other registers. There is a special code for moving data from the memory into the register. As relates to the other commands, the MOD R/M byte is present. Having converted the hex code into binary code, you'll see that the MOD field in all commands equals zero (00B), the REG field encodes the register, and the R/M field equals 101B. It would be logical to assume that the MOD and R/M fields define a certain addressing mode, as with all previously-presented commands, except the one that uses the EAX register. This is so. The current mode assumes that the effective address is determined by only one number — the offset in a 32-bit register. By the way, what would happen if you interchanged the operands in the previously-described commands? Only the command code would change. Everything else should not change, because neither the addressing method nor the register used in the command has changed.

Consider the MOV [EBX], ECX command. As you can see, this command uses indirect addressing through the EBX register. The code of such operations in this command is 89H. The MOD R/M byte contains information about the registers and the mode of addressing — 0B. It can be clearly seen that the MOD field contains 00 and the REG and R/M fields contain the codes of the ECX and EBX registers, respectively. Now, take on a more complicated task: Investigate the MOV [EBX + 10], ECX command. For this command, the disassembler produces the following sequence of bytes: 89 4B 0A. As you can see, the command code remained the same. Obviously, the last byte is the offset. The structure of the MOD R/M byte appears as follows: 01001011B. As a result, in comparison to the MOV [EBX], ECX command, only the MOD field has changed. The reason for this is clear: It occurred because the addressing has changed. I hope that you would be able to compose the following table (Table 1.27) explaining the behavior of the MOD R/M byte on your own.

Table 1.27. MOD R/M byte structure in 32-bit addressing

Effective address	MOD field value	R/M field value
[EAX]	00	000
[EBX]	00	011
[ECX]	00	001
[EDX]	00	010
[ESI]	00	110
[EDI]	00	111
Offset32	00	101
[...]	00	100
Offset8[EAX]	01	000
Offset8[EBX]	01	011
Offset8[ECX]	01	001
Offset8[EDX]	01	010
Offset8[ESI]	01	110
Offset8[EDI]	01	111

continues

Table 1.27 Continued

Effective address	MOD field value	R/M field value
Offset8[EBP]	01	101
Offset8[...]	01	100
Offset32[EAX]	10	000
Offset32[EBX]	10	011
Offset32[ECX]	10	001
Offset32[EDX]	10	010
Offset32[ESI]	10	110
Offset32[EDI]	10	111
Offset32[EBP]	10	101
Offset32[...]	10	100
EAX/AX/AL	11	000
EBX/BX/BL	11	011
ECX/CX/CL	11	001
EDX/DX/DL	11	010
ESP/SP/AH	11	100
EBP/BP/CH	11	101
ESI/SI/DH	11	110
EDI/DI/BH	11	111

In Table 1.27, Offset8 stands for the 1-byte offset, Offset32 stands for the 4-byte offset, and the [...] string means that for this combination of the MOD and R/M fields the MOD R/M byte will be followed by the SIB byte.

NOTE

Consider Table 1.27 more carefully. As you can see, the MOD R/M byte doesn't allow you to define such an important property of relative addressing as the scaling coefficient. Another byte is used for this purpose, the SIB byte. The value of the R/M field set to 100B indicates that the SIB byte must be present.

1.4.4. The SIB Byte

Finally, it is time to consider the SIB byte. Its name stands for scale index base. Accordingly, this byte has the following three fields (see Fig. 1.6).

❏ Bits 7–6, the Scale field, specify the scaling coefficient.
❏ Bits 5–3, the Index field, specify the register — index.
❏ Bits 2–0 define the register that is the Base.

Consider the fragment in Listing 1.23, written in Assembly language.

Listing 1.23. A fragment of the test program for studying the role of the SIB byte

```
MOV  [EAX*4][EBX+5],  EAX
MOV  [EBX*4][EAX+5],  EAX
MOV  [ECX*8][EDX+5],  EAX
MOV  [EDX*8][ECX+5],  EAX
```

Here are the bytes corresponding to the preceding commands (Listing 1.24).

Listing 1.24. The machine code corresponding to the fragment shown in Listing 1.23

```
89  44  83   05
89  44  98   05
89  44  CA   05
89  44  D1   05
```

The operation code in all cases equals 89H. The 44H hex number is nothing but the MOD R/M byte. Convert it to the binary format: 44H = 01000100B. Thus, it becomes clear that MOD = 01. This means that the offset must be present in this command. This is so: The offset equals 5, and the byte representing it is the last byte. The REG field is 000B, which means that the data are copied from the EAX register. As relates to the R/M field, it equals 100B, and this is exactly the exception (see Table 1.27), which means that the SIB byte must follow it. By the way, note that all of the preceding commands differ only by this byte. Start investigation from the first command. For this command, the code is as follows: 83H = 10000011B. The Scale field, equal to 10B, sets the scaling coefficient. The Index field is 000B; this is the index register. It equals EAX. The EAX register is used for forming the resulting address. The Base field equals 011B and defines the base register, which equals the EBX register. Thus, everything is clear with this byte. Now it would be expedient to consider the general method of using the SIB byte (Table 1.28).

Table 1.28. Structure of the SIB byte

Scaling index	Scale field value	Index field value
[EAX]	00	000
[EBX]	00	011
[ECX]	00	001
[EDX]	00	010
[EBP]	00	101
[ESI]	00	110
[EDI]	00	111
Unused	00	100
[EAX*2]	01	000
[EBX*2]	01	011
[ECX*2]	01	001
[EDX*2]	01	010
[EBP*2]	01	101
[ESI*2]	01	110
[EDI*2]	01	111
Unused	01	100
[EAX*4]	10	000
[EBX*4]	10	011
[ECX*4]	10	001
[EDX*4]	10	010
[EBP*4]	10	101

continues

Table 1.28 Continued

Scaling index	Scale field value	Index field value
[ESI*4]	10	110
[EDI*4]	10	111
Unused	10	100
[EAX*8]	11	000
[EBX*8]	11	011
[ECX*8]	11	001
[EDX*8]	11	010
[EBP*8]	11	101
[ESI*8]	11	110
[EDI*8]	11	111
Unused	11	100

Hopefully, the difference between MOV [EAX*8] [EBX + 10], ECX and MOV [EAX] [EBX*8 + 10], ECX is now clearer. In the first command, the scaling index is represented by the EAX register; in the second command, this role is delegated to the EBX register and, accordingly, the situation is opposite for the base. Also, it becomes clear that commands such as MOV [EAX*4] [EBX*2], EAX are technically impossible.

1.4.5. Simple Example of Manual Disassembling

Now, having gained the necessary experience, you can try to disassemble the code shown in Fig. 1.5. The 55H code stands for the PUSH EBP command. This can be easily discovered if you recall that the code of the PUSH command is 50H and the code of the EBP register equals five (101B). After these codes comes the 8DH code. Clearly, this isn't a prefix, because the prefix codes are well known. Principally, it is possible to consult the manual or enter the command under the debugger. It turns out that this code corresponds to the LEA command. Because the command must have two operands, it is obvious that the command must have the MOD R/M byte. The next byte is ECH. After representing it in the binary format, you'll obtain the following result: ECH = 11101100B. If everything is correct, then the first 2 bits define register addressing, in which case the data are stored directly in the register (see Table 1.27). In this case, the next 3 bits (REG) define the register, into which the data will be loaded, and the last bits define the register, from which the data will be obtained. This source register happens to be the ESP register (the 100B code).

The LEA command normally is used for obtaining the address of some variable. How would the command code appear if this is the case? The situation is clear and straightforward. Assume that you have encountered the following command: LEA EBP, DATA1. The result of its disassembling will appear as follows: 8D 2D 00 10 40 00. Clearly, the last 4 bytes of this byte sequence stand for the variable address. How would the MOD R/M byte appear? This is 2DH = 00101101B. Pay attention to the last 3 bits and consult Table 1.27 (with MOD = 00). The last 3 bits specify the 101B number, which means that the effective address will be the offset within a segment — in other words, the direct address of the variable. Hence, it becomes clear that the second byte is followed by the offset.

Now recall Fig. 1.3. The next byte equals 53H. Thus, it is clear that in this case you are dealing with the PUSH EBX command (the 3 = 011B code stands for the EBX register). The next byte is C7H. This is the code of the MOV command, where the destination is either a register or a memory cell (the DWORD data type) and the source is an immediate operand. Clearly, the next byte must be the MOD R/M byte. The value of this byte is 05H = 00000101B. Hence, it is possible to conclude that an immediate operand is loaded into a memory cell. The next 4 bytes must be the address of that cell. Here they are: D0 86 40 00. Now, it becomes possible to determine that the address of the required cell is 004086D0H. Finally, the last byte of this command is 32H. Thus, it is possible to draw the following conclusion: You have decoded the MOV DWORD PTR [004086D0H], 32 command. Why DWORD, you might ask? This is because the command code is C7H. If the command were MOV BYTE PTR [004086D0H], 32, then the C6H code would be used. Now, consider the commands decoded after carrying out this exercise (Listing 1.25).

Listing 1.25. The commands decoded using the manual disassembling technique

```
PUSH EBP
LEA EBP, ESP
PUSH EBX
MOV DWORD PTR [4086D0H], 32
```

Manual disassembling is a tedious job, isn't it? However, having mastered the techniques described in this section and with some hands-on practice, you'll discover that there isn't anything particularly difficult about it.

As it turns out, some microprocessor commands can be represented by at least two different sets of codes. Here is a typical example of such a situation. The MASM32 translator converts the MOV EBX, 34H command into the following sequence of codes: BB 34 00 00 00. In this case, the code of the EBX register is encoded in the first 3 bits of the command code (011B). However, there is another possibility of encoding the same command from a more general point of view — namely, using the MOD R/M byte. When using this representation, the command will appear as the following sequence of bytes: C7 C3 34 00 00 00. As you can see, the second variant of the command representation is 1 byte longer.

1.4.6. Disassembling Problems

The commonly-adopted point of view is that Assembly language is practically the same as machine language. Apparently, it is possible to draw a seemingly obvious conclusion that the code of any Assembly program can be unambiguously reconstructed by the machine code. However, despite this opinion, the situation is not that simple. There are certain problems, which will be covered in this section.

The first problem relates to the reconstruction of the data structure. The only possibility of determining the data structure is analyzing the way, in which these data are used in commands. This is where the problem arises. The data can be accessed in different ways. For example, consider a command that at first glance can be disassembled easily — let this be the MOV DWORD PTR [4086D0H], 32 command. This command shows that some data element (variable) is located at the 4086D0H address. The addressing mode is direct, so everything is clear. However, what would you say about the MOV EAX, [EBX] command? To find out what is stored in the EBX register, it is necessary to analyze the program code. You are lucky if the command being analyzed is preceded, for example, by the sequence in Listing 1.26.

Listing 1.26. The command sequence clarifying that some 32-bit variable is located at the 4176A8H address

```
MOV EAX, 4176A0H

ADD EAX, 8

MOV EBX, EAX
```

On the basis of these commands, it becomes clear that some 32-bit variable is stored at the 4176A8H address. However, the actual address is often formed several hundred commands from the command that uses it. Sophisticated manipulations often are used to form that address. If this is the case, then such an address can be determined only by executing the program step by step, in other words, by using debugging mechanisms.

Furthermore, obtaining the variable address often is not enough; it is also necessary to know its size. For example, when dealing with an array, it isn't easy to determine how many elements are contained there. Even knowing the address of the next variable doesn't always help, because there might be additional alignment bytes between two variables.

This situation is further aggravated by the availability of two different commands that allow you to obtain an address of some object in memory. Traditionally, the LEA command was intended for obtaining the address of the specified variable, for example: LEA EAX, al. Thus, having encountered a byte sequence such as 8D 05 08 10 40 00, you would immediately discover that the address equal to 401008H is loaded into the EAX register. (The 8DH code corresponds to the LEA command, and 05H stands for the MOD R/M byte. Recall that such an analysis has already been conducted several times.) However, there is another command in Assembly language that does the same thing, namely, the MOV reg32, offset var command. The offset keyword makes the assembler substitute the variable address instead of the variable value into the command. Thus, it is difficult to understand without code analysis whether you are dealing with an immediate operand or an address. Note that sometimes carrying out such an analysis might be a difficult task.

Another problem relates to determining jump addresses and procedure addresses. Control can be passed to the procedure not only by the CALL command but also by the JMP or even RET command. Listing 1.27 shows an example program that demonstrates the four methods of calling procedures. With all that being so, the last three methods of calling procedures might result in serious complications, which under certain conditions prevent the researcher from determining that a certain code section is in fact a procedure called from some other location.

The code of the program illustrating different methods of calling procedures is provided in Listing 1.27.

Listing 1.27. A test program illustrating different methods of calling procedures

```
.586P
.MODEL FLAT, STDCALL
TEXT SEGMENT
START:
; Explicit call
        CALL PR1
        LEA  EAX, PR1
; Implicit call
        CALL EAX
        PUSH OFFSET L1
; Return address in the stack
        JMP  EAX
L1:
        PUSH OFFSET L2
        PUSH EAX
; Now the stack top contains the procedure address.
; The next stack element contains the return address from the procedure.
        RETN            ; The call using the RET command
L2:
        RETN
PR1 PROC
        RETN
PR1 ENDP
TEXT ENDS
END START
```

The most important problem is finding the correct address, from which the required block of commands starts. If the procedure couldn't be identified using *cross-references*, then you might hope that you'll at least correctly decode the block where procedures are located. Alas, even this goal isn't always guaranteed to be reached — at least programmatically. It isn't clear where the block of procedures starts. Assume, however, that you have located the first procedure, to which there is a direct call. Further assume that you have located its end. Unfortunately, no one can guarantee that another procedure is located directly after it. Any number of NOP instructions can separate two procedures. For instance, MASM32 can insert such operations using the ALIGN directive.

Various issues of recognizing data, procedures, and other program structures will be covered in more detail in *Chapter 3*.

1.4.7. x87 Floating-Point Unit Commands

You'd probably like to know more about the arithmetic coprocessor. Is there any principal difference between the FPU commands and the normal commands of the Intel Pentium microprocessor? Running a few steps forward, I'll answer that there are no principal differences. However, there are certain specific features. The minimum length of an FPU command is 2 bytes. The first byte of a command, which was always called the operation code for the processor commands, but which isn't called an opcode for FPU commands (see later in this chapter), always has the 5 most significant bits set to 11011B. This means that the most significant nibble of the first byte of an FPU command is always equal to DH. This allows investigators to easily identify a coprocessor command within a sequence of bytes in the main memory.

In addition to the first byte, an FPU command contains the MOD R/M byte and, possibly, an operand pointing to the memory location from which or into which the operand is copied. For example, consider the FLD QWORD PTR [20814000H] command that pushes into the coprocessor stack some long floating-point number from the memory location pointed at by the operand or address. This command is represented by the following sequence of bytes: DD05 20814000. The first byte will appear as follows in the binary format: 11011101B. The 5 most significant bits were already mentioned, while the 3 least significant bits are of great interest to investigators. This command is part of the group of FPU commands intended for manipulations over operands located in the main memory. If the least significant bit of this byte equals one, this means that the command passes the data from the coprocessor stack into the memory or copies the data from the memory. All other commands have this bit set to zero. For example, these might be arithmetic or comparison operations. Bytes 2 and 1 for the commands under consideration determine the type of the memory format (MF). The following four values are possible:

❏   00 — A short floating-point number (32 bits)
❏   01 — A short integer binary number (32 bits)

❐   10 — A long floating-point number (64 bits)

❐   11 — A 10-byte number (80 bits)

In this case, you are dealing with the value 10, in other words, with a long floating-point number. Thus, it becomes possible to state that the first byte of the FPU command code *can no longer be considered an operation code.*

Now, consider the structure of MOD R/M byte: 05H = 00000101B. Thus, the following are true: MOD = 00B, REG = 000B, and R/M = 101B. Having consulted Table 1.27, you can draw an obvious conclusion — namely, that the address is defined by the direct offset (by the R/M value). Thus, the 3 bits in the middle (called REG) are nothing but the operation code.

Consider the code of another command: FADD ST(1), ST(0) (see Table 1.21). This command adds the operands located in ST(0) and ST(1) and loads the result into the ST(1) register. The command code equals DC C1. In binary representation, this code will appear as follows: 11011100 11000001. Consider the first byte. Bit 0 is set to zero and is the part of the operation code in arithmetic and comparison operations, where coprocessor registers participate. The value of bit 1 defines whether or not the stack is popped after the operation. In this command, the stack is not popped, because the value of bit 1 is set to zero. Bit 2 shows whether the result is returned into the stack top (0) or into some other register (1). In the case being considered, the result is returned into the ST(1) register. Now, proceed with the analysis of the second byte. The MOD field is set to 11B, which means that the operation is executed over the operands stored in registers. The R/M field stores the 001B value, which defines the second register participating in the operation (ST(1)). The first register is always the ST(0) register. Finally, the code of the operation just considered is 0000B.

Now, consider the FSQRT command that computes the square root from the operand located at the top of the stack. For this and similar commands, including (except for transcendental functions) loading of some constants and some arithmetic operations, it is typical to use only one stack register — ST(0). The code of this operation is D9 FA, which in the binary format appears as follows: 11011001 11111010. For such an operation, all bits are constant except for the first 4 bits of the second byte of the operation (1010B), which define the operation being executed.

Finally, there is another type of operation that controls the FPU. These operations do not accept any operands. An example of such an operation is the FINIT operation (see Table 1.23), which initializes the coprocessor at start-up. The code of this operation is DB E3, or 11011011 11100011 in the binary format. For these operations, as in the previous case, only the first 4 bits of the second byte are significant. These bits define, which operation is being executed.

Thus, the section on Intel Pentium microprocessor command formats has been completed.

1.5. Structure of the Portable Executable Module

The main goal of this section is to describe the structure of a PE module, a type of executable (EXE) module. Because the main goal of any investigator is studying executable modules, it is necessary to know their structure. This information is of special importance, because this structure is typical not only for executable files but also for DLLs, object modules (OBJ files), and drivers.

1.5.1. General Approach

The PE format was introduced in the UNIX operating system, where its analogue is known as the common object file format (COFF). Microsoft revised this format by introducing considerable modifications to it. Nowadays, it is widely used. As already mentioned, this format is used not only for executable modules but also for DLLs, as well as for kernel-mode drivers. The most interesting issue is that the PE standard also covers OBJ files. You main goal is to master the PE format at such a level that you can understand its structure and use this knowledge in practice.

The main feature of any PE module is the simplicity of loading it into the memory. No additional tuning is needed for this purpose. In essence, a PE module is a snapshot of a main memory region.

Fig. 1.7 shows the general design of the PE format. The first section (in Fig. 1.7, it is shown on the top) deserves the closest attention. Here, the developers have ensured backward compatibility to the MS-DOS operating system. To gain sound understanding of the operating mechanisms of the PE format, it is necessary to consider this section in detail. Thus, any executable module starts with the DOS section, which is necessary when the program is started in the MS-DOS environment. The first 2 bytes (MZ) represent the signature that confirms that you are dealing with an MS-DOS executable module. The MZ signature is the initials of the Microsoft programmer, Mark Zbikowski, who developed the structure of MS-DOS executable modules. If you start a PE program under MS-DOS, the loader of this operating system would read this signature, recognize the module as a normal MS-DOS program, and start it for execution in a normal way. This is so because the MZ signature in a correct PE module is followed by the MS-DOS header, which, in turn, is followed by a small stub procedure. This stub usually displays a text screen informing the user that the current program cannot be executed under the MS-DOS operating system, after which it terminates the operation. The standard stub is shown in Listing 1.28.

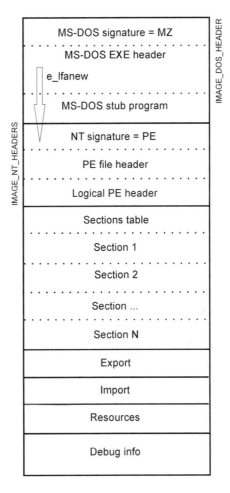

Fig. 1.7. The PE file structure

Listing 1.28. The standard MS-DOS stub

```
PUSH CS
; Data register matches the code register.
POP DS
MOV DX, OFFSET MSG
MOV AH, 9
; Output the MSG text string.
INT 21H
MOV AX, 4C01H
; Exit the program with code 1.
INT 21H
MSG DB ' This program cannot be run in DOS mode $'
```

This code might be different. However, it doesn't matter much, because pure MS-DOS can no longer be encountered. Therefore, this stub never gains control. The most convenient way of parsing the MZ header is to study the IMAGE_DOS_HEADER structure that can be found in the winnt.h[i] file. This structure is shown in Listing 1.29.

Listing 1.29. The IMAGE_DOS_HEADER structure

```
struct IMAGE_DOS_HEADER {       // DOS EXE header
      WORD    e_magic;          // Magic number
      WORD    e_cblp;           // Bytes on the last page of the file
      WORD    e_cp;             // Pages in the file
      WORD    e_crlc;           // Relocations
      WORD    e_cparhdr;        // Size of the header in paragraphs
      WORD    e_minalloc;       // Minimum extra paragraphs needed
      WORD    e_maxalloc;       // Maximum extra paragraphs needed
      WORD    e_ss;             // Initial (relative) SS value
      WORD    e_sp;             // Initial SP value
      WORD    e_csum;           // Checksum
```

---

[i] All structures used in the PE header are taken from the header files.

```
    WORD    e_ip;               // Initial IP value

    WORD    e_cs;               // Initial (relative) CS value

    WORD    e_lfarlc;           // File address of the relocation table

    WORD    e_ovno;             // Overlay number

    WORD    e_res[4];           // Reserved words

    WORD    e_oemid;            // OEM identifier (for e_oeminfo)

    WORD    e_oeminfo;          // OEM information (e_oemid specific)

    WORD    e_res2[10];         // Reserved words

    LONG    e_lfanew;           // File address of the new EXE header

}
```

Only three fields of this structure are of interest from the standpoint of parsing the MZ header. The e_magic field represents the MZ signature. The e_lfarlc field (located at the 18H offset from the start of the file) was initially intended for storing the address of the *relocation table*. The relocation table was used by the MS-DOS loader to configure relative addresses used within a program. If this field contains the 40H byte, then this file is a PE module.[i] Apparently, however, Windows doesn't check the contents of this field; consequently, it is not expedient to consider that the field value equal to 40H is a sure indication of a PE value. Finally, the e_lfanew field contains the relative address (at the offset counted from the start of the file), from which the PE header starts (see Fig. 1.7). This address must contain the PE module signature, the P and E characters, respectively.

Listing 1.30 shows a simple program you can use to determine whether this file is a loadable PE module. The name of the module to be checked must be specified in the command line.

Thus, you have become acquainted with the IMAGE_DOS_HEADER structure. The IMAGE_NT_HEADERS structure that represents the PE header will be covered in later sections. This structure is defined in the windows.h file. Accordingly, the IMAGE_DOS_SIGNATURE and IMAGE_NT_SIGNATURE constants defining the MZ (5A4Dh) and PE (4550h) signatures are also contained in this header file.

---

[i] Or this file is an NE module used under Windows 3.1. Such programs are rarely encountered nowadays.

Listing 1.30. A simple program for determining whether this file is a loadable PE module

```c
#include <windows.h>
#include <stdio.h>
HANDLE openf(char *);
HANDLE hf;
IMAGE_DOS_HEADER id;
IMAGE_NT_HEADERS iw;
// The main function
int main(int argc, char* argv[])
{
        DWORD n;
        int er = 0;
        LARGE_INTEGER l;
// Check whether parameters are present.
        if(argc < 2){printf("No parameters!\n"); er = 1; goto _exit;};
// File name is the first in the list.
        if((hf = openf(argv[1])) == INVALID_HANDLE_VALUE)
        {
                printf("No file!\n");
                er = 2;
                goto _exit;};
// Determine the file length.
                GetFileSizeEx(hf, &l);
// Read the MS-DOS header.
                if(!ReadFile(hf, &id, sizeof(id), &n, NULL))
        {
                printf("Read DOS_HEADER error 1!\n");
                er = 3;
                goto _exit;};
        if(n < sizeof(id))
        {
                printf("Read DOS_HEADER error 2!\n");
                er = 4;
```

```
                goto _exit;};
// Check the MS-DOS signature ('MZ').
        if(id.e_magic != IMAGE_DOS_SIGNATURE)
        {
                printf("No DOS signature!\n");
                er = 5;
                goto _exit;}
        printf("DOS signature is OK!\n");
        if(id.e_lfanew > l.QuadPart)
        {
                printf("No NT signature!\n");
                er = 6;
                goto _exit;};
// Move the pointer.
        SetFilePointer(hf, id.e_lfanew, NULL, FILE_BEGIN);
// Read the NT header.
        if(!ReadFile(hf, &iw, sizeof(iw), &n, NULL))
        {
                printf("Read NT_HEADER error 1!\n");
                er = 7;
                goto _exit;};
        if(n < sizeof(iw))
        {
                printf("Read NT_HEADER error 2!\n");
                er = 8;
                goto _exit;};
// Check the NT signature ('PE').
        if(iw.Signature != IMAGE_NT_SIGNATURE)
        {
                printf("No NT signature!\n");
                er = 9;
                goto _exit;}
        printf("NT signature is OK!\n");
// Close the file descriptor.
_exit:
```

```
        CloseHandle(hf);
        return er;
};
// Function opens the file for reading.
HANDLE openf(char *nf)
{
        return CreateFile(nf,
                GENERIC_READ,
                FILE_SHARE_WRITE | FILE_SHARE_READ,
                NULL,
                OPEN_EXISTING,
                NULL,
                NULL);
};
```

Naturally, the program in Listing 1.30 cannot guarantee that you are or are not dealing with the correct PE header. To achieve this, more detailed analysis of the PE header will be required.

In *Appendix 1*, the example program analyzes the PE header in more detail. This program was written on the basis of the example presented in Listing 1.30. In addition to the analysis of the file headers, this program displays the contents of the import, export, and resource sections.

1.5.2. The Portable Executable Header

Now, consider the PE header. As already mentioned, this header is in the form of the IMAGE_NT_HEADERS structure (Listing 1.31).

Listing 1.31. The IMAGE_NT_HEADERS structure

```
struct IMAGE_NT_HEADERS {
    DWORD Signature;
    IMAGE_FILE_HEADER FileHeader;
    IMAGE_OPTIONAL_HEADER32 OptionalHeader;
}
```

As you can see, this structure is made up of two parts, IMAGE_FILE_HEADER and IMAGE_OPTIONAL_HEADER32. It also contains the Signature field, which is PE. Consider the IMAGE_FILE_HEADER structure, also known as the main header (Listing 1.32).

Listing 1.32. The IMAGE_FILE_HEADER structure

```
struct IMAGE_FILE_HEADER {
        WORD    Machine;
        WORD    NumberOfSections;
        DWORD   TimeDateStamp;
        DWORD   PointerToSymbolTable;
        DWORD   NumberOfSymbols;
        WORD    SizeOfOptionalHeader;
        WORD    Characteristics;
}
```

The fields of this structure are briefly outlined as follows:

- ❑ Machine — This is the type of processor. For Intel i80x86 processors, this value is 014ch.
- ❑ NumberOfSections — This shows the number of sections in the PE module.
- ❑ TimeDateStamp — This gives the date and time of the file creation.
- ❑ PointerToSymbolTable — This field is used for debugging. As a rule, its value is zero.
- ❑ NumberOfSymbols — This field is used for debugging. As a rule, its value is zero.
- ❑ SizeOfOptionalHeader — This shows the size of the second part of the PE header (see the description of the IMAGE_OPTIONAL_HEADER32 structure). As a rule, this value is 224 bytes.
- ❑ Characteristics — This field contains informational bits (flags). In particular, bit 13 specifies whether this module is a DLL (0) or an EXE module (1).

Now, consider the second part of the PE header — an optional header (IMAGE_OPTIONAL_HEADER32). The fields of this header are shown in Listing 1.33.

Listing 1.33. The IMAGE_OPTIONAL_HEADER32 structure

```
struct IMAGE_OPTIONAL_HEADER {
        WORD     Magic;
        BYTE     MajorLinkerVersion;
        BYTE     MinorLinkerVersion;
        DWORD    SizeOfCode;
        DWORD    SizeOfInitializedData;
        DWORD    SizeOfUninitializedData;
        DWORD    AddressOfEntryPoint;
        DWORD    BaseOfCode;
        DWORD    BascOfData;
        DWORD    ImageBase;
        DWORD    SectionAlignment;
        DWORD    FileAlignment;
        WORD     MajorOperatingSystemVersion;
        WORD     MinorOperatingSystemVersion;
        WORD     MajorImageVersion;
        WORD     MinorImageVersion;
        WORD     MajorSubsystemVersion;
        WORD     MinorSubsystemVersion;
        DWORD    Win32VersionValue;
        DWORD    SizeOfImage;
        DWORD    SizeOfHeaders;
        DWORD    CheckSum;
        WORD     Subsystem;
        WORD     DllCharacteristics;
        DWORD    SizeOfStackReserve;
        DWORD    SizeOfStackCommit;
        DWORD    SizeOfHeapReserve;
        DWORD    SizeOfHeapCommit;
        DWORD    LoaderFlags;
        DWORD    NumberOfRvaAndSizes;
    IMAGE_DATA_DIRECTORY DataDirectory[IMAGE_NUMBEROF_DIRECTORY_ENTRIES];
    }
```

The fields of this structure are as follows:

❏ `Magic` — This field defines the main intention of this module. In particular, for a normal executable file this field is `010BH`.

❏ `MajorLinkerVersion` — This is the major version number of the linker used for building this file.

❏ `MinorLinkerVersion` — This is the minor version number of the linker used to create this file.

❏ `SizeOfCode` — This field specifies the size (in bytes) of the executable code contained in the file.

❏ `SizeOfInitializedData` — This is the size of the initialized data section.

❏ `SizeOfUninitializedData` — This is the size of the uninitialized data section.

❏ `AddressOfEntryPoint` — This shows the *relative virtual address*, the address in the virtual address space of the executable module, of the instruction, from which the program execution starts. Accordingly, if the relative address, from which the module starts execution, is `1000H` and the module will load at the `400000H` address (see the `ImageBase` field), then the point, from which the program starts execution, will be located at the `401000H` address.

❏ `BaseOfCode` — This gives the relative virtual address of the first program section.

❏ `BaseOfData` — This gives the relative virtual address, from which the first data section starts. Usually, data sections start after the executable code sections.

❏ `ImageBase` — This gives the virtual address (not a relative address), from which the module will be loaded. If the loader places this module so that it starts exactly from this address, it won't need to correct addresses further and the loading process will be fast. If the loader cannot place the module at this address, then additional address tuning will be required. For executable modules, this value is usually equal to `400000H`.

❏ `SectionAlignment` — This value defines section alignment in memory. All sections in memory must start from values that are multiples of this value.

❏ `FileAlignment` — This value defines section alignment within a file. All sections in the file must start from the address that is a multiple of this value.

❏ `MajorOperatingSystemVersion` — This is the most significant number of the Win32 subsystem required to start the program.

❏ `MinorOperatingSystemVersion` — This is least significant number of the Win32 subsystem required to start the program.

- ❑ MajorImageVersion — This is the major version number specified at linking time (the most significant part of *n*). For link.exe, the command-line option specifying this number must appear as follows: /version:n.m.

- ❑ MinorImageVersion — This is a minor version number specified at compile time (least significant part of *m*).

- ❑ MajorSubsystemVersion, MinorSubsystemVersion — These are the most significant and least significant numbers of the subsystem versions. These fields typically are not used.

- ❑ Win32VersionValue — Although the name of this field is meaningful, most articles related to various issues with PE headers state that its value must be zero.

- ❑ SizeOfImage — This gives the total size of the PE header (headers and sections) in memory, aligned by SectionAlignment.

- ❑ SizeOfHeaders — This gives the size of all headers plus the size of the sections table.

- ❑ CheckSum — This is a checksum of the file. For executable modules, this value is zero.

- ❑ Subsystem — This field specifies, for which subsystem a given module is intended. The values of this field are as follows: 0000H for unknown subsystem, 0001H for device driver, 0002H for Windows GUI, 0003H for console application, 0005H for OS/2, and 0007H for Posix.

- ❑ DllCharacteristics — This field fell out of use starting from Windows NT 3.5.

- ❑ SizeOfStackReserve — This field specifies the required amount of stack memory.

- ❑ SizeOfStackCommit — This gives the amount of memory allocated for the stack.

- ❑ SizeOfHeapReserve — This is the amount of memory required for the local heap.

- ❑ SizeOfHeapCommit — This is the amount of memory allocated for the local heap.

- ❑ LoaderFlags — Starting from Windows NT 3.5, this field is out of use.

- ❑ NumberOfRvaAndSizes — This field is reserved for further extensions of the format (the size of array containing some structures). As a rule, this field is set to 10H.

- ❑ DataDirectory — This is an array of structures (Listing 1.34). For the moment, the IMAGE_NUMBEROF_DIRECTORY_ENTRIES value is 16. Each structure is made up of two elements, each element being 4 bytes in size. Only the first 12 structures are used. The first element of the structure describes the data location (relative virtual address), and the second element specifies the data size. Array elements are as follows:

0 — Table of exported functions

1 — Table of imported functions

2 — Resource table

3 — Table of exceptions

4 — Security table

5 — Sections table

6 — Debug table

7 — Description strings

8 — Operating speed of the computer, measured in million instructions per second (MIPS)

9 — Thread local storage (TLS)

10 — Configuration table area

11 — Table of import addresses

Listing 1.34. The IMAGE_DATA_DIRECTORY structure

```
struct IMAGE_DATA_DIRECTORY {

DWORD   VirtualAddress;

DWORD   Size;

}
```

1.5.3. Sections Table

The sections table comes immediately after the optional PE header. It is possible to compare the value of the SizeOfOptionalHeader field (see the IMAGE_FILE_HEADER structure) to the sizeof(IMAGE_NT_HEADERS) - sizeof(IMAGE_FILE_HEADER) - 4 value. It is then possible to access the following address counting from the start of the file: e_lfanew + sizeof(IMAGE_NT_HEADERS).

The sections table is made up of structures, each 40 bytes in size. The number of sections is taken from the NumberOfSections field (see the IMAGE_FILE_HEADER structure from Listing 1.32). Thus, obtaining the list of sections is a trivial task. Listing 1.35 shows the structure that is an element of the sections table.

Listing 1.35. An elementary structure that makes up a typical element of the sections table

---

```
struct IMAGE_SECTION_HEADER {
    BYTE      Name[IMAGE_SIZEOF_SHORT_NAME];
    union {
            DWORD    PhysicalAddress;
            DWORD    VirtualSize;
    } Misc;
    DWORD   VirtualAddress;
    DWORD   SizeOfRawData;
    DWORD   PointerToRawData;
    DWORD   PointerToRelocations;
    DWORD   PointerToLinenumbers;
    WORD    NumberOfRelocations;
    WORD    NumberOfLinenumbers;
    DWORD   Characteristics;
}
```

Consider the fields of this structure:

❑ `Name` — The section name. The `IMAGE_SIZEOF_SHORT_NAME` value equals 8. If the number of symbols in the name is less than 8, then the remaining bits are filled with zeros.

❑ `VirtualSize` — The memory amount required for the section.

❑ `VirtualAddress` — The relative virtual address, at which the loader must download the section.

❑ `SizeOfRawData` — The size of the virtual section aligned according to the value of the `FileAlignment` field to the nearest greater value (see the `IMAGE_OPTIONAL_HEADER` structure in Listing 1.33).

❑ `PointerToRawData` — The offset within a file, at which this section is located.

❏ `PointerToRelocations`, `PointerToLinenumbers`, `NumberOfRelocations`, and `NumberOfLinenumbers` — Fields used in OBJ files; they won't be considered here.

❏ `Characteristics` — The flags that characterize this section (Table 1.29).

Table 1.29. Flags that characterize a section

Value	Description
00000020H	This section contains the program code.
00000040H	This section contains initialized data.
00000080H	This section contains uninitialized data.
00000200H	This section is used by the compiler.
00000800H	This section is used by the compiler.
04000000H	This section cannot be cached.
08000000H	This section has no paged organization.
10000000H	This is a shared section.
20000000H	This is an executable section.
40000000H	This is a read-only section.
80000000H	This is a writable section.

The names and purposes of the sections can differ at the compiler's discretion.

NOTE

You can create custom sections and assign custom names to them. For example, you can write an Assembly program and assign an arbitrary name to the section or segment, in which the executable code would reside. The program would operate as normal; however, some debuggers and disassemblers would be confused because the entry point to the program is located in a section with a name unknown to them.

Here is an incomplete list of sections created by compilers from Microsoft and Borland.

❏ `.text` — This section contains executable code (Microsoft).

❏ `CODE` — This section contains executable code (Borland).

❏ `.data` — This section contains uninitialized global variables (Microsoft).

❏ `DATA` — This section contains uninitialized global variables (Borland).

- ❏ .bss — All data in this section are uninitialized. The section size within a file is zero.
- ❏ .CRT — This is another section for initialized data (Microsoft).
- ❏ CRT — This is the data section (Borland).
- ❏ .rdata — This section contains read-only data (constants and debug information).
- ❏ .rsrc — This section contains information about resources.
- ❏ .edata — This section contains information about exported functions.
- ❏ .idata — This section contains information about imported functions.
- ❏ .reloc — This is the settings table. Information contained here might be needed for the Windows loader if for some reason it will have to load the module at an address other than the address specified in the PE header. The table contains the relative addresses of those memory cells that contain the addresses used in the program, the values of which might be modified during the loading. This table is also called the relocation table. More detailed information about investigation of the relocation table can be found in *Section 2.1.1*.
- ❏ .icode — This jumps to the import function of older versions of tlink32.exe.
- ❏ .debug — This section contains debug information.

Thus, using the relocation table, you'll be able to compute the position of the section in a file, as well as its size. After you achieve this, you'll be able to view the information stored in this section, obtain its listing, or even try to disassemble executable code.

Special attention should be drawn to import and export tables and to the section containing resource information. These issues will be covered in the next few sections. However, before proceeding with this investigation, it is necessary to clarify how the PE image appears in the virtual memory. It is different from a copy of the PE module. The simplified algorithm used for loading the module appears as follows:

1. All headers, including the DOS header, PE header (IMAGE_NT_HEADERS), and sections table, are loaded into the memory.
2. Sections start to be loaded into the memory. Still, their relative virtual addresses must be aligned according to the value of the SectionAlignment field (see the description of the IMAGE_OPTIONAL_HEADER structure).

What conclusions can be drawn from this information? First, it is necessary to understand how the offset of a specific object within a file can be determined by its virtual address. This important issue is related to the import and export table. In general, the algorithm for obtaining the offset is as follows:

1. The section where the given object resides is determined by the virtual address.
2. On the basis of the sections table, the section offset within the PE file is determined.
3. The offset of the object within a section is determined.
4. The offset of the object can be obtained by adding the section offset within a file and the object offset within the section.

An example C++ function for determining the offset within the PE file by the relative virtual address is presented in Listing 1.36. Accordingly, it is assumed that the iw = IMAGE_NT_HEADERS global structure is read beforehand and the ais global array made up of the IMAGE_SECTION_HEADER structures (see Listing 1.35) is filled. The vsm input parameter is the relative virtual address of the required object. The function would return the offset of that object within the PE file.

Listing 1.36. The C++ function for determining the object offset in the PE file by its relative virtual address

```
DWORD getoffs(DWORD vsm)
{
        DWORD fi = 0;
        if(vsm < ais[0].VirtualAddress) return fi;
        for(int i = 0; I < iw.FileHeader.NumberOfSections; i++)
        {
                if(vsm < ais[i].VirtualAddress && i > 0){
                fi = ais[i - 1].PointerToRawData +
                                        (vsm - ais[i -1].VirtualAddress);
                        break;};
        };
        if(i == iw.FileHeader.NumberOfSections)
        fi = ais[i - 1].PointerToRawData + (vsm - ais[i - 1].VirtualAddress);
        return fi;
};
```

1.5.4. Import Table

It should be pointed out that if you want to find the import section by searching the .idata name in the sections table, you'll fail. Linkers (at least the ones supplied by Microsoft) do not create such a section. Thus, it will be necessary to use the DataDirectory array from the IMAGE_OPTIONAL_HEADER structure (see Listing 1.33). To carry out an elementary investigation of executable modules, it is possible to use the program presented in *Appendix 1*. You'll immediately notice that in many executable modules there is no .idata section, although the import table is present. If the .idata section is present, then the import table is located there.

Recall that the DataDirectory array is made up of 12 significant elements (the total number of elements is 16). Each element of this array is made up of two fields: VirtualAddress for the virtual address of the object, and Size for the object size (see Listing 1.34). The import table is defined by the second element (index of one). This is the only reliable evidence that allows you to determine the location of the import table. However, this is enough. Recall the considerations at the end of the previous section, and then recall Listing 1.36. Thus, there mustn't be any problems related to finding the import table. Now it only remains to understand its structure.

In the beginning of the import table there is an array of structures, which are shown in Listing 1.37.

Listing 1.37. The array of structures in the beginning of the import table

---

```
struct IMAGE_IMPORT_DESCRIPTOR {
union {
        DWORD    Characteristics;
        DWORD    OriginalFirstThunk;
    };
        DWORD    TimeDateStamp;
        DWORD    ForwarderChain;
        DWORD    Name;
        DWORD    FirstThunk;
}
```

This array is terminated by the element with zero fields. It is necessary to point out again that at least two fields must be checked for zero values, for example, Characteristics and Name. Now consider the fields in Listing 1.37:

- ❏ Characteristics — Relative virtual address of another array containing relative virtual addresses of imported functions.
- ❏ TimeDateStamp — Date and time of the file or DLL creation, or zero.
- ❏ ForwarderChain — Usually 0FFFFFFFFh.
- ❏ Name — Address of the ASCII string containing the name of the import library (a DLL). Thus, every element of an array corresponds to its DLL.
- ❏ FirstThunk — Relative virtual address of an array containing addresses of the names of imported functions. This is a second copy of the array pointed at by the Characteristics field. If the Characteristics field is zero (this is typical for some compilers other than that supplied by Microsoft), then it is necessary to check the FirstThunk field, which points at the second copy of the array.

NOTE

Hopefully, you understand that in this case you are dealing with DLLs implicitly related to the executable module, not to those that are loaded during the call to the LoadLibrary API function.

Now, consider arrays pointed at by the Characteristics and FirstThunk fields. It is necessary to point out again that these are two different arrays, although their elements point at the same names of imported functions. These arrays are made up of the structures presented in Listing 1.38.

Listing 1.38. The IMAGE_THUNK_DATA32 structure

```
struct IMAGE_THUNK_DATA32 {
union {
        DWORD ForwarderString;
        DWORD Function;
        DWORD Ordinal;
        DWORD AddressOfData;
        } u1;
}
```

As you can see, the IMAGE_THUNK_DATA32 structure, in essence, is made up of a single field; however, it is in four different forms. This field specifies the relative virtual address of the name of the imported function for a given DLL. If the most significant word of the field equals 8000H, then the least significant word contains the ordinal number of the imported function (export by ordinal). The array must be terminated by a double word set to zero.

Finally, it is necessary to consider the structure of the imported function name. Without diving deep into details, note that the function name is a simple ASCII string terminated by zero. However, this name starts at the address specified by the IMAGE_THUNK_DATA32 structure plus 2 bytes. The preceding 2 bytes contain the ordinal number for the given imported function from the given DLL.

The array pointed at by the FirstThunk field from the IMAGE_IMPORT_DESCRIPTOR structure (see Listing 1.37) deserves special attention. The CALL commands, which call imported functions, point at the elements of this array directly (for example, CALL DWORD PTR [address] or as follows: MOV ESI, address/CALL ESI) or by calling the stub (JMP DWORD PTR [address]). When the module loads, the loader determines the actual addresses of functions in the memory by their names or ordinals and then places these addresses into this array. The array pointed at by the Characteristics field doesn't change in the course of loading. A detailed example illustrating the procedure of searching for the name of imported function will be provided in *Section 1.6.1*.

1.5.5. Export Table

The export table is necessary for DLLs to ensure that the application can correctly call the functions provided by the DLLs. As with the import table, to investigate the export table it is necessary to use the DataDirectory array from the IMAGE_NT_HEADERS structure, because the .edata section might be missing from the executable module. In this case, you'll need the first element of the array (index of zero).

The IMAGE_EXPORT_DIRECTORY structure is located at the specified address. This structure contains all information required for investigating exported functions (Listing 1.39).

Listing 1.39. The IMAGE_EXPORT_DIRECTORY structure

```
struct IMAGE_EXPORT_DIRECTORY {
    DWORD    Characteristics;
    DWORD    TimeDateStamp;
```

```
    WORD     MajorVersion;
    WORD     MinorVersion;
    DWORD    Name;
    DWORD    Base;
    DWORD    NumberOfFunctions;
    DWORD    NumberOfNames;
    DWORD    AddressOfFunctions;
    DWORD    AddressOfNames;
    DWORD    AddressOfNameOrdinals;
}
```

Consider the fields of the IMAGE_EXPORT_DIRECTORY structure:

- Characteristics — This field is reserved. To all appearances, it is always set to zero.
- TimeDateStamp — This shows the data and time of creation of export data, or zero.
- MajorVersion — This gives the major part of the export table version. It usually is zero.
- MinorVersion — This gives the minor version of the export table version. It usually is zero.
- Name — This is the name of exporting module. In principle, it must not match the file name.
- Base — This is the ordinal number of the exported function. Exported functions, besides the name, have an ordinal number, by which they also can be accessed.
- NumberOfFunctions — This shows number of elements in the array of addresses of exported functions.
- NumberOfNames — This gives number of elements in the array of the exported function names.
- AddressOfFunctions — This is a relative virtual address of the array of virtual addresses of exported functions.
- AddressOfNames — This is the relative virtual address of the array, where relative virtual addresses of exported functions are contained.

❑ AddressOfNameOrdinals — This is the relative virtual address of the 16-bit array (ordinals array), containing index values for the array of exported functions. To obtain the function ordinal, it is necessary to add the value of the Base field to the index value.

To gain a proper understanding of the mechanisms of obtaining information about exported functions, it is necessary to understand the relationships among the following three arrays: array of function addresses, names array, and ordinals array. The ordinals array is a link between the first two arrays. The number of elements in the names array equals the number of elements in the ordinals array. Thus, to obtain the function address by its name, it is necessary to complete the following steps:

1. Find the function in the names array by the function name.
2. Obtain the index, by which the required name can be found in the names array, and then find the element with this value of the index in the ordinals array.
3. Take the value of the element found in the ordinals array. This value will serve as an index for the array of function addresses. After that, it is enough to access the array of function addresses and obtain the required address.

Analyze the program presented in *Appendix 1* to understand how to work with the export table. Experiment with locating the export table for different programs and DLL files.

1.5.6. Resource Section

As in previous cases, to obtain the resource block, it is necessary to use the DataDirectory array from the IMAGE_NT_HEADERS structure. You'll need the array element with an index equal to two. In contrast to the previously-considered objects of a PE module, the resource section has a hierarchical tree structure. In practice, four levels of this structure are used. In addition to this, all addresses used within the resource section are counted from the start of the resource section (in other words, these are not relative virtual addresses). This is natural, because resources are loaded into the memory as they are accessed, not during the loading of the module.

In essence, to understand the structure of resources, only the two structures shown in Listings 1.40 and 1.41 will be needed.

Listing 1.40. The IMAGE_RESOURCE_DIRECTORY structure

```
struct IMAGE_RESOURCE_DIRECTORY {
    DWORD    Characteristics;
    DWORD    TimeDateStamp;
    WORD     MajorVersion;
    WORD     MinorVersion;
    WORD     NumberOfNamedEntries;
    WORD     NumberOfIdEntries;
}
```

Consider the fields of the IMAGE_RESOURCE_DIRECTORY structure:

- ❏ Characteristics — This is the flags field, which, to all appearances, is not used nowadays.
- ❏ TimeDateStamp — This field specifies the data and time of resource creation.
- ❏ MajorVersion and MinorVersion — These fields specify the major and minor parts of the resource version. They are practically useless.
- ❏ NumberOfNamedEntries — This is the total number of named resources.
- ❏ NumberOfIdEntries — This field gives the total number of resources specified by resource identifiers.

Listing 1.41. The IMAGE_RESOURCE_DIRECTORY_ENTRY structure

```
struct IMAGE_RESOURCE_DIRECTORY_ENTRY {
    ULONG    Name;
    ULONG    OffsetToData;
}
```

The fields of the IMAGE_RESOURCE_DIRECTORY_ENTRY structure are as follows:

- ❏ Name — This field might be interpreted differently, depending on the level and on the value of the most significant bit. All of these cases will be considered in the sections that follow.

❏ OffsetToData — This field specifies the address computed in relation to the start of the resource section. The objects that can be pointed at by this address will be considered separately.

Thus, by going to the address specified in the second element (index of two) of the DataDirectory array, you'll access the realm of resources. This is where the first hierarchical level starts. It is necessary to point out that if the value of the address is zero, this might mean only that the resource block is missing.

First Level of the Hierarchy

At the top (the first) level of the resource hierarchy, the IMAGE_RESOURCE_DIRECTORY structure resides (see Listing 1.42). The only field that can provide the possibility of investigating the resources is the NumberOfIdEntries field. At the first level, this field contains the number of resource types stored in the PE header. The NumberOfNamedEntries field doesn't have any meaning at the first level.

What can you achieve if you know the number of resource types? As it turns out, this is the key field, because the IMAGE_RESOURCE_DIRECTORY structure is directly followed by the array of IMAGE_RESOURCE_DIRECTORY_ENTRY structures (see Listing 1.41). Their number equals the value stored in the NumberOfIdEntries field, so you'll have no problems reading them one by one. The Name field of the IMAGE_RESOURCE_DIRECTORY_ENTRY structure at the first level contains the resource type identifier. Resource type identifiers can be found in the winuser.h file of the Visual Studio .NET product (Listing 1.42).

Listing 1.42. Fragment of the winuser.h file

```
#define RT_CURSOR          1
#define RT_BITMAP          2
#define RT_ICON            3
#define RT_MENU            4
#define RT_DIALOG          5
#define RT_STRING          6
#define RT_FONTDIR         7
#define RT_FONT            8
#define RT_ACCELERATOR     9
#define RT_RCDATA          10
```

```
#define RT_MESSAGETABLE          11
#define RT_GROUP_CURSOR          12
#define RT_GROUP_ICON            14
#define RT_VERSION               16
#define RT_DLGINCLUDE            17
#define RT_PLUGPLAY              19
#define RT_VXD                   20
#define RT_ANICURSOR             21
#define RT_ANIICON               22
#define RT_HTML                  23
#define RT_MANIFEST              24
```

Thus, at the first level of the resource hierarchy, it is possible to find out how many types of resources are in the module, and to identify them all.

The OffsetToData fields of all elements point to the IMAGE_RESOURCE_DIRECTORY structures located at the second level of the hierarchy.

Second Level of the Hierarchy

The second level of the hierarchy also starts with the IMAGE_RESOURCE_DIRECTORY structures. The number of such structures equals the number of resource types in the module (see the previous section). In these structures, the following two fields are the most important: NumberOfNamedEntries and NumberOfIdEntries. The first field contains the number of named resources, and the second field gives the number of resources specified by resource identifiers. Thus, at the second level, each IMAGE_RESOURCE_DIRECTORY structure is directly followed by an array of the IMAGE_RESOURCE_DIRECTORY_ENTRY structures. The number of elements in such arrays equals the value of the NumberOfNamedEntries+NumberOfIdEntries field. The fields of the IMAGE_RESOURCE_DIRECTORY_ENTRY structures that make up the array deserve special attention. The Name field must now be interpreted differently. If the most significant bit of this field is set to zero, then the field itself represents the resource identifier. If the most significant bit is set to one, then the other bits must be interpreted as the offset of the name of the given resource relative to the start of the block of resources. The structure of the name is as follows: The starting 2 bytes specify the name length in characters (not in bytes), followed by the name itself in Unicode notation.

Again, consider the `OffsetToData` field. This field for each `IMAGE_RESOURCE_DIRECTORY_ENTRY` structure of the second level points at the same structure, except that it belongs to the third level.

Third Level of the Hierarchy

Thus, branching finished at the second level. The array of the `IMAGE_RESOURCE_DIRECTORY_ENTRY` structures at the third level corresponds to the same structures of the second level. Consider how the fields of these structures should be interpreted at the third level. The `Name` field now defines the number (the identifier) of the resource description language. All identifiers are defined in the winnt.h file. They start with the `LANG_` prefix and won't be listed here. As relates to the `OffsetToData` field, it again points at the `IMAGE_RESOURCE_DIRECTORY_ENTRY` structure, except that it belongs to the fourth level.

Fourth Level of the Hierarchy

At the fourth level of the hierarchy, the `Name` field of the `IMAGE_RESOURCE_DIRECTORY_ENTRY` structure defines the size of the binary image of the given resource. The address (relative to the start of the resource section, as usual) is the address of the memory area where the binary resource description is located. This address is defined by the `OffsetToData` field.

At this point, the description of resources is completed. It is only necessary to mention that the program presented in *Appendix 1* analyzes only two levels of resources. In most cases, this is enough.

1.5.7. About Debug Information

This description of the PE module structure won't be complete without at least a brief description of the debug information. The program presented in *Appendix 1* only informs you of the presence of such information (symbolic table and debug info) and the addresses (offsets), at which this information is located within the module being investigated.

Symbolic Table

The location of the symbolic table can be determined using the `FileHeader` header. The `PointerToSymbolTable` field contains the relative virtual address of the symbolic table. If this field is zero, then the symbolic table is missing. What is the symbolic table? The term doesn't reflect the actual meaning. In this case, the term *symbol* must be interpreted as an identifier of the high-level programming language, such as a variable or a function. The symbolic table contains the following information: the symbolic name (the variable or function name), the relative virtual address of the symbol, the type of the symbol (the variable or function), and its memory class (automatic, register, label, etc.). All this information about the identifier is packed into the IMAGE_SYMBOL structure, the description of which can be found in the winnt.h file.

Debug Information

In essence, the debug info must be interpreted as information about the numbers of the code lines of specific program. This information is stored in the PE module in a location other than the symbolic table. Locating this information is not a trivial task. Achieving this goal requires additional effort. First, it is necessary to locate the IMAGE_DEBUG_DIRECTORY header. It is pointed at by the sixth (index of six) element of the DataDirectory array from the IMAGE_NT_HEADERS structure. If the PE file contains several types of debug info, then there is an individual IMAGE_DEBUG_DIRECTORY structure for each of them. The TYPE field of this structure defines the type of debug info. The types of debug info are defined in the winnt.h file. They are specified in the IMAGE_DEBUG_TYPE_ constants. For example, the value 1 corresponds to the debug info in COFF, while the value 9 (IMAGE_DEBUG_TYPE_BORLAND) corresponds to the Borland debug info. The PointerToRawData field of the IMAGE_DEBUG_DIRECTORY structure must contain the offset of the debug info in COFF counted from the start of the debug info block, if the TYPE field is set to one. At this location, the IMAGE_COFF_SYMBOLS_HEADER must reside. This is the key issue. The structure contains information both about the symbolic table (which earlier was found using different method; see the previous section) and about the table of line numbers. The NumberOfSymbols field must contain the number of the identifiers in the symbolic table. This number will equal the contents of the NumberOfSymbols field in the IMAGE_FILE_HEADER structure (see Listing 1.32). The LvaToFirstSymbol field will contain the offset of the symbolic table counted from the start of the IMAGE_COFF_SYMBOLS_HEADER structure. Thus, you'd access the symbolic table using another, more academic method. Finally, the LvaToFirstLinenumber field contains the offset of the COFF line numbers table counted from the start of the structure.

1.6. Debugging and Disassembling Assembly Programs

This section is dedicated to Assembly language because debugging and disassembling programs written in this language usually is convenient and easy.

1.6.1. Examples of Code Disassembling

Consider several examples that, in my opinion, will help you quickly master this process.

Searching for Imported Functions

Consider an elementary example program written in Assembly language. The source code of this program is shown in Listing 1.43.

Listing 1.43. An elementary Assembly program

```
.586P
.MODEL FLAT, STDCALL
includelib f:\masm32\lib\user32.lib
EXTERN          MessageBoxA@16:NEAR
; Data segment
_DATA SEGMENT
TEXT1 DB 'No problem!', 0
TEXT2 DB 'Message', 0
_DATA ENDS
; Code segment
_TEXT SEGMENT
START:
        PUSH OFFSET 0
        PUSH OFFSET TEXT2
        PUSH OFFSET TEXT1
        PUSH 0
        CALL MessageBoxA@16
        RETN
_TEXT ENDS
END START
```

The program in Listing 1.43 is a trivial one. Its only goal is to display the `MessageBox` dialog. To obtain an executable module, issue the following two commands:

```
ML  /c /coff  prog.asm
LINK /subsystem:console prog.obj
```

That you are building a console application doesn't matter in this case. Alternatively, you could use the `/subsystem:windows` linking options and try to explain the difference in the behavior of both programs.

As a result of translation, you'll obtain the executable file called prog.exe. All of these issues are self-evident for any programmer involved in Assembly programming. However, the disassembling procedure is difficult, even for such a trivial example. For disassembling, it is possible to use any suitable program, such as dumpbin.exe supplied as part of Microsoft Visual Studio .NET. Issue the following command: `dumpbin /disasm prog.exe >prog.txt`. The contents of the output file, called prog.txt, are shown in Listing 1.44.

Listing 1.44. The result of disassembling the prog.exe program using the dumpbin.exe utility

---

```
Microsoft (R) COFF/PE Dumper Version 7.10.3077
Copyright (C) Microsoft Corporation.  All rights reserved.

Dump of file r8.exe

File Type: EXECUTABLE IMAGE

  00401000: 6A 00                 push        0
  00401002: 68 0C 30 40 00        push        40300Ch
  00401007: 68 00 30 40 00        push        403000h
  0040100C: 6A 00                 push        0
  0040100E: E8 01 00 00 00        call        00401014
  00401013: C3                    ret
  00401014: FF 25 00 20 40 00     jmp         dword ptr ds:[00402000h]

  Summary

        1000 .data
        1000 .rdata
        1000 .text
```

The dumpbin.exe program turned out to be efficient enough and disassembled this module satisfactorily. On the basis of the disassembled listing, it is easy to recognize the call to the imported MessageBox function. In particular, this follows from the parameter values. After carrying out the dumpbin /rawdata /section:.data prog.exe >prog.txt command, you'll obtain the contents of the .data section, where initialized data must reside (Listing 1.45).

Listing 1.45. The contents of the .data section of the test example in Listing 1.44

```
RAW DATA #3
00403000: 4E 6F 20 70 72 6F 62 6C 65 6D 21 00 4D 65 73 73   No problem!.Mess
00403010: 61 67 65 00                                       age.
```

If you compare the parameter addresses from Listing 1.43 with the data from Listing 1.44, you can make sure that the CALL instruction is the call to the imported MessageBox function.

However, not all questions that arise when viewing Listing 1.44 have been solved. The call is carried out at the address where the JMP command is located. To understand what this means, it is necessary to recall *Section 1.5.4*, where the import table was considered. I'd like to remind you that the import table is made up of an array of IMAGE_IMPORT_DESCRIPTOR structures (see Listing 1.37). The number of structures in the array equals the number of the DLLs in use. The matter concerns implicit linking. In this structure, there is the FirstThunk field, which must point to the array of the IMAGE_THUNK_DATA32 structures (for every DLL). In essence, these structures are made up of the pointers to the names of imported functions. After loading the executable module, the loader places there the addresses of the functions in the DLL instead of the addresses of the function names. The jmp dword ptr ds:[00402000h] command calls the imported function, the address of which must be located at the 00402000h address. Thus, it is possible to conclude that the 00402000h virtual address is the virtual address of the array element pointed at by the FirstThunk field. If you use the program presented in *Appendix 1*, you'll be able to obtain the relative virtual address and the offset for the array of IMAGE_THUNK_DATA32 structures (in the program being described, this array is called AdresImpArray). The relative virtual address turns out to equal 2000h. Everything is correct here, because the virtual loading address is 400000h. As relates to the offset, it is 600h. Having obtained this information, you can locate the array of IMAGE_THUNK_DATA32 structures within the prog.exe file. This can be done using the simplest 16-bit hex viewer (for instance, you can use the one that is part of the FAR Manager). As it turns out, the 38 20 00 00 sequence of bytes is located at the 600h address, in other words, the number 2038h. This number is nothing but the relative virtual address (minus 2 bytes) of the name of the imported MessageBox function. In other words, the relative virtual address of the function name and, after loading, of the function as such is 203Ah. Again, you can use the program from *Appendix 1* to make sure that everything is correct and that the offset of the function name within the prog.exe file must be located at the 63Ah address. Open the prog.exe file and make sure that the MessageBoxA string is located at this offset.

Perhaps, these considerations seem too complicated and bulky to you. If so, try to draw the same conclusion using the hiew.exe program. This program is one of the best hex editors, indispensable when correcting executable modules. In addition, it provides the possibility of disassembling PE modules. All examples and explanations provided in this book relate to version 6.11 of this program. To proceed, load the prog.exe executable module into hiew.exe. Consider what you'd discover at the 401000H address in the disassembling mode (Listing 1.46).

Listing 1.46. The results produced by hiew.exe when disassembling the prog.exe test program

---

```
.00401000:      6A00              push 00
.00401002:      680C304000        push 000403000C
.00401007:      680C304000        push 0004030000
.0040100C:      6A00              push 00
.0040100E:      E801000000        call .000401014
.00401013:      C3                retn
.00401014:      FF2500204000      jmp MessageBoxA
```

As you can see, hiew.exe is a more advanced program than dumpbin.exe, because it has recognized the call to the MessageBoxA function. On the basis of the jmp command, it is possible to determine the jump address. This is the 402000h address, as should be expected (do not forget how the bytes of integer numbers are stored, and that the first 2 bytes of the command code are the code byte and the MOD R/M byte, as explained in *Section 1.4*). Now, switch to the hex viewing mode and go to the obtained address. At that address, as expected, the following sequence of bytes is located: 38 20 00 00. This is the 2038h number, representing a relative virtual address. To obtain the virtual address, it is necessary to add the base loading address of the module, which is 400000h. The address of the string that must contain the name of the imported function (which, in this case, is MessageBoxA) is obtained as follows: 400000h + 2038h + 2h = 40203Ah. Go to the obtained address, and you'd discover the required name.

It would be interesting to view what the result would be if you compiled the program using TASM32. To achieve this, replace the MessageBoxA@16 name (Listing 1.43) with MessageBoxA, and the user32.lib import library with the Borland import32.lib library. To compile and link the program, use the following commands:

```
tasm32 /ml prog.asm
tlink32 -ap prog.obj
```

After compiling and linking, run hiew.exe and load the prog.exe executable module. Note that Borland's compiler creates larger executable modules than the similar Microsoft compiler. Listing 1.47 shows the disassembled text of the prog.exe module compiled and linked using TASM32. Compare it to the text provided in Listing 1.46. As you can see, the text is practically identical, but the addressing is slightly different.

Listing 1.47. The disassembled text of the prog.exe module compiled and linked using TASM32

```
.00401000:     6A00              push 00
.00401002:     680C204000        push 00040200C
.00401007:     680C204000        push 0004020000
.0040100C:     6A00              push 00
.0040100E:     E801000000        call .000401014
.00401013:     C3                retn
.00401014:     FF2530304000      jmp MessageBoxA
```

Go to the 403030h address, which is the address of the array element pointing at the name of the imported function. There you'll find the following sequence of bytes: 44 30 00 00. This means that the name of the imported function must be located at the following address: 40000h + 3044h.

Difficulties with Recognizing Executable Code

Although it might seem that there mustn't be any special problems related to disassembling executable modules written in Assembly languages, some problems still arise.

Consider the following test program (Listing 1.48). First compile it using MASM32.

Listing 1.48. The test Assembly program for illustrating difficulties with disassembling

---

```
.586P
.MODEL FLAT, STDCALL
includelib f:\masm32\lib\user32.lib
EXTERN          MessageBoxA@16:NEAR
; Data segment
_DATA SEGMENT
TEXT1 DB 'No problem!', 0
TEXT2 DB 'Message', 0
_DATA ENDS
; Code segment
_TEXT SEGMENT
START:
        PUSH OFFSET 0
        PUSH OFFSET TEXT2
        PUSH OFFSET TEXT1
        PUSH 0
        CALL MessageBoxA@16
        RETN
        DB 50
l1:
        RETN
_TEXT ENDS
END START
```

The program in Listing 1.48 appears strange. For example, for what purpose is the l1 label intended if there are no jumps to it? Note that the label will be needed in the future. What purpose does the DB 50/RETN sequence serve if it doesn't execute? All of these issues will be clarified in due order. The main goal of this program is to determine how contemporary disassemblers would react to such a fragment. I assume that all disassemblers would understand the entire code fragment following the first RETN command incorrectly. By the way, how should it be interpreted? This is simply the 32 C3 sequence of bytes that corresponds to the XOR AL, BL command. This assumption turns out to be true, because all disassemblers, including the fabulous IDA Pro, considered the RETN command to be followed by the XOR AL, BL command.

NOTE

I was truly surprised by the OllyDbg debugger and disassembler. After loading this code, it displayed the DB 50/RETN sequence. I thought that this was mystical, and for a couple of seconds believed in the eminence of this debugger. Then I replaced the byte sequence with a single XOR AL, BL command. The debugger continued to blindly state that this was DB 50/RETN. So, it was a disappointment.

Now, modify this program by a single command: MOV EBX, OFFSET 11 (Listing 1.49). This command is meaningless. However, consider what the popular disassemblers would state.

Listing 1.49. The modified code of the test program shown in Listing 1.48

```
.586P
.MODEL FLAT, STDCALL
includelib f:\masm32\lib\user32.lib
EXTERN          MessageBoxA@16:NEAR
; Data segment
_DATA SEGMENT
TEXT1 DB 'No problem!', 0
TEXT2 DB 'Message', 0
_DATA ENDS
; Code segment
_TEXT SEGMENT
START:
        MOV  EBX, OFFSET 11
        PUSH OFFSET START
```

```
        PUSH  OFFSET  0

        PUSH  OFFSET  TEXT2

        PUSH  OFFSET  TEXT1

        PUSH  0

        CALL  MessageBoxA@16

        POP   EDX

        ADD   EDX, ll - START

        CALL  EDX

        RETN

        DB  50

ll:

        RETN

_TEXT ENDS

END START
```

Now check the compiled code using three different disassemblers. Hiew.exe doesn't notice anything, which means that its interpretation of the code that follows the RETN command didn't change. The respectable W32Dasm program behaves the same way. IDA Pro (admittedly a superior product) reacts to the new command immediately. The fragment of the disassembled listing produced by IDA Pro is shown in Listing 1.50.

Listing 1.50. A fragment of the disassembled text produced by IDA Pro

```
.text:00401000 ; ------- S U B R O U T I N E ----------------------------

.text:00401000

.text:00401000

.text:00401000               public start

.text:00401000 start    proc near              ; DATA XREF: start + 5↓o

.text:00401000               mov     ebx, offset nullsub_1

.text:00401005               push    offset start

.text:0040100A               push    0               ; uType

.text:0040100C               push    offset Caption  ; lpCaption

.text:00401011               push    offset Text     ; lpText

.text:00401016               push    0               ; hWnd
```

```
.text:00401018              call     MessageBoxA
.text:0040101D              pop      edx
.text:0040101E              add      edx, 28h
.text:00401024              call     edx
.text:00401026              retn
.text:00401026 start        endp
.text:00401026
.text:00401026 ;------------------------------------------------------------
.text:00401027              db 32h
.text:00401028 ; [00000001 BYTES: COLLAPSED FUNCTION nullsub_1. PRESS KEYPAD "+"
.text:00401028 ; TO EXPAND]
```

Note how the MOV EBX, OFFSET 11 command has been disassembled. The nullsub_1 name means that this label points at the procedure comprising only one RETN command — a blank procedure (null). The comment inserted by the 00401028 address means that the procedure is collapsed. To expand the procedure (in other words, to view its text), it is enough to press the <+> key on the numeric keypad. In this case, the expanded procedure contains only one command — RETN.

Thus, IDA Pro has separated the husk from the grain. In other words, it has separated the RETN command from the 32H code. Is this an advantage or is it a drawback? Are you surprised by this question? Assume that the source code contained simply a MOV EBX, N command, where N is some number. This number would happen to fall into some address range; however, it isn't an address of any command. Nevertheless, the disassembler would conclude that a procedure is located at this address. Such errors are not serious because there are no jumps to this address. There are also no jumps to the window procedure; however, in that case the address is determined by the call of one of the API functions (see *Section 1.3*).

Anyway, such erroneous detection of a procedure doesn't imply serious complications. However, if this turns out to be an address of some command, to which there will later be a "secret" jump (secret jumps will be covered further on in more detail), this might be helpful for the purposes of analyzing the code. Developers of IDA Pro were thinking logically when they considered that a number that has fallen into the range of command addresses is likely to represent an address. In my opinion, this was a correct choice.

Now continue the empirical investigation. This time, replace the MOV EBX, OFFSET 11 command with the CALL 11 command. How would the most popular disassemblers handle this situation? IDA Pro tracks the procedure address and marks it in the listing. Hiew.exe still doesn't recognize a procedure, although it displays the CALL command. There is no reason to expect anything different from it, because its main goal is not disassembling. As relates to W32Dasm, this time this disassembler has put on a good show. Listing 1.51 shows a fragment of the listing produced by this program.

Listing 1.51. A fragment of the disassembled listing produced by W32Dasm

```
//******************** Program Entry Point ********
:00401000 E823000000              call 00401028
:00401005 6800104000              push 00401000
:0040100A 6A00                    push 00000000


* Possible StringData Ref from Data Obj ->"Message"

                                 |

:0040100C 680C304000              push 0040300C


* Possible StringData Ref from Data Obj ->"No problem!"

                                 |

:00401011 6800304000              push 00403000
:00401016 6A00                    push 00000000


* Reference To: user32.MessageBoxA, Ord:019Dh

                                 |

:00401018 E80D000000              Call 0040102A
:0040101D 5A                      pop edx
:0040101E 81C228000000            add edx, 00000028
:00401024 FFD2                    call edx
:00401026 C3                      ret
:00401027 32                      BYTE 32h


* Referenced by a CALL at Address:
|:00401000

|

:00401028 C3                      ret
```

As you can see, W32Dasm recognizes the `00401028h` address as a procedure address (`Referenced by a CALL at Address 00401000`).

Thus, the material provided in this section demonstrates that there are certain difficulties with disassembling code written in Assembly programming language. No disassembler is capable of exhaustively analyzing the code, so human investigators won't remain jobless.

Secret Jumps and Secrets of Jumps

I'd like to explain secret jumps. There are the following widely used commands for passing control: `JMP` and the group of conditional jumps, such as `JXX`, `CALL`, `RETN`, and `LOOP`. At the same time, jump commands can imitate different jump commands from the same group. The only reason such a programming style might be used is to confuse potential investigators of the program code. This section will cover this topic to help you take countermeasures against such tricks.

Consider the `JMP` command. This is the simplest command from the preceding list, provided that the jumps are considered within the framework of the flat memory model. At first glance, everything is clear and straightforward. The command carries out the jump to the specified address. When this happens, the contents of all registers (except for `EIP`) don't change. However, in addition to the standard jumps such as `JMP l1` (where `l1` is simply a label), there are indirect jumps:

❑   `JMP DWORD PTR [lo]` — The `lo` variable specifies some jump address.

❑   `JMP EBX` — The `EBX` register contains the jump address.

❑   `JMP DWORD PTR [EBX]` — The `EBX` register contains the address of some variable which, in turn, contains the jump address.

For example, what should you do if you see the `JMP EAX` command but do not know what is contained in the `EAX` register? This content might be formed several hundred commands from the given command. In such a situation, no disassembler would help you. There are only two ways out: Manually analyze the text of the disassembled program, or resort to the debugger. After you finally determine the address contained in the required register, you'll be able to use the disassembler and insert a comment, specifying this value. Most contemporary disassemblers have already implemented this function. However, I'm not going to rush forward. In *Chapter 2*, when considering contemporary disassemblers, I'll cover this functional capability in more detail. For the moment, the most important goal is to understand the essence of the problem and find approaches to solving it.

However, the problem being considered is complicated because any of the previously-listed commands can "masquerade" as a different command. For example, the LOOP command might play the role of a near jump (127 bytes forward or 128 bytes back) instead of providing evidence of the presence of a loop.

Here are several examples. For instance, consider the program presented in Listing 1.52.

Listing 1.52. An example demonstrating nonstandard use of the RET command

```
.586P
.MODEL FLAT, STDCALL
includelib f:\masm32\lib\user32.lib
EXTERN          MessageBoxA@16:NEAR
_DATA SEGMENT
; The address is stored here.
mem1   DD OFFSET l2
TEXT1 DB 'No problem!', 0
TEXT2 DB 'Message', 0
_DATA ENDS
_TEXT SEGMENT
START:
        MOV  EAX, mem1
; The next two commands are equivalent to JMP l2.
        PUSH EAX
        RETN
l1:
        RETN
l2:
        PUSH OFFSET 0
        PUSH OFFSET TEXT2
        PUSH OFFSET TEXT1
        PUSH 0
        CALL MessageBoxA@16
        RETN
_TEXT ENDS
END START
```

The program shown in Listing 1.52 demonstrates nonstandard use of the RET command. The PUSH/RET combination of commands is equivalent to the JMP command. Furthermore, it is possible to invent even trickier code; for example, consider Listing 1.53.

Listing 1.53. A fragment of code demonstrating another imitation of the JMP command

```
MOV   EAX, mem1
SUB   ESP, 4
MOV   DWORD PTR [ESP], EAX
RETN
```

As a result, a simple jump to the 12 address takes place. At the same time, commands might be mixed with other commands, in which case it would be difficult to determine correctly, to which location the jump actually takes place. The main idea here is that the tricks with jumps to addresses stored in the stack can be complicated indefinitely because it is possible to place an arbitrary number of jump addresses into the stack. Furthermore, the commands can be mixed in any order. Assembly language provides unlimited possibilities in this respect.

The situation with conditional jumps is similar. It often is impossible to determine whether the jump condition is satisfied by analyzing the code. As a result, it becomes unclear, to which branch of the program control would be passed, and it becomes difficult even to determine whether any of the branches would be executed. For example, consider the sequences of commands provided in Listing 1.54.

Listing 1.54. A sequence of commands, for which it is hard to guess where the jump takes place

```
...
CMP EAX, 100
JA 11
...
11:
```

For such code fragments, it is difficult to determine where the jump takes place. This is because it is difficult to track what might be contained in the EAX register.

In essence, the JA command in Listing 1.54 might play the role of the JMP command, because in practice the number contained in the EAX register might be greater than 100, in which case the program fragment that follows the JA command has no practical meaning. Only a debugger might be of any help. Nevertheless, even the debugger cannot ensure the necessary results, because there is always a nonzero probability of program execution going the other way.

The technique I will describe now is called *code overlapping*. The main essence of this technique is as follows: Part of the command code might become a stand-alone command, the meaning of which is often difficult to guess. Consider the program fragment presented in Listing 1.55.

Listing 1.55. An example illustrating the code overlapping technique

```
MOV  AX, 015EBH
JMP  $ - 2
PUSH OFFSET 0
PUSH OFFSET TEXT2
PUSH OFFSET TEXT1
PUSH 0
CALL MessageBoxA@16
11:
RETN
```

Guessing that the 015EBH code is simply JMP SHORT 11 and that the MOV AX, 015EBH command simply disguises this jump to the 11 label is not a trivial task.

Using Debug Information

The previous section explained the possibilities of confusing potential code investigators, in other words, protecting the program from anyone who would analyze it with malicious intentions. There also is the reverse of the coin. Often, the developer must disassemble his or her own program to understand how it works and to eliminate implementation errors and bugs. For this purpose, debug info is often used (see *Section 1.5.7*).

Most contemporary debuggers and disassemblers interpret the debug info well and are capable of correctly reconstructing the program being investigated. Assembly language, unfortunately, uses the debug info inefficiently and mainly relates to the variable names. Principally, variable names are satisfactorily identified by disassemblers, such as IDA Pro. The only fault of IDA Pro is that it cannot determine the true name of a variable if the module doesn't contain the debug info.

To include the debug info when translating a program using MASM32, it is necessary to include the /zi command-line option in the ml.exe command line and use the /DEBUG command-line option in the link.exe command line. The debug info is added into the file that has the same name as the executable module and the PDB file name extension (PDB stands for program database). It is also possible to use the /PDB:NONE command-line options, in which case the debug info will be placed into the executable module. Finally, it is possible to specify the type of the debug info, such as /DEBUGTYPE:{CV|COFF}, where CV designates the debug info intended for the CodeView debugger and COFF stands for the debug info in COFF. Similarly, when using the TASM32 assembler, the debug info can be included in the executable module. To achieve this, the tasm32.exe command line must include the /zi command-line option (include all debug info), and the tlink32.exe must include the /v command-line option. If these requirements have been observed, all information related to variables and operations over them will be placed into the executable module. Later, this information will be available to disassemblers and debuggers. Note that all information will be stored, even information about variables that are not used in the program.

1.6.2. About Dynamic Modification of the Executable Code

On one hand, self-modifying code doesn't correspond to the "code and data" programming paradigm, according to which the program is made up of the code that must be executed and the data that must be read and, if necessary, modified. On the other hand, there exists the Von Neumann principle, the rough interpretation of which doesn't make any principal difference between the data and the code. According to this interpretation, both the code and the data are simply sequences of bytes or bits (according to your preference). Therefore, dynamic code modification is an excellent technique that allows you to disguise the intentions of the program.

Programmers who have experience with MS-DOS programming know that code modification during its execution is a simple matter. Under MS-DOS, it is possible to modify the content of any memory cell, no matter what is contained there — the code or the data. Under Windows, code cannot be modified directly. Also, it is impossible to execute code located in the data segment or in the dynamic memory area. To obtain the possibility of doing so, the program must run in ring 0. Thus, for a normal program, all possibilities of dynamic code modification are prohibited. However, there are several ways out, which will be covered in this section.

Execution in the Stack

Code execution in the stack is probably the best method of self-modification that a program can implement. Memory pages allocated for the stack have attributes that allow reading and writing of data from and to the stack and even allow code to be executed there. The code can be modified as it is moved. Finally, Assembly commands can be stored in the data segment then moved to the stack and executed there. High-level programming languages allow you to use the stack, although with several limitations — sometimes considerable. Assembly language freely allows you to use the stack without encountering any serious difficulties. However, some problems can arise even here.

For instance, consider a simple console application (Listing 1.56).

Listing 1.56. A simple console application intended for investigating the code self-modification problem

```
.586P
.MODEL FLAT, STDCALL
includelib f:\masm32\lib\user32.lib
EXTERN MessageBoxA@16:NEAR
;-----------------------------------------------
_DATA SEGMENT
TEXT1 DB 'I am in the stack!', 0
TEXT2 DB 'Message from the stack', 0
_DATA ENDS
_TEXT SEGMENT
START:
; Call a procedure
        CALL PROC1
        RETN
        PROC1 PROC
```

```
        PUSH 0
        PUSH OFFSET TEXT2
        PUSH OFFSET TEXT1
        PUSH 0
        CALL MessageBoxA@16
        RETN
PROC1 ENDP
_TEXT ENDS
END START
```

Name this program prog.asm. To compile and link it, issue the following commands:

```
ML /c /coff prog1
LINK /SUBSYSTEM:CONSOLE prog1.obj
```

As a result, the prog.exe executable module will appear, which would display MessageBox with a corresponding message when it is started for execution.

Now, try to launch a frontal attack at the problem. Copy the contents of the PROC1 procedure into the stack and try to run the procedure there. The program that illustrates this approach is shown in Listing 1.57.

Listing 1.57. A program that copies the contents of PROC1 into the stack and tries to run it there

---

```
.586P
.MODEL FLAT, STDCALL
includelib f:\masm32\lib\user32.lib
EXTERN MessageBoxA@16:NEAR

;-----------------------------------------------
_DATA SEGMENT
TEXT1 DB 'I'm in the stack!', 0
TEXT2 DB 'Message from the stack', 0
_DATA ENDS
_TEXT SEGMENT
```

```
START:
; Prepare the stack.
      MOV EDX, ESP
      MOV ECX, OFFSET L1
      SUB ECX, PROC1
; Allocate space in the stack.
      SUB ESP, ECX
; Copy the code into the allocated space.
      MOV EDI, ESP
      LEA ESI, PROC1
      CLD
      REP MOVSB
; Call the procedure from the stack.
      CALL ESP
; Restore the stack.
      MOV ESP, EDX
      RETN
      PROC1 PROC
      PUSH 0
      PUSH OFFSET TEXT2
      PUSH OFFSET TEXT1
      PUSH 0
      CALL MessageBoxA@16
      RETN
PROC1 ENDP
_TEXT ENDS
END START
```

The result will be disappointing. When you start this program for execution, the operating system would display an error message. Using the OllyDbg debugger, try to find out why this happens. Start the program under the debugger, and execute it in step-by-step mode. Having reached the CALL ESP command, press the <F7> key. You'll find yourself in the stack location, where the procedure was copied. At first glance, it seems that the code has been copied correctly (Listing 1.58).

Listing 1.58. The stack location, to which the code of the PROC1 procedure has been copied

000CFFB0	6A	00	PUSH	0
000CFFB2	68	0B304000	PUSH	40300B
000CFFB7	68	00304000	PUSH	403000
000CFFBC	6A	00	PUSH	0
000CFFBE	E8	02000000	CALL	000CFFC5
000CFFC3	C3		RETN	

However, the address at which the procedure was called, also resides in the stack. Is it possible to find any jump to MessageBox? Everything is straightforward. In the CALL MessageBoxA@16 command, the Assembly translator substitutes relative addresses. This is the cause of the problem! What could be done about it? Do you really need to correct the address when moving the code to the stack? Fortunately, there is another way of calling the procedure. This call appears as follows: LEA EBX, MessageBoxA@16/CALL EBX. Check whether this works by rewriting the program (Listing 1.59).

Listing 1.59. A modified version of the program presented in Listing 1.57

```
.586P
.MODEL FLAT, STDCALL
includelib f:\masm32\lib\user32.lib
EXTERN MessageBoxA@16:NEAR

;-------------------------------------------------

_DATA SEGMENT
TEXT1 DB 'I'm in the stack!', 0
TEXT2 DB 'Message from the stack', 0
_DATA ENDS
_TEXT SEGMENT
START:
; Prepare the stack.
      MOV EBP, ESP
      MOV ECX, OFFSET L1
      SUB ECX, PROC1
```

```
; Allocate space in the stack.
      SUB ESP, ECX
; Copy the code.
      MOV EDI, ESP
      LEA ESI, PROC1
      CLD
      REP MOVSB
; Call the procedure from the stack.
      CALL ESP
; Restore the stack
      MOV ESP, EBP
      RETN
      PROC1 PROC
      PUSH 0
      PUSH OFFSET TEXT2
      PUSH OFFSET TEXT1
      PUSH 0
      LEA EBX, MessageBoxA@16
      CALL EBX
      RETN
PROC1 ENDP
L1:
_TEXT ENDS
END START
```

Translate and run the program. This time there is no error; however, the MessageBox looks somewhat crippled. To be more precise, it doesn't contain any text. An attempt at running the program under the debugger doesn't provide any positive result. Although, this time it is possible to make sure that the call to MessageBox is carried out at the correct address. What's wrong? Conduct the following experiment. Replace the CALL ESP command with CALL PROC1; in other words, check whether the procedure as such would execute. Strangely, the result will be the same. What could be the cause of this error? Because the procedure executed correctly earlier, try to remove commands for copying the procedure into the stack, removing one command at a time. This will help you detect, which command produces the error. As it turns out, this is the SUB ESP, ECX command. At this point, some suspicions should arise. What's wrong with this command? Such commands are widely and extensively used by all assemblers and compilers. The value stored in ECX is not large enough to go beyond the stack boundaries, and even if this happened it would cause a different error. After some consideration, the following idea comes to mind: The address in the stack must be a multiple of four. In the program under consideration, this requirement has not been met. Try to correct the contents of ECX before subtracting it from ESP. There are different methods of achieving this goal. For instance, this might be done as follows: SHL ECX, 2. In other words, multiply the ECX content by four. The same result might be obtained as follows (if you consider four to be too large): AND ECX, FFFFFFFCH/SHL ECX, 1. In both cases, the result will be positive, because the code copied into the stack will work correctly. However, the simplest way of correcting this program is using the ALIGN 4 directive to ensure that the addresses of the PROC1 procedure and the L1 label are aligned by a double word. The final version of the program that copies the procedure into the stack and executes it there appears as in Listing 1.60.

Listing 1.60. The final version that copies the procedure code into the stack and executes it there

```
.586P
.MODEL FLAT, STDCALL
includelib f:\masm32\lib\user32.lib
EXTERN MessageBoxA@16:NEAR
;------------------------------------------------
_DATA SEGMENT
TEXT1 DB 'I'm in the stack!', 0
TEXT2 DB 'Message from the stack', 0
_DATA ENDS
_TEXT SEGMENT
START:
; Prepare the stack.
        MOV EBP, ESP
        MOV ECX, OFFSET L1
        SUB ECX, PROC1
; Allocate the space in the stack.
        SUB ESP, ECX
```

```
; Copy the code into the stack.
      MOV EDI, ESP
      LEA ESI, PROC1
      CLD
      REP MOVSB
; Call the procedure from the stack.
      CALL ESP
; Restore the stack.
      MOV ESP, EBP
      RETN
      ALIGN 4
      PROC1 PROC
      PUSH 0
      PUSH OFFSET TEXT2
      PUSH OFFSET TEXT1
      PUSH 0
      LEA EBX, MessageBoxA@16
      CALL EBX
      RETN
      PROC1 ENDP
      ALIGN 4
L1:
_TEXT ENDS
END START
```

Thus, everything is straightforward — provided that you follow some simple rules: Procedures must be called through a register, and code must be aligned by the 4-byte boundary.

However, there is another problem. What should you do with jumps? If a jump uses a 4-byte address that must be stored in relocatable fragment, then the code copied into the stack won't work correctly. This problem also has a simple solution: All such jumps must be short jumps. No special steps must be taken, because the assembler automatically makes all jumps short if they are carried out within the range of 128 bytes. You'll only need to ensure that all required jumps and procedure calls fall within this interval.

Using the WriteProcessMemory Function

Another method of modifying the code dynamically at run time is to use the WriteProcessMemory API function. Using this function, it is possible to write the data into the process address space. The area, into which it is necessary to write the data, must be available for writing; otherwise, the write operation won't be carried out and the function would return a nonzero value (in a successful write operation, the function returns zero). Consider parameters of this function in more detail.

❑ Parameter 1 — This is the descriptor of the process into whose address space the function is going to write the data.

❑ Parameter 2 — This is the address of the process memory, into which the function is going to write.

❑ Parameter 3 — This is the pointer to the data buffer, from which the data will be written into the process memory.

❑ Parameter 4 — This is the number of bytes that will be written into the process memory.

❑ Parameter 5 — This is the pointer to the variable that will store the number of bytes written into the process memory. If this parameter is zero, it will be ignored.

As already mentioned, before writing anything into the process memory, it is necessary to obtain the process descriptor. To achieve this, it is enough to open the process using the OpenProcess function. This function is used any time some other function requires the descriptor of the process to execute. Consider the parameters of this function:

❑ Parameter 1 — This is the desired level of access to the process. All access levels are mapped to constants and listed in the documentation and header files. The names of these constants start with the PROCESS_ prefix. For writing into the process memory, the combination of the following two constants is needed: PROCESS_VM_OPERATION and PROCESS_VM_WRITE.

❑ Parameter 2 — This parameter can take two values. If this parameter is set to one, then the descriptor can be inherited; otherwise (the parameter is set to zero), the descriptor cannot be inherited.

❑ Parameter 3 — This is the identifier of the process that you need to open.

Finally, it is necessary to describe how the process identifier can be obtained. Because you are studying the task of writing into your own code, it is possible to use the `GetCurrentProcessId` API function. This function doesn't require any parameter and returns the identifier of the calling process.

An example of a self-modifying program is shown in Listing 1.61. This console program writes the `C3H` code at the `RETE` address. If this hasn't been done, the program will fall into an endless loop and will never complete its execution without external influence.

Listing 1.61. An example of a self-modifying program that uses the WriteProcessMemory function

```
.586P
.MODEL FLAT, STDCALL
PROCESS_VM_OPERATION    =       0008H
PROCESS_VM_WRITE        =       0020H
PROCESS_VM_OW           =       PROCESS_VM_OPERATION OR PROCESS_VM_WRITE

includelib f:\masm32\lib\user32.lib
includelib f:\masm32\lib\kernel32.lib
EXTERN OpenProcess@12:NEAR
EXTERN WriteProcessMemory@20:NEAR
EXTERN GetCurrentProcessId@0:NEAR
;-------------------------------------------------
_DATA SEGMENT
OPC         DB 0C3H
_DATA ENDS
_TEXT SEGMENT
START:
        CALL GetCurrentProcessId@0
; EAX contains the identifier of the current process.
        PUSH EAX
        PUSH 1
        PUSH PROCESS_VM_OW
        CALL OpenProcess@12
; EAX contains the descriptor of the opened process.
```

```
        PUSH 0
        PUSH 1
        PUSH OFFSET OPC
        PUSH OFFSET RETE
        PUSH EAX
        CALL WriteProcessMemory@20
RETE:
        JMP  RETE
        RETN
_TEXT ENDS
END START
```

NOTE

After the descriptor of some object has been used, it is necessary to close it using the CloseHandle function. In the preceding example, the system closes all handles automatically.

The use of the WriteProcessMemory function is characterized by certain drawbacks compared with code execution in the stack. First, this function corrects the code of the current process; however, it cannot increase the memory size to add new code. Furthermore, code execution in the stack is stealthier than the use of the WriteProcessMemory function, which can be easily detected by any literate code digger.

Using the VirtualProtectEx Function

Instead of writing into the process memory using the WriteProcessMemory function, it is possible to use the VirtualProtectEx API function to allow access to the required bytes (or pages where the required bytes reside) then use the normal MOV command.

Listing 1.62 presents a program similar to the one shown in Listing 1.61. The difference between these programs is that the program in Listing 1.62 uses the VirtualProtectEx function. Like the previous example, the C3H byte is written at the RETE address; however, this time this goal is achieved using a simple MOV command.

Listing 1.62. An example of self-modifying code that uses the VirtualProtectEx command

```
.586P
.MODEL FLAT, STDCALL
PROCESS_VM_OPERATION    = 0008H
PROCESS_VM_WRITE        = 0020H
PROCESS_VM_OW           = PROCESS_VM_OPERATION OR PROCESS_VM_WRITE
PAGE_WRITECOPY          = 8
PAGE_EXECUTE            = 10h
includelib f:\masm32\lib\user32.lib
includelib f:\masm32\lib\kernel32.lib
; Imported functions
EXTERN OpenProcess@12:NEAR
EXTERN FlushInstructionCache@12:NEAR
EXTERN VirtualProtectEx@20:NEAR
EXTERN GetCurrentProcessId@0:NEAR
;-----------------------------------------------
_DATA SEGMENT
HANDLE  DD ?
NN      DD ?
_DATA ENDS
_TEXT SEGMENT
START:
        CALL GetCurrentProcessId@0
; Open the current process.
        PUSH EAX
        PUSH 1
        PUSH PROCESS_VM_OW
        CALL OpenProcess@12
; Allow copying of the byte at the RETE address.
        MOV  HANDLE, EAX
        PUSH OFFSET NN
```

```
        PUSH PAGE_WRITECOPY
        PUSH 1
        PUSH OFFSET RETE
        PUSH EAX
        CALL VirtualProtectEx@20
; Change the byte at the RETE address.
        LEA  EAX, RETE
        MOV  BYTE PTR [EAX], 0C3H
; Return the initial attribute to the byte.
        PUSH OFFSET NN
        PUSH PAGE_EXECUTE
        PUSH 1
        PUSH OFFSET RETE
        PUSH HANDLE
        CALL VirtualProtectEx@20
; Flush the cache.
        PUSH 1
        PUSH OFFSET RETE
        PUSH HANDLE
        CALL FlushInstructionCache@12
RETE:
        JMP  RETE
        RETN
_TEXT ENDS
END START
```

Consider the parameters accepted by the `VirtualProtectEx` function:

❏ Parameter 1 — Handle of the process whose memory has to be modified.
❏ Parameter 2 — Address of the memory region whose attribute is going to be modified.
❏ Parameter 3 — Size of the memory region to be modified. The attribute is changed for all memory pages containing the bytes of the memory region to be modified.

❏ Parameter 4 — Set of attributes (see Listing 1.62).

❏ Parameter 5 — Address of the variable that will store the old attribute of the first of the range of pages (if there are several pages).

In addition, the program contains a function that wasn't described earlier. This is the `FlushInstructionCache` function. It is needed to flush the buffer containing commands. If this has not been done, the processor will probably used old commands for execution without noticing any changes introduced into the memory. The parameters of this function are as follows.

❏ Parameter 1 — Descriptor of the process whose memory is going to be changed.

❏ Parameter 2 — Address of the memory region that has been changed.

❏ Parameter 3 — Size of the modified memory region.

At this point, coverage of self-modifying code has been completed. Do not forget about this capability when starting code analysis.

Chapter 2:

THE CODE INVESTIGATOR'S TOOLKIT

T his chapter is dedicated to various software tools for investigating and patching executable modules.

2.1. Overview of the Code Investigator's Toolkit

In this section, I briefly overview of the software tools most often used for code investigation. I'll also provide several examples illustrating the use of these instruments.

Some programs covered here were created by enthusiastic individuals; therefore, their life cycle is short. The main goal of this chapter is not only to describe these tools but also to show you what instruments are available for studying the executable code and what can be expected from these tools. The principles of using such programs are similar in many respects. For example, all debuggers implement such an instrument as breakpoints. After you become acquainted with the operating principle of one debugger, you'll feel at ease with the other representatives of this class of programs and will be able to use them in your day-to-day activities.

2.1.1. Disassemblers

The Dumpbin.exe Program

The dumpbin.exe utility is supplied as part of the Visual Studio .NET distribution set. It is used for investigation of loadable object modules in the COFF format and outputs the information into the current console. Console output can always be redirected into a file. Proceeding this way, you'll be able to study the disassembled code in detail. Despite its console nature, this is a useful program suitable for analysis of small programs.

The command-line options of this program are as follows:

❑ /ALL — Displays all available information about the module, except for the Assembly code.

❑ /ARCH — Outputs the contents of the .arch section of the module header.

❑ /ARCHIVEMEMBERS — Displays minimal information about elements of the object library.

❑ /DEPENDENTS — Displays the names of DLLs, from which the module imports functions.

❑ /DIRECTIVES — Displays the contents of the .drectve section created by the compiler (only for object modules).

❑ /DISASM — Disassembles the contents of the module sections using debug info (if present).

❑ /EXPORTS — Displays the names exported by the module.

❑ /FPO — Outputs frame pointer omission (FPO) to the console.

❑ /HEADER — Outputs to the console the headers of the module and all its sections. In case of the object library, it displays the headers of all its modules.

❑ /IMPORTS — Displays the names imported by this module.

❑ /LINENUMBERS — Displays the numbers of the object module lines (if any).

❑ /LOADCONFIG — Displays the IMAGE_LOAD_CONFIG_DIRECTORY structure used by the loader and defined in the winnt.h file.

❑ /LINKERMEMBER[:{1|2}] — Outputs all names in the object library, which are defined as public:

  • /LINKERMEMBER:1 — Outputs in the order, in which object modules appear in the library

  • /LINKERMEMBER:2 — First displays the offset and index of object modules, followed by the alphabetically ordered lists of names for each module

  • /LINKERMEMBER — Uses a combination of options 1 and 2

❑ /OUT — Specifies that the output must occur into the file instead of the console. For example: /OUT:ED.TXT. It is also possible to redirect the output into the file using the redirection character (>).

❑ /PDATA — Outputs the contents of exception tables (for reduced instruction set computing processors).

❐   /RAWDATA — Outputs the dump of each file section. The following variants of this option are possible: /RAWDATA:BYTE, /RAWDATA:SHORTS, /RAWDATA:LONGS, /RAWDATA:NONE, and /RAWDATA:, *number*. Here, the number parameter defines the line width.

❐   /RELOCATIONS — Outputs all relocations within the relocation table.

❐   /SECTION:*section* — Defines the specific section.

❐   /SUMMARY — Displays minimal information about sections.

❐   /SYMBOLS — Outputs the symbolic table of the COFF file.

The following is an example of command-line use:

```
dumpbin  /disasm  prog.exe  >prog.txt
```

Thus, the disassembled program code will be redirected into the prog.txt file.

A specific feature of the dumpbin.exe program is that it disassembles only sections with known names (see *Section 1.5.3*). If you place executable code into a section with an arbitrary name (one that is not predefined), then the program won't output disassembled code, although it would still produce a dump.

As an example, consider the investigation of the relocations table of a DLL (see *Section 1.5.3*) using the dumpbin.exe program. For this investigation, I have chosen a simple DLL written in Assembly language. Assume that the name of this library is prog.dll. To begin the investigation, issue the dumpbin/disasm prog.dll command. Listing 2.1 provides the code lines that represent the disassembled listing of the executable code of this module. Some of the code lines are supplemented with my comments.

Listing 2.1. Disassembled listing of the executable code produced by the dumpbin.exe utility

```
10001000: B8 01 00 00 00    mov  eax, 1    ; Start of entry point
procedure
10001005: C2 0C 00          ret  0Ch
10001008: 55                push ebp       ; Start of exported function
10001009: 8B EC             mov  ebp, esp
1000100B: 83 7D 08 01       cmp  dword ptr [ebp + 8], 1
1000100F: 75 13             jne  10001024
10001011: 6A 00             push 0
10001013: 68 26 30 00 10    push 10003026h
```

```
10001018:  68 3E 30 00 10      push 1000303Eh
1000101D:  6A 00               push 0
1000101F:  E8 04 00 00 00      call 10001028 ; API call
10001024:  5D                  pop  ebp
10001025:  C2 04 00            ret  4
10001028:  FF 25 00 20 00 10   jmp  dword ptr ds:[10002000h]
```

Now output the relocation table and try to find out, which commands correct the addresses when loading this library. To achieve this, issue the `dumpbin` `/relocations prog.dll` command. The result of command execution is shown in Listing 2.2.

Listing 2.2. The result of execution of the dumpbin /relocations prog.dll command

```
BASE RELOCATIONS #4
      1000 RVA,        10 SizeOfBlock
    14  HIGHLOW              10003026
    19  HIGHLOW              1000303E
    2A  HIGHLOW              10002000
```

Most interesting is the leftmost column, which contains the operand offset that must be taken into account when loading this DLL into the main memory. For example, the value `14` means that the address value is `10001014`. Thus, you come to the `push 10003026h` command. The operand of this command is some address that must be corrected if this DLL is going to be loaded by a base address other than `10000000h`.

The IDA Pro Disassembler

This famous disassembler, which hasn't been outperformed yet, will be covered in detail in *Chapter 5*. When I was writing this book, I considered version 4.7; according to information published at the product's official site, **http://www.idapro.com**, the differences between this version and the newly-released version 4.9 are minor for the tasks that will be considered in this book.

By the way, IDA Pro is not only a disassembler but also a debugger. Nevertheless, I'll consider this product mainly as a disassembler because disassembling functions fulfill its main role.

W32Dasm

This disassembler will be covered in detail in *Section 2.2*. This program, like IDA Pro, also provides debugging capabilities. However, to all appearances, the project isn't being developed anymore. Version 10 of this product, which will be considered in this book, apparently was created by individuals other than the initial development team. You also can find version 8.98 of this product on the Internet.

Specialized Disassemblers

What are specialized disassemblers? I consider specialized the disassemblers that are oriented toward specific compilers. Note that I don't mean decompilers. Translation of the executable code into the program source code — in other words, decompilation — is in general impossible. Specialized disassemblers recognize language structures, such as classes, events, and methods, and disassemble them. In this respect, Delphi is mentioned most often because analysis of programs written in Delphi is complicated when using a normal disassembler. The only program

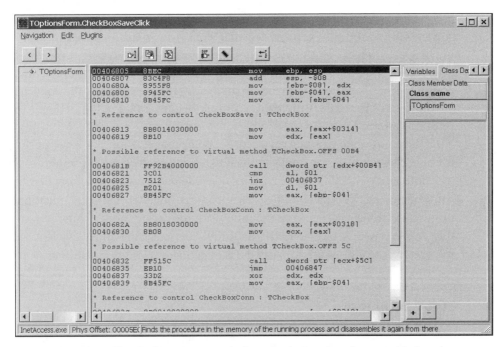

Fig. 2.1. The DeDe program window displaying the disassembled code
of a button-click event in an application

known to me that satisfactorily tackles the task of disassembling programs written using Delphi and C Builder is the DeDe disassembler (DeDe stands for Delphi Decompiler). The official site of the developer of this disassembler can be found at **http://dafixer.cjb.net/**.

Using DeDe, you'll gain a complete understanding of the hierarchy of the program objects within minutes. Furthermore, you'll be capable of viewing Assembly code of any event, such as clicking a button or an event related to form creation. Fig. 2.1 shows one of the program windows, displaying the disassembled code of the button-clicking event.

2.1.2. Debuggers

Debuggers are programs that allow step-by-step execution of programs in machine code. All known programming environments have built-in debuggers. These built-in tools won't be considered here. The main goal of this material is to consider independent standalone debugging tools. Most contemporary debuggers can correctly interpret the structure of the debug info produced by the main contemporary compilers, provided that such information is present in the module being debugged. In this case, they are capable of debugging programs both at the level of Assembly code and at the level of the application source code, which considerably simplifies the program analysis. However, such situations are rarely encountered. As a rule, only programming beginners leave the debug info in the release version.

Another specific feature typical for contemporary debuggers is support of some features characteristic for disassemblers: for example, recognition of library and API functions and possibilities of correcting the code and providing comments. Thus, the convergence of debuggers and disassemblers is obvious. Earlier, I mentioned that most disassemblers can execute the module in the debug mode. Thus, as you can see, this convergence is bidirectional. As you'll see later, the most efficient approach to code investigation is the combined use of debuggers and disassemblers.

Turbo Debugger

Turbo Debugger was one of the most popular debuggers during the 1990s. Unfortunately, nowadays it is no longer supported by Borland. The version from the 1990s, which is freely distributed over the Internet, is unstable under Windows NT/2000/XP/2003.[i] Nevertheless, it is possible to use this debugger for educational purposes and for debugging small applications (Fig. 2.2).

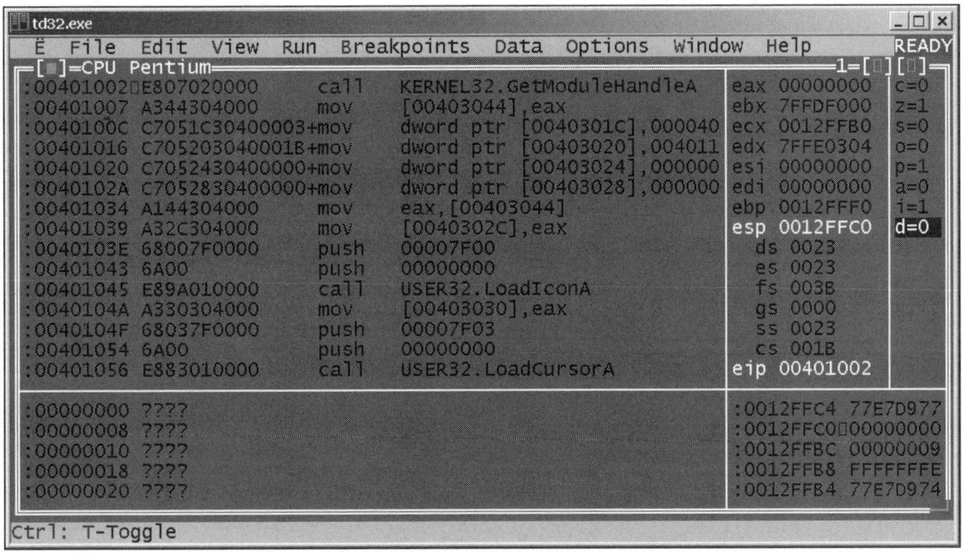

Fig. 2.2. The Turbo Debugger window with a program loaded for debugging

Debugging Tools for Windows

The Debugging Tools for Windows set of programs is supplied as part of the driver development kit (DDK) for Microsoft's Windows XP distribution. Recently, it was possible to download this package directly from Microsoft's Web site: **http://www.microsoft.com.** This toolset allows debugging of both user-mode applications and kernel-mode drivers. It includes version 6.0 of the windbg.exe debugger (Fig. 2.3), equipped with a GUI. A detailed description of this debugger won't be provided here. It is only necessary to mention that this is an event-driven debugger: The user sets breakpoints to specific API functions or attempts to access

---

[i] Here is a quotation from the warning published on the official Borland site: "The Turbo Debugger is provided 'as is,' without warranty of any kind. Borland does not offer technical support or accept bug reports on this version and it will not be updated or upgraded. The latest, supported version of our debugger is available in Borland C++ Builder."

a specific memory area of the application being debugged. Then the user starts working in the debug mode and waits for the debugger to break program execution because of the call to the chosen function or an attempt at accessing the specified memory region. After that, it is possible to find the code that tried to call the function or access the memory, and analyze that fragment. This working mechanism will be covered in detail in *Chapter 4*, when the SoftIce debugger is covered in more detail.

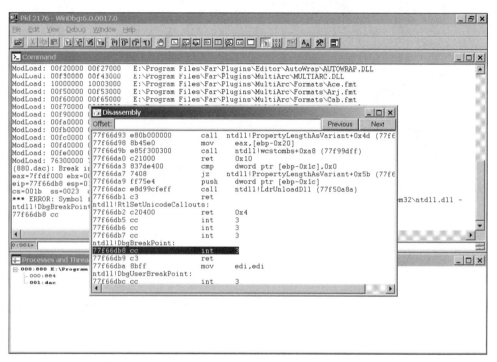

Fig. 2.3. Graphical user interface of the windbg.exe program

The OllyDbg Debugger

OllyDbg is one of the best application-level debuggers. It will be covered in more detail in *Section 2.3*. The discussion forum concerning this debugger can be found at the following address: **http://ollydbg.win32asmcommunity.net/stuph/**. The official site of the product is **http://www.ollydbg.de**.

The SoftIce Debugger

The most powerful debugging tool is indisputably SoftIce, originally from NuMega Lab. In 1997, this company was purchased by Compuware. The name SoftIce refers to how, when this debugger is actuated, all other software running on the computer is "frozen." You'll obtain a "snapshot" of the entire system. *Chapter 4* is dedicated to this excellent product.

Information about this debugger, as well as other NuMega Lab products, can be found at the following address: **http://www.compuware.com/products/numega.htm**.

2.1.3. Hexadecimal Editors

What are hex editors? Hex is an abbreviation of hexadecimal, which means that these editors work with hexadecimal numbers, or, to be precise, with data in the hex format. Normally, they are used for editing files; however, they also might edit disk regions. Advanced hex editors can disassemble binary code and introduce modifications by specifying command mnemonic.

The WinHex Program

This program provides a rich set of functional capabilities. For example, it can do the following:

- ❏ Work with various files and recognize a large number of formats. It carries out lots of operations over files, including encrypting, comparing, splitting, and merging files.
- ❏ Carry out low-level disk operations. This program is indispensable when recovering lost or damaged files.
- ❏ Edit files located directly in the memory.

The site of the developers of this program can be found at **http://www.x-ways.net/**. However, this program lacks disassembling capabilities, which somewhat reduces its value for code investigation.

The Hacker Viewer (hiew.exe) Program

This program is widely used and is popular with programmers involved in investigation and correction of the executable code. Its name stands for Hacker's view.

The main task carried out by this program is viewing and editing loadable modules. The advantage of this program is that editing is possible in three modes: binary, text, and Assembly code.

This program has a console interface (Fig. 2.4). All commands are executed using functional keys (including combinations with the <Alt> and <Ctrl> keys). For example, by pressing <F4>, you'll be able to choose the method of representing binary files: text, Assembly, or binary mode. By pressing <F3> (provided that you are viewing a file in the binary or Assembly mode), you'll gain the possibility of editing the file. If you are working in the Assembly viewing mode and press <F2> after <F3>, then you'll be able to edit the machine command in the symbolic view. I won't concentrate your attention on the commands of this program because they are simple and self-evident. Furthermore, the complete list of these commands can be obtained by pressing <F1>. Now, consider a simple example illustrating the use of this program.

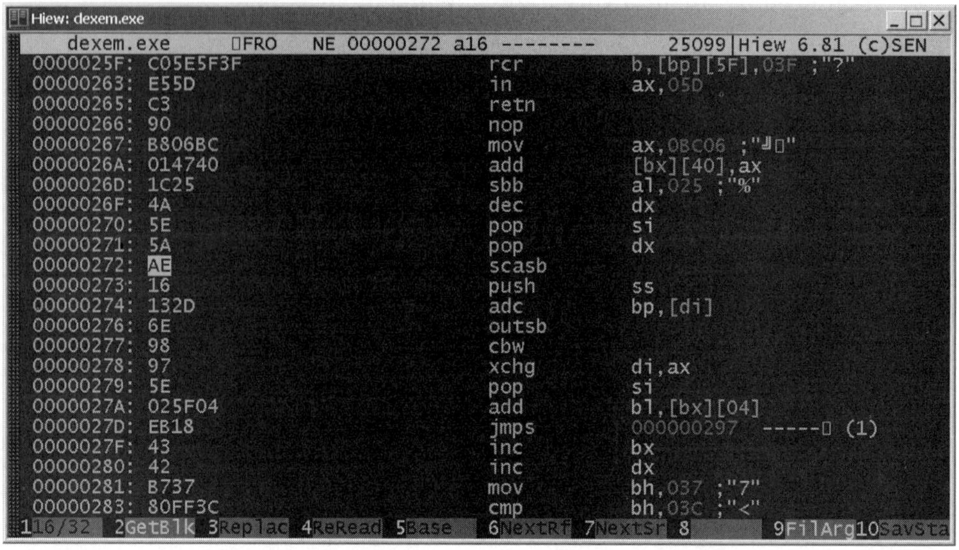

Fig. 2.4. The hiew.exe program interface

Listing 2.3 presents a simple console program written in the Assembly language. This program displays a text string on the screen.

Listing 2.3. A simple console application that displays a text string

```
.586P
.MODEL FLAT, stdcall
; Constants
STD_OUTPUT_HANDLE equ -11
INVALID_HANDLE_VALUE  equ -1
; Prototypes of external procedures
EXTERN  GetStdHandle@4:NEAR
EXTERN  WriteConsoleA@20:NEAR
EXTERN  ExitProcess@4:NEAR
; Linker directives for linking libraries
includelib f:\masm32\lib\user32.lib
includelib f:\masm32\lib\kernel32.lib

;------------------------------------------------------------------------
; Data segment
_DATA SEGMENT
      BUF    DB   "Output string", 0
      LENS   DWORD ?  ; Number of displayed characters
      HANDL DWORD ?
_DATA ENDS
; Code segment
_TEXT SEGMENT
START:
; Obtain the output handle.
      PUSH STD_OUTPUT_HANDLE
      CALL GetStdHandle@4
      CMP  EAX, INVALID_HANDLE_VALUE
      JE  _EX
      MOV  HANDL, EAX
; String output
      PUSH 0
      PUSH OFFSET LENS
      PUSH 17
      PUSH OFFSET BUF
```

```
        PUSH HANDL

        CALL WriteConsoleA@20

_EX:

        PUSH 0

        CALL ExitProcess@4

_TEXT ENDS

END START
```

The program shown in Listing 2.3 is easy and correct. Now assume that in the course of debugging you have accidentally changed a single command. For instance, assume that you replaced the JE command with JNE. As a result, after translation the program ceased to operate. Is it possible to correct the error without resorting to editing the Assembly code? The answer is yes. To achieve this, it is necessary to disassemble the program, find an error, and then use hiew.exe. In general, it is possible to do without the disassembler, using only hiew.exe, because it is suitable for disassembling small programs. Nevertheless, to make this example more illustrative, this investigation will be conducted in two stages.

Disassemble the module using the dumpbin.exe utility. The disassembled code is provided in Listing 2.4.

Listing 2.4. Disassembled code of the simple console program provided in Listing 2.3

```
Dump of file cons1.exe
File Type: EXECUTABLE IMAGE


    00401000: 6AF5                push    0F5h
    00401002: E82B000000          call    00401032
    00401007: 83F8FF              cmp     eax, 0FFh
    0040100A: 751E                jne     0040102A
    0040100C: A316304000          mov     [00403016], eax
    00401011: 6A00                push    0
    00401013: 6812304000          push    403012h
    00401018: 6A11                push    11h
    0040101A: 6800304000          push    403000h
```

```
0040101F: FF3516304000      push    dword ptr ds:[00403016h]
00401025: E80E000000        call    00401038
0040102A: 6A00              push    0
0040102C: E80D000000        call    0040103E
00401031: CC                int     3
00401032: FF2508204000      jmp     dword ptr ds:[00402008h]
00401038: FF2500204000      jmp     dword ptr ds:[00402000h]
0040103E: FF2504204000      jmp     dword ptr ds:[00402004h]
```

The disassembled code allows you to easily detect the error. By the way, the cmp eax, 0FFFFFFFFh command must be interpreted as cmp eax, -1. Memorize the required code: 83F8FFH. Now start hiew.exe, press <F7>, and search for the required combination. Having located it, press <F3> then <F2>. Then replace the JNE command with JE. Press <F9> to save the change. Thus, you have corrected the program without retranslating it. It is also possible to find the required command at the 00401007H address, because hiew.exe correctly displays the virtual addresses of the disassembled sections.

In addition to the PE format, hiew.exe supports other executable file formats, such as MZ, NE, LX, LE, and ELF. The author of this program is Eugene Suslikov. The program support site address is **http://www.serje.net/sen/**.

The biew.exe Editor

In its interface and system of commands, this program is close to hiew.exe. It also supports a large number of executable file formats. The program support site is **http://biew.sourceforge.net**. The latest released version is 5.6.2.

2.1.4. Other Utilities

There are lots of programs intended to help investigators understand the structure of the executable module and analyze the executable code contained there. All such utilities carry out specialized functions. For example, PE browsers allow you to obtain the most complete information about the executable module. An example of such a simple browser is the program presented in *Appendix 1*. More advanced browsers allow you to edit the PE header by correcting the field contents, adding new sections, etc. Two other types of researcher tools will be covered in the next few sections. Individual programs won't be covered in detail, first because they are numerous and second because most of them are no longer supported by their authors.

Resource Viewers

There are lots of programs capable of viewing the resources of executable modules. Programs capable of extracting resources and saving them in binary format or in the form of a text files with the .rc file name extension are less numerous. Careful attention must be drawn to more advanced programs capable of editing resources directly in the executable module.

Fig. 2.5 shows the dialog of the Resource Hacker program, allowing you to edit resources directly in executable modules. Pay special attention to the left pane of the window, where all resources of a given program are listed in the form of a hierarchical structure. The right pane of the window contains the resource code in the RC format. You can directly modify the resource code in the right window pane and then press the **Compile Script** button to compile the resource code and place it into the executable module. Using the **Show Dialog** button, it is possible to open the dialog editor, edit the resource using visual GUI tools, and then place it again into the executable module.

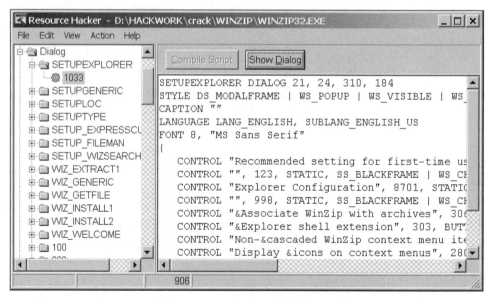

Fig. 2.5. Resource Hacker is one of the most advanced resource editors,
allowing you to edit resources directly in the executable module

Monitors

Monitors are a special kind of program intended for tracking specific events occurring in the system. In relation to the disassembling tasks, monitors trace specified actions carried out by programs being investigated. There are two types of monitors that are of the most interest to code investigators: registry monitors that track all attempts at accessing the system registry, and file monitors that trace attempts at accessing the entire file system.

Fig. 2.6 shows the window of the Registry Monitor (regmon.exe) utility, which tracks attempts of the application programs at accessing the system registry. Having obtained and saved such a log (see Fig. 2.6), it is possible to easily determine, which actions were carried out by a specific program and what that program attempted to do with the system registry. This information provides an important clue for searching the required location in the executable code. File monitors operate in a similar way; however, as mentioned before, they trace all attempts at accessing the entire file system.

There is another type of program working with the system registry, namely, registry scanners. Scanners can determine, which registry entries were accessed during the specified time interval. Often, such programs are even more convenient than monitors.

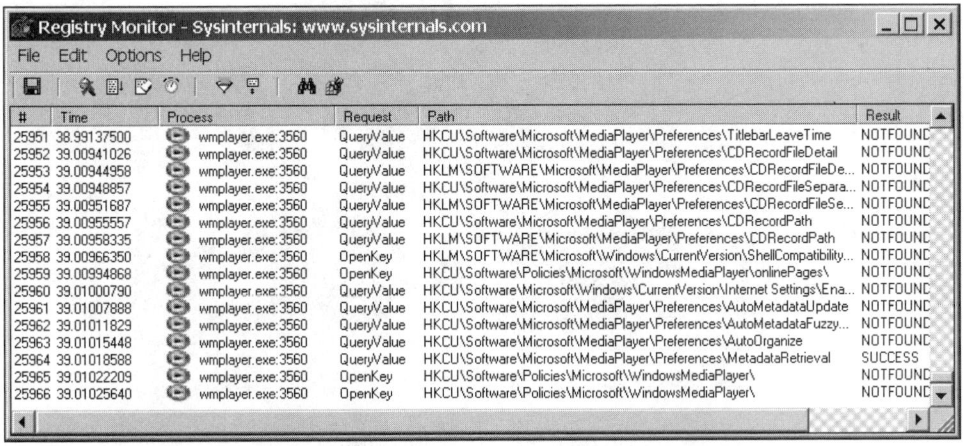

Fig. 2.6. The Registry Monitor by Mark Russinovich,
a program that tracks all attempts at accessing
the system registry carried out by application programs

2.2. The W32Dasm Debugger and Disassembler

The Windows Disassembler (W32Dasm) program is a symbiosis of a powerful debugger and a disassembler. Versions 8.93 and 10 of this program, which are the most widely used nowadays, can work not only with PE modules but also with DOS, NE, and LE modules. In this section, this program will be covered in detail.

2.2.1. Getting Started

Program Appearance and Settings

The main window of the W32Dasm program is shown in Fig. 2.7. The main menu is supplemented by the toolbar, elements of which are activated depending on the situation.

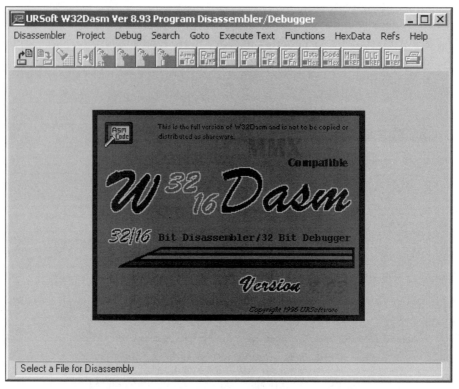

Fig. 2.7. The main window of the W32Dasm program

As already mentioned, this program is a combination of a debugger and a disassembler. This is reflected by the presence of the two menu items: **Disassembler** and **Debug**. Accordingly, there are individual settings both for the disassembler and for the debugger. For the disassembler, there are only three options related to the analysis of the cross-references in conditional jumps, unconditional jumps, and procedure calls. By default, all three options are set. It is undesirable to disable these options because this reduces the information content of the disassembled code. Principally, disabling these options might be necessary if you are going to disassemble a large program, because this would slightly speed up the process of program code analysis.

Debugger options are more numerous; however, all of them are self-evident. The **W32Dasm Debugger Options** window is shown in Fig. 2.8. As you can see, all debugger options relate to the specific features of loading processes, threads, and DLLs.

To start working with the chosen executable module, it is necessary to choose the required file by selecting the **Disassembler | Open File...** menu options. After that, the program will carry out analysis of that module and produce the disassembled text, along with detailed information about the sections existing in the module.[i] W32Dasm correctly recognizes API functions and supplies them with informative comments (Fig. 2.9).

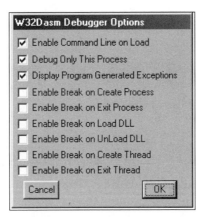

Fig. 2.8. The W32Dasm Debugger Options window

---

[i] Although W32Dasm is capable of working with modules of different types, only PE modules will be covered here.

```
* Possible Reference to String Resource ID=00001: "!>>1I5=85"
                                         |
:00401013 6A01                           push 00000001
:00401015 FF3518304000                   push dword ptr [00403018]

* Reference To: USER32.LoadStringA, Ord:01A8h
                                         |
:0040101B E8AE000000                     Call 004010CE
```

Fig. 2.9. A fragment of the disassembled text

Having completed the work with the module, it is possible to create a working project using the **Disassembler | Save Disassembler...** menu commands. By default, the project will be saved in the wpjfiles subdirectory of the W32Dasm working directory. Every project includes two files: the file with the .alf file name extension, containing the disassembled text, and another file with the .wpj file name extension, which represents the project as such. If you want to start another working session, you can open the saved project using the **Project | Open...** menu commands.

2.2.2. Working with the Disassembled Code

Navigating the Disassembled Code

When navigating the disassembled code, the current line is highlighted in a different color. In addition, jumps and procedure calls are highlighted specially. Navigation over the disassembled code is also simplified by the **Goto** menu item. The available options are as follows:

❑ **Goto Code Start** — This means go to the start of the listing.

❑ **Goto Program Entry Point** — This is the most important menu item, allowing you to go to the program entry point.

❑ **Goto Page** — This menu item allows you to go to the page with the specified number. By default, each page contains 50 lines of code.

❑ **Goto Code Location** — This means jump to the specified address. If the address is missing, then the range and proximity to other addresses are taken into account.

The **Search** menu command is another method of navigating the disassembled text. This command doesn't differ from similar commands found in other programs.

If the current line contains a jump or procedure call, you can jump to the appropriate address by clicking the respective toolbar button. You can continue navigating in this way until you detect the required program fragment. The most advantageous point here is that it is also possible to move in the inverse direction. All required toolbar buttons will be automatically highlighted.

Furthermore, those addresses, to which the jump is carried out, contain lists of source addresses, from which the jumps were carried out. If you highlight the line, in which the address is located, and double-click it with the right mouse button, you'll go to the required line of code.

Displaying Data

There are several methods of working with the data.

First, there is the **HexData | Hex Display of Data...** menu item, which you can use to view the contents of data segments in hex or string representations. In addition, the program code can be viewed in hex format. For this purpose, use **HexData | Hex Display of Code...** menu command sequence.

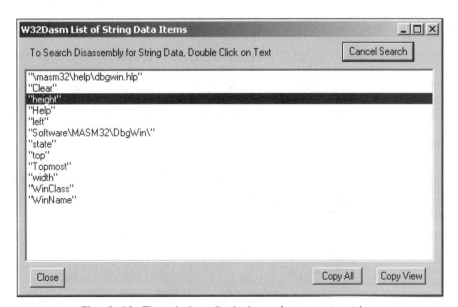

Fig. 2.10. The window displaying references to strings

Second, there is the **Refs | String Data References** menu item. This is a powerful and useful tool. When you choose this menu item, the list of code lines, to which there are references from the program text, will appear. This list includes everything the disassembler could detect when analyzing the program. By selecting the required line, you can double-click it and jump to the required program location. If this line is referenced from several locations, you can continue double-clicking to visit all required locations. Fig. 2.10 displays the window containing references to string data types.

As you can see from Fig 2.10, it is possible to copy either selected string or all strings into the clipboard.

Outputting Imported and Exported Functions

The list of imported functions and modules is located in the beginning of the disassembled text (Fig. 2.11). In addition, the list of imported functions can be obtained by choosing the **Functions | Imports** menu options. If you select a specific function from the list and double-click it, you'll obtain all program locations, from which that function is called.

To obtain the list of exported functions, choose the **Functions | Exports** menu commands.

```
++++++++++++++++++++ IMPORTED FUNCTIONS ++++++++++++++++++++
Number of Imported Modules =    7 (decimal)

   Import Module 001: ADVAPI32.dll
   Import Module 002: KERNEL32.dll
   Import Module 003: MPR.dll
   Import Module 004: COMCTL32.dll
   Import Module 005: GDI32.dll
   Import Module 006: SHELL32.dll
   Import Module 007: USER32.dll

++++++++++++++++++++ IMPORT MODULE DETAILS ++++++++++++++++++
   Import Module 001: ADVAPI32.dll

 Addr:000D9660 hint(0000) Name: RegCloseKey
 Addr:000D966E hint(0000) Name: RegOpenKeyExA
 Addr:000D967E hint(0000) Name: RegQueryValueExA
 Addr:000D9692 hint(0000) Name: RegSetValueExA

   Import Module 002: KERNEL32.dll
```

Fig. 2.11. A fragment of the list of imported modules and functions

Displaying Resources

Resources (or, to be precise, two main resources — menu and dialog) are also described in the beginning of the disassembled text. It is possible to work with the list of resources in special windows that can be opened by choosing the **Refs | Menu References** and **Refs | Dialog references** options from the menu. String resources can be viewed in the previously-mentioned window for viewing string references (see Fig. 2.10). Unfortunately, this version of the program doesn't recognize other types of resources.

Text Operations

Strings of the disassembled text can be copied to the clipboard or printed. To select the string, move the cursor to its leftmost position and click the left mouse button. To select a group of code lines, use the <Shift> key as well. To copy or print the selected fragment, click a special toolbar button, which is highlighted when the fragment is copied to the clipboard or sent to the printer.

2.2.3. Debugging Programs

In this section, I briefly cover the functional possibilities of application debugging using the W32Dasm debugger.

Loading a Program for Debugging

There are two methods of loading a module for debugging. To load a module that has already been disassembled, choose the **Debug | Load Process** menu commands. The **Debug | Attach to an Active Process** menu options allow you to attach and debug the process loaded into the memory. When the debugger loads, two windows appear on the screen. The first one is the information window (Fig. 2.12).

The second window is the control window (Fig. 2.13).

The information window contains several list windows, including the contents of the central processing unit (CPU) registers, processor flag values, breakpoints, the contents of segment registers, base addresses, and two data displays. Later in this chapter, I will explain the functions of the buttons located in this window.

Now, consider the control window. The **Run** button starts the program loaded into the debugger, and the **Pause** button pauses its execution. The **Terminate** button stops the program's execution and removes it from the debugger. The **Step Into**

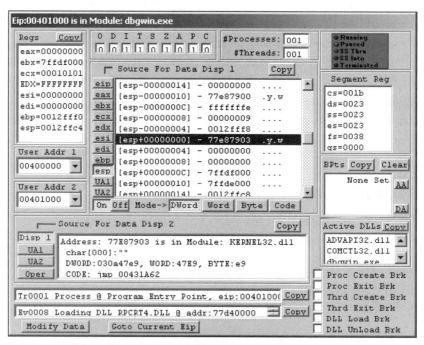

Fig. 2.12. The information window of the debugger

Fig. 2.13. The control window of the debugger

and **Step Over** buttons are intended for step-by-step execution of the program being debugged. The first button executes all instructions sequentially, and the second button executes instructions by stepping over the code of procedures and repeating chains of commands. In addition, there are **AutoStep Into** and **AutoStep Over** buttons for automatic step-by-step execution of the debugged program. With an API function, even the use of the **Step Into** button will not result in step-by-step execution of the function code because this code is not available to user programs. A convenient feature is that in the course of step-by-step execution, the cursor moves synchronously not only in the debugger but also in the disassembler window.

Note that if you are attaching to the process loaded into the memory, then this process will be unloaded from the memory when exiting the debugger, which might result in incorrect operation of the operating system.

Working with Dynamic Link Libraries

To debug a DLL, you can proceed as follows: Load the program that accesses the required DLL into the debugger. Then, view the list of used DLLs. To work with a particular DLL, you might be required to start the program and execute one of its functions. After you double-click the required library, you'll see its disassembled code in the disassembler window and will be able to work with the library code.

Setting Breakpoints

You can set breakpoints in the disassembled listing. To achieve this, go to the required line of code and press <F2> or press <Ctrl> and click the left mouse button. The breakpoint will immediately appear in the information window and in the control window; the marked command will have the BP* prefix. The existing breakpoint can be deleted in the same way it was set. It is also possible to deactivate the existing breakpoint. To achieve this, go to the information window and open the list of existing breakpoints. Choose the required address and right-click it with the mouse. The asterisk near the breakpoint will disappear, and the line of code in the disassembler window will change from yellow to green.

To quickly jump to the required breakpoint, choose it from the list in the information window and double-click it with the mouse. Finally, it is possible to set breakpoints to specific events, such as loading and unloading a DLL or creating and deleting a thread. These goals are achieved by setting an appropriate flag in the information window.

Modifying Code, Data, and Registers

The debugger allows you to modify the code that you loaded previously. To do so, click the **Patch Code** button in the control window (Fig. 2.14). It is important to note that only the code loaded into the debugger is modified, not the disassembled text. Having found the required location in the code being debugged, you can modify this code and immediately test the result of modification by running the program. If your modification was correct, you can proceed with modifying the module.

To modify the registers and memory cells of an executable process, there is a special button — the **Modify Data** button in the information window. The window opened with this button is shown in Fig. 2.15. At first glance, it might seem that this window is cluttered with elements; however, after you carefully study this window, you'll discover that there isn't anything redundant there. The top part of the window displays the current values of the main processor flags, which you can change. To modify the content of a register or memory cell, first set the modifier value using **Enter Value**. Then choose the required register and click the button next to it.

Fig. 2.14. The window for modifying the code being debugged

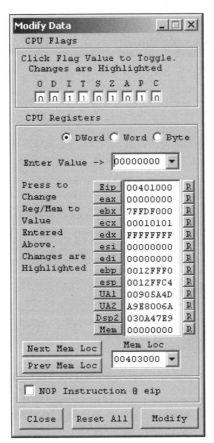

Fig. 2.15. The window for modifying the contents
of registers and memory cells

To restore the previous value, click the **R** button to the right of the register field. To change the content of the memory cell, first write the cell address to the **Mem Lock** field and then use the **Mem** button above it. Other operations that can be carried out in this window are self-evident.

Outputting Information about an Application Programming Interface

The debugger allows you to output additional information about executed API functions. To use this functionality, go to the control window and set the following flags: **Enable Documented API Detail** and **Stop Auto On API**. Then, press <F5>

to start program execution. Every time the program encounters an API function, it will stop and the screen will display information about the specific function.

Searching for the Required Locations in a Program

Quite often, it is necessary to find a location within the disassembled code that corresponds to a specific location within the executable program. The most efficient way of achieving this goal is as follows: Load the required module into the debugger. Start it for execution, step to the required position, and click the **Terminate** button. As a result, the highlighted string in the disassembled code will be at the required position. Bear in mind that some programs introduce modifications that remain in force. For instance, the hotkeys can be classified as such modifications.

The use of W32Dasm will be covered in more detail later in this book.

2.3. The OllyDbg Debugger

This is an excellent debugger in its class. For example, it is capable of determining procedure parameters and loops, and of detecting constants, arrays, and strings. Such features have never been typical of the instruments in its class. This debugger supports all processors of the 80x86 family and correctly interprets most numeric formats. It is possible to load an executable module into this debugger, as well as to connect to the running process. In general, there are rich possibilities, some of which will be covered here.

2.3.1. Getting Started with OllyDbg

Debugger Windows

The main window of OllyDbg is shown in Fig. 2.16. In addition to the traditional main menu and the toolbar, the main window contains four informational panes. These are the disassembler window (top left), data window (bottom left), registers window (top right), and stack window (bottom right). In addition, other windows are available for use. The list of all available windows is presented in the **View** menu. Some of these windows will be described in this section; other ones you'll have to study on your own if you like this debugger and are going to use it regularly. I strongly recommend that you do so.

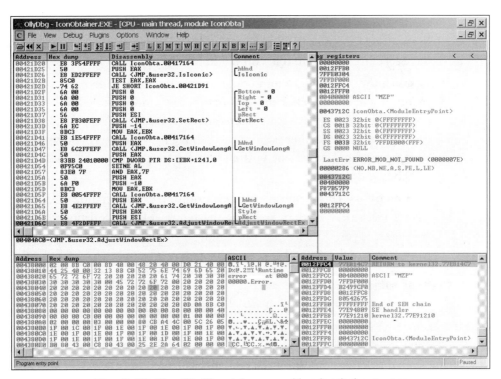

Fig. 2.16. The OllyDbg debugger with a loaded program

Now, consider the windows shown in Fig. 2.16. These windows are the most important ones, without which it is impossible to debug applications.

The Disassembler Window

The disassembler window contains four columns:

❑ **Address** — The command address column. This column contains the virtual address of the command, which is assigned when the command is loaded into the memory. By double-clicking this column, you'll convert all addresses into offsets counted from the current address ($, $-2, $+4, etc.).

❑ **Hex dump** — The command code column. In this case, you'll see the code as such and the operand value. In addition, the column provides various icons that allow you to understand the program logic: For instance, they specify commands, to which there are jumps (>) and commands that carry out the jumps (ˆ for up and ˇ for down). The same column marks the loops that the debugger has successfully recognized. When you double-click this column, the address shown in the first column is highlighted in red. This means that you have set a breakpoint to that command (address).

❑ **Disassembly** — This column contains the Assembly mnemonics for the command. If you double-click this command, the window for editing the Assembly command will appear. Here you can correct the command. The corrected command will be further used in the debugging process. Furthermore, the corrected program text can be written into the executable module. That's a great possibility, isn't it?

❑ **Comment** — This column contains additional information about the command. Here the program specifies the names of API functions, library functions, etc. If you double-click this column, you'll be able to add your comment to each line of the Assembly code.

The Data Window

By default, this window contains three columns: **Address**, **Hex dump**, and the column for text interpretation of the contents of the cell (**ASCII**, **Unicode**, etc.). Interpretation of the second and third columns can be changed. For instance, you can choose to display and interpret cell contents as Unicode.

The Registers Window

The registers window can contain three sets of registers: general-purpose registers and FPU registers, general-purpose registers and MMX registers, and general-purpose registers and 3DNow registers. By double-clicking this window, you'll gain the possibility of editing the contents of the appropriate register.

The Stack Window

The stack window displays the stack content. The first column (**Address**) contains the cell address within the stack, the second column (**Value**) displays the cell content, and the third column (**Comment**) contains the possible comment to the cell value (see Fig. 2.16).

More about the Windows

When starting to work with the debugger, bear in mind the following issues:

❑ By double-clicking the right mouse button within any window, you'll call the context menu. This menu is different for different windows. I strongly recommend that you carefully study these menus. Some information on this topic will be provided further on in this chapter.

❐ Window contents are interdependent. For instance, consider the registers. By clicking one of the general-purpose registers with the right mouse button, it is always possible to interpret its contents as an address in the data area (**follow in dump**) or as an address in the stack area (**follow in stack**).

Debug Execution

Debugging is analyzing a program by executing it in different modes. This section covers different program execution modes in OllyDbg.

Assume that the executable code is loaded into the debugger. The disassembler window displays the Assembly code. The main modes of program execution available to you are as follows:

❐ Step-by-step execution that bypasses procedures (**step over**). When you press <F8>, the current Assembly command is executed. By executing commands sequentially, you can watch three other windows to view how the contents of registers, the data section, and the stack section are changed. A specific feature of this mode is that if the next command happens to be the procedure call (CALL), then all commands that make up the procedure will be automatically executed as a single instruction.

❐ Step-by-step execution that steps into the procedure (**step into**). To execute the program in this mode, press <F7>. The main difference from the previous mode is that when CALL commands are encountered, all instructions that make up the procedure will be executed sequentially.

Both of the preceding methods (**step over** and **step into**) can be automated using *animation*. This can be achieved by pressing the <Ctrl>+<F8> and the <Ctrl>+<F7> keyboard combinations for each mode, respectively. After you press these keyboard shortcuts, the **step over** and **step into** commands will be executed in the automatic mode with a small delay, one after another. After executing each instruction, the debugger windows will be refreshed so that you'll be able to trace the changes. The execution can be paused at any time by pressing the <Esc> key. Also, execution stops automatically when breakpoints are encountered (see *Section 2.3.2*) and when the program being debugged generates an exception.

Another method of the step-by-step program execution is the *trace mode*. Trace mode is similar to animation, but this time the debugger windows are not refreshed at each step. Two methods of tracing corresponding to **step over** and **step into** are executed using the <Ctrl>+<F12> and <Ctrl>+<F11> shortcuts. Tracing can be stopped with the same methods used for stopping animation. After execution of each command, information related to its execution is loaded into the special tracing buffer, which you can view using the **View | Run trace** menu commands. If desired, the contents of the trace buffer can be saved into a text file. Also, it is possible to define the conditions, under which the tracing would stop (**set trace condition**) — <Ctrl>+<T> (the breakpoint). The following trace conditions can be specified:

❒ The range of addresses, in which the break would take place
❒ Conditional expressions, such as EAX>100000, for which tracing would be stopped provided that the condition is true
❒ A number of some command or a command set, for which tracing would stop

It is possible to instruct the debugger to execute the code until the return from the procedure is encountered (**execute till return**). In other words, the entire code of the current procedure will be executed, and the procedure would return control. To achieve this goal, the <Ctrl>+<F9> shortcut is used.

Finally, if in the course of tracing you have found yourself somewhere deep within the system code, it is possible to exit it by using the **execute till user code** command — the <Alt>+<F9> shortcut.

2.3.2. Breakpoints

Breakpoints are a powerful debugging tool. They allow you to understand program execution logic in the finest detail, providing snapshots of the registers, stack, and data at specified moments.

Ordinary Breakpoints

Ordinary breakpoints are set at a chosen command. To achieve this, use the <F2> key in the disassembler window or double-click the second column of this window (**Hex dump**). As a result, the address of the command (**Address**) in the first column will be highlighted in red. This type of breakpoint is helpful for finding the correlation between program execution logic (displaying specific windows, messages, etc.) and specific sections of program code. In addition, it is possible to check the status of registers, a variable, or the stack in any breakpoint of this type. If you press <F2> or double-click a breakpoint a second time, the breakpoint will be removed. Bear in mind that the break occurs before execution of the command, to which the breakpoint has been set.

Conditional Breakpoints

Conditional breakpoints are set by pressing the <Shift>+<F2> combination. In this case, the window with the combo box, into which the breakpoint can be entered will appear. The combo box field allows you to enter the condition, under which command execution must be interrupted provided that this condition is true. The debugger supports complex expressions containing various conditions. Here are several examples:

- ❑ EAX == 1 — This condition instructs the debugger to interrupt execution at the marked command (before its execution). Program execution will be interrupted provided that the content of the EAX register is one.

- ❑ EAX = 0 and ECX > 10 — These conditions instruct the debugger to interrupt program execution at the marked command provided that the content of the EAX register is zero and the content of the ECX register is greater than ten.

- ❑ [STRING 427010] == "Error" — Program execution will be interrupted provided that the "Error" string is found at the 427010H address. Also, it is possible to write the following condition: EAX == "Error". In this case, the content of EAX will always be interpreted as a pointer to string.

- ❑ [427070] = 1231 — This condition defines the breakpoint in case the content of the 427070H memory cell is equal to 1231H.

- ❑ [[427070]] = 1231 — Indirect addressing is used. It is assumed that the cell with the 427070H address, in turn, contains the address of another cell, the content of which will be compared with the 1231H number.

Conditional Breakpoints with a Log

Conditional logging breakpoints are an extension for conditional breakpoints. To set a conditional logging breakpoint, press the <Shift>+<F4> shortcut.

Any time such a breakpoint is actuated, this event is recorded in the log. To view the log contents, press the <Alt>+<L> shortcut or select the **View | Log** commands from the menu. It is possible to specify the record, as well as the expression whose value will appear in the log. Finally, it is possible to set the counter, which will specify how many times the record must be written into the log and whether it is necessary to interrupt program execution any time the breakpoint conditions are satisfied.

Breakpoint to Windows Messages

Because messages arrive to the window function (or, to be precise, to the window class function), to set a breakpoint to some windows message it is necessary to ensure that the application window is opened — in other words, that the windowing application has been started for execution. For simplicity, I have loaded a simple application with a single window into the debugger. Press the <Ctrl>+<F8> shortcut to start this application. The application window activates after a short delay (about 1 second). Pay attention to the part of the program that executes continuously. This is the message-processing loop. To reach the window function, it is necessary to call the list of windows created by the application being investigated. This can be achieved using the **View | Windows** menu. The result of this command is shown in Fig. 2.17.

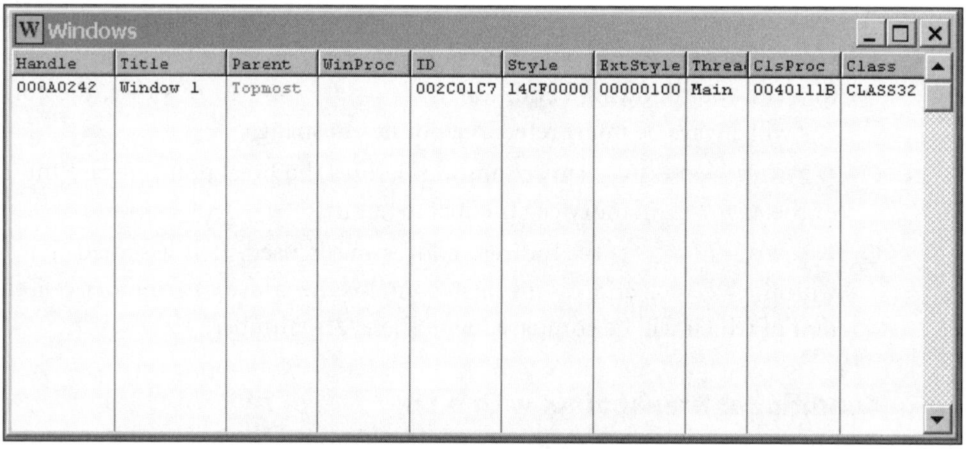

Fig. 2.17. The window displaying the list of windows created by
the application being investigated

The window displayed in Fig. 2.17 allows the investigator to discover the window descriptor, its name, its identifier, and, most importantly, the address of the window procedure (`ClsProc`). The information about the address of the window procedure allows the investigator to find the window function and set there either a normal or a conditional breakpoint. However, when working with window functions, it is best to set breakpoints at window messages.

Thus, click the window shown in Fig. 2.17 and choose **Message breakpoint on ClassProc** from the context menu. Another window will appear, in which it is possible to set the following breakpoint parameters:

❑ Choose the message from the drop-down list. Note the following:
  ● Instead of the message as such, it is possible to choose an event, which might be indicated by several messages, such as creation or deletion of a window or a keyboard event.
  ● It is possible to choose user-defined messages.
❑ List the windows that will be tracked to determine whether this message arrives from one of them. Include the given window, all windows with a given title, or all windows.
❑ Define a counter to determine how many times the breakpoint is actuated.
❑ Specify whether the program execution should be interrupted when the breakpoint is actuated.
❑ Define whether the record should be written into the log when the breakpoint is actuated.

On your own, practice setting the preceding breakpoints. Also, trace the contents of the stack window, a useful and instructive occupation.

Breakpoints to the Import Functions

To obtain the list of all names imported into the module being debugged, press the <Ctrl>+<N> shortcut. Further, click the window with right mouse button, and you'll be able to carry out the following actions:

❑ Set a breakpoint at the call of the imported function (**Toggle breakpoint on import**)
❑ Set a conditional breakpoint at the call to the imported function (**Conditional breakpoint on import**)

❑ Set a conditional breakpoint with logging at the call to the imported function (**Conditional log breakpoint on import**)

❑ Set breakpoints at all links to the specified name (**Set breakpoint on every reference**)

❑ Set breakpoints with logging at all references to the given name (**Set log breakpoint on every reference**)

❑ Remove all breakpoints (**Remove all breakpoints**)

Breakpoints at the Memory Area

The OllyDbg debugger allows you to set a single breakpoint at the memory area. To achieve this, choose the disassembler window or the data window. Then use the context menu and choose the **Breakpoint | Memory on access** commands or **Breakpoint | Memory on write** commands. After that, the newly-specified breakpoint will be ready to use. The first type of a breakpoint is possible both for the code and for the data, and the second type is possible only for the code. Breakpoints can be deleted by choosing the **Breakpoint | Remove memory breakpoint** commands from the context menu.

Breakpoints in the Memory Window

The memory window displays the memory blocks reserved for the program being debugged or by the program being debugged on its own. In this window, it is also possible to set one breakpoint. To achieve this, use the right-click menu and choose the **Set memory breakpoint on access** command or the **Set memory breakpoint on write** command. To remove the breakpoint, right-click the memory window and choose the **Remove memory breakpoint** command.

Hardware Breakpoints

Normal breakpoints use the standard INT 3 interrupt vector. The use of such breakpoints can considerably slow down the execution of the program being debugged. However, Intel Pentium microprocessors also provide four debug registers — DR0–DR3 (see *Section 1.2.1*). These registers can contain four breakpoints, virtual addresses of the current program. When the address used by a command turns out to equal the address contained in one of these registers, the processor generates an exception that is trapped by the debugger. Hardware breakpoints do not slow down the execution of the program being debugged. However, there are only four of them. To set a hardware breakpoint, go to the disassembler window and choose the **Breakpoint | Hardware on execution** commands from the context menu. As an alternative, use the **Breakpoint | Hardware on access** or **Breakpoint | Hardware on write** commands from the main menu. To delete hardware breakpoints, use the **Breakpoint | Remove hardware breakpoints** commands from the context menu.

2.3.3. Other Capabilities

The Watch expressions Window

OllyDbg provides a special window for watching expressions. Recall that you encountered expressions when I described conditional breakpoints. It is possible to use complex expressions containing both memory cells and registers, and these expressions might be as complicated as desired. To open the **Watch expressions** window, use the **View | Watches** menu commands. When the **Watch expressions** window opens, click the right mouse button and choose the **Add Watches** command. After that, you can define an expression that the debugger will watch — in other words, display its value. Fig. 2.18 shows the **Watch expressions** window containing a list of four expressions, the values of which are watched and displayed when executing any processor command.

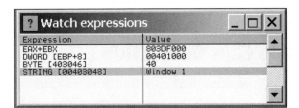

Fig. 2.18. The Watch expressions window

Searching for Information

OllyDbg allows you to search for any kind of information. Consider some of its functional capabilities.

By pressing the <Ctrl>+<B> shortcut, the search window appears, in which you can define the string that will be sought in the module loaded into the debugger.

The search string can be entered in the form of the sequence of characters, sequence of bytes, or sequence of Unicode characters.

For searching, use the <Ctrl>+<F> shortcut (for a single command) or the <Ctrl>+<S> combination (for a sequence of commands).

The <Ctrl>+<L> combination repeats the last search operation.

Correcting an Executable Module

OllyDbg provides excellent capabilities of correcting executable modules. You can save the module being debugged, along with corrections, and even create a new executable module. This can be achieved easily. Just click the right mouse button in the disassembler window and choose the **Copy to execution | Selection** commands from the context menu. As a result, the entire disassembled module will be copied into the new window. After that, click the right mouse button in that window and choose the **Save file** command. You'll have the possibility to choose the name, under which to save the new executable module. This is convenient: First, you can create any number of versions of the corrected file. Second, the check for the correctness of the modified code is carried out without exiting the debugger.

There are still lots of important and interesting issues related to OllyDbg. Alas, everything has its natural end, and the limited volume of this book requires me to proceed with considering several other topics that are no less interesting and important.

2.4. Examples of Executable Files Correction

The examples provided here are not too difficult. They are given for the following purposes:

❏ To demonstrate the possibilities of the previously described tools
❏ To demonstrate some standard techniques for investigation and correction of executable code
❏ To stop tempting you with promises and jump into code disassembling

All techniques of correcting executable code are provided here for educational purposes only.

2.4.1. Example 1: Eliminating an Annoying Message

Recently I purchased a CD containing an encyclopedia in the field of history. After installing it on my computer and making sure that everything worked, I forgot about this program. A week later, I discovered that when this program was started for execution, an annoying message box appeared on the screen (Fig. 2.19).

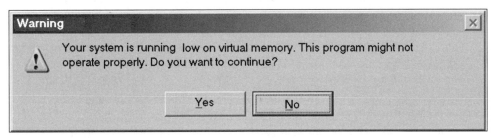

Fig. 2.19. The annoying error message that appeared when
the encyclopedia was started

If the **Yes** button is clicked, the program would continue to operate normally. After several minutes of consideration, I decided that this happened because a couple of days ago I moved all swap files to the same partition. Because I didn't intend to recover the initial state and the program continued to operate normally, I decided to correct its executable code to remove the annoying message.

Thus, I proceeded as follows. To all appearances, this message is displayed in a standard `MessageBox` window. First, the presence of an icon on the left indicates such a window (in this case, it is an exclamation mark). Second, such windows usually contain two buttons — **Yes** and **No**. How do you reach this call?

Searching with OllyDbg

There are several ways of accessing the `MessageBox` window using the debugger. The easiest way of doing this is to set a breakpoint to the imported `MessageBox` name (see *Section 2.3.2*), and then start the program (<Ctrl>+<F8>) and wait for the interrupt. However, this time the situation is much simpler. The message appears at the initial stages of the program start-up, and this location can be easily detected by step-by-step program execution (press <F8>).

Fig. 2.20 shows the debugger window displaying the required program fragment. Note that slightly above the `MessageBox` function there is the `GlobalMemoryStatus` API call. Obviously, the execution of this function results in the error message.

In this case, you do not even need to investigate how this function operates. The important issue is that the call to this function is directly followed by the code lines provided in Listing 2.5.

Listing 2.5. Code lines directly preceding the call displaying the warning message

---

```
00494039          813D 287A4900          CMP DWORD PTR DS:[497A28], 989680
00494043          7D 1F                  JGE SHORT RHistory.00494064
```

It is easy to replace the JGE SHORT 00494064 command with the JMP SHORT 00494064 command. Thus, you'll bypass the call to the MessageBox window. In this chapter I have described hiew.exe, an excellent program that can be used for correcting executable modules. However, it is also possible to correct executable modules using OllyDbg. It is a wonderful feeling to know that any task can have several solutions and that you can use any of them. I hope that you experience this feeling many times!

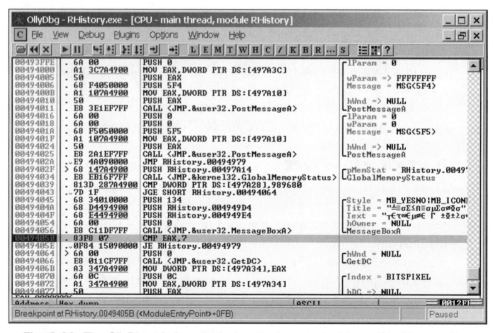

Fig. 2.20. The OllyDbg window displaying the fragment of the call to MessageBox

Searching with W32Dasm

Now, try to locate the required fragment using W32Dasm. It is possible to use the list of imported functions and, having found MessageBox by double-clicking the line of code containing this function name, to find all locations where this function is called. It is also possible to use the debugger built into W32Dasm. This method will be illustrated here.

Use the **Debug | Load Process** menu commands. The window will appear where it is necessary to specify the program loading parameters. Click the **Load** button. The debugger window will appear (Fig. 2.21). Click the **AutoStep Over** button and wait for the required message to appear. When the message appears, click the **Terminate** button. You'll find yourself in the required location of the program (disassembled code). The further steps are exactly as described earlier — start hiew.exe and introduce the required corrections.

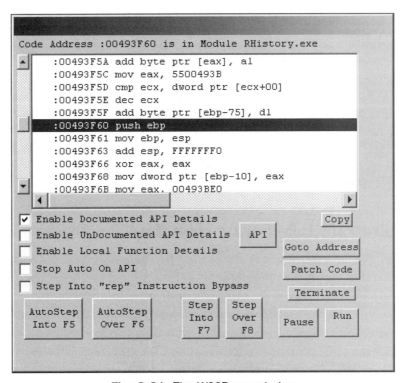

Fig. 2.21. The W32Dasm window

Searching with IDA Pro

The procedure of searching for the required program fragment in IDA Pro also is traditional. First, it is necessary to find the MessageBox name in the list of functions. Then double-click the name to go to the code fragment shown in Fig. 2.22. This is a "stub" called from the other locations within the program. Pay special attention to the ellipsis. If you right-click it and select the **Jump to cross reference** item in the context menu, the window will open, which would display all program addresses, from which the MessageBox function is called. Now you won't have any difficulties checking all of these function calls and finding the required location within the program.

```
CODE:00405E1C ; ------------- S U B R O U T I N E -------------------------------------
CODE:00405E1C
CODE:00405E1C ; Attributes: thunk
CODE:00405E1C
CODE:00405E1C                  public MessageBoxA_0 ; weak
CODE:00405E1C MessageBoxA_0    proc near              ; CODE XREF: sub_408560+99↓p
CODE:00405E1C                                         ; sub_4297F0+43↓p ...
CODE:00405E1C                  jmp     ds:__imp_MessageBoxA_0
CODE:00405E1C MessageBoxA_0    endp
CODE:00405E1C
CODE:00405E1C ; -------------------------------------------------------------------
```

Fig. 2.22. Fragment of the disassembled program code produced by IDA Pro

NOTE

When correcting the executable code (usually, this is done to remove the protection), conditional jump commands are often encountered. Because such commands are often preceded by comparison commands (CMP), there is a common opinion that to crack a program the cracker needs to know only one Assembly command. This is not quite true. In difficult situations, the code investigator must literally "grind" the Assembly code.

2.4.2. Example 2: Removing Limitations on Program Use

The task of removing limitations of trial versions is not too difficult. At the same time, it is one of the most common. This problem can be solved using W32Dasm. For code correction, the hiew.exe program is traditionally used.

The program considered in this section, Allscreen, is a shareware program allowing you to produce snapshots of individual windows or fragments of the screen. I downloaded its shareware release quite a long time ago. This program is written in Delphi. However, as will be shown in this section, it is possible to solve the problem without even knowing, in which programming language it was written. Nevertheless, it should be pointed out that the DeDe disassembler (see *Section 2.1.1*), which I praised earlier, failed to determine the program structure. This is probably because an old version of compiler was used for program translation.

Thus, when you start the allscreen.exe program, the dialog shown in Fig. 2.23 appears on the screen. When you carefully study cracking and related issues, you'll discover that usually the cracker must look for the program fragment corresponding to some visual effect, such as opening or closing a window or text output.

When the user clicks the **Accept** button, there is a delay of about 6 seconds (Fig. 2.24), after which the program operates normally.

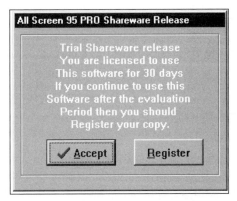

Fig. 2.23. The window that appears at start-up
of the Allscreen program

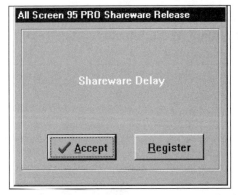

Fig. 2.24. The delay window displayed by
the Allscreen program

Fig. 2.25. The message informing the user about expiration of the trial period

After 15 runs, the program displays the window shown in Fig 2.25, and terminates.

To remove the protection, the cracker must solve the following two problems:

❑ Eliminate the annoying delay

❑ Ensure that the program continues to operate correctly after the trial period expires

The Delay Procedure

The window shown in Fig. 2.25 is a blunder of the program's authors. The window, along with its contents, can be hidden within the resources. However, when a new record appears in that window, it is nothing but the program code. Thus, start W32Dasm and load the allscreen.exe program there. Open the string data reference (SDR) window, find the Shareware Delay string there, and double-click it. You'll find yourself in the required program location. This program fragment is shown in Listing 2.6.

Listing 2.6. Fragment of the Allscreen code required for removing the delay procedure

---

```
* Referenced by a (U)nconditional or (C)onditional Jump at Address:
|:004420BC(C)
|
:00442123 33D2                    xor edx, edx
:00442125 8B83B0010000            mov eax, dword ptr [ebx + 000001B0]
:0044212B E8541DFDFF              call 00413E84
:00442130 33D2                    xor edx, edx
:00442132 8B83B4010000            mov eax, dword ptr [ebx + 000001B4]
```

```
:00442138 E8471DFDFF          call 00413E84
:0044213D 33D2                xor edx, edx
:0044213F 8B83B8010000        mov eax, dword ptr [ebx + 000001B8]
:00442145 E83A1DFDFF          call 00413E84
:0044214A BA50000000          mov edx, 00000050
:0044214F 8B83BC010000        mov eax, dword ptr [ebx + 000001BC]
:00442155 E8D618FDFF          call 00413A30


* Possible StringData Ref from Code Obj ->"Shareware Delay"
                              |

:0044215A BAA8214400          mov edx, 004421A8
:0044215F 8B83BC010000        mov eax, dword ptr [ebx + 000001BC]
:00442165 E8EE1DFDFF          call 00413F58
:0044216A 33D2                xor edx, edx
:0044216C 8B83C0010000        mov eax, dword ptr [ebx + 000001C0]
:00442172 E80D1DFDFF          call 00413E84
:00442177 33D2                xor edx, edx
:00442179 8B83C4010000        mov eax, dword ptr [ebx + 000001C4]
:0044217F E8001DFDFF          call 00413E84
:00442184 33D2                xor edx, edx
:00442186 8B83C8010000        mov eax, dword ptr [ebx + 000001C8]
:0044218C E8F31CFDFF          call 00413E84
:00442191 8B83CC010000        mov eax, dword ptr [ebx + 000001CC]
:00442197 E8E8D4FFFF          call 0043F684
:0044219C 5B                  pop ebx
:0044219D C3                  ret
```

I have provided a larger code fragment in Listing 2.6, having included several preceding lines of code. In essence, this listing shows the entire delay procedure. There is no practical sense in trying to understand the meaning of each individual CALL command, although it can be easily discovered (by conducting a small experiment) that, for example, CALL 00413E84 removes a string from the screen.

To eliminate the delay, it is enough to "exclude" this fragment from the program. The easiest way of achieving this is to insert POP EBX/RET commands into the start of this code fragment (the 00442123 address) using some hex editor (hiew.exe, for example). After starting the corrected program for execution, the delay is eliminated (see for yourself).

Removing the Limitation on the Number of Program Runs

Now consider the second problem — removing the limitation on program runs. After you carefully consider the window (see Fig. 2.25), it will be clear that this window is formed by the program. This means that you can try to find the text displayed on the screen within the program. As in the previous case, the string can be found in the SDR window. Double-click this line of code to find yourself in the required program location (Listing 2.7).

Listing 2.7. Fragment of Allscreen responsible for limiting the number of runs

---

```
:00443326 8BC0              mov eax, eax
:00443328 53                push ebx
:00443329 8BD8              mov ebx, eax
:0044332B 803DEC56440001    cmp byte ptr [004456EC], 01
:00443332 7546              jne 0044337A
:00443334 A124564400        mov eax, dword ptr [00445624]
:00443339 E84E2CFEFF        call 00425F8C
:0044333E A1D8564400        mov eax, dword ptr [004456D8]
:00443343 E87816FEFF        call 004249C0
:00443348 FF05F0564400      inc dword ptr [004456F0]
:0044334E C605EC56440000    mov byte ptr [004456EC], 00
:00443355 833DF05644000F    cmp dword ptr [004456F0], 0000000F
:0044335C 7E1C              jle 0044337A
:0044335E 6A00              push 00000000
:00443360 668B0DB0334400    mov cx, word ptr [004433B0]
:00443367 B202              mov dl, 02


* Possible StringData Ref from Code Obj ->"This Software Has Been Used Over"
                                |
:00443369 B8BC334400        mov eax, 004433BC
:0044336E E8BDAEFEFF        call 0042E230
:00443373 8BC3              mov eax, ebx
```

```
:00443375 E84214FEFF          call 004247BC
```

```
* Referenced by a (U)nconditional or (C)onditional Jump at Addresses:
:00443332(C), :0044335C(C)
                              |
:0044337A 33D2                xor edx, edx
:0044337C 8B83F4010000        mov eax, dword ptr [ebx + 000001F4]
:00443382 E8A52DFFFF          call 0043612C
:00443387 33D2                xor edx, edx
:00443389 8B83F8010000        mov eax, dword ptr [ebx + 000001F8]
:0044338F E8982DFFFF          call 0043612C
:00443394 33D2                xor edx, edx
:00443396 8B83FC010000        mov eax, dword ptr [ebx + 000001FC]
:0044339C E88B2DFFFF          call 0043612C
:004433A1 33D2                xor edx, edx
:004433A3 8B8314020000        mov eax, dword ptr [ebx + 00000214]
:004433A9 E87E2DFFFF          call 0043612C
:004433AE 5B                  pop ebx
:004433AF C3                  ret
```

As in the previous case, Listing 2.7 presents the entire code fragment required to achieve the cracking goal. View several preceding lines of code, and you'll easily discover "suspicious" commands (Listing 2.8).

Listing 2.8. Commands you must correct to remove the limitation on program runs

```
cmp dword ptr [004456F0], 0000000F
jle 0044337A
```

Recall that the program ceases to operate after 15 runs (0FH in hex representation). The easiest way of removing the limitation is to overwrite the code fragment spanning the addresses from 0044335EH to 00443375H with NOP (90H) commands. Use hiew.exe for this purpose. As a result, the program would operate without any limitations on the number of runs.

2.4.3. Example 3: Cracking an Evaluation Copy

General Considerations

The next example considers how to make a fully featured program out of the 30-day evaluation copy of the Intel C++ 4.5 compiler. I'm not going to add functional capabilities missing from the evaluation version of the compiler. This example only demonstrates the principal possibility of removing the time limitation for the use of the evaluation copy.

After you install the compiler on your computer, it will be located in the ...\compiler45\bin directory. The program name is icl.exe. Start this program, and it will output the following strings to the console:

```
Intel(R) C/C++ Compiler Version 4.5 00015

Copyright (C) 1985-2000 Intel Corporation. All rights reserved.

Evaluation copy.

Icl: NOTE: This is day 1 of 30 day evaluation period.

Icl: Command line error: no files specified.
```

The last output line is clear because the C program name wasn't specified in the command line. If you specify the name of some C program, the compiler would be functional. However, after a month it would cease to operate and, instead of compiling your programs, would display the following string: The evaluation period has expired.

Now, start IDA Pro and try to find the strings that appear in the compiler's console output. Listing 2.9 shows what I located as a result of searching the program code.

Listing 2.9. Strings in the Intel C compiler console output, which were found in IDA Pro

---

```
data:00419C20 aCopyrightC1985 db 'Copyright (C) 1985-2000 Intel
Corporation.  All rights reser'
.data:00419C20                      ; DATA XREF: sub_404574 + 31↑o
.data:00419C20                      ; sub_40C974 + 21↑o
.data:00419C20                      db 'ved.', 0Ah
.data:00419C20                      db 'Evaluation copy', 0
```

Note that the entire listing represents a single string. This is an important issue, especially if you assume that the Evaluation copy message isn't related to any check for the program's operability. Any attempt at locating a string like This is day, however, didn't succeed. Even if I could locate such a string, I'd most likely discover a call to some library function, such as puts or printf. Then I'd have to go one level higher to discover the strings where the limitations for the program use are checked. So, I decided to use the debugger for further analysis of the program.

Searching in the Debugger

Before starting the debugger, I found the address of the main function using IDA Pro. This address turned out to be 00402000H, so, after starting OllyDbg, I immediately set the breakpoint to that address and started program analysis from that point.

To try this, locate the main function and start step-by-step program execution (<F8>), checking the contents of the console window after each procedure call. You'll soon locate the fragment in Listing 2.10.

Listing 2.10. Tracing the console output of the evaluation copy of the Intel C compiler

```
0040204A       E8 71040000        CALL   icl.004024C0
0040204F       0FB6C0             MOVZX EAX, AL
00402052       85C0               TEST   EAX, EAX
00402054       0F84 E5000000      JE     icl.0040213F
0040205A       E8 D1780000        CALL   icl.00409930
0040205F       0FB6C0             MOVZX EAX, AL
00402062       85C0               TEST   EAX, EAX
00402064       0F84 C4000000      JE     icl.0040212E
```

As it turns out, the procedure with the 0040204AH address outputs the Evaluation copy string, and the procedure located at the 0040205AH address outputs the string informing the user about the 30-day evaluation period. Based on the assumption made at the end of the previous section, consider the second procedure (0040205AH), skipping the first one. An attempt at replacing the JE command with JNE doesn't produce the desired result. When running the program in step over mode, you'll find that this procedure returns one. Thus, I've made a simple assumption, namely, that only the contents of the EAX register are of any interest in this procedure. Thus, replace CALL icl.00409930 with MOV EAX, 1 (the number of bytes in both commands is equal) and save the executable module. Test it for usability. It works, and it continues to work after the 30-day trial period expires.

2.4.4. Example 4: Removing Protection

In this example, I demonstrate how crackers often achieve their goals by taking a lengthy and tedious route instead of using the easy and fast approach. This time, consider the GetPixel program intended for taking color pixels from the screen. I obtained this module with the crack (crack.exe). Because I required a demonstration example, I decided to remove the protection without any help (after all, this is an interesting and instructive occupation). Note that although this program was written in Visual Basic I didn't use this knowledge for code investigation. For all I know, Visual Basic decompilers never produce useful results.

Step 1: Attempt To Register the Program

Fig. 2.26 shows the registration window of the GetPixel program. According to the intention of the program's author, this window must be used for user registration. The **Name** and **Registration Code** fields are intended for supplying the user name and registration code. When the user clicks the **OK** button, the program checks the supplied name and password. When I supplied an arbitrary name and an arbitrary password, the program displayed an error message. Well, I didn't expect it to behave differently.

After this first failed attempt, I tried to make the program register my name and the password. Using logic, I started this small investigation by searching for strings containing Registration.

Open the famous IDA Pro disassembler and load the program there. In the strings window, I located three strings containing this word: Register Successfully!, Registration, and Register Fail!. It seems that I chose a correct approach. Start with the first phrase. Double-click this string, and you'll find yourself in the required location of the disassembler window (Listing 2.11).

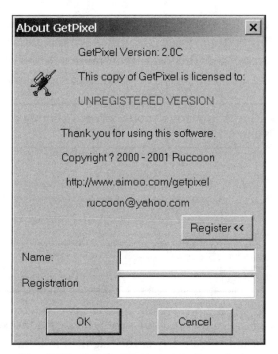

Fig. 2.26. The GetPixel registration window

Listing 2.11. The fragment of disassembled code containing the Register Successfully! string

```
.text:00409720          aRegisterSucces:  ; DATA XREF: .text:00417ECE↓o
.text:00409720          unicode 0, <Register Successfully!>, 0
```

Follow the cross-reference, and you'll find the fragment in Listing 2.12.

Listing 2.12. The code fragment, to which the cross-reference (Listing 2.11) points

```
.text:00417EC5     lea     edx, [ebp - 134h]
.text:00417ECB     lea     ecx, [ebp - 34h]
.text:00417ECE     mov     dword ptr [ebp - 12Ch], offset aRegisterSucces
; "Register Successfully!"
.text:00417ED8     mov     dword ptr [ebp - 134h], 8
.text:00417EE2     call    ds:__vbaVarDup
```

It is difficult to determine what the __vbaVarDup function represents; however, it appears much like a message about successful registration. Now, study the program code located near these strings in more detail. Slightly above the code provided in Listing 2.12, I discovered the fragment shown in Listing 2.13.

Listing 2.13. The "suspicious" code located slightly above the fragment shown in Listing 2.12

```
.text:00417E76       push      ecx
.text:00417E77       push      edx
.text:00417E78       push      4
.text:00417E7A       call      edi ; __vbaFreeVarList
.text:00417E7C       add       esp, 20h
.text:00417E7F       cmp       [ebp - 1A8h], bx
.text:00417E86       jz        loc_4181A4
```

This looks suspicious. Find out what is located at the loc_4181A4 address. Jump to that address, and you'll discover the fragment in Listing 2.14.

Listing 2.14. Code fragment located at the loc_4181A4 address of the GetPixel program

```
.text:00418268       mov       dword ptr [ebp - 12Ch], offset aRegisterFailed
; "Register Failed!"
.text:00418272       mov       dword ptr [ebp - 13Ch], offset aPleaseVisit
; "Please visit"
.text:0041827C       mov       dword ptr [ebp - 14Ch], offset aHttpWww_aimoo_
; "http://www.aimoo.com/getpixel"
.text:00418286       mov       dword ptr [ebp - 15Ch], offset aToGetYourRegis
; "to get your register code"
.text:00418290       call      ebx
; __vbaVarCat
```

This is a message about failed registration that invites the user to visit the developer's site. Thus, this indicates that the chosen way is the correct one. Start hiew32.exe and find the .text:00417E86 address there. Overwrite 6 bytes with

NOP instructions. Then exit and start the program. When the program starts, repeat the registration attempt by supplying any arbitrarily chosen name and password. You'll receive the message that you are now a registered user. Does this mean that the problem has been solved and you can rejoice? No!

Step 2: Remove the Nag Screen

Soon you'll discover that the problem is far from solved. If you didn't quit the program after "successful" registration, the registration window would display that the registration was carried out successfully. However, after restarting the program, the registration window would again state that this copy wasn't a registered one. Furthermore, after restart, the window shown in Fig. 2.27 would start to appear with a certain level of probability. If this window appears and the user clicks the **Yes** button, the program tries to connect to the developer's site; otherwise, it continues normal operation.

After carefully looking at the contents of the directory, where the program was installed, I discovered the clickme.reg file containing the script for writing a correct user name and password into the registry (provided that the user knows the correct user name and password). Open the registry, and you'll discover that the user name and the password you specified when attempting to register the program were written into the location specified by the clickme.reg script. Apparently, the program compares this user name and password to some reference value at start-up. You do not know these values (and, rushing somewhat ahead, you'll never know them). After that, the program specifies that this is an unregistered copy (see Fig. 2.26). In addition, it occasionally displays the nag screen (see Fig. 2.27).

It is necessary to remove the nag screen. Open the strings window in IDA and search for the How do you feel me? string. Having located it, consider the code section that contains a reference to this string. This code fragment is provided in Listing 2.15.

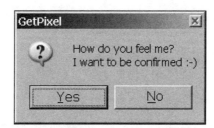

Fig. 2.27. The nag screen

Listing 2.15. The GetPixel code fragment that contains a reference to "How do you feel me?"

```
.text:0040B217    push    eax
.text:0040B218    mov     dword ptr [ebp - 0D0h], offset aHowDoYouFeelMe
                                        ; "How do you feel me?"
.text:0040B222    mov     dword ptr [ebp - 0E0h], offset aIWantToBeConfi
                                        ; "I want to be confirmed :-)"
.text:0040B22C    call    esi             ; __vbaVarCat
.text:0040B22E    lea     ecx, [ebp - 0E8h]
.text:0040B234    push    eax
.text:0040B235    lea     edx, [ebp - 98h]
.text:0040B23B    push    ecx
.text:0040B23C    push    edx
.text:0040B23D    call    esi ; __vbaVarCat
.text:0040B23F    push    eax
.text:0040B240    call    ds:rtcMsgBox
```

It is obvious that the `call rtcMsgBox` command is the call to the `MessageBox` function. This function is unneeded, so you can overwrite it with NOP instructions. However, don't rush forward without taking all required actions. The `MessageBox` function must provide the user with a choice, and it is assumed that the user chooses **No**. Scroll the listing down and locate the required code fragment (Listing 2.16).

Listing 2.16. The GetPixel fragment for the Yes/No choice when the nag screen is displayed

```
.text:0040B2B6    call    ds:__vbaVarTstEq
.text:0040B2BC    test    ax, ax
.text:0040B2BF    jz      short loc_40B305
.text:0040B2C1    mov     esi, ds:__vbaStrToAnsi
.text:0040B2C7    push    1
.text:0040B2C9    lea     edx, [ebp - 60h]
.text:0040B2CC    push    offset aC      ; "C:\\"
.text:0040B2D1    push    edx
.text:0040B2D2    call    esi            ; __vbaStrToAnsi
.text:0040B2D4    push    eax
```

```
.text:0040B2D5      push     0
.text:0040B2D7      lea      eax, [ebp - 5Ch]
.text:0040B2DA      push     offset aHttpWww_aimoo_
                                          ; "http://www.aimoo.com/getpixel"
.text:0040B2DF      push     eax
.text:0040B2E0      call     esi            ; __vbaStrToAnsi
.text:0040B2E2      ush      eax
.text:0040B2E3      push     0
.text:0040B2E5      push     0
.text:0040B2E7      call     sub_407CB0
.text:0040B2EC      call     ds:__vbaSetSystemError
```

If the condition requiring the contents of the EAX register to be zero has not been observed, the program attempts to connect to the author's site. To avoid this action, it is necessary to replace JZ with JMP SHORT. That's all!

Start hiew32.exe and modify the two previously-mentioned fragments (see Listing 2.15, overwrite the MessageBox function with NOP instructions, and replace JZ with JMP SHORT in Listing 2.16). Do not forget that it is necessary to overwrite both the function call and the PUSH instruction preceding it. As a result, the nag screen won't appear.

Step 3: Complete the Registration

Now it remains to complete the final step, which consists of making the program to believe that the registry contains the correct registration data. Apparently, it would be logical to assume that there must be some procedure that checks the password for correctness.

I should admit that at this stage it took me about an hour to locate this procedure. I used both a disassembler and a debugger (OllyDbg). I had to guess how to access that procedure. Now I'm going to explain you how I did this.

First, it is necessary to note the names of the registry entries that have to be filled in the course of registration. These are the License and RegUser fields. The License field must contain the password. Now search for this string.

The string can be easily found. It occurs in two locations. This is an encouraging indication, because there are two calls to the password: at program start-up and from the registration window. Look at the disassembled program code, and you'll discover that in the first case the rtcGetSetting function is used and in the second case the `rtcSaveSetting` function is used. Everything is clear now. The first function reads the password, and the second function writes it. Information about both functions can be found in the Microsoft Developer Network (MSDN). The first function deserves the most attention.

Go to the required program fragment, scroll the listing down, and try to understand the program logic. When scrolling down, trace only those procedures that are not supplied as part of some library. One such procedure, most likely, will be the one that checks the password and user name for correctness.

First, the code fragment in Listing 2.17 attracted my attention.

Listing 2.17. A candidate for the role of the password-checking procedure

```
.text:0040AE00        lea      edx, [ebp - 78h]
.text:0040AE03        push     edx
.text:0040AE04        call     sub_415160
```

What value is placed into the EDX register? Start the debugger and set a breakpoint to the 40AE03 address. Then look, at which location in the stack the EDX register points. It turns out to be the name read from the system registry. There is no password here. Consequently, this procedure is not the one you are looking for. It is necessary to continue the search. In the course of this search, another procedure should attract your attention (Listing 2.18).

Listing 2.18. Another candidate for the role of the password-checking procedure

```
.text:0040AE5C        lea      edx, [ebp - 88h]
.text:0040AE62        lea      eax, [ebp - 78h]
.text:0040AE65        push     edx
.text:0040AE66        push     eax
.text:0040AE67        call     sub_416070
```

Use the debugger to find out that EDX points to the string made up of the user name and the password (as it turns out, they were combined somewhere). Execute this procedure under the debugger, and it will return the value of zero in the EAX register. Note that 0 in most programming languages corresponds to FALSE. Well, it seems that the time has come for a small experiment.

Start hiew32.exe, and replace the fragment shown in Listing 2.19 with the MOV EAX, 1 command, overwriting all other bytes of the procedure (Listing 2.18) with 90H values.

Listing 2.19. The code fragment that must be replaced with the MOV EAX, 1 command

```
.text:0040AE65        push     edx
.text:0040AE66        push     eax
.text:0040AE67        call     sub_416070
```

Start the program, open the registration window, and try to register again. This time you'll succeed.

Step 4: Use an Unexpected Solution

Now it is time to point out that there is much easier way of achieving the correct result. Probably, you have already guessed what I mean. It is necessary to access the 00416070H address, which is the address where the password-checking procedure starts, and insert two commands at its beginning: MOV EAX, 1/RETN 8. Nothing else will be needed. All three steps described earlier will become unnecessary. It was tempting to demonstrate for you an easy and ready-to-use solution. However, several considerations prevented me from doing this:

❑ In practice, most problems are not solved in the easiest way. An easy and elegant solution is usually found later, when the desired result has already been achieved. Thus, learning on the basis of elegant solution is not the correct approach.

❑ The approach to solving the problem chosen by the investigator doesn't matter. What matters is that the task has finally been solved.

A question may come to your mind. In the solution that I demonstrated here, I acted on the basis of information obtained from the script found in the working directory of the program. On the basis of this script, I discovered where the user name and password are written in the course of program registration. What would I do if there were no script? There is no problem here. If this were the case, it would be possible to use some registry monitor tracing all attempts at accessing the registry. If you have no registry monitors at your disposal, it is possible to resort to direct analysis of the disassembled code. For example, functions such as rtcSaveSetting and rtcGetSetting are the first candidates for such an analysis.

Chapter 3

MAIN PARADIGMS OF THE EXECUTABLE CODE ANALYSIS

I n *Section 2.4*, I provided several simple examples of analysis and correction of executable code. The main goal of this chapter is to provide some theoretical basis. Using the material provided here, you'll be able to investigate more difficult cases.

When studying code analysis, it is necessary to understand that this is not the same thing as decompilation (conversion of binary executable code into a program written in some high-level programming language). Although I will provide analysis of the algorithmic structure and main constructs of high-level programming languages in this chapter, its main goal isn't reconstruction of the program's source code (which in general is impossible). Rather, the main aim of this material is to provide an understanding of the program operating logic. Examples in *Section 2.4* demonstrate code analysis techniques aimed at solving specific tasks (code analysis in the specified context). These problems were solved without even trying to understand, which constructs of specific programming language were used. However, you won't be able to solve more difficult problems without knowing these constructs, understanding how they are converted during the compilation, and discovering the form, in which they are present in the binary code after the compilation is completed.

Even for a single programming language there might be lots of different compilers — consider the C++ programming language. In addition, every compiler usually has several compilation modes, which, as a rule, are related to the methods of optimizing the resulting code and adding various check procedures into it (such as checks for going beyond the buffer limits). All of these concepts are illustrated in Fig. 3.1. In general, it is impossible to study this entire hierarchy. This is not a serious problem, however, because studying this is unnecessary. The only thing that you need to do is understand the patterns, according to which the executable code is formed.

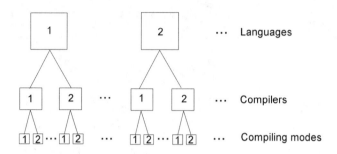

Fig. 3.1. The language–executable code hierarchy

I hope that the material provided in this chapter will help you master these patterns. The executable code in this chapter is all analyzed on the basis of IDA Pro, which is the best contemporary disassembler. Reference information about this disassembler will be provided in *Chapter 5*.

3.1. Data Identification

Data identification was covered in *Section 1.6*; however, there I mainly described Assembly language. Analysis of code written using Assembly language is, on one hand, easier and on the other hand, more difficult than analyzing the code written in some high-level programming language. This task is easier because you are writing the same code that will be placed into the compiled program. This task is more difficult because Assembly language practically doesn't limit the options of the programmer. Thus, everything depends on the programmer's self-discipline and formulated tasks. If your goal is to confuse any potential investigator of your code, you won't be able to find a language better than Assembly. When you are writing a program in some high-level programming language, you can't predict what will result after your source code is compiled. Furthermore, most programmers writing their programs in Visual C++ or Delphi never think what the compiler would produce on the basis of their source code. When analyzing such a code, investigators must solve the following problems:

❏ "Grind" the specific features of compiler operation
❏ "Squeeze" their way through the programmer's working style

This section concentrates on the topic of identifying the data used in high-level programming languages.

3.1.1. Global Variables

There is a common opinion that global variables are harmful for programming. Nevertheless, most programmers always used them in the past, use them now, and will continue to use them in the future. Therefore, mastering the technique of recognizing global variables is a must.

Optimization Influence

Optimization by Execution Speed and Code Size

I'll start investigation of the optimization influence with a simple program written in C++.[i] This program is presented in Listing 3.1. There are three global variables in this program, one of which is not initialized.

Listing 3.1. Simple C++ program containing three global variables, one uninitialized

---

```
#include <stdio.h>
int a, b = 20, s = 0;
void main()
{
        a = 10;
        s = a + b;
        printf("%d", s);
};
```

Consider what the Microsoft Visual C++ (Visual Studio .NET 2003) compiler would produce out of this program. Load the executable module, compiled using the "no optimization" option, into the IDA Pro disassembler. The disassembled code is presented in Listing 3.2. I hope that you won't have any difficulties studying this disassembled text, which I have followed with brief comments.

---

[i] The same relates to the C programming language because this program doesn't use any capabilities introduced with the arrival of the C++ language. However, I won't concentrate on these minor details. I always mean the two most widely used C++ compilers, namely, Microsoft Visual C++ and Borland C++.

Listing 3.2. Disassembled code of the program (Listing 3.1) compiled without optimization

```
.text:00401000 _main    proc near                    ; CODE XREF: start + 16E↓p
.text:00401000          push    ebp
.text:00401001          mov     ebp, esp
.text:00401003          mov     dword_4086E0, 0Ah ; a = 10
.text:0040100D          mov     eax, dword_4086E0 ; a -> eax
.text:00401012          add     eax, dword_408040 ; a + b -> eax
.text:00401018          mov     dword_4086E4, eax ; eax -> s
.text:0040101D          mov     ecx, dword_4086E4 ; s -> ecx
.text:00401023          push    ecx
.text:00401024          push    offset unk_4060FC ; Formatted printf string
.text:00401029          call    _printf
.text:0040102E          add     esp, 8
.text:00401031          xor     eax, eax
.text:00401033          pop     ebp
.text:00401034          retn
.text:00401034 _main    endp
```

Having carefully analyzed Listing 3.2, you'll immediately note the following interesting issues:

❑ IDA Pro has excellently handled the job of recognizing global variables. This is not surprising. The text contains direct references to global variables (dword_4086E0, dword_4086E4, and dword_408040). Assembly commands directly refer to the variable size. Determining the sizes of variables is an important issue related to disassembling. It is not always possible to determine the variable size exactly. Note that the b (dword_408040) variable is located separately from the other two variables. The compiler considers a (dword_4086E0) and s (dword_4086E4)[i] variables uninitialized ones. This topic will be covered in more detail later in this section, when discussing variable size and location (see "*Variable Size, Location, and Type*").

---

[i] Start-up initialization of the s variable doesn't make sense because the initial value of s is not used anywhere.

❏ Even a beginner will immediately note that the compiled text is redundant:

- There are the so-called prologue (PUSH EBP/MOV EBP, ESP) and epilogue (POP EBP) of the function. These will be covered in more detail in *Section 3.2.1*. Both of these elements are redundant in this function, because the EBP register is used for addressing of the stack variables and parameters, which are not present in this program.

- The a variable is initialized, then it is used in the addition operation. Because its value is not printed and is not further used, it is possible to use a simple constant instead of the a variable.

- Unnecessary memory reservation for the s variable immediately attracts attention. Because the result of addition is loaded into the EAX register, it is most logical to use it as the s variable. In other words, it would be expedient to make s a register variable.

Listing 3.3 presents the disassembled code of the same program (see Listing 3.1) compiled with the "create fast code" option. As you can see, now the code doesn't create any function prologue or epilogue. For the moment, this issue is not the main one.

Consider how the sum (the s variable) is obtained. The summing is carried out by adding the register content and a constant. This operation is carried out much faster than adding the register content and a variable. Pay special attention to the command grouping. First, the values are pushed onto the stack; then, they are followed by two data exchange commands. This approach is based on the Pentium processor properties. It is known as *command pairing*. Its main idea is that two commands that satisfy specific predefined conditions are executed in parallel, which means that two commands are carried out as a single command. Thus, the compiler has met some of the optimization requirements.

NOTE

Contemporary Intel-compatible processors have two pipelines of executing instructions. These pipelines are known as U pipelines and V pipelines. Under certain circumstances, the processor would execute two commands sequentially in different pipelines. As the result, the execution speed would be practically doubled. There are instructions that can be executed only in the U pipeline, and other instructions can be used only in V pipeline. Finally, there are instructions that can be executed in both pipelines. Knowing this, it is possible to group commands to increase the program execution speed as much as possible. Contemporary compilers "know" this processor feature. So, if you encounter an unusual order of instructions in the executable code, you should recall instruction pairing.

Listing 3.3. Disassembled code (Listing 3.1) compiled with the "create fast code" option

```
.text:00401000 _main    proc near                   ; CODE XREF: start + 16E↓p
.text:00401000          mov  eax, dword_408040      ; b -> eax
.text:00401005          add  eax, 0Ah               ; The sum is here.
.text:00401008          push eax
.text:00401009          push offset unk_4060FC
.text:0040100E          mov  dword_4086E0, 0Ah      ; 10 -> a
.text:00401018          mov  dword_4086E4, eax      ; eax -> s
.text:0040101D          call _printf
.text:00401022          add  esp, 8
.text:00401025          xor  eax, eax
.text:00401027          retn
.text:00401027 _main    endp
```

Try to optimize by the code size. Disassembling shows that the change in the code size is minimal (compared with that in Listing 3.3): the ADD ESP, 8 command (which takes 3 bytes) is replaced with the POP ECX/POP ECX pair of commands (each command is 1 byte).

Why did I provide all these examples? My goal wasn't to study optimization techniques (this topic deserves a separate book). I simply wanted to prepare you (and provide a certain theoretical background) to perceive that the code you will analyze might be quite unusual as the result of optimization. Nevertheless, in the future I'll explain lots of optimization methods many times.

NOTE

The examples provided in this section, among other things, demonstrate that trying to provide better optimization than the compiler does (especially as relates to the execution speed) is not a simple job. The test example (see Listing 3.1) considered in this section is simple. The situation will become more complicated with a real-world Assembly program comprising hundreds of commands. Manual optimization of such programs becomes difficult. Thus, in most cases you'll have to rely on the compiler, especially when dealing with such products as Microsoft Visual C++, long famous for its optimization capabilities.

Evaluating Execution Time

When optimizing program code, evaluating the execution time of a specific program fragment becomes the most important issue. The simplest way of achieving this goal is to use two API functions. The first function is QueryPerformanceCounter. Its only argument is the pointer to the LARGE_INTEGER structure. If the function is executed correctly, this structure would store the number of processor clocks elapsed since program start-up. The second function is QueryPerformanceFrequency. Its argument also contains the pointer to the LARGE_INTEGER structure; however, this time the structure contains the clock frequency. Thus, if t1 and t2 stand for the number of clocks elapsed from the start and to the end of the program fragment being investigated, respectively, and fr is the clock frequency, then the number of milliseconds required for executing the given program fragment can be computed by the following formula: (t2 - t1)*1000/fr. This is only a rough evaluation, because in the multitasking environment exact computations of the execution time of the chosen program fragment are out of the question.

Pointers to Global Variables

It is impossible to imagine the C programming language without pointers. Pointers are quintessential of this programming language and determine its fate. Instead operating over a variable, it is possible to operate over the pointer to that variable. To operate over pointers, compilers use indirect addressing. This fact, however, is self-evident. If s is some pointer to data, then the MOV EDX, s command allows the data to be accessed through [EDX]: for example, the MOV EAX, [EDX] command moves a 4-byte value from the data area into the EAX register.

Listing 3.4. Sample program, in which one global variable is defined using a pointer

---

```
#include <stdio.h>
#include <stdlib.h>
int   a, b = 20;
int *s;
void main()
{
        s = (int*)malloc(4);
        a = 10;
```

```
        *s = a + b;
        printf("%d", *s);
        free(s);
};
```

Listing 3.4 demonstrates a sample program, in which one of the global variables is defined by a pointer. The disassembled listing of this program is provided in Listing 3.5.

Listing 3.5. Disassembled code of the program presented in Listing 3.4

```
.text:00401000 _main  proc  near              ; CODE XREF: start + 16E↓p
.text:00401000        push  ebp
.text:00401001        mov   ebp, esp
.text:00401003        push  4                  ; Reserve 4 bytes.
.text:00401005        call  _malloc
.text:0040100A        add   esp, 4             ; Clear the stack.
.text:0040100D        mov   dword_4086C0, eax  ; This variable
                                               ; contains a pointer.
.text:00401012        mov   dword_4086C4, 0Ah  ; a = 10
.text:0040101C        mov   eax, dword_4086C4  ; a -> eax
.text:00401021        add   eax, dword_408040  ; a + b -> eax
.text:00401027        mov   ecx, dword_4086C0  ; ECX contains the
                                               ; pointer address.
.text:0040102D        mov   [ecx], eax         ; The sum is located
                                               ; at the address
                                               ; referenced by the
                                               ; pointer.
.text:0040102F        mov   edx, dword_4086C0  ; Pointer -> edx
.text:00401035        mov   eax, [edx]         ; Sum -> eax
.text:00401037        push  eax                ; The sum is pushed
                                               ; into the stack.
.text:00401038        push  offset unk_4060FC  ; The formatted string
.text:0040103D        call  _printf
.text:00401042        add   esp, 8
```

```
.text:00401045        mov    ecx, dword_4086C0   ; Pointer -> ecx.
.text:0040104B        push   ecx
.text:0040104C        call   _free               ; Release the pointer.
.text:00401051        add    esp, 4
.text:00401054        xor    eax, eax
.text:00401056        pop    ebp
.text:00401057        retn
.text:00401057        _main  endp
```

Note that Listing 3.5 uses indirect addressing twice (through the ECX and EDX registers). The second case, in which indirect addressing is used (through EDX), looks strange because ECX already contains the address of the s variable. Why use EDX? This is a rhetorical question. After all, I compiled the program having specified that no optimization was needed by the compiler. Thus, the compiler has simply generated one fragment for writing through the pointer and another fragment for reading through the pointer.

What conclusions can be drawn on the basis of this material? Notice that indirect addressing is used when briefly viewing the disassembled code. This means that pointers must be present in the program being investigated.

Global Variables and Constants

Consider an intricate issue: How do you distinguish the address of some global variable from a normal constant?

Listing 3.6. Distinction between an address of a global variable and a normal constant

```
#include <stdio.h>
int a, b, c;
void main()
{
        a = 10;
        b = 20;
        c = 0x4086d0;
        printf("%d %d %d\n", a, b, c);
};
```

Consider the example program shown in Listing 3.6. Variables a, b, and c are assigned the values of some numeric constants, then the standard printf library function is used to output them to the console. The C program is correct and unambiguous; it cannot be interpreted incorrectly. However, consider how IDA Pro interprets the executable code of this program (Listing 3.7).

Listing 3.7. Disassembled code of the program shown in Listing 3.6

```
.text:00401000 _main            proc near              ; CODE XREF: start + 16E↓p
.text:00401000                  push     ebp
.text:00401001                  mov      ebp, esp
.text:00401003                  mov      dword 4086C8, 0Ah
.text:0040100D                  mov      dword_4086C0, 14h
.text:00401017                  mov      dword_4086C4, offset unk_4086D0
.text:00401021                  mov      eax, dword_4086C4
.text:00401026                  push     eax
.text:00401027                  mov      ecx, dword_4086C0
.text:0040102D                  push     ecx
.text:0040102E                  mov      edx, dword_4086C8
.text:00401034                  push     edx
.text:00401035                  push     offset aDDD   ; "%d %d %d\n"
.text:0040103A                  call     _printf
.text:0040103F                  add      esp, 10h
.text:00401042                  xor      eax, eax
.text:00401044                  pop      ebp
.text:00401045                  retn
.text:00401045 _main            endp
```

Consider Listing 3.7, obtained using IDA Pro, more carefully. The dword_4086C8 label is the a variable, dword_4086C0 corresponds to the b variable, and dword_4086C4 stands for the c variable. What does this mean? The dword_4086C4 variable is used to load the address of the unk_4086D0 memory cells. Why? What is the role of these cells? The number 0x4086D0 is simply a constant! However, IDA Pro considered this number to be an address. Strange! It should be pointed out that the unk_ prefix means that the disassembler has doubts and is not sure what is hidden by that address. However, the disassembler's doubts do not matter!

In the course of analysis, you must draw an unambiguous conclusion. In this example, the text is simple; therefore, it is not difficult to make the right decision. You must not have any doubts, even though IDA Pro has some. However strange this might seem at first, in this situation the W32Dasm disassembler has done a good job. This is not because of its outstanding capabilities in the field of recognizing addresses and constants. This is because of its lack of such capabilities, which causes this disassembler to interpret everything (or practically everything) as constants.

What would happen if the `c` variable is assigned the `0x4086c0` value? I hope that you have already guessed. In this case, IDA Pro will obtain additional confirmation that this is an address of some variable. Instead of the `mov dword_4086C4, offset unk_4086D0` command, another command would appear in the listing: `mov dword_4086C4, offset dword_4086c0`. Thus, the disassembler no longer doubts that it is dealing with a variable. However, you know that this is not so. Furthermore, you will easily draw the right conclusion using the disassembled listing.

However, another problem remains. Any disassembler is a program; therefore, it needs a strict criterion that can be implemented algorithmically. In the case being considered, there are no commands that would confirm (or refute) the assumption that it is dealing with an address except for the range. Falling into this range makes a constant a candidate for being an address. What would this range be in the case in question? Everything is straightforward here. First, there is a range of addresses allocated for the data. IDA Pro considers a constant falling into this range one of the indications of a data address. However, there also is the range of code addresses. For example, if a constant is equal to `0x401000`, the disassembler would consider that it deals with the address of the `_main` function. Note that in this case IDA Pro will not "suspect" that the constant represents an address; it would be sure that this is an address.

What conclusion can be drawn on the basis of these considerations? My conclusion is *de omnibus dubitandum*. In other words, you can never be certain of anything. If the suspicious constant is treated like an address — for instance, using the `LEA` command — then it is possible to speak about an address with greater certainty. Furthermore, if you notice that the constant is then used in indirect addressing or as a function parameter (which represents an address by definition), then you shouldn't have any doubts.

Variable Size, Location, and Type

Long ago, when MS-DOS was dominant, I encountered in a Pascal manual a statement declaring that the use of 1-byte variables instead of 2-byte ones speeds up program operation. I doubted this statement, so I investigated the Assembly code of such a program. It turned out that the statement was far from true. Has the situation changed? How do 32-bit operating systems behave? Is there any practical advantage in using 1- and 2-byte variables instead of 4-byte ones? Where are variables located, and how can disassemblers determine their size? All of these questions will be answered in this section.

To begin the investigation, recall the material provided in *Section 1.1.3*. Consider the code fragment shown in Listing 3.8 (it is similar to the one shown in Listing 1.2).

Listing 3.8. Fragment of the test C program for studying variable size, location, and type

---

```
BYTE e = 0xab;

WORD c = 0x1234;

DWORD b = 0x34567890;
```

If you view the memory, you will discover that all variables are aligned by a boundary that is a multiple of four. However, it turns out that this alignment is only due to the order, in which these variables were declared. For example, consider code, in which variables are declared in a different order (Listing 3.9).

Listing 3.9. Fragment of Listing 3.8, in which variables are declared in a different order

---

```
WORD c = 0x1234;

BYTE e = 0xab;

DWORD b = 0x34567890;
```

In this case, the compiler will place variables in memory so that the first two variables will be located in two neighboring words. The b variable will be aligned by the 4-byte boundary, as in the previous case. There are optimal rules for the alignment of different data types. Table 3.1 outlines information about the alignment of data of different sizes.

Table 3.1. Optimal requirements for alignment of data of different sizes

Data size	Alignment
1 byte	1 (no alignment)
2 bytes	2
4 bytes	4
6 bytes	8
8 bytes	8
10 bytes	16
16 bytes	16

Consider another example (Listing 3.10).

Listing 3.10. Simple example illustrating optimal alignment of data of different sizes

```
#include <stdio.h>
#include <windows.h>
WORD b = 10;
BYTE a;
DWORD c;
void main()
{
        a = 10;
        c = 30;
        printf("%d %d %d\n", a, b, c);
};
```

This is a simple example. However, even here there is a particular feature that will be helpful for investigating some patterns of memory allocation for different variables. The a and c variables are not initialized. They are assigned their values directly in the program text. The b variable is initialized. Is there any difference among these variables? As it turns out, there is. Compile the program using the Microsoft Visual C++ compiler, then disassemble the resulting executable module using IDA Pro. Analyze the resulting listings, and you'll find that in IDA Pro all variables will be located in the .data section. However, recall the material provided in *Section 1.5.3*, where it was explained that initialized variables must be placed into the .data section and uninitialized ones must be added to the .bss section. Curiously, listings produced by IDA Pro clearly show that although all variables are located within the same section, they are placed into different parts of that section: First, there is an initialized variable, then, after a long-enough interval, there are two uninitialized variables. To understand the reason behind such behavior, compile the program with the /Fas command-line option. An intermediate Assembly listing will be generated in the course of compiling. View this listing, and you'll discover an interesting phenomenon: Two segments are present in the listing, one with the _data name (containing an initialized variable) and another one called _bss (containing uninitialized variables). Later, these segments must transform into appropriate sections. However, the compiler knows the names of the _bss and _data segments and later combines them into the single .data section. With all that being so, the data located in the _bss segment always follow the data from the _data segment. To check this statement, write a simple Assembly program containing two data segments (_bss and _data). After linking, only one data section called .data will remain. However, if you slightly change the segment names, for example, replacing _bss with _bss1, then the executable module will have two sections: .data and _bss1 (including the underscore character). After checking this statement for the Microsoft Visual C++ compiler, test the behavior of other compilers. In my experiments, compiling the program from Listing 3.10 using Borland C++ v. 5.00 showed that this compiler behaves similarly. In this case, the Assembly code contained two data segments, with the _data and _bss names.

Consider another issue. How is it possible to determine the variable size in the course of disassembling? The generalized answer to this question is as follows: This goal can be achieved by analyzing the commands that operate over a specific variable. This answer is self-evident because the variable behaves in a specific way depending on the operations that are carried out over it. Recall the material provided in *Section 1.4*, where the format of the Intel microprocessor commands was described. For instance, consider a simple operation that assigns some integer value to a numeric variable. In C, this operation appears, for example, as follows: b = 10. Accordingly, an Assembly command in general will appear as follows: MOV [mem], 10. However, you know that in Assembly such operations require the variable type to be specified explicitly (for example, byte ptr). This requirement is well-grounded. There is a significant difference between placing the number 10 into a WORD variable and placing it into a DWORD variable. Because there is a significant difference in the mathematics, there also must be a difference in the command format.

Consider the complete command codes for the commands assigning values to variables of three types: BYTE, WORD, and DWORD (Listing 3.11).

Listing 3.11. Complete codes of commands assigning values to three types of variables

```
C605 C8864000 14           MOV byte ptr [04086C8], 20
66 C705 C8864000  0A00     MOV word ptr [04086C8], 10
C705 C4864000 1E000000     MOV dword ptr [04086C4], 30
```

Note that MOD R/M bytes for all three commands are identical. The reason is clear: The first operand is an offset for all three commands. Curiously, the code of the command operating over a WORD operand differs by the presence of the 66H prefix from the code of the command operating over the DWORD operand. This prefix specifies that the operand has the WORD type, not the DWORD type. The command, in which the first operand has the BYTE type, has its individual code. Thus, it becomes clear how the disassembler obtains information about the variable size: It simply analyzes the program code.

Until now, floating-point numbers have not been covered. Now it is time to consider them. Consider the program shown in Listing 3.12.

Listing 3.12. Simple program for investigating the behavior of floating-point variables

```c
#include <stdio.h>
#include <windows.h>
double s, d;
int i;
void main()
{
        s = 0.00;
        d = 1.034;
        for(i = 0; i < 100; i++)
                s = s + i/d;
    printf("%f\n", s);
};
```

As you can see, the program in Listing 3.12 has two double variables. Recall the material provided in *Section 1.1.3* — to be precise, in its "Real Numbers" subsection, where floating-point numbers were described. The format of double numbers used in the C++ language corresponds to the format of long floating-point numbers supported by the Intel microprocessor, or, to be precise, by its FPU (see *Section 1.2.3*). Listing 3.13 contains the disassembled code of the main function from Listing 3.12.

Listing 3.13. Disassembled code of the main function from Listing 3.12

```
.text:00401000  _main          proc near    ; CODE XREF: start + 16E↓p
.text:00401000          var_8 = qword ptr -8
.text:00401000
.text:00401000                 push    ebp
.text:00401001                 mov     ebp, esp
.text:00401003                 fld     ds:dbl_408108
.text:00401009                 fstp    dbl_40A9D0
.text:0040100F                 fld     ds:dbl_408100
.text:00401015                 fstp    dbl_40A9C0
.text:0040101B                 mov     dword_40A9C8, 0
.text:00401025                 jmp     short loc_401034
.text:00401027 loc_401027:                  ; CODE XREF: _main + 55↓j
.text:00401027                 mov     eax, dword_40A9C8
.text:0040102C                 add     eax, 1
.text:0040102F                 mov     dword_40A9C8, eax
.text:00401034
.text:00401034 loc_401034:                  ; CODE XREF: _main + 25↑j
.text:00401034                 cmp     dword_40A9C8, 64h
.text:0040103B                 jge     short loc_401057
.text:0040103D                 fild    dword_40A9C8
.text:00401043                 fdiv    dbl_40A9C0
.text:00401049                 fadd    dbl_40A9D0
.text:0040104F                 fstp    dbl_40A9D0
.text:00401055                 jmp     short loc_401027
.text:00401057 ;------------------------------------------------------------
.text:00401057
```

```
.text:00401057 loc_401057:                        ; CODE XREF: _main + 3B↑j
.text:00401057                 fld     dbl_40A9D0
.text:0040105D                 sub     esp, 8
.text:00401060                 fstp    [esp + 8 + var_8]
.text:00401063                 push    offset unk_4080FC
.text:00401068                 call    _printf
.text:0040106D                 add     esp, 0Ch
.text:00401070                 xor     eax, eax
.text:00401072                 pop     ebp
.text:00401073                 retn
.text:00401073 _main           endp
```

The disassembled listing created by IDA Pro deserves special comments:

❏ For the moment, skip the strange var_8 variable, which will be considered later. Also, skip the function prologue. The four commands that following the prologue are interesting. They represent nothing but the assignment of initial values to the s and d variables. For this purpose, the compiler has reserved places for two floating-point constants (dbl_408108 and dbl_408100) beforehand. Using a sequence of two commands (fld and fstp), the constant is loaded into an appropriate variable (these commands can be found in Table 1.19). Both constants and variables (dbl_40A9D0 and dbl_40A9C0) take 8 bytes, which is quite natural. The next command, resetting the dword_40A9C8 integer variable to zero, is self-evident. It simply assigns an initial value to the loop counter.

❏ Later, there is a jump into the loop body to the loc_401034 label. Before this label, there are three commands, which are intended to increase the loop counter (i++). Therefore, skip these commands the first time. A possible exit from the loop is checked by the cmp dword_40A9C8 and 64h/jge short loc_401057 commands. Naturally, 64h corresponds to 100.

❏ Then, there are four commands whose goal can be guessed by the code of the source program. They correspond to s = s + i/d. The algorithm implemented by these commands is as follows: The fild dword_40A9C8 command loads the integer loop counter into the top of the coprocessor stack, st(0). The next command, fdiv, divides the loop counter by the dbl_40A9C0 variable (this is d). Then, the fadd command adds the division result to the dbl_40A9D0 variable, where the sum will be accumulated. Finally, because the addition result is located in the coprocessor stack, the `fstp` command is used to place it into the `dbl_40A9D0` variable. The coprocessor stack is popped, which means that, for example, the content of `ST(1)` is moved to `ST(0)`. Later, an unconditional jump returns control to the start of the loop.

❑ Then, there is the call to the `printf` function. It is necessary to push a floating-point number into the stack. This is an instructive technique. The `fld dbl_40A9D0` command pushes the computed sum into the coprocessor stack. The next command, `sub esp, 8`, reserves space in the stack for an 8-byte value. This command is equivalent to the two `push` commands. Then, the `fstp [esp + 8 + var_8]` command places the sum from the coprocessor stack into the normal stack. The next `push` command sends the formatted string into the stack.

The case just considered, in which initial values of floating-point variables are stored in constants and then loaded into variables, is practiced by the Microsoft Visual C++ compiler. The Borland C++ compiler uses another technique, which is less illustrative. The disassembled code of the executable module produced by the Borland C++ compiler is shown in Listing 3.14.

Listing 3.14. Disassembled code of the executable module produced by Borland C++

```
.text:0040111B         mov      dword ptr dbl_40C2C4, 95810625h
.text:00401127         mov      dword ptr dbl_40C2C4 + 4, 3FF08B43h
```

As you can see, two strange constants are loaded into the memory. From this listing, it is hardly possible to determine that this is a floating-point number and then to determine that number. When analyzing this code, it is impossible to do without the information provided in *Section 1.1.3*. The same problem is also encountered in Microsoft Visual C++, provided that you operate over `float` variables. Such variables are short real numbers taking only 32 bits. Therefore, a normal `MOV` command is used for assigning this type of value to a variable. However, for any operations over such variables, coprocessor commands are used. Thus, I strongly recommend that you gain a sound understanding of the structure of real numbers (*Section 1.1.3*).

Thus, if you encounter FPU commands, you must immediately understand that it will be necessary to spend time investigating floating-point variables.

When dealing with an integer variable, it is important to discover whether it is signed or unsigned. For example, how would you distinguish int variables from unsigned int (DWORD) ones? The general principle is as follows: Analyze the operations over the variables of interest and, on the basis of this analysis, determine their types. A more specific method of determining the type of integer variables is analysis of the conditional constructs, in which they participate. For example, the JL conditional jump command is used for comparing signed numbers, and the JB command is its analogue used for unsigned numbers.

It only remains to answer a single question: Will any performance gain be obtained if you use integer variables smaller than 4 bytes? The answer to this question consists of the following issues:

- ❏ Using shorter variables allows you to economize on memory.
- ❏ However, it complicates the algorithm in the compiled code, because 32-bit variables must be used in the program anyway. Complication of the algorithm slows down the execution and results in the growth of the required memory.

Complex Data Types

Strings

Programming languages interpret string data types as sequences of encoded characters. As a rule, ASCII encoding is used. When using this type of encoding, 1 byte is allocated for encoding each character. Nowadays, Unicode encoding is gaining popularity. When using this type of encoding, 2 bytes are allocated for encoding a single character.

Strings look much like arrays. The difference between them is that the string structure contains information that can be used to easily determine its length. There are two different approaches to solving this problem.

- ❏ The end of the string must be marked in some way. Some specific code can be used for this purpose, made up of 1 or more bytes. In C, the NULL (zero) code is traditionally used for this purpose (it should not be confused with the 0 character). When using Unicode, strings are terminated by two characters with the zero code. In addition, some contemporary compilers can terminate strings with an entire sequence of seven 0 bytes, thus adapting strings for processing in double-word blocks. Taking into account growing memory resources, this approach doesn't seem too wasteful. This mechanism is characterized by the following two drawbacks:

- To discover the string length, it is necessary to view the entire string, no matter how long it might be. Furthermore, all string operations must be based on checking for the presence of the string terminating character, which makes these operations somewhat slower.
- When this approach is used, 0 bytes cannot be used directly within a string.
- ❏ Information about the string length (or about its end) must be stored somewhere within the string. Using the starting bytes of the string for this purpose is a natural approach. For example, this approach is used in Pascal and in Delphi. This might be only a single byte, in which case the string might not be longer than 255 characters. In Delphi, however, it is possible to create strings with a 4-byte length field. In this case, the maximum possible string length is comparable to the amount of the address space allocated to a process under the Windows operating system.

In addition to the two preceding approaches, it is possible to use a combined approach. In this case, the string length is specified before the string but the string terminator marks its end. This approach is convenient for compatibility. However, because of its redundancy, it is a constant source of headaches for programmers.[i]

NOTE

Programmers with experience in MS-DOS programming, certainly, would immediately recall function 9 of the `int 21h` interrupt, using which it is possible to output a character string to the screen. This system procedure used the dollar sign ($) as a terminator. This terminator is inconvenient and was moved out of use long ago.

To begin investigation of the string data type, consider a simple example of using Unicode strings (Listing 3.15).

Listing 3.15. Simple example illustrating the use of Unicode strings

---

```
#include <stdio.h>
wchar_t  s[] = L"Hello, programmer!";
wchar_t  f[] = L"%s\n";
```

---

[i] A typical complication is deciding what to do if, for example, information about the string length doesn't correspond to the location of the terminator.

```
void main()
{
    wprintf(f, s);
};
```

Recall that `wchar_t` specifies the Unicode string type, `L` stands for the macro converting an ASCII string to a Unicode string, and `wprintf` is the function for console output of Unicode strings (an analogue of the `printf` function used for console output of ASCII strings). Note that the format string (`f`) for the `wprintf` function also must be in Unicode encoding. Consider how IDA Pro disassembles the call to the `wprintf` function (Listing 3.16).

Listing 3.16. Disassembled listing of the call to the wprintf function

```
.text:00401003          push  offset aHelloProgramme ; "Hello, programmer!"
.text:00401008          push  offset aS              ; "%s\n"
.text:0040100D          call  _wprintf
```

This is great, isn't it? IDA Pro has done an excellent job recognizing a Unicode string. Here are these strings as they appear in the data section (Listing 3.17).

Listing 3.17. Unicode strings from Listing 3.15 as they appear in the data section

```
.data:00409040          aHelloProgramme:              ; DATA XREF: _main + 3↑o
.data:00409040          unicode 0, <Hello, programmer!>, 0
```

If desired, you can press the <A> key to convert this string into the sequence of ASCII characters. You'll then discover that the codes of ASCII characters belonging to the range from 0 to 127 are converted to Unicode without changes by adding a most significant 0 byte (complementing a byte with a word). Thus, conversion of an English text from ASCII to Unicode is a trivial task.

The next example (Listing 3.18) relates to Delphi.[i]

---

[i] Here and further on, I use the Delphi compiler supplied as part of Borland Delphi 7.0.

Listing 3.18. Example illustrating the use of Delphi strings

```
var
  s1:widestring;
  s2:string; {by default this is an AnsiString}
  s3:shortstring;
begin
  s1 := 'Hello world!';
  s2 := 'Hello programmers!';
  s3 := 'Hello hackers!';
  writeln(s1);
  writeln(s2);
  writeln(s3);
end.
```

The program in Listing 3.18 uses three types of strings available in Delphi. What would you see when analyzing the disassembled code produced by IDA Pro? What could be more interesting than programming, except for investigation of the executable code?

Compile this program, load it into IDA Pro, and analyze it automatically. Then, try to find the strings of interest in the **Strings** window. Strangely, only the Hello world! string can be found there. Hope remains that other strings are near, so you'd be able to find them quickly. This hope is not vain. Here is the code fragment that you needed (Listing 3.19).

Listing 3.19. Code fragment containing strings from the program in Listing 3.18

```
CODE:0044CC4D             align 10h
CODE:0044CC50             dd 18h
CODE:0044CC54 aHelloWorld:
CODE:0044CC54                              ; DATA XREF: sub_44CBAC + 21↑o
CODE:0044CC54             unicode 0, <Hello world!>, 0
CODE:0044CC6E             align 10h
CODE:0044CC70             dd 0FFFFFFFFh, 12h
CODE:0044CC78 aHelloProgramme db 'Hello programmers!', 0
```

```
CODE:0044CC78                          ; DATA XREF: sub_44CBAC + 30↑o
CODE:0044CC8B        align 4
CODE:0044CC8C dword_44CC8C   dd 6C65480Eh, 68206F6Ch, 656B6361h, 217372h
CODE:0044CC8C                          ; DATA XREF: sub_44CBAC + 3A↑o
```

Very well! The disassembler has recognized the s2 string (Listing 3.18). It hasn't placed it into the **Strings** window; however, this is a minor drawback. It would be interesting to find out what is located at the 0044CC8C address, because the reference to that block from the program code is also present. Move the cursor to that string and press the <A> key (it is also possible to use the **Options | Ascii string style** menu commands and click the **Pascal style** button in the dialog box that would appear on the screen. Then the wonder would happen (Listing 3.20).

Listing 3.20. Fragment of the disassembled test program (Listing 3.18) with the s3 string

```
CODE:0044CC8C aHelloHackers    db 14, 'Hello hackers!'
CODE:0044CC8C                          ; DATA XREF: sub_44CBAC + 3A↑o
CODE:0044CC9B                    db   0
```

As you can see, the third string also has been discovered. Why didn't the disassembler find it immediately? To all appearances, the cause lies in the byte with the 14 value, to which the reference was pointing. This is the string length byte. However, the disassembler, when analyzing the reference, considered that because this is the start of the string, then the text cannot contain a character with the code 14. In principle, this assumption was correct; however, the disassembler never guessed that this is the string length byte.

Thus, it becomes possible to draw conclusions. In case of a short string (shortstring), the reference points to the string length byte. By the way, pay attention that the string is terminated by the NULL character, which is not taken into account when computing the string length (which is correct).

Now consider two other strings. The string located at the 0044CC78 address also is null-terminated. Note that the reference again points to the start of the string and the string is null terminated. What about the string length? This issue is interesting. The string is preceded by two 4-byte values. The 12h number specifies the string length. As you can see, 4 bytes are allocated for the string length. However, the string structure includes 4 more bytes. This is the so-called reference count. Thus, for strings of this type the reference points directly to the string contents. The text information itself is preceded by 8 bytes of auxiliary information.

The last string type is Unicode. The Unicode string starts at the `0044CC54` address. In contrast to the previous case, the string structure includes a 4-byte length, but there is no reference count. In this case, the reference from the program code points to the string contents. The disassembler has located this string because of this. The string is terminated by two 0 bytes.

To conclude the discussion of strings, consider the simple test program shown in Listing 3.21. Compile this program using Microsoft Visual C++.

Listing 3.21. Simple C program illustrating string operations

---

```
#include <stdio.h>
#include <string.h>
char s[] = "Good-bye!";
void main()
{
        strcat(s," My love!");
        printf("%s\n", s);
}
```

The disassembled code of the program presented in Listing 3.21 is shown in Listing 3.22.

Listing 3.22. Disassembled code of the program shown in Listing 3.21

```
.text:00401000 _main          proc near            ; CODE XREF: start + 16E↑p
.text:00401000                push    ebp
.text:00401001                mov     ebp, esp
.text:00401003                push    offset aMyLove  ; char *
.text:00401008                push    offset aGoodBye ; char *
.text:0040100D                call    _strcat
.text:00401012                add     esp, 8
.text:00401015                push    offset aGoodBye ; "Good-bye!"
.text:0040101A                push    offset aS       ; "%s\n"
```

```
.text:0040101F                call    _printf
.text:00401024                add     esp, 8
.text:00401027                xor     eax, eax
.text:00401029                pop     ebp
.text:0040102A                retn
.text:0040102A _main         endp
```

Listing 3.22 is easy and is not worth special comments. It should only be mentioned that both strings are excellently recognized by IDA Pro.

Introduce a small modification into the program shown in Listing 3.21. Make the s variable local by moving its definition into the main function. After compiling the program and disassembling its code, you'll obtain an unusual disassembled code (Listing 3.23).

Listing 3.23. Disassembled code of the modified program (Listing 3.21)

```
.text:00401000 _main          proc near              ; CODE XREF: start + 16E↓p
.text:00401000 var_C          = byte ptr -0Ch
.text:00401000 var_8          = dword ptr -8
.text:00401000 var_4          = word ptr -4
.text:00401000
.text:00401000                 push    ebp
.text:00401001                 mov     ebp, esp
.text:00401003                 sub     esp, 0Ch
.text:00401006                 mov     eax, ds:dword_4060FC
.text:0040100B                 mov     dword ptr [ebp + var_C], eax
.text:0040100E                 mov     ecx, ds:dword_406100
.text:00401014                 mov     [ebp + var_8], ecx
.text:00401017                 mov     dx, ds:word_406104
.text:0040101E                 mov     [ebp + var_4], dx
.text:00401022                 push    offset aMyLove          ; char *
.text:00401027                 lea     eax, [ebp + var_C]
.text:0040102A                 push    eax                     ; char *
.text:0040102B                 call    _strcat
.text:00401030                 add     esp, 8
.text:00401033                 lea     ecx, [ebp + var_C]
```

```
.text:00401036                 push    ecx
.text:00401037                 push    offset aS        ; "%s\n"
.text:0040103C                 call    _printf
.text:00401041                 add     esp, 8
.text:00401044                 xor     eax, eax
.text:00401046                 mov     esp, ebp
.text:00401048                 pop     ebp
.text:00401049                 retn
.text:00401049 _main           endp
```

Consider Listing 3.23 more carefully. The code is unusual. The disassembler has determined only one string (a literal). However, the first parameter of the strcat function is the address of the string that the disassembler failed to locate. This can be stated doubtlessly because strcat is a well-known library function. However, what about commands ranging from the 00401006 to the 0040101E address? What do they mean? They move 10 bytes of data into the stack area (recall that the string must be stored in the stack). At the same time, the string in question is exactly 10 bytes in size (taking into account the 0 byte). Thus, it is an intricate method used by the compiler to pass the string from the data section to the stack area. Consider the memory address 004060FC, from which the block passed into the stack starts. Here is this block (Listing 3.24).

Listing 3.24. Memory block passed to the stack

```
.rdata:004060FC dword_4060FC    dd 646F6F47h    ; DATA XREF: _main + 6↑r
.rdata:00406100 dword_406100    dd 6579622Dh    ; DATA XREF: _main + E↑r
.rdata:00406104 word_406104     dw 21h          ; DATA XREF: _main + 17↑r
```

Press the <A> key and convert the block to the ASCII format. After that, the "lost" string will be found. The conclusion is easy and straightforward: The disassembler failed to locate one of the strings because the compiler treated it simply as a block of data.

Arrays

As shown in the previous section, although strings have a structure that allows you to determine the data size, even such a powerful disassembler as IDA Pro is not always capable of recognizing a string, to speak nothing about arrays. This is because the array size is not explicitly specified in the structure. There are difficulties related to determining the array size. However, arrays can be clearly identified. Consider a simple example. In the program shown in Listing 3.25, an integer array is filled with integer numbers ranging from zero to nine. After compiling this program using Microsoft Visual Studio and loading the executable code into IDA Pro, the disassembled code shown in Listing 3.26 will be obtained.

Listing 3.25. Simple C program for investigating array identification in the executable code

```c
#include <stdio.h>
int a[10];
void main()
{
        for(int i = 0; i < 10; i++) a[i] = i;
};
```

Listing 3.26. Disassembled code of the program shown in Listing 3.25

```
.text:00401000 _main          proc near          ; CODE XREF: start + 16E↓p
.text:00401000                var_4  = dword ptr - 4
.text:00401000                push   ebp
.text:00401001                mov    ebp, esp
.text:00401003                push   ecx
.text:00401004                mov    [ebp + var_4], 0
.text:0040100B                jmp    short loc_401016
.text:0040100D loc_40100D:                        ; CODE XREF: _main + 29↓j
.text:0040100D                mov    eax, [ebp+var_4]
.text:00401010                add    eax, 1
.text:00401013                mov    [ebp + var_4], eax
.text:00401016 loc_401016:                        ; CODE XREF: _main + B↑j
.text:00401016                cmp    [ebp + var_4], 0Ah
.text:0040101A                jge    short loc_40102B
.text:0040101C                mov    ecx, [ebp + var_4]
```

```
.text:0040101F                     mov     edx, [ebp + var_4]
.text:00401022                     mov     dword_4072C0[ecx*4], edx
.text:00401029                     jmp     short loc_40100D
.text:0040102B loc_40102B:                         ; CODE XREF: _main + 1A↑j
.text:0040102B                     xor     eax, eax
.text:0040102D                     mov     esp, ebp
.text:0040102F                     pop     ebp
.text:00401030                     retn
.text:00401030 _main              endp
```

You encountered the method of loop organization shown in Listing 3.13. As you have certainly guessed, var_4 is nothing but the stack variable — the loop counter. Pay special attention to the mov dword_4072C0[ecx*4], edx command, which is the key to understanding the operating logic of this program. There is no doubt that this is an array: dword_4072C0 is the start of this array, ecx contains the current index value, and the scaling coefficient equal to four indicates that each element of this array is 4 bytes in size. The array size in this program can be clearly identified. However, you should not rely on the assumption that the number of array elements is always determined by the number of iterations in the loop that processes this array. The programmer might use different parts of the array in different sections of the program. With all this being so, these fragments of the array must not begin from the starting point of that array. Thus, with high probability it is possible to state that the array size is no less than the specified value.

Some problems might arise when using arrays in functions. The argument accepted by the function is simply a pointer. This pointer might be passed farther through a sequence of functions. Assume that in the last function you see some parameter used as a pointer to an array. To locate that array, you'll have to traverse the entire sequence of functions in the reverse direction, which would require time and patience. In such situations, it is better to use the debugger, set a breakpoint to the function where the pointer behaves like a pointer to an array, and obtain the value of that pointer. Having accomplished this, it is necessary to return to disassembler, locate the required array at the address determined using the debugger, and find cross-references from the program code to that array. After that, it will be possible to continue analysis of the executable code.

Structures

A structure is a generalization of an array. In contrast to arrays, which are made up of the elements of the same type, structures can comprise elements of different types. As with arrays, structure elements are accessed on the basis of the base address, which defines the starting point of the structure instance. However, the problem is more complicated than with arrays. Sometimes, it is difficult to make sure that data items of different types belong to the same structure. Consider a C program illustrating the behavior of structures (Listing 3.27).

Listing 3.27. Sample program for investigating the behavior of structures

```c
#include <stdio.h>
#include <windows.h>
struct a {
        char s[10];
        BYTE b;
        int i;
};
a a1;
void main()
{
        for(int j = 0; j < 10; j++) a1.s[j] = 'A';
        a1.b = 10;
        a1.i = 10000;
};
```

Compile this program using the Microsoft Visual C++ compiler, then disassemble the executable code using IDA Pro. The disassembled text of this program is shown in Listing 3.28.

Listing 3.28. Disassembled text of the program shown in Listing 3.27

```
.text:00401000 _main            proc near        ; CODE XREF: start + 16E↓p
.text:00401000                  var_4 = dword ptr -4
.text:00401000                  push    ebp
```

```
.text:00401001                mov      ebp, esp
.text:00401003                push     ecx
.text:00401004                mov      [ebp + var_4], 0
.text:0040100B                jmp      short loc_401016
.text:0040100D loc_40100D:                       ; CODE XREF: _main + 26↓j
.text:0040100D                mov      eax, [ebp + var_4]
.text:00401010                add      eax, 1
.text:00401013                mov      [ebp + var_4], eax
.text:00401016 loc_401016:                       ; CODE XREF: _main + B↑j
.text:00401016                cmp      [ebp + var_4], 0Ah
.text:0040101A                jge      short loc_401028
.text:0040101C                mov      ecx, [ebp + var_4]
.text:0040101F                mov      byte_4072C0[ecx], 41h
.text:00401026                jmp      short loc_40100D
.text:00401028 loc_401028:                       ; CODE XREF: _main + 1A↑j
.text:00401028                mov      byte_4072CA, 0Ah
.text:0040102F                mov      dword_4072CC, 2710h
.text:00401039                xor      eax, eax
.text:0040103B                mov      esp, ebp
.text:0040103D                pop      ebp
.text:0040103E                retn
.text:0040103E _main         endp
```

Carefully consider the text shown in Listing 3.28. In this text, you will encounter three different types of data determined by the following pointers: byte_4072C0 (array), byte_4072CA (byte), and dword_4072CC (double word). At the same time, there are no clear indications that these variables must be joined into the same structure. This is of no importance in the current context. Hence, the program must contain operations that would disclose the structure as an integral entity.

Consider the program shown in Listing 3.29. As you can see, the a structure is the parameter of the init procedure. Then consider how this situation is reflected in the program's executable code (Listing 3.30). This program is artificial because the structure passed to the function is not used and is not passed back.

Listing 3.29. Behavior of the structure passed to some function as a parameter

```
#include <stdio.h>
#include <windows.h>
struct a {
        char s[10];
        BYTE b;
        int i;
};
a a1;
void init(a);
void main()
{
        init(a1);
};
void init(a c)
{
        for(int j = 0; j < 10; j++) c.s[j] = 'A';
        c.b = 10;
        c.i = 10000;
};
```

Listing 3.30 presents the disassembled code of the main function of the program in Listing 3.29. The sub_401040 procedure, the call to which is carried out by 0040102B, is the init function. The lines of code preceding this procedure are of great interest. Pay special attention to the sub esp, 10h command. It is the equivalent of four PUSH commands. However, note that the size of the structure under consideration is exactly 16 bytes. After the command allocating the space in the stack is the mov eax, esp command. Thus, the EAX register points to the start of the stack area. This stack area is filled with the data. The impression is that you are dealing with 4 double words. IDA Pro has come to the same conclusion. That 16 bytes are allocated simultaneously (the structure length is exactly 15 bytes, but taking into account that the i field is aligned by the 4-byte boundary, the result is 16) must make you vigilant. Nevertheless, this alone doesn't prove anything. To discover what was passed to the function, it is necessary to analyze the code of that function (Listing 3.31).

Listing 3.30. Disassembled text of the main function of the program shown in Listing 3.29

```
.text:00401000  main        proc near          ; CODE XREF: start + 16E↓p
.text:00401000              push    ebp
.text:00401001              mov     ebp, esp
.text:00401003              sub     esp, 10h
.text:00401006              mov     eax, esp
.text:00401008              mov     ecx, dword_4072C0
.text:0040100E              mov     [eax], ecx
.text:00401010              mov     edx, dword_4072C4
.text:00401016              mov     [eax + 4], edx
.text:00401019              mov     ecx, dword_4072C8
.text:0040101F              mov     [eax + 8], ecx
.text:00401022              mov     edx, dword_4072CC
.text:00401028              mov     [eax + 0Ch], edx
.text:0040102B              call    sub_401040
.text:00401030              add     esp, 10h
.text:00401033              xor     eax, eax
.text:00401035              pop     ebp
.text:00401036              retn
.text:00401036  _main       endp
```

Listing 3.31. Disassembled text of the init function (Listing 3.29)

```
.text:00401040 sub_401040    proc near          ; CODE XREF: _main + 2B↑p
.text:00401040        var_4  = dword ptr -4
.text:00401040        arg_0  = byte  ptr  8
.text:00401040        arg_A  = byte  ptr  12h
.text:00401040        arg_C  = dword ptr  14h
.text:00401040              push    ebp
.text:00401041              mov     ebp, esp
.text:00401043              push    ecx
.text:00401044              mov     [ebp + var_4], 0
.text:0040104B              jmp     short loc_401056
.text:0040104D loc_40104D:                       ; CODE XREF: sub_401040 + 24↓j
```

```
.text:0040104D                 mov      eax, [ebp + var_4]
.text:00401050                 add      eax, 1
.text:00401053                 mov      [ebp + var_4], eax
.text:00401056 loc_401056:                ; CODE XREF: sub_401040 + B↑j
.text:00401056                 cmp      [ebp + var_4], 0Ah
.text:0040105A                 jge      short loc_401066
.text:0040105C                 mov      ecx, [ebp + var_4]
.text:0040105F                 mov      [ebp + ecx + arg_0], 41h
.text:00401064                 jmp      short loc_40104D
.text:00401066 loc_401066:                ; CODE XREF: sub_401040 + 1A↑j
.text:00401066                 mov      [ebp + arg_A], 0Ah
.text:0040106A                 mov      [ebp + arg_C], 2710h
.text:00401071                 mov      esp, ebp
.text:00401073                 pop      ebp
.text:00401074                 retn
.text:00401074 sub_401040     endp
```

Consider the code of the init function (see Listing 3.31). Principally, this text is similar to that provided in Listing 3.28. However, this time, taking into account the analysis of the code of the main function (see Listing 3.30), it is possible to understand its meaning. Thus, 16 bytes were passed to the function (4 times, 4 bytes at a time). The function first processes an array (10 bytes in size), then a 0 byte (arg_0), then a 1-byte value (arg_A), and finally a 4-byte value (arg_C). At this point, it is logical to assume that the object you are dealing with is a structure. What allows you to draw such a conclusion? For instance, the 3 independent (at first glance) double words were sent to the stack and the first 10 bytes are combined to form an array within the procedure can confirm this assumption.

Thus, it is possible to conclude that the structures can be disclosed when they are passed as parameters. However, it is necessary to admit that these considerations are too heuristic to delegate this task to a disassembler. An interesting point here is that the Borland C++ compiler in a similar situation acts in approximately the same way as Microsoft Visual C++. Compile the program presented in Listing 3.29 using the Borland C++ compiler, then disassemble it using IDA Pro. The disassembled fragment of the executable code responsible for calling the Init function is shown in Listing 3.32.

Listing 3.32. Fragment calling Init (compiled by Borland C++ and disassembled by IDA Pro)

```
.text:00401108          mov     al, byte_40C2C6
.text:0040110E          shl     eax, 10h
.text:00401111          mov     ax, word_40C2C4
.text:00401118          push    eax
.text:00401119          push    dword_40C2C0
.text:0040111F          push    dword_40C2BC
.text:00401125          push    dword_40C2B8
.text:0040112B          call    sub_401134
```

This fragment is notable by a strange variable — word_40C2C4. Where could such a variable of the WORD type come from? After all, there are no such variables in the program. Nevertheless, the total amount of data passed through the stack is 16 bytes as in the previous case — to be precise, 15 bytes. Is Borland more accurate than Microsoft? This is unlikely.

However, there are situations, in which the disassembler can unambiguously determine that it is dealing with a structure. These are situations, in which structures are used as parameters when calling well-known library or API functions. The code fragment shown in Listing 3.33 demonstrates the call to the RegisterClass API function. I have intentionally provided the code lines preceding this call. These code lines contain commands that fill the WndClass structure, which the disassembler recognizes excellently. It cannot fail to recognize this structure, because its address is the parameter of the well-known API function.

Listing 3.33. Disassembled code showing the call to the RegisterClass API function

```
.text:0040104D          mov     [ebp+WndClass.style], 0
.text:00401054          mov     [ebp+WndClass.lpfnWndProc], offset sub_401140
.text:0040105B          mov     [ebp+WndClass.cbClsExtra], 0
.text:00401062          mov     [ebp+WndClass.cbWndExtra], 0
.text:00401069          mov     edx, [ebp + hInstance]
.text:0040106C          mov     [ebp + WndClass.hInstance], edx
.text:0040106F          push    7F00h                ; lpIconName
```

```
.text:00401074      mov      eax, [ebp + hInstance]
.text:00401077      push     eax                  ; hInstance
.text:00401078      call     ds:LoadIconA
.text:0040107E      mov      [ebp + WndClass.hIcon], eax
.text:00401081      push     7F00h                ; lpCursorName
.text:00401086      push     0                    ; hInstance
.text:00401088      call     ds:LoadCursorA
.text:0040108E      mov      [ebp + WndClass.hCursor], eax
.text:00401091      mov      [ebp + WndClass.hbrBackground], 6
.text:00401098      mov      [ebp + WndClass.lpszMenuName], 0
.text:0040109F      lea      ecx, [ebp + ClassName]
.text:004010A2      mov      [ebp + WndClass.lpszClassName], ecx
.text:004010A5      lea      edx, [ebp + WndClass]
.text:004010A8      push     edx                  ; lpWndClass
.text:004010A9      call     ds:RegisterClassA
```

In Listing 3.33, the address of the WndClass structure is counted in relation to the contents of the EBP register, which means that the structure is defined as a stack local variable (see *Section 3.1.2*). However, the essence of these considerations won't change if you make it a global variable. In this case, the structure is identified because it is used as a parameter.

3.1.2. Local Variables

As a rule, local variables are interpreted as variables defined directly within a procedure or a function. As you know, the stack is used for this purpose. In my opinion, this is only a particular case. I understand local variables widely, not only as variables defined in the stack (they might be called stack variables) but also as temporary variables (local in relation to the program run time) and as variables stored in registers.

Variables Defined in the Stack

Variables defined in the stack (stack variables) were already mentioned several times. The program in Listing 3.34 uses only local variables and two functions: main and add. Note that the add function accepts three arguments and that the first argument is a pointer. The s variable is modified in the add function.

Listing 3.34. Example program illustrating the use of local variables

```c
#include <stdio.h>
int add(int *, int, int);
void main()
{
        int i = 10, s, j;
        s = 12; j = 20;
        printf("%d\n", add(&s, i, j));
};
int add(int *s1, int i1, int j1)
{
        int n;
        *s1 = *s1 + 10;
        n = *s1 + j1 + i1;
        return n*n;
};
```

The disassembled text of the `main` function from Listing 3.34 is presented in Listing 3.35. Note that when compiling the test program, the option preventing optimization was set.

Listing 3.35. Disassembled text of the main function from Listing 3.34

```
.text:00401000 _main           proc near         ; CODE XREF: start + 16E↓p
.text:00401000         var_C   = dword ptr -0Ch
.text:00401000         var_8   = dword ptr -8
.text:00401000         var_4   = dword ptr -4
.text:00401000             push    ebp
.text:00401001             mov     ebp, esp
.text:00401003             sub     esp, 0Ch
.text:00401006             mov     [ebp + var_4], 0Ah
.text:0040100D             mov     [ebp + var_8], 0Ch
.text:00401014             mov     [ebp + var_C], 14h
.text:0040101B             mov     eax, [ebp + var_C]
.text:0040101E             push    eax
```

```
.text:0040101F                 mov      ecx, [ebp + var_4]
.text:00401022                 push     ecx
.text:00401023                 lea      edx, [ebp + var_8]
.text:00401026                 push     edx
.text:00401027                 call     sub_401050
.text:0040102C                 add      esp, 0Ch
.text:0040102F                 push     eax
.text:00401030                 push     offset unk_4060FC
.text:00401035                 call     _printf
.text:0040103A                 add      esp, 8
.text:0040103D                 xor      eax, eax
.text:0040103F                 mov      esp, ebp
.text:00401041                 pop      ebp
.text:00401042                 retn
.text:00401042 _main           endp
```

Skip the standard function prologue, and look at the sub esp, 0CH command. Here, 12 bytes are reserved for local variables — this is the area between the previous value of the stack pointer (to which the EBP register points) and the new value. This corresponds to three variables (see Listing 3.34). Nevertheless, IDA Pro declares these variables as var_4, var_8, and var_C. What do the _4, _8, and _C suffixes mean? These are addresses where the variables are located in relation to the boundary, from which the area of stack variables starts. The address of this boundary is stored in the EBP register.

Next are the commands for data initialization. Note that there is no difference between variables initialized when declared and variables assigned some values in the program.

Addresses from 0040101B to 00401026 are occupied by the commands that send parameters into the stack for calling the add function. Pay special attention to the var_8 variable, which, doubtlessly, corresponds to the s variable in the program source code. To handle this variable, the lea edx, [ebp + var_8]/push edx commands are used, which means that the address of this variable is sent into the stack. This is natural, because in the program it is explicitly specified that the pointer is passed. However, I'd like to warn you against drawing premature conclusions. Compilers often handle pointers with undue familiarity. For the s variable, the pointer is passed to the function used in the program for modifying the s variable.

If this were not so (if the s variable were not modified in the add function), then the compiler would be able to pass the variable to the function. This approach produces the same result, but it is much easier. Thus, two other variables, i (var_4) and j (var_C), are passed into the stack by value.

The result of the function call, which, as expected, is stored in the EAX register (nevertheless, see *Section 3.2.1*), is passed to the function as a parameter for console output.

It is time to consider the code of the add function. The disassembled text is shown in Listing 3.36.

Listing 3.36. Disassembled text of the add function (Listing 3.34)

```
.text:00401050 sub_401050    proc near          ; CODE XREF: _main + 27↑p
.text:00401050              var_4  = dword ptr -4
.text:00401050              arg_0  = dword ptr   8
.text:00401050              arg_4  = dword ptr   0Ch
.text:00401050              arg_8  = dword ptr   10h
.text:00401050              push   ebp
.text:00401051              mov    ebp, esp
.text:00401053              push   ecx
.text:00401054              mov    eax, [ebp + arg_0]
.text:00401057              mov    ecx, [eax]
.text:00401059              add    ecx, 0Ah
.text:0040105C              mov    edx, [ebp + arg_0]
.text:0040105F              mov    [edx], ecx
.text:00401061              mov    eax, [ebp + arg_0]
.text:00401064              mov    ecx, [eax]
.text:00401066              add    ecx, [ebp + arg_8]
.text:00401069              add    ecx, [ebp + arg_4]
.text:0040106C              mov    [ebp+var_4], ecx
.text:0040106F              mov    eax, [ebp + var_4]
.text:00401072              imul   eax, [ebp + var_4]
.text:00401076              mov    esp, ebp
.text:00401078              pop    ebp
.text:00401079              retn
.text:00401079 sub_401050    endp
```

IDA Pro assigns the function parameter names starting with the `arg` prefix. Thus, as expected, the function has obtained three parameters: `arg_0`, `arg_4`, and `arg_8`. As in case of the stack variables, offsets 0, 4, and 8 are counted in relation to the content of the `EBP` register; however, this time the offset is counted downward into the area of higher addresses.

Note that at first glance, no space is reserved in the stack for the `var_4` variable (in the program, the name of this variable is `n`). This issue is an interesting one. Why does the compiler reserve stack space for variables in the `main` function? To reserve the stack space, the `push ecx` command is used. This can be easily discovered by checking the stack balance in the beginning and in the end of the procedure. To achieve this, count the number of bytes pushed into the stack in the beginning and popped from the stack in the end. The `PUSH` command is often used for reserving stack space when there is only one stack variable.

It would be interesting to find the parameter that is a pointer to variable among all function parameters. Here, everything is simple. This parameter was the last to be pushed. Because the stack grows upward, toward lower addresses, this parameter will have the smallest offset in the direction of higher addresses. This will be `arg_0`. Here is the sequence of commands that discloses this: `mov eax, [ebp + arg_0]`/`mov ecx, [eax]`/`add ecx, 0Ah`. This corresponds to `*s1 = *s1 + 10`.

All further computations are self-evident. They correspond to `n = *s1 + j1 + i1`. The `imul` instruction stands for the `n*n` operation.

Again, it is necessary to mention the optimization. Optimization can change the program code to such an extent that it becomes impossible to recognize it. This is especially true for Microsoft Visual C++. For instance, try to compile the program (see Listing 3.34) using the "create compact code" option. Before compiling, insert some output operator into the `add` function — for example, `printf("%d\n", n)`. Otherwise, the optimizer will do without any function call and replace it with the constant that it computes on its own (yes, this is so[i]). Now, consider what would happen to the `main` function after optimization (Listing 3.37).

Listing 3.37. Disassembled code of the optimized main function

```
.text:00401029 _main           proc near       ; CODE XREF: start + 16E↓p
.text:00401029                 var_4 = dword ptr -4
.text:00401029                 push    ebp
```

---

[i] When optimizing a program for maximum operating speed, even this trick won't help!

```
.text:0040102A                 mov      ebp, esp
.text:0040102C                 push     ecx
.text:0040102D                 push     14h
.text:0040102F                 lea      eax, [ebp + var_4]
.text:00401032                 push     0Ah
.text:00401034                 push     eax
.text:00401035                 mov      [ebp + var_4], 0Ch
.text:0040103C                 call     sub_401000
.text:00401041                 push     eax
.text:00401042                 push     offset unk_4060FC
.text:00401047                 call     _printf
.text:0040104C                 add      esp, 14h
.text:0040104F                 xor      eax, eax
.text:00401051                 leave
.text:00401052                 retn
.text:00401052 _main           endp
```

Listing 3.37 is an instructive one. The main issue, to which it is necessary to pay attention in the course of analysis, is that only one stack variable has been defined. It would be desirable to guess, which variable this is, even without viewing the listing. This is the s variable. It is this variable whose contents will be modified in the add function. In other words, s is a variable. However, i and j are not variables; rather, they are in essence constants because they are not modified in the course of program execution. The optimizer treats them accordingly. Instead of allocating stack memory for them, it is possible to simply send numeric constants as parameters to the add function. This goal is achieved by the push 14h and push 0Ah commands. The address of the s variable is sent to the stack: lea eax, [ebp + var_4]/.../push eax.

Also, it is necessary to pay attention to another issue: Memory for the stack variable is allocated using the push ecx command, which can confuse the code investigator. However, the optimizer's main goal in this case is to make the code as compact as possible, and it does its best to achieve this. This also explains why only a single leave command is used to restore the stack in the end of the procedure.

Thus, the following conclusion can be drawn in relation to stack variables: If the value of a stack variable is not changed in the course of program execution, the optimizer can replace it with a constant. This information is not particularly important for a simple analysis of the program's actions. However, in my opinion, for a sound understanding of the program operating logic this issue is important.

Also, it is possible to obtain useful information if you compile the program shown in Listing 3.34 using the Borland C++ v. 5.0 compiler. The result of disassembling the executable code of the main function is shown in Listing 3.38.

Listing 3.38. Disassembled main function from Listing 3.34 compiled using Borland C++ 5.0

```
.text:00401108 _main          proc near        ; DATA XREF: .data:0040A0B8↓o
.text:00401108          var_4 = dword ptr -4
.text:00401108          argc  = dword ptr  0Ch
.text:00401108          argv  = dword ptr  10h
.text:00401108          envp  = dword ptr  14h
.text:00401108                 push    ebx
.text:00401109                 push    esi
.text:0040110A                 push    ecx
.text:0040110B                 mov     ebx, 0Ah
.text:00401110                 mov     [esp + 4 + var_4], 0Ch
.text:00401117                 mov     esi, 14h
.text:0040111C                 push    esi
.text:0040111D                 push    ebx
.text:0040111E                 lea     eax, [esp + 0Ch + var_4]
.text:00401122                 push    eax
.text:00401123                 call    sub_401140
.text:00401128                 add     esp, 0Ch
.text:0040112B                 push    eax
.text:0040112C                 push    offset format    ; Format
.text:00401131                 call    _printf
.text:00401136                 add     esp, 8
.text:00401139                 pop     edx
.text:0040113A                 pop     esi
.text:0040113B                 pop     ebx
.text:0040113C                 retn
.text:0040113C _main          endp
```

Different compilers are characterized by different styles. For instance, in contrast to Microsoft's compiler, which, just to be on the safe side, resets the EAX register to zero even when the main function is declared as void, Borland's compiler interprets the void type literally, which means that it doesn't pay attention to the contents of the EAX register. Another specific feature of Borland's compiler is that it actively uses the ESI and EBX registers. Note that according to generally adopted conventions, a function must not change the contents of the EBX, EBP, ESP, ESI, and EDI registers; so, Borland's compiler must insert PUSH EBX/PUSH ESI commands in the beginning of the function and POP ESI/POP EBX commands in the end of function. I suspect that this is just an inherited legacy. In older Intel processors, the CX and DX registers could not be used for addressing.

Like Microsoft's compiler, Borland's compiler analyzes the text and discovers that the i and j variables are constants in their essence. Therefore, it doesn't reserve the memory in the stack for them and uses constants instead. Stack memory is reserved only for the s variable (var_4). Note that this also is carried out using a single PUSH command (push ecx).

Consider the most interesting issue. Borland's compiler doesn't use the EBP register here; it uses the ESP register instead. This is a well-known optimization technique, so you should know about it. However, you might object: The contents of the ESP register changes. You'd be right. But the compiler does not forget about this; it handles this problem excellently by dynamically tracking all changes of the ESP register and correcting the addressing as appropriate. Look, in the beginning was the mov [esp + 4 + var_4], 0Ch command followed by two PUSH commands. The content of ESP was reduced by eight. Therefore, the compiler uses the lea eax, [esp + 0Ch + var_4] command. Everything is correct, because 4 + 8 = 12 = 0Ch. IDA Pro, fortunately, also understands these issues and specifies the var_4 variable in both commands.

Temporary Variables

What are temporary variables? I consider as such the variables used for storing intermediate results of computations. In the course of computations, the processor registers are widely used. Therefore, it is possible to state that the registers are used as temporary variables. Note that you have already encountered such variables. For example, consider Listing 3.13, and recall how the loop was organized there (the 00401027–0040102F addresses). The EAX register plays the role of temporary variable, which for the time of loop execution stores the loop counter. When using real variables for storing intermediate results, the FPU registers are also used. As a rule, these are the first three registers of the coprocessor: ST(0), ST(1), and ST(2). If you recall Listing 3.13, the comments that follow it emphasized the method of start-up initialization of floating-point variables: The floating-point variable is first loaded into the ST(0) coprocessor register using the FLD command. Then, from the ST(0) register the variable is loaded into the memory area allocated for the floating-point variable (using the FSTP command).

How many registers might be needed if the expression to be computed is a complex one? Simple considerations are as follows: Operations over numeric variables are binary operations. Two operands participate in each operation. The result can be placed either into a third operand or into one of the operands participating in the previous operation. The result of execution of any specific operation might be the operand of another binary operation. However, again two operands participate in the binary operation and the result is placed into one of them. These considerations are also applicable if there are parentheses in the expression. Thus, it is possible to conclude that two operands are enough for storing intermediate results. However, what should you do if the operands are 64-bit ones (and you have a 32-bit processor)? The C++ compiler can use library procedures (such as _alldiv), which are provided especially for such cases. Nevertheless, as you'll see later, sometimes the compiler still uses the stack for temporary variables.

It is time to study an instructive example. Some program that carries out numeric computations would be suitable for this purpose. The program in Listing 3.39 provides an example of such a computation, where both integer and floating-point values are used in the expression to be computed.

Listing 3.39. Use of temporary variables on the example of numeric computations

```
#include <stdio.h>
void main()
{
        double i, j, s;
        int k, d;
        i = 10; j = 20; k = 30; d = 40;
        s = ((k - 1)*(d - 1))*((i - 1)/(j - 1));
        printf("%f\n", s);
};
```

The disassembled code of the main function of this program, obtained using the IDA Pro disassembler, is shown in Listing 3.40.

Listing 3.40. Disassembled code of the main function of the program in Listing 3.39

```
.text:00401000  _main           proc near      ; CODE XREF: start + 16E↓p
.text:00401000         var_2C = qword ptr -2Ch
.text:00401000         var_24 = dword ptr -24h
.text:00401000         var_20 = qword ptr -20h
.text:00401000         var_18 = dword ptr -18h
.text:00401000         var_14 = dword ptr -14h
.text:00401000         var_10 = qword ptr -10h
.text:00401000         var_8  = qword ptr -8
.text:00401000              push    ebp
.text:0040100              mov     ebp, esp
.text:00401003              sub     esp, 24h
.text:00401006              fld     ds:dbl_408110
.text:0040100C              fstp    [ebp + var_8]
.text:0040100F              fld     ds:dbl_408108
.text:00401015              fstp    [ebp + var_20]
.text:00401018              mov     [ebp + var_14], 1Eh
.text:0040101F              mov     [ebp + var_18], 28h
.text:00401026              mov     eax, [ebp + var_14]
.text:00401029              sub     eax, 1
.text:0040102C              mov     ecx, [ebp + var_18]
.text:0040102F              sub     ecx, 1
.text:00401032              imul    eax, ecx
.text:00401035              mov     [ebp + var_24], eax
.text:00401038              fild    [ebp + var_24]
.text:0040103B              fld     [ebp + var_8]
.text:0040103E              fsub    ds:dbl_408100
.text:00401044              fld     [ebp + var_20]
.text:00401047              fsub    ds:dbl_408100
.text:0040104D              fdivp   st(1), st
.text:0040104F              fmulp   st(1), st
```

```
.text:00401051              fst       [ebp + var_10]
.text:00401054              sub       esp, 8
.text:00401057              fstp      [esp + 2Ch + var_2C]
.text:0040105A              push      offset unk_4080FC
.text:0040105F              call      _printf
.text:00401064              add       esp, 0Ch
.text:00401067              xor       eax, eax
.text:00401069              mov       esp, ebp
.text:0040106B              pop       ebp
.text:0040106C              retn
.text:0040106C _main        endp
```

For storing local variables, 36 bytes are allocated (sub esp, 24h). This is 4 bytes more than required for five variables. The compiler has allocated the stack memory for storing a temporary variable, although at first glance it might do without it. This is because it is also possible to use the reserves (such as the EDX register) or leave the result in the EAX register (as will be explained later). Microsoft's compiler tries to avoid using the EBX, EDI, and ESI registers for computations because doing so would make it necessary to take steps for recovering these registers in the end of the function.

The start-up initialization commands occupy addresses from 00401006 to 0040101F. As before, for initializing floating-point variables the compiler uses floating-point constants,[i] which are stored in the data segment. In this case, the constant is first loaded into the ST(0) FPU register using the fld command and then into appropriate variable (using the fstp command). Integer variables are initialized by directly loading specific values into them using the mov command.

Next, direct computations start. This stage requires more detailed consideration:

❐ Commands from 00401026 to 0040102F load the k and d variables into registers and further prepare them for multiplication. The preparation consists of subtracting one from them. Thus, the EAX register will contain the k – 1 value, and

---

[i] In the C++ language, constants stored in the data segment and having, like variables, strictly defined types, are called type safe constants. Constants used only directly in the program code are called literal constants.

ECX will contain the d - 1 value. Then it is possible to carry out multiplication. Next, the `imul eax, ecx` command is executed, and the multiplication result is loaded into the EAX register. In other words, the following operation is executed: `(k - 1)*(d - 1) -> EAX`. Later, it is necessary to decide where the computation result must be stored. The EAX register at first seems suitable because it appears that this register won't be used in later computations. However, there is a small problem here. The resulting integer value must participate in computations with real numbers. At the same time, the `fld` command loads values from the memory into FPU stack. Thus, the compiler made a reasonable decision to use a temporary variable for storing an intermediate result (the intermediate result will be stored directly in the stack).

❐ Consider further computations. The result of computing the `(k - 1)*(d - 1)` expression is loaded onto the top of the FPU stack (into the ST(0) register) using the `fild` command. Then the `fld` command moves the current ST(0) value into ST(1) and loads the i variable into ST(0). Next, the `fsub ds:dbl_408100` command (located at the 0040103E address) computes the i - 1 expression, leaving the result in the ST(0) register. The next `fld` command loads the j variable into ST(0). As this happens (pay attention!), the previous value of ST(0) is moved into ST(1) and the previous value of ST(1) is moved into ST(2). Thus, ST(2) plays the role of a temporary variable. The next `fsub` command computes the j - 1 value. Then the `fdivp st(1), st` command carries out division and pops the stack. As a result, the quotient goes into ST(0) and the value in ST(2) moves into ST(1). The `fmulp st(1), st` command carries out multiplication and pops the stack, which means that the final result goes into ST(0). The last stroke is carried out by the `fst [ebp + var_10]` command, which corresponds to ST(0) -> s. Note that the `fst` command loads the value into the variable without popping the stack.

❐ To load a floating-point value into the stack, a well-known technique encountered earlier is used: The `sub esp, 8` command, equivalent to the two PUSH commands, prepares the space for a floating-point variable. Then the `fstp` command (popping the coprocessor stack) places the result of computations into the stack for further use with the `printf` function.

Thus, temporary variables are used by the compiler for computations. The role of temporary variables can be delegated to general-purpose registers, FPU registers, and stack variables.

Temporary variables are often used when the result of execution of one function is used in another function (Listing 3.41).

Listing 3.41. Temporary variables when the result of executing a function is used in another

---

```
#include <stdio.h>
int add(int, int);
int sub(int, int);
void main()
{
        int i = 10, j = 20;
        printf("%d\n", add(i, sub(i, j)));
};


int add(int a, int b)
{
        return a + b;
};
int sub(int a, int b)
{
        return a - b;
};
```

In the program shown in Listing 3.41, the result of the sub function is used in the add function, and the result of the add function, in turn, is used by the printf function. Listing 3.42 shows the fragment of the disassembled code of this program related to temporary variables.

Listing 3.42. Disassembled code of Listing 3.41 for processing intermediate variables

---

```
.text:00401014        mov      eax, [ebp + var_8]
.text:00401017        push     eax
.text:00401018        mov      ecx, [ebp + var_4]
.text:0040101B        push     ecx
```

```
.text:0040101C          call      sub_401060
.text:00401021          add       esp, 8
.text:00401024          push      eax
.text:00401025          mov       edx, [ebp + var_4]
.text:00401028          push      edx
.text:00401029          call      sub_401050
.text:0040102E          add       esp, 8
.text:00401031          push      eax
.text:00401032          push      offset unk_4060FC
.text:00401037          call      _printf
.text:0040103C          add       esp, 8
```

The var_4 and var_8 variables correspond to the i and j variables in the program source code. First, the sub_401060 (sub) function is called. As should be expected, the result of this function is loaded into the EAX register. Later, the EAX register is used as a variable, which is then used as a parameter when calling the add function (sub_401050). Similarly, the result of the add function is loaded into the EAX register and used as a parameter when calling the printf function.

Register Variables

The C programming language makes provision for the register type of variables. Initially, it was assumed that variables declared as register must be stored in registers whenever possible. Contemporary compilers ignore this keyword (although it is considered valid for compatibility). Nowadays, compilers act as they consider expedient, according to the specified optimization options. Consider the example program shown in Listing 3.43. Compile this program using the Microsoft Visual C++ compiler, with the "create compact code" option.

Listing 3.43. Example program illustrating the use of register variables

```
#include <stdio.h>
void main()
{
        int i, j, s;
        i = 0; j = 1; s = 0;
```

```
for(i = 0; i < 100; i++, j++) s = s + j;
printf("%d %d %d \n", i, j, s);
};
```

The disassembled code of this program is shown in Listing 3.44.

Listing 3.44. Disassembled code of the program shown in Listing 3.43

```
.text:00401000 _main        proc near           ; CODE XREF: start + 16E↓p
.text:00401000              xor     eax, eax
.text:00401002              push    64h
.text:00401004              inc     eax
.text:00401005              xor     ecx, ecx
.text:00401007              pop     edx
.text:00401008 loc_401008:                      ; CODE XREF: _main + C↓j
.text:00401008              add     ecx, eax
.text:0040100A              inc     eax
.text:0040100B              dec     edx
.text:0040100C              jnz     short loc_401008
.text:0040100E              push    ecx
.text:0040100F              push    eax
.text:00401010              push    64h
.text:00401012              push    offset aDDD ; "%d %d %d \n"
.text:00401017              call    _printf
.text:0040101C              add     esp, 10h
.text:0040101F              xor     eax, eax
.text:00401021              retn
.text:00401021 _main        endp
```

Note that although three local variables are defined in the source program, the stack is not used for storing variables in the resulting code. This is exactly the case, in which the compiler has used registers for storing variables. Also note that for code size minimization, the compiler didn't insert a prologue and an epilogue into the main function.

Thus, the ECX register is used for storing the s variable (the xor ecx, ecx command corresponds to s = 0). The xor eax, eax/.../inc eax commands relate to the j variable. As relates to the i variable, the compiler has introduced an interesting modification to reduce the code size. Instead of increasing a value of some variable and comparing it with 100, some variable is first assigned the value of 100 and after each iteration the value of this variable is decremented and compared with 0. This approach is easier and faster. The role of this register variable is delegated to the EDX register.

Finally, because in the end of the loop there is no variable that would contain the value of 100 (as there should be, according to the source code of the program), the number 100 is simply pushed into the stack using the push 64h command.

3.2. Identifying Program Structures

Understanding the program structure of the executable module is often more important than recognizing variables, because it allows you to understand the program's operating logic.

3.2.1. Procedures and Functions

You have already encountered procedures and functions[i] many times. The main goal of this section is to generalize accumulated experience and investigate new features.

Passing Parameters

Until now, it was silently assumed that data are passed to the procedure through the stack. This mechanism, which will be considered in the next section, is common. However, this approach is not the only available one.

For the moment, abstract from compilers and simply consider how and in which way it is possible to pass parameters to the procedure. If you are working in Assembly, you'll be able to add all of these mechanisms to your arsenal. Furthermore, nothing can prevent you from combining several such mechanisms simultaneously. However, when working with compilers created for high-level programming languages, it is necessary to account for generally-adopted conventions, which will be covered in the next few sections.

---

[i] In high-level programming languages, the commonly-adopted practice is to distinguish between procedures and functions. From the standpoint of the disassembled text, there is no difference between these two concepts.

Passing Parameters through the Stack

Passing parameters through the stack is the most common and widely used mechanism. This approach allows you to create recursive procedures, but the use of other approaches makes recursion problematic. As a rule, parameters are placed into the stack using the PUSH commands. However, another method is possible, which you have encountered multiple times. It is possible to manually change the value of the stack pointer and then use normal MOV commands to place the parameters into the allocated region. For example, if two parameters are loaded into the EAX and EBX registers, respectively, then it is possible to place them into the stack using the following sequence of commands: SUB ESP, 8/MOV [ESP], EAX/MOV [ESP], EBX. This is equivalent to the two PUSH EAX/PUSH EBX commands (recall that the stack grows upward in the direction of smaller addresses).

When passing parameters, the most important issue is the order, in which the parameters appear in the stack. When receiving parameters from the stack, the called procedure follows a strictly defined order, which must be observed when calling that procedure. However, this is only one problem. The second problem is clearing the stack. After the called procedure has executed all required operations and returned control into the calling program fragment, the parameters passed to the procedure remain in the stack. If the procedure is called multiple times, this, in the long run, might crash the program. There are two practical approaches to solving this problem. The first method is used only in the C++ programming language. Using this method, the stack is released after the return from the called procedure. It is convenient because it is possible to use procedures with a variable number of parameters.

NOTE

The printf standard C library function is an example of such a procedure. The first parameter of this function is always a string that might contain special substrings (called *format specifiers*). Format specifiers start with the % character. The number of such specifiers is equal to the number of additional parameters of the printf function.

As a rule, the stack is restored using the ADD ESP, 4*N command, where N is the number of 32-bit parameters.[i] However, alternative ways, such as using SUB ESP, -4*N or even POP commands, are possible. It is important to understand their meaning.

---

[i] One parameter of the double type must be interpreted as two 32-bit parameters.

Sometimes the compiler, for economy, restores the stack after calling several procedures.

The second method of stack recovery consists of using the RETN 4*N command immediately after exiting the procedure. Again, N specifies the number of 32-bit parameters. This approach was initially used in Pascal compilers. This approach is slightly faster. However, it makes it problematic to call a procedure with a variable number of parameters.

Passing Parameters through the Data Segment

The use of global variables for passing information into a procedure suggests itself. However, this approach is a persistent source of headaches. To avoid errors, you'll have to allocate an individual set of global parameters for every procedure, which requires additional memory resources. The use of global variables also makes recursive calls problematic, because you won't be able to use the same variables if they are already in use. However, this drawback doesn't mean that this approach is not used. Nothing prevents you from using it when writing a program in C++ or Delphi.

The preceding approach can be improved by using a specially organized memory block for passing parameters. You'll probably have to organize such a block individually for each procedure, although, in theory, it is possible to create a structure of universal buffer for passing parameters to all called procedures. The structure of such a buffer can be organized to make it possible to use recursive procedure calls.

Passing Parameters through Program Code

Passing parameters through program code looks somewhat exotic. However, it is a realistic method, provided that you use Assembly language. For example, consider the algorithm in Listing 3.45.

Listing 3.45. Algorithm for passing parameters through the program code

---

```
...
CALL PROC1
    DB "This parameter is passed through the program code", 0
; The PROC1 procedure will return control here.

...

PROC1 PROC
; Pop the return address from the stack.
```

```
; Define the parameter addresses and length.
; Modify the return address in the stack.
; Process.
; Return from the procedure.
        RETN
PROC1 ENDP
```

As you can see, this method doesn't contain anything too difficult or impossible. However, its implementation in a high-level programming language requires additional effort.

Passing Parameters through Registers

The method of passing parameters through registers is fast. However, it has certain limitations, because registers are few. This approach is mainly used with other mechanisms, such as passing parameters through the stack. When using this combined approach, the first parameters are usually passed through registers and the remaining parameters are passed through the stack. Later in this chapter, this approach will be covered in more detail.

Conventions for Passing Parameters

Consider compilers of high-level programming languages. As you would expect, they mainly pass parameters through the stack. The main calling conventions used by contemporary compilers are listed in Table 3.2.

Table 3.2. Standard calling conventions used by contemporary compilers

Calling convention	Order of parameters	Stack-clearing method	Comment
C convention (__cdecl)	From right to left	By the calling program	The compiler automatically inserts the underscore character (_) before the function name.
Standard calling convention (__stdcall)	From right to left	By the called procedure	The compiler automatically inserts the underscore character (_) before the function name. The function name is terminated by the @ suffix followed by the number specifying the total length of all parameters (in bytes).

continues

Table 3.2 Continued

Calling convention	Order of parameters	Stack-clearing method	Comment
Pascal calling convention (PASCAL)	From left to right	By the called procedure	This calling convention is used in Pascal and Delphi.
Fast calling convention, also known as register call (__fastcall)	From left to right	By the called procedure	Microsoft's C++ compiler employs two registers (ECX and EDX). If this is not enough for passing all parameters, then the remaining parameters are passed through the stack. The Borland C++ compiler uses three registers (EAX, EDX, and ECX).

NOTE

The calling conventions listed in Table 3.2 are not the only available ones. In different programming languages, there are language-specific conventions. For example, Delphi supports the safecall convention, and Basic has its individual calling convention. Some calling conventions have been gradually moved out of use. For example, the Pascal (__pascal) calling convention is no longer supported in Microsoft Visual C++.

When writing programs in C++, the most common calling conventions are __cdecl (when working with normal and library functions) and __stdcall (when calling most API functions).

As an illustration of the use of register calling conventions (fast function calls), consider the simple program shown in Listing 3.46.

Listing 3.46. Simple program illustrating the use of the __fastcall calling convention

```
#include <stdio.h>
int __fastcall  add(int, int, int);
void main()
{
        int i = 10, j = 20, k = 30;
        printf("%d\n", add(i, j, k));
```

```
};

int __fastcall add(int a, int b, int c)
{
        return a + b + c;
};
```

As you can see, the program in Listing 3.46 contains a function declared as __fastcall. First, consider the disassembled text of the executable code of this program produced by the Microsoft Visual C++ compiler (Listing 3.47).

Listing 3.47. Disassembled text (Listing 3.46) produced by Microsoft Visual C++

```
.text:00401000 _main          proc near            ; CODE XREF: start + 16E↓p
.text:00401000      var_C = dword ptr -0Ch
.text:00401000      var_8 = dword ptr -8
.text:00401000      var_4 = dword ptr -4
.text:00401000          push    ebp
.text:00401001          mov     ebp, esp
.text:00401003          sub     esp, 0Ch
.text:00401006          mov     [ebp + var_4], 0Ah
.text:0040100D          mov     [ebp + var_C], 14h
.text:00401014          mov     [ebp + var_8], 1Eh
.text:0040101B          mov     eax, [ebp + var_8]
.text:0040101E          push    eax
.text:0040101F          mov     edx, [ebp + var_C]
.text:00401022          mov     ecx, [ebp + var_4]
.text:00401025          call    sub_401040
.text:0040102A          push    eax
.text:0040102B          push    offset unk_4060FC
.text:00401030          call    _printf
.text:00401035          add     esp, 8
.text:00401038          xor     eax, eax
.text:0040103A          mov     esp, ebp
.text:0040103C          pop     ebp
.text:0040103D          retn
.text:0040103D _main          endp
```

The code presented in this listing is well known. However, there is one issue that you did not encounter earlier. According to the program (see Listing 3.46), the add function must have three parameters. Obviously, sub_401040 corresponds to the add function. Later, the mov eax, [ebp + var_8]/push eax commands send the last variable into the stack (this is the k variable). The values of the i and j variables are placed into the ECX and EDX registers, respectively. This corresponds to the fastcall calling convention typical for the Microsoft Visual C++ compiler. The documentation supplied with the compiler states that it uses the __fastcall calling convention whenever possible. As you can see, this is true. If the number of parameters is increased, then the compiler will pass the remaining parameters in a normal way, namely, through the stack. This can be easily explained because the procedure that will be called also needs registers. So, as the number of parameters is increased, the number of general-purpose registers will not be enough and it will be necessary to create local stack variables.

Listing 3.48 presents the disassembled code of the same program compiled using the Borland C++ compiler.

Listing 3.48. Disassembled code (Listing 3.46) compiled using the Borland C++ compiler

```
.text:00401108 _main      proc near       ; DATA XREF: .data:0040A0B8↓o
.text:00401108      argc  = dword ptr  10h
.text:00401108      argv  = dword ptr  14h
.text:00401108      envp  = dword ptr  18h
.text:00401108            · push    ebx
.text:00401109              push    esi
.text:0040110A              push    edi
.text:0040110B              mov     ebx, 0Ah
.text:00401110              mov     esi, 14h
.text:00401115              mov     edi, 1Eh
.text:0040111A              mov     ecx, edi
.text:0040111C              mov     edx, esi
.text:0040111E              mov     eax, ebx
.text:00401120              call    sub_401138
.text:00401125              push    eax
.text:00401126              push    offset format    ; Format
```

```
.text:0040112B                        call      _printf
.text:00401130                        add       esp, 8
.text:00401133                        pop       edi
.text:00401134                        pop       esi
.text:00401135                        pop       ebx
.text:00401136                        retn
.text:00401136 _main                 endp
```

As you can see from Listing 3.48, the Borland C++ compiler sends parameters sequentially into the EAX, EDX, and ECX registers. Note that the Borland's compiler uses register variables in the EBX, ESI, and EDI registers instead of stack variables. In contrast to the Microsoft Visual C++ compiler, the Borland C++ compiler is serious about the __fastcall modifier and doesn't neglect the instruction for using registers as the number of parameters increases.

Stack Structures

Throughout this chapter, I have provided lots of different listings, in which I try to draw your attention to the locations of the return address, parameters, and local and temporary variables within the stack. The main goal of this section is to generalize accumulated experience and supply new information.

The standard stack structure in the course of a procedure call is shown in Fig. 3.2. This illustration shows the stages that the stack undergoes. The process of stack modification starts from the procedure call (stages 1–3), during which the parameters are placed into the stack and the procedure is called. During stages 4–5, memory is allocated and the registers that will be used within the procedure, whose values must not be changed after the call, are saved into the stack.

Consider the stages shown in Fig. 3.2 in more detail:

❐ Usually, parameters are placed into the stack using reg32 or PUSH DWORD PTR mem commands, where reg32 is a 32-bit register and mem is the address of the memory area (direct or indirect). However, another method of placing parameters into the stack is possible. First, the area for parameters is allocated in the stack. This can be carried out, for example, as follows: SUB ESP, N. Here, N is the number of bytes required for storing parameters, aligned by the 4-byte boundary. Then, the parameters are loaded into the stack using standard MOV commands. For example, this task can be carried out as follows: MOV DWORD

PTR [ESP], EAX/MOV DWORD PTR [ESP + 4], EBX, etc. When dealing with double operands (which are 8 bytes in size), the FSTP command is used to place them into the stack, for example: FSTP DWORD PTR [ESP]. Thus, 8 bytes from the ST(0) FPU register will be sent to the stack (see Listing 3.12 and the comments that follow it).

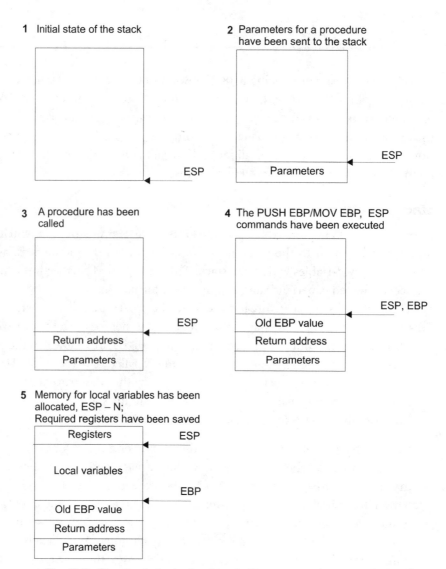

1 Initial state of the stack

ESP

2 Parameters for a procedure have been sent to the stack

ESP

Parameters

3 A procedure has been called

ESP

Return address

Parameters

4 The PUSH EBP/MOV EBP, ESP commands have been executed

ESP, EBP

Old EBP value

Return address

Parameters

5 Memory for local variables has been allocated, ESP – N; Required registers have been saved

Registers   ESP

Local variables

EBP

Old EBP value

Return address

Parameters

Fig. 3.2. Standard stack structure in the course of a procedure call

❏ The CALL command places the return address into the stack directly after parameters (if there are any). To correctly return from the procedure, this address must be located on the top of the stack. In addition, the CALL command jumps to the address specified to it. Now all work related to stack modification is delegated to the procedure. As a rule, the procedure starts with the PUSH EBP command. This command immediately assumes further use of EBP, and this register probably will be used for addressing the stack variable and parameters. The presence of the MOV EBP, ESP command confirms this assumption. For what purpose is this necessary? The ESP register is bound to the PUSH and POP commands that change it automatically. Consequently, if the parameter nearest to the stack top was located in the start of the procedure at the [ESP + 4] address, then after the execution of the PUSH command it will be located at the [ESP + 8] address. Thus, the EBP register is used to fix the reference point, from which locations of the parameters and stack variables are counted.

❏ The next step in the procedure of forming the stack structure is allocation of the memory area for storing local variables. Note that if the use of local variables is not presumed, then the compiler skips this step. As a rule, stack allocation is carried out by the SUB ESP, N command, where N stands for the number of allocated bytes, aligned by the 4-byte boundary. In some cases, however, it is possible to use the ADD ESP, -N command or several PUSH commands. The use of the PUSH command is convenient, because within the same command it is possible to combine stack allocation and variable initialization (see Listing 3.36 and the comments that follow it). The sequence of the PUSH EBP/MOV EBP, ESP/SUB ESP, N commands can be replaced with a single ENTER N command, which, however, is rarely used by the compilers because of its slowness.

❏ Finally, if it is presumed that the EBX, ESI, and EDI registers are used in the procedure, they also must be saved in the stack.

❏ In the end of the procedure, the stack must be returned to the state, in which the address of return from the procedure was located on its top. In addition, it is necessary to restore the EBP, EBX, ESI, and EDI registers (provided that they were modified). The most common is the sequence of MOV ESP, EBP/POP EBP commands, which the compiler often replaces with a single leave command.

❏ If the preceding method was strictly observed, then there will be no problems with recognizing the procedure in the course of disassembling, even if the procedure was called using indirect call commands (CALL reg32, CALL [reg32], and CALL [mem]). However, contemporary compilers, because of optimization, abandon the use of the EBP register for addressing stack variables and parameters (see Listing 3.38 and the comments that follow it).

☐ In my opinion, the most interesting issue is the one related to nested procedures. In C++, nested functions are not possible. Pascal, in contrast, allows such constructs (Listing 3.49).

Listing 3.49. Pascal program with nested procedures

```
program Project1;
var
a:integer;
procedure proc1(a1:integer);
var  b, g, d, e:integer;
  procedure proc2(a1:integer);
  var c:integer;
  begin
    c := 30;
    writeln(a1, b, c, d, e, g);
  end;
begin
  b := 20; g := 30; d := 40; e := 50;
    proc2(a1);
end;
begin
  a := 10;
  proc1(a);
end.
```

Listing 3.50 provides the disassembled starting (main) part of the program (see Listing 3.49) compiled using Delphi.

Listing 3.50. Disassembled code of the program shown in Listing 3.49, compiled using Delphi

```
CODE:004039B4                 public start
CODE:004039B4    start:
CODE:004039B4                 push    ebp
```

```
CODE:004039B5                 mov      ebp, esp
CODE:004039B7                 add      esp, 0FFFFFFF0h
CODE:004039BA                 mov      eax, ds:off_4040A8
CODE:004039BF                 mov      byte ptr [eax], 1
CODE:004039C2                 mov      eax, offset dword_403994
CODE:004039C7                 call     sub_403860
CODE:004039CC                 mov      ds:dword_40565C, 0Ah
CODE:004039D6                 mov      eax, ds:dword_40565C
CODE:004039DB                 call     sub_403938
CODE:004039E0                 call     sub_403394
```

Listing 3.50 shows the starting part of the program (see Listing 3.49). Of the three procedure calls shown in this listing, one is the call to the procedure directly present in the application program (proc1). This is the sub_403938 procedure. The other two procedures are system procedures executed when starting (start-up initialization) and when exiting the program. The sub_403938 procedure obtains its only parameter through the EAX register. The __fascall calling convention is "flourishing" in Delphi, although it wasn't declared in the program. I have even declined optimization when compiling this program. However, as you can see, Delphi made an independent decision. The dword_40565C name corresponds to the a variable in the program source code, and it is the one passed to the procedure through the register. Also, pay attention to the add esp, 0FFFFFFF0h command. I hope that you without trouble can guess that this is the add esp, -16 command, which is equivalent to sub esp, 16. In other words, 16 bytes are reserved.

Listing 3.51 provides the disassembled text of the compiled proc1 (sub_403938) procedure.

Listing 3.51. Disassembled text of the compiled proc1 procedure

```
CODE:00403938  sub_403938     proc near        ; CODE XREF: CODE:004039DB↓p
CODE:00403938          var_14  = dword ptr -14h
CODE:00403938          var_10  = dword ptr -10h
CODE:00403938          var_C   = dword ptr -0Ch
CODE:00403938          var_8   = dword ptr -8
CODE:00403938          var_4   = dword ptr -4
CODE:00403938                  push     ebp
```

```
CODE:00403939                    mov      ebp, esp
CODE:0040393B                    add      esp, 0FFFFFFECh
CODE:0040393E                    mov      [ebp + var_14], eax
CODE:00403941                    mov      [ebp + var_4], 14h
CODE:00403948                    mov      [ebp + var_10], 1Eh
CODE:0040394F                    mov      [ebp + var_8], 28h
CODE:00403956                    mov      [ebp + var_C], 32h
CODE:0040395D                    push     ebp
CODE:0040395E                    mov      eax, [ebp + var_14]
CODE:00403961                    call     sub_4038DC
CODE:00403966                    pop      ecx
CODE:00403967                    mov      esp, ebp
CODE:00403969                    pop      ebp
CODE:0040396A                    retn
CODE:0040396A    sub_403938      endp
```

Note that four local variables are defined in the proc1 procedure. However, as you can see, five local variables are defined in the executable code. The var_14 variable is allocated for storing the parameter passed to the procedure (mov [ebp + var_14], eax); in other words, it is a temporary variable. The add esp, 0FFFFFFECh command is equivalent to add esp, -20. Everything is correct here (there are five variables, and $20 = 4*5$).

There are even more interesting issues. For instance, consider the call to the proc2 procedure, to which the call sub_4038DC command in Listing 3.51 corresponds. Note that this time the parameter also is passed to the procedure through the EAX register. However, what does the push ebp command mean? Is it another parameter? In the source code of the program, there were no additional parameters. Furthermore, this doesn't correspond to the __fascall convention. Recall that the proc2 procedure is nested, and it must have access to the local variables of the proc1 procedure. This is why the EBP register is secretly passed to the proc2 procedure through this value. This is necessary to provide the nested procedure with access to local variables of the proc1 procedure. Also, note that the pop ecx command that follows the procedure call simply releases the stack from this "illegal" parameter.

Listing 3.52 provides the disassembled code of the proc2 procedure (see Listing 3.49).

Listing 3.52. Disassembled code of the proc2 procedure from Listing 3.49

```
CODE:004038DC  sub_4038DC     proc near       ; CODE XREF: sub_403938 + 29↓p
CODE:004038DC         var_8  = dword ptr -8
CODE:004038DC         var_4  = dword ptr -4
CODE:004038DC         arg_0  = dword ptr  8
CODE:004038DC                push    ebp
CODE:004038DD                mov     ebp, esp
CODE:004038DF                add     esp, 0FFFFFFF8h
CODE:004038E2                mov     [ebp + var_4], eax
CODE:004038E5                mov     [ebp + var_8], 1Eh
CODE:004038EC                mov     eax, ds:off_4040A4
CODE:004038F1                mov     edx, [ebp + var_4]
CODE:004038F4                call    sub_402B78
CODE:004038F9                mov     edx, [ebp + arg_0]
CODE:004038FC                mov     edx, [edx - 4]
CODE:004038FF                call    sub_402B78
CODE:00403904                mov     edx, [ebp + var_8]
CODE:00403907                call    sub_402B78
CODE:0040390C                mov     edx, [ebp + arg_0]
CODE:0040390F                mov     edx, [edx - 8]
CODE:00403912                call    sub_402B78
CODE:00403917                mov     edx, [ebp + arg_0]
CODE:0040391A                mov     edx, [edx - 0Ch]
CODE:0040391D                call    sub_402B78
CODE:00403922                mov     edx, [ebp + arg_0]
CODE:00403925                mov     edx, [edx - 10h]
CODE:00403928                call    sub_402B78
CODE:0040392D                call    sub_402BA8
CODE:00403932                pop     ecx
CODE:00403933                pop     ecx
CODE:00403934                pop     ebp
CODE:00403935                retn
CODE:00403935  sub_4038DC     endp
```

The abundance of procedure calls immediately attracts attention. But you know that in the source code (see Listing 3.49), there is only the `writeln` function. However, `writeln` is not a function but an operator. The compiler transforms this operator into two procedure calls. The first procedure (`sub_402B78`) forms some resulting string, which will be printed. The number of calls to this procedure matches the number of parameters in the `writeln` operator. When the resulting string is formed, the `sub_402BA8` procedure is called, which outputs the string to the console.

Pay special attention to the `add esp, 0FFFFFFF8h` command. The memory for two stack variables is reserved. The parameter passed to the procedure is placed into the `var_4` variable. The `var_8` variable corresponds to the `c` local variable, which is assigned the value of 30 (`1Eh`).

In addition to the two local variables, the procedure has the `arg_0` parameter, which is nothing but the `EBP` value passed from the `proc1` procedure, using which it is possible to access local variables of the `proc1` procedure.

If you view the source code of the program, you'll immediately note that the `proc2` procedure prints the values of `a1` (the values passed from `proc1` as a parameter), `c` (local variable of the `proc1` procedure), and the values of four variables defined in `proc1`.

The previously-considered `arg_0` parameter is used for obtaining the values of variables defined in `proc1`. For example, consider how the value of the `b` variable is retrieved: `mov edx, [ebp + arg_0]`/`mov edx, [edx - 4]`. Again, parameters are passed through registers. As relates to the `EAX` register, some `ds:off_4040A4` parameter is placed there, the value of which is unknown. As you probably can guess, this parameter is required for the operation of the `sub_402B78` procedure.

Identifying Procedures and Functions

To identify a specific procedure, you need to determine the addresses of its start and its end. Second, it is necessary to determine the number and type (or at least the size) of the passed parameters, the stack variables used by this procedure, and the type of its return value. Consider the possibilities are available for completing this task:

❑ The procedure call can be used. The `CALL addr` command explicitly specifies that some procedure is located at the `addr` address. However, there are two possible problems:

 • An indirect procedure call, such as `CALL [EAX]`, causes difficulties for disassemblers. It is necessary to either resort to using a debugger or analyze the disassembled text manually. Furthermore, if the value of the EAX register is subject to change depending on the values of some other parameters, it becomes problematic to locate all procedures called using this method.

- From *Section 1.6.1*, you know that there are lots of methods of calling procedures. This can be achieved even using the RET command. If you are dealing with a program written in Assembly or containing Assembly inserts, and the program's author aims to confuse potential code investigators, there are lots of possibilities of achieving this goal. However, if nonstandard procedure calls are used, this might be disclosed by the presence of commands like ADD ESP, N, SUB ESP, -N, or one or more POP instructions. If you encounter such patterns, this must inspire you to investigate the code more closely.

❑ Functions can be identified by locating the standard function prologue. As a rule, the standard function prologue is made up of three commands directly following each other: PUSH EBP, MOV EBP, ESP, and SUB ESP, N. The final command might be different, for example, ADD ESP, -N or simply one or more sequential PUSH commands. It also is possible to do without stack allocation for local and temporary variables. This is the case when there are no such variables or if registers are used for passing such variables. Besides this, the procedure might start with the commands for saving the values of the EBX, ESI, and EDI registers. In the course of optimization, the compiler might do without the standard prologues and address all stack variables and parameters using the ESP register. Finally, instead of the standard prologue it is possible to use the ENTER N command. The end of the function is easier to locate when the starting point of that function is known. However, in some cases the end of the function is the first to be located.

❑ The procedure end can be easily located if a standard epilogue is present: MOV ESP, EBP/POP EBP. Sometimes, this sequence of commands is replaced with the LEAVE command. The epilogue is followed by the RETN command. In general, any RETN command (especially RETN N) must make the code investigator vigilant. Having encountered it, you should always check whether this is the procedure end. This is a good criterion; however, it is not always applicable. In particular, if the function contains more than one __try/__except blocks, the Microsoft Visual C++ compiler might generate several standard epilogues (for optimization). Thus, even the IDA Pro disassembler might be easily confused in such situations.

❑ As mentioned earlier, it is easier to find the procedure end if the procedure start has been determined. This usually will be the first RETN command encountered.

However, it is possible to exit in the middle of a procedure. In this case, some unconditional jump must precede the RETN command, which passes control to some location beyond the RETN command. For example, the pattern might appear as shown in Listing 3.53.

Listing 3.53. Sequence of commands typical for exiting in the middle of a procedure

```
    CMP    EAX, 1
    JNZ    L1
    RETN
L1:
```

Thus, it is possible to search for the procedure end starting from the L1 (label). If the procedure has to return something when terminating its execution (when it is a function), then the command setting the value of the EAX register must be present near its end. Such commands might appear as XOR EAX, EAX (return false) or MOV EAX, 1 (return true), or these might be some commands that modify the EAX value (MOV, ADD, SUB, etc.). If the type of the return value is 8 bytes is size, then this value is returned in the EDX:EAX pair of registers. Finally, values of the double type are returned in the ST(0) FPU register.

NOTE

If the return value is a structure, then the pointer to that structure, instead of the structure, is returned in the EAX register. The structure itself is created in the calling function. When the function of the "structure" type is called, the pointer to that structure is passed in the EAX register. Thus, the function will work with the structure that has already been created, and after completion it will return the pointer to the same structure.

❑ Most procedures and functions have either variables defined in the stack or parameters passed through the stack. This is an important indication because you will certainly encounter commands with addressing through the EBP or ESP registers. By carefully viewing the code above and below the encountered command, it is possible to determine the procedure start.

❑ When stack variables are addressed in a standard way (through the EBP register), it won't be difficult to determine the amount of stack memory allocated to them (SUB ESP, N or any similar command). As relates to the parameters passed to the procedure, here the situation is slightly more complicated, because it is not known beforehand how much memory has been allocated for them. The easiest way of solving this problem is to find the call to this procedure, because all parameters are usually loaded into the stack using PUSH commands or another obvious method (for instance, see Listing 3.13 and the comments that follow it). If the location, from which the procedure under consideration was called, is not known beforehand, then it will be necessary to analyze its code. First, it will be necessary to find the maximum offset in relation to the EBP value in the direction of higher addresses. Because the return address and old EBP value were loaded into the stack after parameters, the first parameter (the one with the minimum address) will be located at the [EBP + 8] address (see Fig. 3.2). Thus, if the maximum offset using the [EBP + N] addressing is equal to max_off, then the number of bytes allocated for parameters will be equal to max_off - 4. Assuming that all parameters are 32 bits in size and have a simple data type (these are not arrays or structures), an approximate number of parameters will be equal to (max_off - 4)/4.

After these theoretical considerations and computations, consider a simple example program written in C++ (Listing 3.54).

Listing 3.54. C++ program illustrating the procedure of identifying function start and end

---

```
#include <stdio.h>
#include <windows.h>
double myfunc(double, __int64, int, BYTE);
void main()
{
        double ff = 10.45;
        __int64 ii = 1000;
        int jj = 200;
        BYTE bb = 50;
        double ss = myfunc(ff, ii, jj, bb);
        printf("%f\n", ff);
};
```

```
double myfunc(double f, __int64 i, int j, BYTE b)
{
        double s;
        s = f + i + j + b;
        printf("%f\n", s);
        return s;
};
```

The disassembled text of the main function from this program is shown in Listing 3.55.

Listing 3.55. Disassembled code of the main function from Listing 3.54

```
.text:00401000 _main          proc near        ; CODE XREF: start + 16E↓p
.text:00401000      var_40  = qword ptr -40h
.text:00401000      var_30  = qword ptr -30h
.text:00401000      var_28  = qword ptr -28h
.text:00401000      var_1C  = dword ptr -1Ch
.text:00401000      var_18  = qword ptr -18h
.text:00401000      var_10  = dword ptr -10h
.text:00401000      var_C   = dword ptr -0Ch
.text:00401000      var_1   = byte ptr -1
.text:00401000              push      ebp
.text:00401001              mov       ebp, esp
.text:00401003              sub       esp, 28h
.text:00401006              fld       ds:dbl_408108
.text:0040100C              fstp      [ebp + var_28]
.text:0040100F              mov       [ebp + var_10], 3E8h
.text:00401016              mov       [ebp + var_C], 0
.text:0040101D              mov       [ebp + var_1C], 0C8h
.text:00401024              mov       [ebp + var_1], 32h
.text:00401028              mov       al, [ebp + var_1]
.text:0040102B              push      eax
.text:0040102C              mov       ecx, [ebp + var_1C]
.text:0040102F              push      ecx
```

```
.text:00401030                 mov      edx, [ebp + var_C]
.text:00401033                 push     edx
.text:00401034                 mov      eax, [ebp + var_10]
.text:00401037                 push     eax
.text:00401038                 fld      [ebp + var_28]
.text:0040103B                 sub      esp, 8
.text:0040103E                 fstp     [esp + 40h + var_40]
.text:00401041                 call     sub_401070
.text:00401046                 add      esp, 18h
.text:00401049                 fstp     [ebp + var_18]
.text:0040104C                 fld      [ebp + var_28]
.text:0040104F                 sub      esp, 8
.text:00401052                 fstp     [esp + 30h + var_30]
.text:00401055                 push     offset unk_4080FC
.text:0040105A                 call     _printf
.text:0040105F                 add      esp, 0Ch
.text:00401062                 xor      eax, eax
.text:00401064                 mov      esp, ebp
.text:00401066                 pop      ebp
.text:00401067                 retn
.text:00401067  _main          endp
```

First, identify four local variables defined in the main function. Discard the var_30 and var_40 names, because these are not variables. These are identifiers used by IDA Pro. For local variables, 40 bytes are allocated. This is too much for five variables. Thus, it is necessary to investigate these variables in more detail and in due order. The var_28 variable stands for the ff variable of the double type. Here, everything is clear: The initial value is loaded from the dbl_408108 constant using the fld/fstp commands. The mov [ebp + var_10], 3E8h/mov [ebp + var_C], 0 commands load the 1000 (3E8h) value into the ii variable. The disassembler didn't understand that this was a single 64-bit variable, and it interpreted this data item as two different variables. The var_1C variable designates the jj variable. Then, there is the var_1 single-byte variable designating bb. Note that although this is a single-byte variable, it takes 4 bytes. This variable is followed by 4 more free bytes, and only after this interval does the var_C variable start.

Thus, the compiler has aligned the data by the 8-byte boundary. This alone appears suspicious and causes the code investigator to assume that instead of two 4-byte variables there is one 8-byte variable. Now only the ss variable remains. Note that after the call to the myfunc function that has the double type, there is the fstp [ebp + var_18] command. This means that the value from the ST(0) FPU register is loaded into the var_18 variable. However, double variables are returned in the ST(0) register. Thus, it is possible to conclude that var_18 stands for the ss variable. Therefore, everything is OK. All variables have been identified, and the extra reservation was caused by data alignment.

Another interesting sequence of commands is as follows: mov al, [ebp + var_1]/ push eax. At first glance, it appears that everything is all right here because, although the variable is 1 byte, it is necessary to load a 4-byte value into the stack. However, the most significant bytes of the EAX register were not cleared. Furthermore, the entire double word is sent to the stack as a parameter. This is possible only if the function strictly accounts for the parameter being 1 byte in size. By the way, pay special attention to the order, in which parameters are sent to the stack (from right to left). It is the calling function that clears the stack. This corresponds to the __cdecl calling convention (see Table 3.2). Then all other parameters are sent into the stack. The ii (var_10, var_c) variable is sent into the stack as two independent 4-byte variables. The ff variable is sent into the stack using the fstp command, as required. Then there is the call to the printf function. This isn't anything unusual. However, I would still like to draw your attention to the following issue: The first parameter of this function is the format string, which specifies all other parameters of the function. This specification is often helpful for determining the variable type and size. This is even truer because the C++ library provides several other functions similar to printf and operating over the format string.

The disassembled code of the myfunc function is provided in Listing 3.56.

Listing 3.56. Disassembled code of the myfunc function from Listing 3.54

```
.text:00401070          sub_401070     proc near      ; CODE XREF: _main + 41↑p
.text:00401070          var_14  = qword ptr -14h
.text:00401070          var_C   = dword ptr -0Ch
.text:00401070          var_8   = qword ptr -8
.text:00401070          arg_0   = qword ptr  8
.text:00401070          arg_8   = qword ptr  10h
.text:00401070          arg_10  = dword ptr  18h
```

```
.text:00401070      arg_14  = byte ptr   1Ch
.text:00401070              push     ebp
.text:00401071              mov      ebp, esp
.text:00401073              sub      esp, 0Ch
.text:00401076              fild     [ebp + arg_8]
.text:00401079              fadd     [ebp + arg_0]
.text:0040107C              fiadd    [ebp + arg_10]
.text:0040107F              movzx    eax, [ebp + arg_14]
.text:00401083              mov      [ebp + var_C], eax
.text:00401086              fild     [ebp + var_C]
.text:00401089              faddp    st(1), st
.text:0040108B              fst      [ebp + var_8]
.text:0040108E              sub      esp, 8
.text:00401091              fstp     [esp + 14h + var_14]
.text:00401094              push     offset byte_408100
.text:00401099              call     _printf
.text:0040109E              add      esp, 0Ch
.text:004010A1              fld      [ebp + var_8]
.text:004010A4              mov      esp, ebp
.text:004010A6              pop      ebp
.text:004010A7              retn
.text:004010A7  sub_401070  endp
```

Start the analysis by considering stack variables. There are only two such variables (the var_14 variable is not taken into account): var_8 and var_c. The var_8 variable takes 8 bytes, which leads to the conclusion that this is nothing but the s variable. This assumption will be further confirmed. No other variables were declared in the myfunc function. Consequently, the 4-byte var_c variable is simply a temporary variable.

It is time to consider the function parameters. Strangely, there are only four parameters. Recall that although there are four parameters, when disassembling the main function IDA Pro considered there to be five variables, which later are used as parameters. Nevertheless, there isn't anything difficult here. When the disassembler processed the main function, it didn't have groundwork for considering var_10 and var_c as a single variable. When processing the myfunc function, the disassembler has well-grounded reasons for considering `arg_8` as a single 8-byte parameter or the `__int64` number (see the `fild` command).

Now, consider the algorithm used for computing the value of the `f + i + j + b` expression. The `fild` command loads a long integer number (the `i` number) onto the top of the FPU stack (namely, into the `ST(0)` register). The next command, `fadd`, adds this number to a real number, `f`. The result is then loaded into `ST(0)` and interpreted as real. The next command, `fiadd`, adds the real number stored in `ST(0)` to the 32-bit integer number `j`. Again, the result is placed into `ST(0)`. Then the `movzx eax, [ebp + arg_14]` command places 1 byte into the `EAX` register and clears the most significant bytes of the register. This issue has already been mentioned in comments that follow Listing 3.55. The byte is sent into the stack as part of a double word, and the calling party doesn't clear the most significant bits, while the called procedure does clear them; otherwise, error would be inevitable. Later, the `var_c` variable is used. The `b` number is loaded into it (`mov [ebp + var_C], eax`), after which the `var_c` variable is loaded into the `ST(0)` register and the old value of `ST(0)` is moved into the `ST(1)` register. Finally, there is the `faddp st(1), st` command, and the result of computing the `f + i + j + b` expression is placed into `var_8` (the `s` variable) by the `fst [ebp + var_8]` command. The stack is not popped, and the result is still contained in `ST(0)`. Thus, the sequence of the `sub esp, 8/fstp [esp + 14h + var_14]` commands places this result into the stack for output using the `printf` function. The final stroke is the `fld [ebp + var_8]` command — the value returned by the function. Here, the compiler has made minor error. It wasn't necessary to use the `fstp` command, and without it the latter command also wouldn't be needed.

Buffer Overflow

Buffer overflow is one of the methods often used by hackers for correcting the software at run time. By skillfully manipulating the input data, the hacker causes buffer overflow and passes control to the shellcode expertly inserted into the program. Here, only one type of overflow error will be considered, namely, stack overflow. Usually, stack overflow manifests in programs written in C++. It consists of intrusion into the executable program code through the program stack.

The stack overflow technique is mainly used for remote attacks. If you need to intrude the program that runs on the local computer, there are more powerful tools for achieving this goal. Besides, cracking some system running on a remote computer requires the intruder to carry out some preliminary investigations. This is why I decided to include this material in this book, even though it mainly relates to remote attacks.

Essence of the Problem

When working with external devices, the program allocates buffers for storing sent and received data. The received data fill the allocated buffers either completely or partially. The program must ensure that the received data do not go beyond the buffer limits. If this happens, other data items of even the executable code might become damaged. If the data being loaded exceed the boundaries of the buffer allocated to them, this might result in a program malfunction or even in a total crash. A specific feature of such errors is that they are exceedingly difficult to detect. In some cases, programmers might gain a false impression that the errors are arbitrary and are not related to specific actions. Exceeding the array boundaries is a typical example of such errors.

Most contemporary compilers are capable of generating the code that can check whether the boundaries of allocated buffers have been exceeded. For example, the Microsoft C++ compiler provides the /GS command-line options. If this option is used, additional code is generated by the compiler, which checks all operations to find out whether the buffer limits have been exceeded. However, only buffers defined in the stack are checked, and this check is superficial. It doesn't guarantee that the data do not fall into another buffer after exceeding limits of the allocated one. The essence of the idea of checking the stack for overflow is to place certain predefined bytes at the boundaries of the allocated buffer. After any operations that write into the allocated buffer, a special procedure that checks these bytes must be called. If these bytes are modified, this is evidence that there was a buffer overflow error. This approach requires additional memory. Furthermore, it considerably slows program execution.

A natural question arises: How can the buffer overflow be exploited by those who try to crack the program or a system? There are several techniques of penetration:

❑ If the buffer is located in the stack, then the most obvious mechanism of intrusion from the outside is modification of the return address from the function. The return address can be modified in such a way that it jumps to another function or to the address that also is located in the stack but contains malicious code instead of normal data. This method is the one that will be covered later in this section.

❏ Another approach is to modify some pointers (including to pointers to functions, the jump table, etc.) at run time in such a way as to point to code other than that initially intended by the program developer. This code was previously inserted by the intruder and will run according to the intruder's plans.

❏ Another approach is to modify data addresses in the course of overflow. The next portion of data will be supplied into a different program location, which would allow the intruder to insert an external code into the program.

Thus, it is possible to state that software is cracked by buffer overflow in the following two stages: It is necessary first to insert malicious code and then to pass control to it. In theory, the first stage might not be needed if the procedure that the hacker requires is part of the program being investigated. In this case, the only thing that the hacker needs is to pass control to that procedure at the required moment.

Why do I pay such attention to stack overflow? Windows protects the executable code from writing there (the topic of self-modification was covered in detail in *Section 1.6.2*). Also, Windows protects the data section from executing some code there. The stack is the only location where it is possible to both write data and execute commands. This fundamental property of the stack is universally applicable to most operating systems. In other words, it is possible to fill the stack buffer with executable code and then make the processor execute it.

Practical Example

As an example, consider the simple program provided in Listing 3.57. The getpassword function checks whether the supplied password is correct and, depending on the password's correctness, returns either false or true.

Listing 3.57. Example of a simple program vulnerable to stack overflow

```
#include <stdio.h>
#include <string.h>
int getpassword(char *);
char *passw = "privet";
int main()
{
        printf("Input password:\n");
        if(!getpassword(passw))printf("You are registered!\n");
```

```
        else printf("You are wrong!\n");
        return 0;
};


int getpassword(char *ss)
{
        char s[13];
        gets(s);
        if(!strcmp(s, ss))return 0;
        else return 1;

}
```

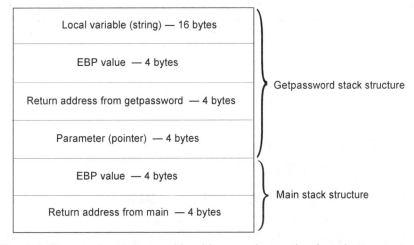

Fig. 3.3. The stack structure, with addresses decreasing from bottom to top

Fig. 3.3 shows the design of the stack of the program presented in Listing 3.57. This is a standard arrangement with prologue and epilogue. As you can see, the general stack structure is divided into the stack structure of the main function and the stack structure of the getpassword function. Note that addresses decrease from bottom to top. The local variable shown in this illustration is the s variable. And, although the size of this parameter was specified to equal 13 bytes, the compiler aligns it by the 4-byte boundary so that the buffer size equals 16 bytes. Data are inserted into the s variable from lower addresses to higher addresses. Thus, the data that overflow the stack overwrite everything located below. The EBP value is the first to be overwritten. After it, there is the address of return from the getpassword function (which is the result longed for by the attacker). If the data go beyond the buffer limits and change the value of the return address, then the function would return control to a different location. But where to? This is the most interesting question. The attacker can place into the stack the address of some function present within the program so that in case of buffer overflow the program would execute according to the different method (which the programmer didn't expect).

It is time to conduct an experiment by changing the return address from the getpassword function. First, it is necessary to carefully study the disassembled code of the program. Listings 3.58 and 3.59 show the disassembled texts of the main and getpassword functions, respectively.

Listing 3.58. Disassembled code of the main function from Listing 3.57

```
.text:00401000  _main        proc near          ; CODE XREF: start + 16E↓p
.text:00401000               push      ebp
.text:00401001               mov       ebp, esp
.text:00401003               push      offset aInputPassword
.text:00401008               call      _printf
.text:0040100D               add       esp, 4
.text:00401010               mov       eax, dword_409040
.text:00401015               push      eax
.text:00401016               call      sub_401050
.text:0040101B               add       esp, 4
.text:0040101E               test      eax, eax
.text:00401020               jnz       short loc_401031
.text:00401022               push      offset aYouAreRegister
.text:00401027               call      _printf
.text:0040102C               add       esp, 4
.text:0040102F               jmp       short loc_40103E
.text:00401031  loc_401031:                     ; CODE XREF: _main + 20↑j
.text:00401031               push      offset aYouAreWrong
.text:00401036               call      _printf
.text:0040103B               add       esp, 4
```

```
.text:0040103E  loc_40103E:                        ; CODE XREF: _main + 2F↑j
.text:0040103E                 xor      eax, eax
.text:00401040                 pop      ebp
.text:00401041                 retn
.text:00401041  _main          endp
```

To start this study, first consider the call to the `sub_401050` function, which is nothing but the designation of the `getpassword` function. The sequence of the `mov eax, dword_409040/push eax` commands corresponds to sending the pointer containing the reference password into the stack. The `dword_409040` global variable contains the address of this string; in other words, it is the pointer variable. Thus, the parameter is sent to the stack, then the `call` command places there the return address (in this case, this is the `0040101Bh` value).

Then pay attention to the `test eax, eax` command and the conditional jump that follows it: `jnz short loc_401031`. This is a normal conditional construct, and the `test` command corresponds to the `if(!)` operator. You have encountered the structure of the `main` function many times.

Listing 3.59. Disassembled code of the getpassword function (Listing 3.57)

```
.text:00401050  sub_401050  proc near            ; CODE XREF: _main + 16↑p
.text:00401050             var_10 = byte ptr -10h
.text:00401050             arg_0  = dword ptr  8
.text:00401050                 push     ebp
.text:00401051                 mov      ebp, esp
.text:00401053                 sub      esp, 10h
.text:00401056                 lea      eax, [ebp + var_10]
.text:00401059                 push     eax
.text:0040105A                 call     _gets
.text:0040105F                 add      esp, 4
.text:00401062                 mov      ecx, [ebp + arg_0]
.text:00401065                 push     ecx      ; char *
.text:00401066                 lea      edx, [ebp + var_10]
.text:00401069                 push     edx      ; char *
.text:0040106A                 call     _strcmp
```

```
.text:0040106F                 add      esp, 8
.text:00401072                 test     eax, eax
.text:00401074                 jnz      short loc_40107A
.text:00401076                 xor      eax, eax
.text:00401078                 jmp      short loc_40107F
.text:0040107A  loc_40107A:                     ; CODE XREF: sub_401050 + 24↑j
.text:0040107A                 mov      eax, 1
.text:0040107F  loc_40107F:                     ; CODE XREF: sub_401050 + 28↑j
.text:0040107F                 mov      esp, ebp
.text:00401081                 pop      ebp
.text:00401082                 retn
.text:00401082  sub_401050     endp
```

First, note that 16 bytes are allocated for storing local variables in this program. This is because all data in the stack are aligned by the 4-byte boundary. So, if you want to overflow the stack, bear in mind the actual size of this buffer.

The lea eax, [ebp + var_10]/push eax sequence of commands simply places the address of this buffer into the stack. It is assumed that the password will be loaded into that buffer. This is the key issue. As you should understand (see Fig. 3.3), this buffer is followed by the content of the EBP register, which, in turn, is followed by the desired return address.

After the call to the gets library function, the strcmp function for comparing strings is called. This function receives the addresses of two strings from the stack. After the execution of this function, there is an ordinary conditional construct (test, then jnz). By the way, note that the strcmp function, like many other string functions, controls the string lengths only by the terminating null; consequently, buffer overflow cannot influence their operation.

Thus, having carefully considered Listings 3.58 and 3.59, it is possible to proceed further. What is the main goal? First, try to modify the return address so that the jump by retn from the getpassword function would pass control to the printf command in the beginning of the main function. From Listing 3.58, it follows that the jump address is equal to 00401003. Recall that in the memory the number is written according to the principle "the most significant byte gets the higher address," and you'll find that the following sequence of bytes must be sent to the buffer: 03 10 40 00. However, it is necessary to fill first the 16-byte buffer then

4 more bytes where the EBP value is stored. Because it is difficult to enter the characters with codes 10h and 03h from the command line, it is recommended that you use the following technique. Prepare the text file with the required string, then use input redirection. Thus, assuming that the program name is prog1.exe and the text file is named pasw.txt, it is necessary to issue the following command: prog1 < pasw.txt. For entering characters with codes smaller than 32, it is possible to use the hiew.exe program (see *Section 2.1.3*). Well, let the string appear as follows:

qqqqqqqqqqqqqqqqqqqq♥►@

Exactly 20 bytes (16 bytes is the size of the string buffer, and 4 bytes are for the contents of EBP) are filled with arbitrary characters (for simplicity, I suggested simply the q character. Then there follow the characters with the codes 03h 10h 40h. And where is the character with code 0? Actually, you do not need it. After all, in the address that you will change, it is present in the position where it is required. Thus, prepare and execute the prog1 < pasw.txt command. The result will be as follows:

```
Input password:
Input password:
You are wrong!
```

Thus, the problem has been solved. After the execution of the getpassword function, the jump passes control to the address specified in the buffer. However, after these strings are displayed, the dialog box warning you that there was an exception will appear (Fig. 3.4). This is natural and can be easily explained. During the second pass, different data fall into the buffer and stack is already corrupted; thus, the application cannot terminate correctly.

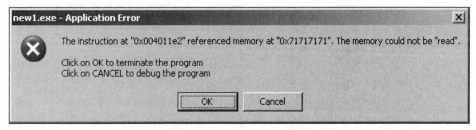

Fig. 3.4. The exception reported by Windows XP after
an artificially-created buffer overflow

The attacker has serious limitations when choosing what bytes are sent into the buffer. For example, the hacker would fail to send characters with codes such as 26 or, say, 0 into the buffer. However, these limitations are not insurmountable for the following two reasons:

- Only a particular case is considered in this example, namely, input using the `gets` console function. In general, the buffer might be intended for arbitrary binary information, in which case the attacker can freely choose the information that will be passed for the input.

- The information that will be sent into the buffer can be encoded so that it won't contain "dangerous" codes. This issue will be described later in this chapter.

Recall that it is possible to run executable code in the stack. What if you place the program code into the stack and pass control to that code? This sounds promising! After all, in the primitive program the buffer size is only 16 bytes. Assume that you are dealing with a buffer that is 16 KB. It is possible to place a program into that buffer that would do anything you like and on behalf of a program that probably has a high privilege level in the system. This security hole has been exploited by crackers for more than 10 years.

What can be placed into the buffer in this particular case? For example, consider the code in Listing 3.60.

Listing 3.60. Executable code that can be placed into the vulnerable buffer (Listing 3.57)

```
MOV   EAX, 0
RETN
```

Is this code suitable? I have intentionally made an error here. Recall that the RETN command has already been executed for jumping to this fragment; so instead of RETN it is necessary to use some kind of JMP command.

If you succeed in achieving this goal, the program will be cracked, because it will always report any supplied password as correct.

From Listing 3.58 it becomes clear that the jump address must be equal to 0040101B. The stack content will not be damaged, and no critical errors will occur.

Disappointingly, the sequence of commands such as MOV EAX, 0/JMP 0040101B is not suitable for passing it into the stack as a string. This is because of the following:

❏ The first command contains zeros. The code of the MOV EAX, 0 command is equal to B8 00000000.

❏ In the second command, the jump address is counted in relation to the command that follows the JMP command. If the starting address of the stack is changed, then this code fragment won't operate correctly.

Thus, to achieve the formulated goal, the two commands from Listing 3.60 must be transformed into a sequence of six commands (Listing 3.61).

Listing 3.61. Executable code that would operate correctly in the vulnerable buffer

```
XOR EAX, EAX          ; 33 C0
XOR ECX, ECX          ; 33 C9
MOV CL, 40H           ; B1 40
SHL ECX, 10H          ; C1 E1 10
MOV CX, 101BH         ; 66 B9 1B 10
JMP ECX               ; FF E1
```

The codes of the commands in Listing 3.61 are specified as comments. The best approach to obtaining the correct codes of all commands is to use some debugger, such as OllyDbg. Thus, you'll require 15 bytes out of 20 allocated bytes (recall that 16 bytes are allocated for the string and 4 bytes are allocated for storing EBP). The remaining 5 bytes of the allocated 20 bytes can contain any information. The return address, which is next, must contain the starting address of the buffer. The buffer address can be determined using the same debugger. In this particular example, it turns out to be equal to 0012FEC8. Thus, it is necessary to add 3 more bytes for the 20-byte string that has already been formed: C8 FE 12.

Here is the content of the pasw.txt file: 3 L3 ▦⊖⊥c☐f‖☐☐ cqqqqqcqqqqq ⌐■☐. To avoid errors, fill the text file using hiew.exe, not using a standard text editor. An attempt at passing some characters through the clipboard inevitably corrupts the code, although the character might remain the same. Thus, having prepared the text file, issue the prog1 < pasw.txt command. The result will be wonderful:

```
You are registered!
```

Thus, the shellcode has been inserted into the program, making the program register the user.

Now, only one issue needs clarification. As you have seen, there are problems with the input of characters that can be sent to the program as a string. The input is not always carried out using the console procedure that treats some characters selectively. If you deal with such an input, then there is no problem.

However, return to the case of console input. What is the solution to this problem? The answer is straightforward. It is necessary to encode the sequence of bytes in such a way as to ensure that the codes incorrectly treated by console input are missing from the string. I won't consider different methods of encoding here. I prefer the following approach (which might require additional memory). The main goal of this approach is as follows: All "invalid" bytes must be encoded (for example, by the XOR command). Each of these bytes must be preceded by a byte specifying that the next byte that follows it is encoded. For this purpose, it is natural to use the NOP command that has the 90H code. The entire fragment must start with the decoder for the remainder of the code. Decoding consists of removing the NOP bytes and decoding the bytes that follow them. Because the bytes that console input functions consider invalid or interpret incorrectly are not numerous, the number of NOP instructions must not be too large.

3.2.2. Conditional Constructs and Logical Operators

When programming in high-level languages such as C and Pascal, most programmers have become used to completed conditional constructs (if—else) and logical operators (AND, OR, etc.). However, there was a time when such possibilities were not available. For instance, consider Fortran or early versions of Basic. For these, unconditional jump operators, such as goto, were helpful, despite strong dislike by ardent supporters of high style in programming. However, the machine language is entirely built on the basis of conditional and unconditional jumps. Like it or not, it is impossible to do without them if you need to check some condition.

Simple Constructs

Consider the simple conditional construct shown in Listing 3.62.

Listing 3.62. Simple conditional construct

```
#include <stdio.h>
void main()
{
        int a, b;
```

```
        scanf("%d", &a);

        scanf("%d", &b);

        if(a >= b)

                printf("a >= b\n");

        else

                printf("a < b\n");

}
```

After compiling the program presented in Listing 3.62 using Microsoft Visual Studio and loading it into the IDA Pro disassembler, you'll obtain the code shown in Listing 3.63.

Listing 3.63. Disassembled code of the program shown in Listing 3.62

```
.text:00401000  _main           proc near         ; CODE XREF: start + 16E↓p
.text:00401000         var_8  = dword ptr -8
.text:00401000         var_4  = dword ptr -4
.text:00401000                 push    ebp
.text:00401001                 mov     ebp, esp
.text:00401003                 sub     esp, 8
.text:00401006                 lea     eax, [ebp + var_4]
.text:00401009                 push    eax
.text:0040100A                 push    offset unk_4080FC
.text:0040100F                 call    _scanf
.text:00401014                 add     esp, 8
.text:00401017                 lea     ecx, [ebp + var_8]
.text:0040101A                 push    ecx
.text:0040101B                 push    offset unk_408100
.text:00401020                 call    _scanf
.text:00401025                 add     esp, 8
.text:00401028                 mov     edx, [ebp + var_4]
.text:0040102B                 cmp     edx, [ebp + var_8]
.text:0040102E                 jl      short loc_40103F
.text:00401030                 push    offset aAB    ; "a >= b\n"
.text:00401035                 call    _printf
```

```
.text:0040103A                  add      esp, 4
.text:0040103D                  jmp      short loc_40104C
.text:0040103F  loc_40103F:                          ; CODE XREF: _main + 2E↑j
.text:0040103F                  push     offset aAB_0 ; "a<b\n"
.text:00401044                  call     _printf
.text:00401049                  add      esp, 4
.text:0040104C  loc_40104C:                          ; CODE XREF: _main + 3D↑j
.text:0040104C                  xor      eax, eax
.text:0040104E                  mov      esp, ebp
.text:00401050                  pop      ebp
.text:00401051                  retn
.text:00401051  _main           endp
```

Pay special attention to the way, in which the scanf function is called. Because its argument requires a pointer to a variable, lea eax, [ebp + var_4]/push eax sends the pointer to the var_4 variable into the stack. Note that Microsoft's compiler treats the var_8 variable in the same way.

The second important issue is how the complete conditional construct is implemented in the executable code. Schematically, this can be represented as shown in Listing 3.64.

Listing 3.64. Implementation of a complete conditional structure in the executable code

```
jl   l1
// a >= b
...
jmp  l2
l1:
// a < b
...
l2:
```

As you can see, to implement a complete conditional construct one conditional jump and one unconditional jump are required. Note that the conditional jump command corresponds to the condition that is the negation of the one in the original program text. If you remove the `else` branch (the incomplete conditional construct) from the program, then the unconditional jump command (`jmp 12`) will be missing from the executable code. Finally, if you replace the `a >= b` condition with `a > b`, then the executable code will contain the `jle` (jump less or equal) command instead of the `jl` command. If the source program uses the less-or-equal condition, for example, `a =< b`, then the executable code will contain `jg` or `jge` commands (for the less condition). The fact that instead of a direct condition its negation is checked in the executable code isn't an axiom. Another approach is possible (Listing 3.65).

Listing 3.65. Alternative implementation of complete conditional constructs

---

```
jge  11
// a < b
...
jmp 12
11:
// a >= b
...
12:
```

As you can see, there isn't anything abnormal in this approach. You can encounter it when analyzing the code created by some compilers. However, I'd like to point out again that decompilation isn't your main goal. You must try to understand the program's operating logic. For this purpose, you do not need to know exactly, which source code was used to generate a specific fragment of the disassembled code.

If variables used within the program being studied are unsigned, then instead of `jl` (`jle`) the `jb` (`jbe`) commands are used, and the `jg` (`jge`) commands are replaced with `ja` (`jae`). In case of the check for equality (`==`) or inequality (`!=`), the `jnz` and `jz` commands are used, respectively. Note that in the previously considered example, the CMP command was used in the executable code for checking the `a > b` condition. This is obvious. This command is also used for checking other conditions: `<`, `<=`, `>=`, `==`, and `!=`. Everything depends on the conditional check that you'll use later — in other words, on the flag or group of flags that you are checking. If you check for equality (or inequality) to zero, the TEST command is often used instead of CMP.

Recall that in many programming languages the `false` value corresponds to 0, and `true` corresponds to some nonzero value (1, for example). In this relation, it is instructive to consider a construct typical for the C++ language (Listing 3.66).

Listing 3.66. Typical C++ construct

```
if(k = (a == b)))
{
} else
{
}
```

It is clear that the `k` variable will be assigned one of the following two values: 1 (if a is equal to b) or 0 (if a is not equal to b). Here is a fragment of the executable code compiled using the Microsoft Visual C++ compiler (Listing 3.67).

Listing 3.67. Executable code generated using Microsoft Visual C++ (Listing 3.66)

```
; Load the a variable into the EAX register.
mov      eax, [ebp + var_4]
; Compute the difference a - b; the variables remain unchanged.
sub      eax, [ebp + var_8]
; Sign inversion is needed to check whether the EAX register contains 0.
neg      eax
; Subtraction takes into account the sign.
; If the EAX register contains a nonzero value,
; then the subtraction result in EAX will be -1;
; otherwise, the EAX register would contain 0.
sbb      eax, eax
; If the EAX register contained -1, the inc command
; will produce 0 (false); otherwise, the result will be 1 (true).
inc      eax
; The value is assigned to the k variable.
mov      [ebp + var_C], eax
; Jump depends on the result in the EAX register.
```

```
jz        short loc_401058

...

jmp       short loc_401065
loc_401058:

...

loc_401065:

...
```

The algorithm of obtaining the value of the `k` variable is a notable one. As you can see, the `CMP` command is not used in this case. Note that the conditional jump is carried out depending on the value contained in the `EAX` register after the `INC EAX` operation. The result of this operation, contained in the `EAX` register, is either `0` (`false`) or `1` (`true`).

Comparison of real numbers deserves special attention (Listing 3.68).

Listing 3.68. Sample program illustrating comparison of real numbers

```c
#include <stdio.h>
void main()
{
        double a, b;
        scanf("%Lf", &a);
        scanf("%Lf", &b);
        if(a >= b)
                printf("%Lf\n", a);
        else
                printf("%Lf\n", b);
}
```

Listing 3.68 presents a simple program for comparing two real numbers of the `double` type. From the language syntax point of view, the difference between this program and a similar one that compares integer variables is minor and relates only to the format of the `scanf` and `printf` functions. However, comparison of real variables must be principally different from comparison of integer numbers at the level of executable code. Consider Listing 3.69, produced by IDA Pro.

Listing 3.69. Disassembled code of the program in Listing 3.68 created by IDA Pro

```
.text:00401000 _main          proc near              ; CODE XREF: start + 16E↓p
.text:00401000         var_18 = qword ptr -18h
.text:00401000         var_10 = qword ptr -10h
.text:00401000         var_8  = qword ptr -8
.text:00401000                 push    ebp
.text:00401001                 mov     ebp, esp
.text:00401003                 sub     esp, 10h
.text:00401006                 lea     eax, [ebp + var_8]
.text:00401009                 push    eax
.text:0040100A                 push    offset unk_4090FC
.text:0040100F                 call    _scanf
.text:00401014                 add     esp, 8
.text:00401017                 lea     ecx, [ebp + var_10]
.text:0040101A                 push    ecx
.text:0040101B                 push    offset unk_409100
.text:00401020                 call    _scanf
.text:00401025                 add     esp, 8
.text:00401028                 fld     [ebp + var_8]
.text:0040102B                 fcomp   [ebp + var_10]
.text:0040102E                 fnstsw  ax
.text:00401030                 test    ah, 1
.text:00401033                 jnz     short loc_40104D
.text:00401035                 fld     [ebp + var_8]
.text:00401038                 sub     esp, 8
.text:0040103B                 fstp    [esp + 18h + var_18]
.text:0040103E                 push    offset aLf   ; "%Lf\n"
.text:00401043                 call    _printf
.text:00401048                 add     esp, 0Ch
.text:0040104B                 jmp     short loc_401063
.text:0040104D loc_40104D:                           ; CODE XREF: _main + 33↑j
.text:0040104D                 fld     [ebp + var_10]
.text:00401050                 sub     esp, 8
.text:00401053                 fstp    [esp + 18h + var_18]
```

```
.text:00401056                 push     offset aLf_0 ; "%Lf\n"
.text:0040105B                 call     _printf
.text:00401060                 add      esp, 0Ch
.text:00401063   loc_401063:                     ; CODE XREF: _main + 4B↑j
.text:00401063                 xor      eax, eax
.text:00401065                 mov      esp, ebp
.text:00401067                 pop      ebp
.text:00401068                 retn
.text:00401068   _main         endp
```

For the moment, you shouldn't see anything unusual in allocating memory for stack variables. The only issue that deserves special mention is that now variables have the double type and, consequently, take 8 bytes. Arguments of the scanf function are pointers to variables rather than actual variables. Hence, the lea (lea eax, [ebp + var_8]/push eax) commands are used. The use of two registers (EAX and ECX) as temporary variables for storing the pointers to variables for further pushing into the stack has no special meaning. It would be possible to do with only one register.

Starting from the 00401028 address, the really interesting commands are encountered. It is necessary to compare two 8-byte floating-point numbers. Here is the sequence of commands that carries out this comparison (Listing 3.70).

Listing 3.70. Sequence of commands that compares two 8-byte floating-point numbers

```
; Load the a variable into ST(0).
fld     [ebp + var_8]
; Compare the content of ST(0) to var_10 (the b variable).
fcomp   [ebp + var_10]
; Save the status word (SW) in the AX register.
fnstsw  ax
; Check bit 0 of the AH register.
test    ah, 1
; Jump if this bit is set.
jnz     short loc_40104D
...
```

```
jmp      short loc_401063
loc_40104D:

. . .

loc_401063:

. . .
```

Although the preceding fragment is supplied with comments, some notes still have to be made. The `fcomp` command compares two operands, and the result of this comparison is reflected by the `C0`, `C2`, and `C3` flags that correspond to bits 8, 9, and 10 of the status word (see *Section 1.2.3*). Table 3.3 outlines the flag values for different situations of comparison.

Table 3.3. Flag values for different situations of comparison

Checked condition	C3 flag	C2 flag	C0 flag
ST(0) > src	0	0	0
ST(0) < src	0	0	1
ST(0) == src	1	0	0
Operands are incomparable	1	1	1

From this table, it follows that if `C0 == 0`, this corresponds to the >= condition. Hence, the `JNZ` (jump if nonzero) command corresponds to printing the message that the `b` variable is the greatest. Some compilers use different techniques. For instance, a complier may copy the coprocessor flags into the flags register using the `SAHF` command. In this case, the `C0` flag is copied into the `CF` flag, `C2` is copied into `PF`, and `C3` goes into `ZF`. Later, it is possible to use conditional jumps. In the case under consideration, this will be the `JZ` command (instead of `JNZ`). What should you do when checking a strict inequality, such as `a > b`? According to the data provided in Table 3.3, the checking command would appear as follows: `TEST AX, 41H`.

Nested Constructs and Logical Operators

In real-world programming, conditional constructs might contain nested logical constructs (Listing 3.71). Consider how nesting might influence the executable code.

Listing 3.71. Example program containing nested conditional constructs

```
// Searching for the maximum number out of three numbers
#include <stdio.h>
void main()
{
        int a, b, c;
        scanf("%d", &a);
        scanf("%d", &b);
        scanf("%d", &c);
        if(a > b)
        {
                if(a > c) printf("%d\n", a);
                else printf("%d\n", c);
        } else
        {
                if(b > c) printf("%d\n", b);
                else printf("%d\n", c);
        }
}
```

The compiler builds the structure of nested conditional constructs according to the same method as the one shown in Listing 3.63. This method is presented in Listing 3.72.

Listing 3.72. Method of nested conditional structures built by the compiler

```
jl l1
// if (1)[i]
// The branch corresponding to a > b
jl l4
// if (2)
// The branch corresponding to a > c
```

---

[i] The number enclosed in parentheses specifies the nesting level.

```
// Output the a value.
...
jmp 12
14:
// else (2)
// The a > c condition is not observed, while the a > b condition is true.
// Output the c value.
...
12:
// The end of the if operator of the first nesting level
jmp 13
// The start of the else operator of the first nesting level
11:
// else (1)
// The a > b condition hasn't been observed.
jl 15
// if (2)
// The b > c condition is true, while the a > b condition is false.
// Output the b value.
...
jmp 13
15:
// else (2)
// The b > c is condition false, and the a > b condition is false.
// Output the c value.
...
13:
// End of the nested construct
```

Carefully consider the method presented in Listing 3.72. As you can see, it is clearly mapped to the method present in the source program (see Listing 3.71). At the same time, any complete conditional construct can be easily converted into incomplete conditional construct by simply discarding an appropriate jmp command.

Contemporary programming languages use OR and AND logical operators instead of large numbers of nested conditional constructs. Using these logical operators, combined conditions are built. In real-world programming, such combined conditions are sophisticated. Kris Kaspersky, in his excellent book *Hacker Debugging Uncovered*, suggests the diagrams technique for analyzing executable code resulting from complex conditional constructs. This approach can be helpful when reconstructing a complex conditional construct. In my opinion, however, it is not always necessary to reconstruct the source code to understand the conditions implemented in the executable code. After all, programmers often use logical operators more for making the code compact than for making their programs readable. This doesn't improve understanding of their programs. Furthermore, most programmers use both logical operators and nested conditional constructs, which makes it problematic to recover source constructs.

Consider the example in Listing 3.73.

Listing 3.73. Example illustrating recognition of logical operators

```
.text:00401000 _main         proc near          ; CODE XREF: start + 16E↓p
.text:00401000      var_C  = dword ptr -0Ch
.text:00401000      var_8  = dword ptr -8
.text:00401000      var_4  = dword ptr -4
.text:00401000           push     ebp
.text:00401001           mov      ebp, esp
.text:00401003           sub      esp, 0Ch
.text:00401006           lea      eax, [ebp + var_4]
.text:00401009           push     eax
.text:0040100A           push     offset unk_4080FC
.text:0040100F           call     _scanf
.text:00401014           add      esp, 8
.text:00401017           lea      ecx, [ebp + var_8]
.text:0040101A           push     ecx
.text:0040101B           push     offset unk_408100
.text:00401020           call     _scanf
.text:00401025           add      esp, 8
.text:00401028           lea      edx, [ebp + var_C]
.text:0040102B           push     edx
.text:0040102C           push     offset unk_408104
.text:00401031           call     _scanf
```

```
.text:00401036                 add     esp, 8
.text:00401039                 mov     eax, [ebp + var_4]
.text:0040103C                 cmp     eax, [ebp + var_8]
.text:0040103F                 jle     short loc_401047
.text:00401041                 cmp     [ebp + var_8], 0
.text:00401045                 jg      short loc_401055
.text:00401047  loc_401047:                          ; CODE XREF: _main + 3F↑j
.text:00401047                 mov     ecx, [ebp + var_4]
.text:0040104A                 cmp     ecx, [ebp + var_C]
.text:0040104D                 jz      short loc_401055
.text:0040104F                 cmp     [ebp + var_C], 0
.text:00401053                 jnz     short loc_401064
.text:00401055  loc_401055:                          ; CODE XREF: _main + 45↑j
.text:00401055                 push    offset aYes  ; "Yes!\n"
.text:0040105A                 call    _printf
.text:0040105F                 add     esp, 4
.text:00401062                 jmp     short loc_401071
.text:00401064  loc_401064:                          ; CODE XREF: _main + 53↑j
.text:00401064                 push    offset aNo   ; "No!\n"
.text:00401069                 call    _printf
.text:0040106E                 add     esp, 4
.text:00401071  loc_401071:                          ; CODE XREF: _main + 62↑j
.text:00401071                 xor     eax, eax
.text:00401073                 mov     esp, ebp
.text:00401075                 pop     ebp
.text:00401076                 retn
.text:00401076  _main          endp
```

Lots of similar listings have already been provided in this book. Thus, you'll easily determine that three stack variables of the integer type are used here (12 bytes are reserved, and three variables of the same type are used). The input of their values using the scanf library function also isn't anything new. The most interesting are the conditional jumps. First, consider the code in general. What would you see? First, all conditional jumps can produce one of the two possible results: printing the "Yes" string (the 00401055 address) or the "No" string (the 00401064 address) using the `printf` function. Consequently, to all appearances you are dealing with the `if-else` conditional construct. Combine all conditions that produce the first result and, accordingly, combine all conditions that lead to the second result. Thus, the jump to the `00401055` address takes place when `var_4 > var_8` and `var_8 > 0`. This condition is an obvious candidate for the role of the following combined condition: `a > b && b > 0`. Let it be designated as condition 1. Because the same result is produced when all conditions except for condition 1 are satisfied, it is possible to assume that you are dealing with the OR logical operator (although, it is not necessary to take this into account to gain a sound understanding of the process). The same result is obtained if the `var_4 = var_C` condition is satisfied. Let it be condition 2. Finally, the same result will be produced if `var_C = 0`. This will be condition 3. In all other cases, the code fragment starting from the `00401064` address is executed. After completing all of these considerations, it is possible to write a conditional construct using the AND and OR logical operators. However, this won't improve your understanding of the code, because you have already understood the operating logic of this fragment.

Thus, what conclusion can be drawn on the basis of these considerations? This conclusion is as follows: Conditions related to one another using logical AND can be easily recognized. Considering them as a combined condition, it is also possible to understand the operating logic of all other conditions (related to the first one using logical OR).

Conditional Constructs without Jumps

It is necessary to mention that conditional and unconditional jumps reset the command queue, which slows down the program execution. Bear this in mind when writing a program in Assembly. Avoid using jumps whenever it is possible to do without them. Instead, it is possible to use the following sets of commands: SETcc r/m (conditional setting of the first bit) and CMOVX (conditional data sending). These commands are described in *Chapter 1* (see Table 1.2). Advanced compilers, such as Visual C++, are aware of this capability. Unfortunately, I failed to make this compiler use any of the conditional move commands. On the other hand, it turned out that Visual C++ actively uses conditional bit setting commands.

The idea of using the commands for conditionally setting the first bit of the byte is trivial. Let some register (for example, EAX) contain the 0 value in the beginning. Then, after using the CMP command, it is possible to use one of the conditional bit setting commands, for instance, the SETLE command (set if lower). After that, execute DEC EAX. Now, if the condition has been satisfied, EAX contains 0;

otherwise, the value contained in EAX is equal to −1 (FFFFFFFFH). If the operand is equal to 0, then the AND instruction with any value of the second operand won't change its content. For instance, consider the fragment in Listing 3.74.

Listing 3.74. Code fragment illustrating the use of the conditional bit setting commands

```
.text:00401013          xor       eax, eax
.text:00401015          cmp       edx, 0Ah
.text:00401018          setle     al
.text:0040101B          dec       eax
.text:0040101C          and       eax, 0FFFFF200h
.text:00401021          add       eax, 1000h
```

As can be easily seen, if the EDX <= 0 condition is satisfied, the EAX register contains the 1000H value; otherwise, it will contain the 200H value. This executable code is equivalent to the if(a > 10) b = 0x200; else b = 0x1000; operator. This code is created by Microsoft's compiler if the "create fast code" option is set.

Choice Operators

As a rule, a long sequence of incomplete conditional operators is replaced with the choice operator. Listing 3.75 provides a typical example of using the choice operator. Consider what Microsoft's compiler would do to this code (Listing 3.76).

Listing 3.75. Typical example of using the choice operator

```
#include <stdio.h>
void main()
{
        char a;
        scanf("%c", &a);
        switch(a)
        {
                case 'A':
                        printf("A\n");
                        break;
```

```
                case 'B':
                        printf("B\n");
                        break;
                default:
                        printf("?\n");
        }
}
```

Listing 3.76. Disassembled listing (Listing 3.74) compiled using Microsoft Visual C++

```
.text:00401000  _main       proc near        ; CODE XREF: start + 16E↓p
.text:00401000        var_8  = byte ptr -8
.text:00401000        var_1  = byte ptr -1
.text:00401000               push    ebp
.text:00401001               mov     ebp, esp
.text:00401003               sub     esp, 8
.text:00401006               lea     eax, [ebp - 1]
.text:00401009               push    eax
.text:0040100A               push    offset unk_4080FC
.text:0040100F               call    _scanf
.text:00401014               add     esp, 8
.text:00401017               mov     cl, [ebp + var_1]
.text:0040101A               mov     [ebp + var_8], cl
.text:0040101D               cmp     [ebp + var_8], 41h
.text:00401021               jz      short loc_40102B
.text:00401023               cmp     [ebp + var_8], 42h
.text:00401027               jz      short loc_40103A
.text:00401029               jmp     short loc_401049
.text:0040102B  loc_40102B:                   ; CODE XREF: _main + 21↑j
.text:0040102B               push    offset byte_408100
.text:00401030               call    _printf
.text:00401035               add     esp, 4
.text:00401038               jmp     short loc_401056
.text:0040103A  loc_40103A:                   ; CODE XREF: _main + 27↑j
```

```
.text:0040103A                push    offset unk_408104
.text:0040103F                call    _printf
.text:00401044                add     esp, 4
.text:00401047                jmp     short loc_401056
.text:00401049  loc_401049:                   ; CODE XREF: _main + 29↑j
.text:00401049                push    offset unk_408108
.text:0040104E                call    _printf
.text:00401053                add     esp, 4
.text:00401056  loc_401056:                   ; CODE XREF: _main + 38↑j
.text:00401056                ; _main + 47↑j
.text:00401056                xor     eax, eax
.text:00401058                mov     esp, ebp
.text:0040105A                pop     ebp
.text:0040105B                retn
.text:0040105B  _main         endp
```

This code is interesting because of a certain redundancy. Two stack variables are defined in the main procedure. The var_1 variable apparently is intended for storing the a variable defined in the program source code (see Listing 3.75), because it is used with the scanf function. The var_8 variable is an auxiliary one. It is used for comparison in commands such as cmp [ebp + var_8], 42h. It is possible to use a single variable, var_1. By the way, note that two single-bit variables are stored in two adjacent 4-byte blocks. This is because of the requirement to meet the data alignment by the 4-byte boundary.

The method for checking conditions is bulky. This is because the check tests whether the condition is satisfied. The method in Listing 3.77 would be more elegant.

Listing 3.77. Alternative and more elegant method for checking conditions

```
cmp     [ebp + var_8], 41h
jnz     l1
...
jmp     _break
l1:
cmp     [ebp + var_8], 42h
```

```
jnz      l2:
...
jmp      _break
l2:
//default
...
_break:
```

Finally, you can encounter the approach shown in Listing 3.78. In particular, Borland C++ 5.0, as well as the Delphi compiler, processes the choice operator in this way. The Microsoft C++ compiler also behaves in this way, provided that the "create fast code" option is set.

Listing 3.78. Processing the typical choice operator

```
mov      dl, [ebp + var_1]
sub      dl, 41h
jz       l1
dec      dl
jz       l2
jmp      l3
l1:
...
jmp      l3
l2:
...
l3:
...
```

On the basis of Listing 3.78, the principle of this approach is easily understandable. The parameter of the switch operator is placed into some temporary variable, which might also be a register. Assume that the values for equality, to which the variable will be checked, are a1, a2, ..., an (in ascending order). The check is carried out as follows: First, the a1 value is subtracted from the temporary variable and the variable is tested for equality to zero. Later, the values a2 – a1, a3 – a2, etc., are subtracted from the variable. After each subtraction, the variable is tested for equality to zero. This approach is especially efficient when all differences (a2 – a1, a3 – a2, etc.) are equal to one. In this case, it is convenient to use the DEC processor command.

3.2.3. Loops

Looping algorithms are a kind of branching in which, depending on the condition, a specific program fragment is executed multiple times. At the level of Assembly language, a conditional or unconditional backward jump is assumed to the instructions with smaller addresses. Contemporary disassemblers and debuggers trace such jumps and mark them in the disassembled text.

Simple Loops

Consider all possible variants of loop organization in Assembly language. This would allow you to easily understand how contemporary compilers treat loops. A typical loop structure is shown in Listing 3.79.

Listing 3.79. Typical loop structure

```
. . .
; Quite often, the JMP L1 instruction is encountered here.
_beg:
; In particular, the commands changing the loop parameter
; appear here.
. . .
CMP EAX, EBX ; Or, perhaps, check for some other condition.
JZ  _end     ; Or, perhaps, some other conditional jump
             ; beyond the loop limits.
; The loop body starts here.
L1:
. . .
; The loop body - any number of commands.
JMP _beg
_end:
```

Listing 3.79 demonstrates a typical loop structure that you can encounter when studying the code generated by various compilers. Note that the jump to the start of the loop body might be present (JMP L1). If such a jump is present, then the loop body will be executed at least once. This corresponds to the postcondition loop ideology. If there is no jump to the loop body, then in general the loop body does not execute even once. This corresponds to the precondition loop ideology.

A typical example of a postcondition loop is presented in Listing 3.80.

Listing 3.80. Typical example of a postcondition loop

```
...
_beg:
; Start of the loop body
...
CMP EAX, EBX  ; Or check for some other condition.
JZ  _beg      ; Or some other conditional jump to the start of the loop
...
```

In this case, you are dealing with a typical example of the postcondition loop. However, it would be an error to consider that the loop type specified in the high-level programming language would automatically correspond to the loop type in the executable code. Contemporary compilers do not simply transform operators of high-level programming languages to machine commands but sometimes inventively reconstruct them (for some cases, the word *inventively* should be enclosed in quotation marks). Thus, if you use a precondition loop in your program but variable values are guaranteed to ensure that the loop will be executed at least once, the compiler can use the postcondition loop in the machine code.

The FOR loops present in the main algorithmic languages are variants of precondition loops. One or more parameters simply participate in formulating the condition. Parameters of such loops, when executing the loop body (or before the next iteration) obtain some constant increment (which might be either positive or negative). The presence of a variable, which is incremented or decremented by a constant value at each iteration, is an important indication that you are dealing with the FOR loop.

After this brief introduction, it is natural to consider several practical examples. For instance, Listing 3.81 provides the simplest example of using the FOR loop.

Listing 3.81. Simple example of using the FOR loop

```c
#include <stdio.h>
void main()
{
    int b = 10;
    for(int i = 0; i < 100; i++)
            printf("%d\n", b);

}
```

Consider how the Microsoft Visual C++ compiler translates this program, pro vided that the "no optimization" option was chosen for compilation (Listing 3.82).

Listing 3.82. Disassembled text compiled using Microsoft Visual C++ without optimization

```
.text:00401000   _main        proc near        ; CODE XREF: start + 16E↓p
.text:00401000        var_8  = dword ptr -8
.text:00401000        var_4  = dword ptr -4
.text:00401000               push    ebp
.text:00401001               mov     ebp, esp
.text:00401003               sub     esp, 8
.text:00401006               mov     [ebp + var_4], 0Ah
.text:0040100D               mov     [ebp + var_8], 0
.text:00401014               jmp     short loc_40101F
.text:00401016   loc_401016:                   ; CODE XREF: _main + 36↓j
.text:00401016               mov     eax, [ebp + var_8]
.text:00401019               add     eax, 1
.text:0040101C               mov     [ebp + var_8], eax
.text:0040101F   loc_40101F:                   ; CODE XREF: _main + 14↑j
.text:0040101F               cmp     [ebp + var_8], 64h
.text:00401023               jge     short loc_401038
.text:00401025               mov     ecx, [ebp + var_4]
.text:00401028               push    ecx
.text:00401029               push    offset unk_4060FC
.text:0040102E               call    _printf
```

```
.text:00401033                add     esp, 8
.text:00401036                jmp     short loc_401016
.text:00401038  loc_401038:                     ; CODE XREF: _main + 23↑j
.text:00401038                xor     eax, eax
.text:0040103A                mov     esp, ebp
.text:0040103C                pop     ebp
.text:0040103D                retn
.text:0040103D  _main         endp
```

First, I'd like to draw your attention to local variables. Obviously, var_4 stands for the b variable. As relates to var_8, it is nothing but the loop parameter. Also, note the mov eax, [ebp + var_8]/add ax, 1/mov [ebp + var_8], eax commands. They immediately attract attention and clearly indicate the FOR loop.

Note that Listing 3.82 corresponds exactly to the program operating method provided in Listing 3.81. The jmp short loc_40101F jump reflects that the initial value of the loop parameter must be 0, and the exit condition of the loop is the equality of the loop parameter to 100. When implementing such an algorithm in Assembly, it would be possible to do without this jump by simply assigning the initial value of −1 to the loop parameter.

From Listing 3.82, it is clear that you are dealing with the precondition loop. However, consider what the result would be if you instructed the compiler to produce compact executable code (Listing 3.83).

Listing 3.83. Disassembled text (Listing 3.81) compiled using the "compact code" option

```
.text:00401000  _main         proc near          ; CODE XREF: start + 16E↓p
.text:00401000                push    esi
.text:00401001                push    64h
.text:00401003                pop     esi
.text:00401004  loc_401004:                      ; CODE XREF: _main + 13↓j
.text:00401004                push    0Ah
.text:00401006                push    offset unk_4060FC
.text:0040100B                call    _printf
.text:00401010                dec     esi
.text:00401011                pop     ecx
```

```
.text:00401012                      pop     ecx
.text:00401013                      jnz     short loc_401004
.text:00401015                      xor     eax, eax
.text:00401017                      pop     esi
.text:00401018                      retn
.text:00401018   _main              endp
```

Listing 3.83 provides a typical example of the postcondition loop. Note that the role of the loop parameter is delegated to the ESI register. At the same time, instead of incrementing the parameter this code decrements it to make it possible to use the condition of comparing this parameter to zero. This technique is often used by the Microsoft Visual C++ compiler to turn a precondition loop to a postcondition loop. In this case, the parameter increment is replaced with the decrement. An interesting issue is that if the for loop is replaced with the while or do-while loop and the "create compact code" optimization option is preserved, the result will be exactly the same as the one shown in Listing 3.82.

Consider how the program shown in Listing 3.81 is treated by the Borland C++ compiler (Listing 3.84).

Listing 3.84. Disassembled text (Listing 3.81) compiled using the Borland C++ compiler

```
.text:00401108   _main              proc near          ; DATA XREF: .data:0040A0B8↓o
.text:00401108            argc     = dword ptr  8
.text:00401108            argv     = dword ptr  0Ch
.text:00401108            envp     = dword ptr  10h
.text:00401108                      push    ebp
.text:00401109                      mov     ebp, esp
.text:0040110B                      push    ebx
.text:0040110C                      push    esi
.text:0040110D                      mov     esi, 0Ah
.text:00401112                      xor     ebx, ebx
.text:00401114   loc_401114:                            ; CODE XREF: _main + 1E↓j
.text:00401114                      push    esi
.text:00401115                      push    offset format    ; Format
.text:0040111A                      call    _printf
```

```
.text:0040111F                 add     esp, 8
.text:00401122                 inc     ebx
.text:00401123                 cmp     ebx, 64h
.text:00401126                 jl      short loc_401114
.text:00401128                 pop     esi
.text:00401129                 pop     ebx
.text:0040112A                 pop     ebp
.text:0040112B                 retn
.text:0040112B    _main        endp
```

The most interesting issue is that the Borland C++ v. 5.0 compiler interprets the same program slightly differently: The precondition loop is transformed to the postcondition loop; however, the loop parameter continues to be incremented (see Listing 3.84). Moreover, note that Microsoft's compiler is more accurate when working with registers: It uses only one register (ESI) that must be stored in the stack.

Loop Optimization

One type of loop optimization was covered in the previous section: conversion of the precondition loop to the postcondition loop. In addition, it was shown that the Microsoft Visual C++ compiler can replace the loop parameter increment with its decrement so that the equality of this parameter to zero is the loop termination condition. However, there are even more efficient methods of loop optimization used by advanced compilers. Here, I'll cover the two most important techniques.

Computation at Compile Time

The programmer often doesn't notice that the result obtained in the course of executing a looping algorithm is self-evident. Advanced compilers, including Microsoft Visual C++, recognize such situations and replace looping algorithms with ready-to-use results. Consider the simple example provided in Listing 3.85.

Listing 3.85. Simple demonstration of computation at compile time optimization

```
#include <stdio.h>
void main()
{
```

```
int i = 0, s = 0, k = 5;
for(i = 0; i < k; i++) s = s + i;
printf("%d\n", s);
}
```

Principally, it is not difficult to evaluate the result of computing the s value: It will be ten. The Microsoft Visual C++ compiler easily solves this problem. Consider the code that it will produce as the result of compiling the program in Listing 3.85 using the "create fast code" option (Listing 3.86).

Listing 3.86. Disassembled text of the program in Listing 3.85

```
.text:00401000 _main       proc near        ; CODE XREF: start + 16E↓p
.text:00401000             push    0Ah
.text:00401002             push    offset unk_4060FC
.text:00401007             call    _printf
.text:0040100C             add     esp, 8
.text:0040100F             xor     eax, eax
.text:00401011             retn
.text:00401011 _main       endp
```

In Listing 3.86, there are no loops. This reconfirms that the compilation process is generally irreversible. However, this is not related to understanding the program operating logic.

Loop Unwinding

Loop unwinding (also known as loop unrolling) is a technique based on the principles of optimizing memory access.

Listing 3.87 presents a test program demonstrating the loop unwinding technique.

Listing 3.87. Test program demonstrating the loop unwinding technique

```
#include <stdio.h>
void main()
{
        int a[100];
```

```
    int i = 0, s = 0;
    for(i = 0; i < 100; i++) a[i] = i;
    for(i = 0; i < 100; i++) s += a[i];
    printf("%d\n", s);
}
```

Listing 3.87 presents a program using the a array. Compile this program using the Microsoft Visual C++ compiler with the "create fast code" option specified. The disassembled text of the executable code of this program is shown in Listing 3.88.

Listing 3.88. Disassembled text of the executable code of the program in Listing 3.87

```
.text:00401000  _main          proc near          ; CODE XREF: start + 16E↓p
.text:00401000        var_194 = dword ptr -194h
.text:00401000        var_190 = dword ptr -190h
.text:00401000        var_18C = dword ptr -18Ch
.text:00401000        var_188 = dword ptr -188h
.text:00401000        var_184 = dword ptr -184h
.text:00401000        var_180 = dword ptr -180h
.text:00401000               sub     esp, 190h
.text:00401006               xor     ecx, ecx
.text:00401008               xor     eax, eax
.text:0040100A               lea     ebx, [ebx + 0]
.text:00401010  loc_401010:                    ; CODE XREF: _main + 17↓j
.text:00401010               mov     [esp + eax*4 + 190h + var_190], eax
.text:00401013               inc     eax
.text:00401014               cmp     eax, 64h
.text:00401017               jl      short loc_401010
.text:00401019               xor     eax, eax
.text:0040101B               push    esi
.text:0040101C               lea     esp, [esp+0]
.text:00401020  loc_401020:                    ; CODE XREF: _main + 3E↓j
.text:00401020               mov     esi, [esp + eax*4 + 194h + var_184]
.text:00401024               mov     edx, [esp + eax*4 + 194h + var_180]
```

```
.text:00401028                 add      edx, esi
.text:0040102A                 add      edx, [esp + eax*4 + 194h + var_188]
.text:0040102E                 add      edx, [esp + eax*4 + 194h + var_18C]
.text:00401032                 add      edx, [esp + eax*4 + 194h + var_190]
.text:00401036                 add      eax, 5
.text:00401039                 add      ecx, edx
.text:0040103B                 cmp      eax, 64h
.text:0040103E                 jl       short loc_401020
.text:00401040                 push     ecx
.text:00401041                 push     offset unk_4060FC
.text:00401046                 call     _printf
.text:0040104B                 add      esp, 8
.text:0040104E                 xor      eax, eax
.text:00401050                 pop      esi
.text:00401051                 add      esp, 190h
.text:00401057                 retn
.text:00401057  _main          endp
```

For storing a local array, 190h bytes are allocated (which is equal to 400) — in other words, 4 bytes per element.

I'd like to immediately draw your attention to two commands: lea ebx, [ebx] and lea esp, [esp]. Neither command changes the contents of the registers; the compiler has inserted them to optimize the execution speed. Earlier in this chapter, I mentioned the optimization technique of command pairing (see the comments that follow Listing 3.2). In this case, the compiler adds commands that do not mean anything but correctly divide the commands by pairs.

The loop, in which the values of array elements are specified, is simple. It is located in the listing from addresses 00401010 to 00401017. Note that addressing of local variables in the stack is not done using the EBP register for the reasons of optimization. On the contrary, the ESP register is used for addressing of local variables. The EAX register plays the role of the i variable (this is an example of using a register variable). Note that in this loop the compiler doesn't use the technique of replacing the loop parameter increment with the decrement, which was described earlier. This is because the loop parameter also plays the role of the array index.

Now, consider the next loop, located from the 00401020 to the 0040103E address. The goal of this loop is to sum all array elements. The sum must be accumulated in the s variable (see Listing 3.87). As can be easily seen, the role of the s variable is delegated to the ECX register (for instance, this can be noticed by the call to the printf function). The most important detail is that the loop is preceded by the PUSH ESI command. The reason for the presence of this command is obvious: The ESI register is further used as a temporary variable, and this register must not be changed after execution of the main function. However, do not forget that addressing is relative to the ESP register and the compiler later corrects the addressing of the array elements. Thus, when computing the array index, it is necessary to subtract one (or to subtract four when computing the element address). The result will be as shown in Listing 3.89.

Listing 3.89. Computing array elements

```
[esp + eax*4 + 194h + var_184] = [esp + eax*4 + 4*4], which corresponds to a[i + 3]

[esp + eax*4 + 194h + var_180] = [esp + eax*4 + 5*4], which corresponds to a[i + 4]

[esp + eax*4 + 194h + var_188] = [esp + eax*4 + 3*4], which corresponds to a[i + 2]

[esp + eax*4 + 194h + var_18C] = [esp + eax*4 + 2*4], which corresponds to a[i + 1]

[esp + eax*4 + 194h + var_190] = [esp + eax*4 + 1*4], which corresponds to a[i]
```

In the beginning, the a[i + 3] and a[i + 4] elements are added, and the result is loaded into the EDX register. Then the a[i + 2], a[i + 1] and a[i] elements are added to the sum. The resulting sum is added to the ECX register, which, as you know, is the s variable. Finally, the index and the loop parameter are increased by five instead of one. Thus, it is possible to state that the compiler has implemented the loop in Listing 3.90.

Listing 3.90. Loop implemented by the compiler

```
for(i = 0; i < 100; i += 5)
{
        s = s + a[i];
        s = s + a[i + 1];
        s = s + a[i + 2];
        s = s + a[i + 3];
        s = s + a[i + 4];

}
```

From the algorithmic point of view, this loop is the full equivalent of the loop in Listing 3.87. From the optimization point of view, it implements *loop unwinding*, which allows you to considerably speed up program execution.

Nested Loops and Loops with Complex Exit Conditions

In the previous section, I considered executable code structures corresponding to the simplest loops. However, looping algorithms might be complicated by the following factors:

- ❑ Loop nesting
- ❑ Complex exit condition
- ❑ Auxiliary loop control operators, such as break and continue

Consider the following two examples. The first example contains simultaneously complex exit condition and auxiliary loop control operators (Listing 3.91). I intentionally did not provide the source code of the C++ program here, because your main goal is to understand the code operating logic, not to discover how the compiler translated the program source code into the executable code.

Listing 3.91. Simultaneous complex loop exit condition and auxiliary loop control operators

```
.text:00401000 _main          proc near          ; CODE XREF: start + 16E↓p
.text:00401000        var_C  = dword ptr -0Ch
.text:00401000        var_8  = dword ptr -8
.text:00401000        var_4  = dword ptr -4
.text:00401000               push    ebp
.text:00401001               mov     ebp, esp
.text:00401003               sub     esp, 0Ch
.text:00401006               mov     [ebp + var_4], 0
.text:0040100D               mov     [ebp + var_C], 0
.text:00401014               mov     [ebp + var_8], 0
.text:0040101B               jmp     short loc_401026
.text:0040101D loc_40101D:                        ; CODE XREF: _main + 51↓j
.text:0040101D                                    ; _main + 74↓j
.text:0040101D               mov     eax, [ebp + var_8]
.text:00401020               add     eax, 1
```

```
.text:00401023                    mov      [ebp + var_8], eax
.text:00401026  loc_401026:                    ; CODE XREF: _main + 1B↑j
.text:00401026                    cmp      [ebp + var_8], 2710h
.text:0040102D                    jge      short loc_401076
.text:0040102F                    cmp      [ebp + var_4], 0C350h
.text:00401036                    jge      short loc_401076
.text:00401038                    mov      ecx, [ebp + var_4]
.text:0040103B                    add      ecx, [ebp + var_C]
.text:0040103E                    add      ecx, [ebp + var_8]
.text:00401041                    mov      [ebp + var_4], ecx
.text:00401044                    mov      [ebp + var_4], 1Eh
.text:0040104B                    cmp      [ebp + var_4], 0
.text:0040104F                    jz       short loc_401053
.text:00401051                    jmp      short loc_40101D
.text:00401053  loc_401053:                    ; CODE XREF: _main + 4F↑j
.text:00401053                    mov      eax, [ebp + var_4]
.text:00401056                    cdq
.text:00401057                    idiv     [ebp + var_8]
.text:0040105A                    mov      [ebp + var_C], eax
.text:0040105D                    cmp      [ebp + var_C], 64h
.text:00401061                    jnz      short loc_401065
.text:00401063                    jmp      short loc_401076
.text:00401065  loc_401065:                    ; CODE XREF: _main + 61↑j
.text:00401065                    mov      edx, [ebp + var_C]
.text:00401068                    mov      [ebp + var_C], edx
.text:0040106B                    mov      eax, [ebp + var_C]
.text:0040106E                    add      eax, 1
.text:00401071                    mov      [ebp + var_C], eax
.text:00401074                    jmp      short loc_40101D
.text:00401076  loc_401076:                    ; CODE XREF: _main + 2D↑j
.text:00401076                                   ; _main + 36↑j ...
.text:00401076                    xor      eax, eax
.text:00401078                    mov      esp, ebp
.text:0040107A                    pop      ebp
.text:0040107B                    retn
.text:0040107B  _main             endp
```

First, consider the fragment located from the `0040101D` to the `00401023` address. This is a typical loop header, or, to be precise, the part of the loop that increments the value of the loop parameter. Accordingly, the entry point into the loop is below this fragment. Entry into the loop is executed by the `jmp short loc_401026` command. You have already encountered such fragments. Thus, the start of the loop is identified clearly: This is the `loc_40101D` label. When viewing the lower part of the listing, pay attention to the `jmp short loc_40101D` command. Because below it there are no commands that would jump to labels between the `0040101D` and the `00401074` addresses, it is possible to assume that this is the last command of the loop. Note that principally the loop under consideration could be nested into another loop; however, the current analysis doesn't relate to this issue. Thus, the loop boundaries have been identified.

Another question arises: What are the loop exit conditions? In essence, it is not important whether this condition is written in the loop header or the exit is carried out by the `break` operator. The issue that does matter is that the exit from the loop is by the `00401076` address. Thus, you'll see the commands in Listing 3.92.

Listing 3.92. Commands for loop exit

```
.text:0040102D                jge      short loc_401076

...

.text:00401036                jge      short loc_401076

...

.text:00401063                jmp      short loc_401076
```

The last jump is slightly below the first two and takes place if the `var_C` variable is equal to `64h` — in other words, to 100. To all appearances, this is the exit by the `break` operator. The first two jumps correspond to the loop header and to the logical AND condition. Thus, without any trouble it is possible to determine that the loop execution condition can be written as `var_8 < 2710h && var_4 < c350h`. Note that the `var_8` variable is the loop parameter (see addresses `0040101D`–`00401023` in Listing 3.91). In essence, only the role of the commands shown in Listing 3.93 needs to be clarified.

Listing 3.93. Commands whose role in the loop structure needs to be clarified

---

```
.text:0040104B            cmp      [ebp + var_4], 0
.text:0040104F            jz       short loc_401053
.text:00401051            jmp      short loc_40101D
```

If the var_4 variable has a nonzero value, then there will be a jump to the start of the loop. This cannot be anything other than the continue operator.

Now, consider an example of nested loops. Manipulations of multidimensional arrays are typical examples of nested loops. Listing 3.94 presents the disassembled code that fills a two-dimensional array. It is necessary to mention that this program was compiled using the Microsoft Visual C++ compiler with the "no optimization" option.

Listing 3.94. Disassembled code that fills a two-dimensional array

---

```
.text:00401000 _main            proc near    ; CODE XREF: start + 16E↓p
.text:00401000      var_198  = dword ptr -198h
.text:00401000      var_194  = dword ptr -194h
.text:00401000      var_190  = dword ptr -190h
.text:00401000              push    ebp
.text:00401001              mov     ebp, esp
.text:00401003              sub     esp, 198h
.text:00401009              mov     [ebp + var_194], 0
.text:00401013              jmp     short loc_401024
.text:00401015 loc_401015:                 ; CODE XREF: _main:loc_401078↓j
.text:00401015              mov     eax, [ebp + var_194]
.text:0040101B              add     eax, 1
.text:0040101E              mov     [ebp + var_194], eax
.text:00401024 loc_401024:                 ; CODE XREF: _main + 13↑j
.text:00401024              cmp     [ebp + var_194], 0Ah
.text:0040102B              jge     short loc_40107A
.text:0040102D              mov     [ebp + var_198], 0
.text:00401037              jmp     short loc_401048
.text:00401039 loc_401039:                 ; CODE XREF: _main + 76↓j
.text:00401039              mov     ecx, [ebp + var_198]
.text:0040103F              add     ecx, 1
.text:00401042              mov     [ebp + var_198], ecx
.text:00401048 loc_401048:                 ; CODE XREF: _main + 37↑j
.text:00401048              cmp     [ebp + var_198], 0Ah
.text:0040104F              jge     short loc_401078
.text:00401051              mov     edx, [ebp + var_194]
```

```
.text:00401057                    add      edx, [ebp + var_198]
.text:0040105D                    mov      eax, [ebp + var_194]
.text:00401063                    imul     eax, 28h
.text:00401066                    lea      ecx, [ebp + eax + var_190]
.text:0040106D                    mov      eax, [ebp + var_198]
.text:00401073                    mov      [ecx + eax*4], edx
.text:00401076                    jmp      short loc_401039
.text:00401078  loc_401078:                ; CODE XREF: _main + 4F↑j
.text:00401078                    jmp      short loc_401015
.text:0040107A  loc_40107A:                ; CODE XREF: _main + 2B↑j
.text:0040107A                    xor      eax, eax
.text:0040107C                    mov      esp, ebp
.text:0040107E                    pop      ebp
.text:0040107F                    retn
.text:0040107F  _main             endp
```

It is not difficult to locate nested loops in this listing. The starting point of the nesting loop at the 00401015 address and the starting point of the nested loop at the 00401039 address can be noticed easily. I'd like to draw your attention to the jmp short loc_401024 and jmp short loc_401048 instructions that carry out initial entries into the nesting and into the nested loops, respectively. Thus, the structure of the nested loops in this case is easy and doesn't require any additional comments.

The most interesting issue here is how the executable code implements the algorithm assigning the value to the two-dimensional array. The parameter of the nesting loop is stored in the var_198 variable. The remaining var_190 variable points to the starting point of the two-dimensional array. Thus, after the mov edx, [ebp + var_194] and add edx, [ebp + var_198] commands, the EDX register will contain the sum of the two index values. If you run a few steps forward to the mov [ecx + eax*4], edx command, which appears like an operator that assigns the value to the array element, it becomes obvious that array elements are assigned values equal to the sum of indexes (the values of the parameters of the nesting and the nested loops). However, look back several commands. What is the meaning of the mov eax, [ebp + var_194]/imul eax, 28h commands? The index value (consider it to be the first) is multiplied by the number of bytes in the row of a two-dimensional array (4*10 = 40 = 28h). Then, by executing the lea ecx, [ebp + eax + var_190] command, the address of the starting point of the current row is loaded into the ECX register. Finally, ecx + eax*4 is the address of the current element of the two-dimensional array. Thus, the algorithm in Listing 3.94 can be clarified easily.

To complete the description of loops, it is necessary to mention that if the same program operating over a two-dimensional array is compiled using the Microsoft Visual C++ "create fast code" option, the result would be interesting. Namely, the nested loop would disappear, because the compiler would unroll it (see Listing 3.93 and the comments that follow it). The nesting loop will be transformed from the precondition loop to the postcondition loop.

3.2.4. Objects

Identification of objects and everything related to them is a more complicated problem than the ones solved earlier. However, you have already encountered most of the material provided here. After all, methods are functions, and object properties are variables.[i] It is time to consider this problem in more detail and in due order.

Identifying Objects

Static Objects

First, consider a simple example intended to demonstrate typical program structures that serve objects. The program in Listing 3.95 has only one class, on the basis of which a single object is created. Note that this is a global static object. In other words, the compiler must take care to allocate memory for storing that object. The most important issue in object-oriented programming is deciding whether the created properties and methods relate to a single object or to several objects simultaneously. It is necessary to answer the following question: If, for example, a method (in essence, representing some function) relates to several objects simultaneously, how does it "know", in relation to which object it has been called from a specific program location?

---

[i] Both methods and variables are called class members.

Listing 3.95. Simple program demonstrating typical program structures for serving objects

```
#include <stdio.h>
class A {
public:
        int b;
        int a;
        int geta(){b = 0; return a;};
        void seta(int);
};
void A::seta(int a1)
{
        a = a1;
        b = 1;
};
A A1;
void main()
{
        A1.seta(10);
        int c = A1.geta();
        printf("%d\n", c);
}
```

Listing 3.96 provides the executable code of the main function from Listing 3.95, disassembled using IDA Pro. The program was compiled using Microsoft Visual C++ with the "no optimization" option.

Listing 3.96. Disassembled code of the main function from Listing 3.95

```
.text:00401020   _main           proc near        ; CODE XREF: start + 16E↓p
.text:00401020           var_4   = dword ptr -4
.text:00401020                   push    ebp
.text:00401021                   mov     ebp, esp
.text:00401023                   push    ecx
.text:00401024                   push    0Ah
```

```
.text:00401026                     mov      ecx, offset unk_4086C0
.text:0040102B                     call     sub_401000
.text:00401030                     mov      ecx, offset unk_4086C0
.text:00401035                     call     sub_401060
.text:0040103A                     mov      [ebp + var_4], eax
.text:0040103D                     mov      eax, [ebp + var_4]
.text:00401040                     push     eax
.text:00401041                     push     offset unk_4060FC
.text:00401046                     call     _printf
.text:0040104B                     add      esp, 8
.text:0040104E                     xor      eax, eax
.text:00401050                     mov      esp, ebp
.text:00401052                     pop      ebp
.text:00401053                     retn
.text:00401053     _main           endp
```

The text presented in Listing 3.96 contains three function calls. The first call is to the printf library function, so it doesn't make sense to consider it in detail. The sub_401000 and sub_401060 functions deserve special attention. In the comments following Listing 3.97, the code of these functions will be described in more detail. Because the source code of the program is available (see Listing 3.95), it is possible to tell for certain that these are the calls to the seta and geta methods, respectively. Note that before calling the method, in both cases, some memory address is sent into the ECX register: offset unk_4086C0. Click the reference, and you will find that this memory area is made up of 8 bytes (at least, IDA Pro has decided so). This must make you vigilant, because the object contains two int properties, which makes exactly 8 bytes. Thus, already on the basis of preliminary considerations it is possible to conclude that when calling a method, one parameter is the address of the object, in relation to which the given method is called (for the Microsoft Visual C++ compiler, the parameter is passed through the ECX register).

NOTE

The pointer to an object used in a method has a special name in the C++ language: this. Using the this pointer, it is possible to access the class members, including the closed ones.

Listing 3.97. Disassembled code (Listing 3.96) corresponding to seta/geta calls (Listing 3.95)

```
.text:00401000   sub_401000   proc near        ; CODE XREF: _main + B↓p
.text:00401000        var_4 = dword ptr -4
.text:00401000        arg_0 = dword ptr  8
.text:00401000                push    ebp
.text:00401001                mov     ebp, esp
.text:00401003                push    ecx
.text:00401004                mov     [ebp + var_4], ecx
.text:00401007                mov     eax, [ebp + var_4]
.text:0040100A                mov     ecx, [ebp + arg_0]
.text:0040100D                mov     [eax + 4], ecx
.text:00401010                mov     edx, [ebp + var_4]
.text:00401013                mov     dword ptr [edx], 1
.text:00401019                mov     esp, ebp
.text:0040101B                pop     ebp
.text:0040101C                retn    4
.text:0040101C   sub_401000   endp


.text:00401060   sub_401060   proc near        ; CODE XREF: _main + 15↑p
.text:00401060.           var_4 = dword ptr -4
.text:00401060                push    ebp
.text:00401061                mov     ebp, esp
.text:00401063                push    ecx
.text:00401064                mov     [ebp + var_4], ecx
.text:00401067                mov     eax, [ebp + var_4]
.text:0040106A                mov     dword ptr [eax], 0
.text:00401070                mov     ecx, [ebp + var_4]
.text:00401073                mov     eax, [ecx + 4]
.text:00401076                mov     esp, ebp
.text:00401078                pop     ebp
.text:00401079                retn
.text:00401079   sub_401060   endp
```

Consider the text of the `sub_401000` function. As already mentioned, to all appearances this is the `seta` function. Note immediately that this function has only one stack variable and one parameter. The stack is released by the `RETN 4` command. The sequence of the `push ecx/mov [ebp + var_4], ecx` commands immediately draws attention. This is a nuisance. The `push` command here is used to reserve memory for the local variable. At the same time, the variable is assigned the value stored in the `ECX` register. The command that follows the `PUSH` command again assigns the same value to the variable. Well, the compiler can be excused for this incident, because, after all, it was not instructed to use optimization. Further operations are the matter of technique: The value considered the object address is loaded into the `EAX` register. The `mov [eax + 4], ecx` command follows (and `ECX` now contains the parameter value). In other words, the `a` object property is located at the offset of 4 bytes in relation to the start of the object. Then there is the sequence of the `mov edx, [ebp + var_4]/mov dword ptr [edx], 1` commands, which corresponds to assignment of the value `1` to the `b` property.

The `sub_401060` function doesn't contain anything new. The `mov eax, [ecx + 4]` command simply returns the `a` property of the `geta` function.

Thus, having considered the example of compilation using the Microsoft Visual C++ compiler, it is possible to note that when calling a method, it is implicitly passed the pointer to the object, in the context of which it is called. In this example, a global object was created. However, there will be no difference when creating an object locally in the stack. Try to conduct this investigation on your own.

If the program presented in Listing 3.95 is compiled using the Borland C++ v. 5.0 compiler, there won't be any significant difference. Again, the method will be informed about the object address by the passing of an additional parameter. This additional parameter is the last to be passed through the stack in relation to all other parameters. I won't provide any additional listings here because they won't teach you anything new.

Dynamic Objects

In real-world programming, new objects are typically created on the fly. The `new` operator is intended specially for this purpose. Consider the program from Listing 3.95 rewritten in terms of dynamically-created objects (Listing 3.98).

Listing 3.98. Example illustrating the use of dynamic objects

---

```c
#include <stdio.h>
class A {
public:
        int b;
        int a;
        int geta(){b = 0; return a;};
        void seta(int);
};
void A::seta(int a1)
{
        a = a1;
        b = 1;
};
void main()
{
        A * A1 = new(A);
        A1 -> seta(10);
        int c = A1 -> geta();
        printf("%d\n", c);
        delete A1;
}
```

Listing 3.99 presents the disassembled text of the executable code created by the Microsoft Visual C++ compiler with the "no optimization" option.

Listing 3.99. Disassembled text of the program shown in Listing 3.98

```
.text:00401020 _main          proc near          ; CODE XREF: start + 16E↓p
.text:00401020      var_10   = dword ptr -10h
.text:00401020      var_C    = dword ptr -0Ch
.text:00401020      var_8    = dword ptr -8
.text:00401020      var_4    = dword ptr -4
.text:00401020               push     ebp
.text:00401021               mov      ebp, esp
```

```
.text:00401023                     sub      esp, 10h
.text:00401026                     push     8
.text:00401028                     call     ??2@YAPAXI@Z      ; Operator new(uint)
.text:0040102D                     add      esp, 4
.text:00401030                     mov      [ebp + var_C], eax
.text:00401033                     mov      eax, [ebp + var_C]
.text:00401036                     mov      [ebp + var_8], eax
.text:00401039                     push     0Ah
.text:0040103B                     mov      ecx, [ebp + var_8]
.text:0040103E                     call     sub_401000
.text:00401043                     mov      ecx, [ebp + var_8]
.text:00401046                     call     sub_401080
.text:0040104B                     mov      [ebp + var_4], eax
.text:0040104E                     mov      ecx, [ebp + var_4]
.text:00401051                     push     ecx
.text:00401052                     push     offset unk_4060FC
.text:00401057                     call     _printf
.text:0040105C                     add      esp, 8
.text:0040105F                     mov      edx, [ebp + var_8]
.text:00401062                     mov      [ebp + var_10], edx
.text:00401065                     mov      eax, [ebp + var_10]
.text:00401068                     push     eax
.text:00401069                     call     j__free
.text:0040106E                     add      esp, 4
.text:00401071                     xor      eax, eax
.text:00401073                     mov      esp, ebp
.text:00401075                     pop      ebp
.text:00401076                     retn
.text:00401076   _main             endp
```

The abundance of redundant code and redundant stack variables in this code fragment is surprising. In this case, however, this is of little or no importance. It is important here that after creation of an object all further actions have principally no differences from the ones encountered in Listing 3.96. Note that the new and delete operators (the call to the j__free procedure) are recognized by the IDA Pro disassembler, which makes further analysis a simple matter.

Virtual Functions

Virtual functions are a kind of payment for the beauty and ease of object-oriented programming theory. Consider the program shown in Listing 3.100, demonstrating a typical example of inheritance.

Listing 3.100. Example program demonstrating a typical example of inheritance

```
#include <stdio.h>
class A {
public:
        int a;
        int seta(int a1){a = a1; return a;};
        void pa(){printf("%d\n", a);}
};
class B:public A {
public:
        int seta(int a1){a = a1 + 1; return a;};
};
void main()
{
        A* A1;
        A1 = new(B);
        A1 -> seta(10);
        A1 -> pa();
        delete A1;
};
```

The B class inherits properties and methods of the A class. In this case, the B class has the seta method that by its name and parameters matches the similar method in class A. If, for example, you create an object on the basis of the B class, then when the seta method is called, the method from the B class will be called. This is a well-known inheritance property. The situation will be slightly different if you first create the pointer to the object of the base class A and then create a new object using the new operator on the base of the B class template (see Listing 3.100). This time, the compiler will orient toward the pointer type. In this case, A1 -> seta(10) will mean the call to the method of the base class. Listing 3.101 shows the disassembled code created by the Microsoft Visual C++ compiler using the "no optimization" option.

Listing 3.101. Disassembled code of the program compiled by Microsoft Visual C++ without optimization

```
.text:00401000 _main        proc near        ; CODE XREF: start + 16E↓p
.text:00401000       var_C  = dword ptr -0Ch
.text:00401000       var_8  = dword ptr -8
.text:00401000       var_4  = dword ptr -4
.text:00401000              push    ebp
.text:00401001              mov     ebp, esp
.text:00401003              sub     esp, 0Ch
.text:00401006              push    4
.text:00401008              call    ??2@YAPAXI@Z      ; Operator new(uint)
.text:0040100D              add     esp, 4
.text:00401010              mov     [ebp + var_8], eax
.text:00401013              mov     eax, [ebp + var_8]
.text:00401016              mov     [ebp + var_4], eax
.text:00401019              push    0Ah
.text:0040101B              mov     ecx, [ebp + var_4]
.text:0040101E              call    sub_401050
.text:00401023              mov     ecx, [ebp + var_4]
.text:00401026              call    sub_401070
.text:0040102B              mov     ecx, [ebp + var_4]
.text:0040102E              mov     [ebp + var_C], ecx
.text:00401031              mov     edx, [ebp + var_C]
.text:00401034              push    edx
.text:00401035              call    j__free
.text:0040103A              add     esp, 4
.text:0040103D              xor     eax, eax
.text:0040103F              mov     esp, ebp
```

```
.text:00401041                    pop      ebp
.text:00401042                    retn
.text:00401042  _main             endp
.text:00401042
.text:00401050
.text:00401050  sub_401050  proc near          ; CODE XREF: _main + 1E↑p
.text:00401050       var_4  = dword ptr -4
.text:00401050       arg_0  = dword ptr  8
.text:00401050                    push     ebp
.text:00401051                    mov      ebp, esp
.text:00401053                    push     ecx
.text:00401054                    mov      [ebp + var_4], ecx
.text:00401057                    mov      eax, [ebp + var_4]
.text:0040105A                    mov      ecx, [ebp + arg_0]
.text:0040105D                    mov      [eax], ecx
.text:0040105F                    mov      edx, [ebp + var_4]
.text:00401062                    mov      eax, [edx]
.text:00401064                    mov      esp, ebp
.text:00401066                    pop      ebp
.text:00401067                    retn     4
.text:00401067  sub_401050  endp
.text:00401067
.text:00401070
.text:00401070  sub_401070  proc near          ; CODE XREF: _main + 26↑p
.text:00401070       var_4 = dword ptr -4
.text:00401070                    push     ebp
.text:00401071                    mov      ebp, esp
.text:00401073                    push     ecx
.text:00401074                    mov      [ebp + var_4], ecx
.text:00401077                    mov      eax, [ebp + var_4]
.text:0040107A                    mov      ecx, [eax]
.text:0040107C                    push     ecx
.text:0040107D                    push     offset unk_4060FC
.text:00401082                    call     _printf
.text:00401087                    add      esp, 8
```

```
.text:0040108A                    mov     esp, ebp
.text:0040108C                    pop     ebp
.text:0040108D                    retn
.text:0040108D  sub_401070  endp
```

This listing doesn't contain anything principally new from the issues investigated in the previous section (see Listing 3.99). Here, 4 bytes are allocated for creating a new object, and the pointer to the newly-created object is passed through the ECX register (see the calls to the sub_401050 and sub_401070 functions). In the functions, the pointer to object is used for accessing the object property. For example, in sub_401050 the code shown in Listing 3.102 can be located.

Listing 3.102. Fragment of the sub_401050 function (Listing 3.101)

```
mov     [ebp + var_4], ecx ; The object address is loaded
                           ; into the stack variable.
mov     eax, [ebp + var_4] ; The address is loaded into the EAX register.
mov     ecx, [ebp + arg_0] ; The parameter value is loaded
                           ; into the ECX register.
mov     [eax], ecx         ; The parameter value is assigned to
                           ; the object property.
```

It is time to consider the concepts of virtual functions and polymorphism. For this purpose, consider the program in Listing 3.103. In comparison to Listing 3.100, another method, seta1, has been added to the base class, and the seta and seta1 methods have been made virtual. If you are acquainted with object-oriented programming, you will immediately guess that in the A1 -> seta(10) and A1 -> seta1(10) calls, the methods of the derived class (the B class) will be used.

Listing 3.103. Program for studying the concepts of virtual functions and polymorphism

```
#include <stdio.h>
class A {
public:
        int a;
```

```
        virtual int seta(int a1){a = a1; return a;};
        virtual int seta1(int a1){a = 2*a1; return a;};
        void pa(){printf("%d\n", a);}
};
class B:public A {
public:
        int seta(int a1){a = a1 + 1; return a;};
        int seta1(int a1){a = 2*a1 + 1; return a;};
};
void main()
{
        A* A1;
        A1 = new(B);
        A1 -> seta(10);
        A1 -> pa();
        A1 -> seta1(10);
        A1 -> pa();
        delete A1;
};
```

Listing 3.104 shows the disassembled executable code of the main function from Listing 3.103. As usual, the program was compiled using the Microsoft Visual C++ compiler with the "no optimization" option.

Listing 3.104. Disassembled code of the main function from Listing 3.103

```
.text:00401000 _main           proc near        ; CODE XREF: start + 16E↓p
.text:00401000      var_10 = dword ptr -10h
.text:00401000      var_C = dword ptr -0Ch
.text:00401000      var_8 = dword ptr -8
.text:00401000      var_4 = dword ptr -4
.text:00401000              push     ebp
.text:00401001              mov      ebp, esp
.text:00401003              sub      esp, 10h
.text:00401006              push     8
.text:00401008              call     ??2@YAPAXI@Z      ; Operator new(uint)
```

```
.text:0040100D                     add     esp, 4
.text:00401010                     mov     [ebp + var_8], eax
.text:00401013                     cmp     [ebp + var_8], 0
.text:00401017                     jz      short loc_401026
.text:00401019                     mov     ecx, [ebp + var_8]
.text:0040101C                     call    sub_4010A0
.text:00401021                     mov     [ebp + var_10], eax
.text:00401024                     jmp     short loc_40102D
.text:00401026   loc_401026:                       ; CODE XREF: _main + 17↑j
.text:00401026                     mov     [ebp + var_10], 0
.text:0040102D   loc_40102D:                       ; CODE XREF: _main + 24↑j
.text:0040102D                     mov     eax, [ebp + var_10]
.text:00401030                     mov     [ebp + var_4], eax
.text:00401033                     push    0Ah
.text:00401035                     mov     ecx, [ebp + var_4]
.text:00401038                     mov     edx, [ecx]
.text:0040103A                     mov     ecx, [ebp + var_4]
.text:0040103D                     call    dword ptr [edx]
.text:0040103F                     mov     ecx, [ebp + var_4]
.text:00401042                     call    sub_401080
.text:00401047                     push    0Ah
.text:00401049                     mov     eax, [ebp + var_4]
.text:0040104C                     mov     edx, [eax]
.text:0040104E                     mov     ecx, [ebp + var_4]
.text:00401051                     call    dword ptr [edx + 4]
.text:00401054                     mov     ecx, [ebp + var_4]
.text:00401057                     call    sub_401080
.text:0040105C                     mov     eax, [ebp + var_4]
.text:0040105F                     mov     [ebp + var_C], eax
.text:00401062                     mov     ecx, [ebp + var_C]
.text:00401065                     push    ecx
.text:00401066                     call    j__free
.text:0040106B                     add     esp, 4
.text:0040106E                     xor     eax, eax
.text:00401070                     mov     esp, ebp
```

```
.text:00401072                  pop     ebp
.text:00401073                  retn
.text:00401073  _main           endp
```

Note that when creating an object, 8 bytes are allocated (push 8) instead of the 4 bytes allocated earlier. Running some steps ahead, I'd like to mention that the additional 4 bytes located in the beginning of the object are allocated for the address of the table of virtual functions.

In the text, you can see that the check is carried out, ensuring that the new operator has allocated memory for the object to be created. If the memory allocation function returns zero (which means that an error has occurred), then the var_10 variable is assigned the value of zero, which finally must cause an exception (the mov edx, [ecx] command if the ECX register contains zero).

Pay special attention to the sub_4010A0 function (see Listing 3.106). This is a special function, which is not present in the program code. Its intention is to place the address of the virtual functions table into the start of the area allocated for the object to be created. The function will return the object address — but with the address of the virtual functions table (in the first 4 bytes). Later, the mechanism in Listing 3.105 will be used.

Listing 3.105. Mechanism used for forming the virtual function address

```
mov     ecx, [ebp + var_4] ; The object's address
mov     edx, [ecx]         ; The contents of the start of the area
                           ; The object is loaded into the EDX register.
                           ; The address of the virtual functions table
mov     ecx, [ebp + var_4]
call    dword ptr [edx]    ; The call to the virtual function
```

Thus, you can see that the virtual function address, in contrast to a normal function, is formed dynamically. Any indirect call (no matter what the compiler might be) must make you vigilant, suspecting a call to a virtual function. In the program being studied, virtual functions are called twice: call dword ptr [edx] (the call to seta) and call dword ptr [edx + 4] (the call to seta1). The EDX register points to the start of the virtual functions table. The table must contain the addresses of two virtual functions.

Consider Listing 3.106, where the disassembled text of the sub_4010A0 function is shown. The main goal of this function is to place the address of the virtual functions table into the start of the area that stores the object.

Listing 3.106. Disassembled code of the sub_4010A0 function

```
.text:004010A0  sub_4010A0      proc near        ; CODE XREF: _main + 1C↑p
.text:004010A0          var_4    = dword ptr -4
.text:004010A0                  push     ebp
.text:004010A1                  mov      ebp, esp
.text:004010A3                  push     ecx
.text:004010A4                  mov      [ebp + var_4], ecx
.text:004010A7                  mov      ecx, [ebp + var_4]
.text:004010AA                  call     ??0ios_base@std@@IAE@XZ
.text:004010AF                  mov      eax, [ebp + var_4]
.text:004010B2                  mov      dword ptr [eax], offset off_407100
.text:004010B8                  mov      eax, [ebp + var_4]
.text:004010BB                  mov      esp, ebp
.text:004010BD                  pop      ebp
.text:004010BE                  retn
.text:004010BE  sub_4010A0  endp
```

The function presented in the listing has an interesting organization. First, the address of the virtual functions table is defined and placed into the start of the area where the object is stored. These commands are in Listing 3.107.

Listing 3.107. Defining and placing the address of the virtual functions table

```
. . .
mov      [ebp + var_4], ecx
. . .
mov      eax, [ebp + var_4]
mov      dword ptr [eax], offset off_407100
. . .
```

The memory area with the off_407100 address stores the virtual functions table. What about the call to the ??0ios_base@std@@IAE@XZ function? Here, it is necessary to understand that the class hierarchy in the text program has only two levels: the base class, A, and the derived class, B. Tables of virtual functions are created for each class. The ??0ios_base@std@@IAE@XZ function places the address of the virtual functions table of the base class into the object. In this case, the address is overwritten with the address of the virtual functions table of class B. Now assume that another class, C, is added to this hierarchy. This class is the descendant of class B. Create an object on the basis of the C class: A1=new(C). How would the compiler treat the tables of virtual functions in this case? Consider Listing 3.108.

Listing 3.108. Virtual functions table in a sophisticated class hierarchy

```
; The main function
_main proc near
        . . .
        call proc1
; Now the object contains the address of the
; virtual functions table of class C.
        . . .
_main endp
. . .
proc1 proc near
        . . .
        call proc2
; Now the object contains the address of the
; virtual functions table of class B.
        . . .
; Now the object contains the address of the
; virtual functions table of class C.
        . . .
        retn
proc1 endp
        . . .
Proc2 proc near
        . . .
```

```
        call ??0ios_base@std@@IAE@XZ

        . . .
; Now the object contains the address of the
; virtual functions table of the base class.

        . . .
; Now the object contains the address of the
; virtual functions table of class B.

        . . .
        retn
proc1 endp
```

Carefully consider the method presented in Listing 3.108. From this method, it must be clear how the addresses of virtual functions are written for the hierarchy of objects with an arbitrary number of members. In particular, from this listing it follows that the greater the number of members, the more time required to complete such an operation, because the number of nested procedures equals the number of classes, including the base class. Also note that the Microsoft Visual C++ compiler places the virtual functions tables of the parent and child classes one after another and that the base class has the greatest address (addresses grow from bottom to top). The functions are placed in the table from bottom to top, according to their declarations in the program text.

Thus, knowing the address of the virtual functions table, you'll easily locate the text of that function. For example, Listing 3.109 shows the code of the seta virtual function defined in class B.

Listing 3.109. Code of the seta virtual function defined in class B

```
.text:004010C0  sub_4010C0  proc near      ; DATA XREF: .rdata:off_407100↓o
.text:004010C0          var_4  = dword ptr -4
.text:004010C0          arg_0  = dword ptr  8
.text:004010C0              push    ebp
.text:004010C1              mov     ebp, esp
.text:004010C3              push    ecx
.text:004010C4              mov     [ebp + var_4], ecx
.text:004010C7              mov     eax, [ebp + arg_0]
.text:004010CA              add     eax, 1
```

```
.text:004010CD                    mov      ecx, [ebp + var_4]
.text:004010D0                    mov      [ecx + 4], eax
.text:004010D3                    mov      edx, [ebp + var_4]
.text:004010D6                    mov      eax, [edx + 4]
.text:004010D9                    mov      esp, ebp
.text:004010DB                    pop      ebp
.text:004010DC                    retn     4
.text:004010DC   sub_4010C0       endp
```

The text of the seta procedure is clear. First, the object address, as before, is contained in the ECX register. The arg_0 parameter is the value that must be assigned to the a property (see Listing 3.103). Finally, when assigning the value, it must be increased by one (Listing 3.110).

Listing 3.110. When assigning the value, it must be incremented by one (Listing 3.109)

```
add     eax, 1
mov     ecx, [ebp + var_4]
mov     [ecx + 4], eax
```

From Listings 3.109 and 3.110, it is clear that the a property is located at the offset 4 bytes from the object start. This is correct, because the first 4 bytes contain the address of the virtual functions table. If optimization options are specified at compile time, the compiler reduces the code. For example, the procedures, where the virtual function address is written to the object, disappear because all operations are carried out directly in the main function (in the example under consideration). In addition, the address of the last class is immediately written into the object.

If you use the Borland C++ v. 5.0 compiler, you won't notice any significant differences. The address of the virtual functions table also is placed in the start of the object. In the course of initialization, it also is overwritten starting from the base class (or, to be precise, starting from the class, in which the virtual keyword appeared first) and ending with the current derived class.

Constructors and Destructors

The need for constructors and destructors is the logical consequence of the concept of object-oriented programming, especially as related to visual programming for the Windows operating system. There is an urgent need for automating some actions that must be carried out when objects are created and when they are destroyed. In particular, this relates to initial values of the object properties that cannot be initialized when they are declared, as was the general practice with the C programming language. On the other hand, calling the initialization procedure every time is bad programming style.[i] Until now, I have not used constructors or destructors in the examples. However, this cannot be said about the compiler. For example, determining the address of the virtual functions table is exactly the operation that must be carried out automatically. This means that you have already encountered constructors in this chapter! You first encountered a constructor in Listing 3.104. This is the `sub_4010A0` procedure that was separately considered in Listing 3.106. The only intention of this procedure is writing the address of the correct virtual functions table into the start of the object. However, if you define the constructor explicitly and carry out specific actions there, these actions will be "in the same company" as the actions for defining the virtual functions table.

Consider the practical example presented in Listing 3.111. In this program, a single class A is defined, in which there is one variable, one virtual method, and special methods: constructor and destructor.

Listing 3.111. Practical example illustrating the use of constructors and destructors

---

```
#include <stdio.h>
class A {
public:
        int a;
        virtual void pa(){printf("%d\n", a);}
        A(){a = 1; printf("Constructor A\n");};
        ~A(){printf("Destructor A\n");};
};
void main()
{
        A* A1;
```

---

[i] When creating a new object, the programmer might forget to call the initialization procedure or might call it more than once.

```
        A1 = new(A);
        A1 -> pa();
        delete A1;
};
```

The disassembled code of the `main` function of this program is presented in Listing 3.112. As before, this code was created using the Microsoft Visual C++ compiler with the "no optimization" option.

Listing 3.112. Disassembled code of the main function from Listing 3.111

```
.text:00401000  _main        proc near           ; CODE XREF: start + 16E↓p
.text:00401000        var_18  = dword ptr -18h
.text:00401000        var_14  = dword ptr -14h
.text:00401000        var_10  = dword ptr -10h
.text:00401000        var_C   = dword ptr -0Ch
.text:00401000        var_8   = dword ptr -8
.text:00401000        var_4   = dword ptr -4
.text:00401000              push    ebp
.text:00401001              mov     ebp, esp
.text:00401003              sub     esp, 18h
.text:00401006              push    8
.text:00401008              call    ??2@YAPAXI@Z ; Operator new(uint)
.text:0040100D              add     esp, 4
.text:00401010              mov     [ebp + var_8], eax
.text:00401013              cmp     [ebp + var_8], 0
.text:00401017              jz      short loc_401026
.text:00401019              mov     ecx, [ebp + var_8]
.text:0040101C              call    sub_401070
.text:00401021              mov     [ebp + var_14], eax
.text:00401024              jmp     short loc_40102D
.text:00401026  loc_401026:                       ; CODE XREF: _main + 17↑j
.text:00401026              mov     [ebp + var_14], 0
.text:0040102D  loc_40102D:                       ; CODE XREF: _main + 24↑j
.text:0040102D              mov     eax, [ebp + var_14]
.text:00401030              mov     [ebp + var_4], eax
```

```
.text:00401033                         mov      ecx, [ebp + var_4]
.text:00401036                         mov      edx, [ecx]
.text:00401038                         mov      ecx, [ebp + var_4]
.text:0040103B                         call     dword ptr [edx]
.text:0040103D                         mov      eax, [ebp + var_4]
.text:00401040                         mov      [ebp + var_10], eax
.text:00401043                         mov      ecx, [ebp + var_10]
.text:00401046                         mov      [ebp + var_C], ecx
.text:00401049                         cmp      [ebp + var_C], 0
.text:0040104D                         jz       short loc_40105E
.text:0040104F                         push     1
.text:00401051                         mov      ecx, [ebp + var_C]
.text:00401054                         call     sub_4010C0
.text:00401059                         mov      [ebp + var_18], eax
.text:0040105C                         jmp      short loc_401065
.text:0040105E    loc_40105E:                            ; CODE XREF: _main + 4D↑j
.text:0040105E                         mov      [ebp + var_18], 0
.text:00401065    loc_401065:                            ; CODE XREF: _main + 5C↑j
.text:00401065                         xor      eax, eax
.text:00401067                         mov      esp, ebp
.text:00401069                         pop      ebp
.text:0040106A                         retn
.text:0040106A    _main             endp
```

The structure of this listing must already be well known to you. However, I'd like to draw your attention to certain issues that have not been covered in sufficient detail yet. On the basis of all previous material, it is clear that the sub_401070 function is the constructor. This is confirmed first by the constructor's proximity to the new operator. Also, important is that after execution of the new operator the check is carried out if the memory has actually been allocated. Consider all listings provided in *Section 3.2.4* more closely. You'll see that such checks appear only with the introduction of virtual functions. However, you already know that if virtual functions are present, the compiler creates a constructor even if it wasn't present in the source code of the program. This probably is the main indication of the constructor call, because the compiler won't allow a constructor to execute if the object hasn't been created.

Consider the end of the function. The call to sub_4010C0 immediately attracts attention. Earlier, in similar programs, there was the call to the j__free function, which was associated with the delete operator (see Listing 3.99 and the comments that follow it). In this case, you are dealing with the destructor, which will be considered in detail in Listing 3.116. Note that the compiler again won't allow the destructor to execute if the object hasn't been created.

As relates to the remaining code, hopefully you'll easily recognize the call dword ptr [edx] command as a call to the A1 -> pa() virtual function. This mustn't cause you any problems after you consider all previously provided examples.

Now, consider the contents of the constructor (Listing 3.113).

Listing 3.113. Disassembled code of the constructor (Listing 3.111)

```
.text:00401070  sub_401070  proc near              ; CODE XREF: _main + 1C↑p
.text:00401070           var_4 = dword ptr -4
.text:00401070                    push    ebp
.text:00401071                    mov     ebp, esp
.text:00401073                    push    ecx
.text:00401074                    mov     [ebp + var_4], ecx
.text:00401077                    mov     eax, [ebp + var_4]
.text:0040107A                    mov     dword ptr [eax], offset off_40710C
.text:00401080                    mov     ecx, [ebp + var_4]
.text:00401083                    mov     dword ptr [ecx + 4], 1
.text:0040108A                    push offset aConstructorA ; "Constructor A\n"
.text:0040108F                    call    _printf
.text:00401094                    add     esp, 4
.text:00401097                    mov     eax, [ebp + var_4]
.text:0040109A                    mov     esp, ebp
.text:0040109C                    pop     ebp
.text:0040109D                    retn
.text:0040109D  sub_401070  endp
```

You must rejoice when viewing this listing. Consider the well-known code fragment (Listing 3.114).

Listing 3.114. Writing the virtual functions table address into the new object instance

```
mov     [ebp + var_4], ecx
mov     eax, [ebp + var_4]
mov     dword ptr [eax], offset off_40710C
```

This is nothing other than writing the address of the virtual functions table into the newly-created object instance. Then there is another easily recognizable pattern (Listing 3.115).

Listing 3.115. Code fragment demonstrating the code of the constructor

```
; Set the property value (a = 1).
mov     dword ptr [ecx + 4], 1
; The call to the printf function
push    offset aConstructorA ; "Constructor A\n"
call    _printf
```

This is the code that was placed into the constructor (see Listing 3.111). There isn't anything to add here because the entire pattern is clear.

Listing 3.116 presents the disassembled code of the destructor (or, to be precise, the procedure, from which the true destructor will be called) from the program shown in Listing 3.111.

Listing 3.116. Disassembled code of the procedure calling the destructor (Listing 3.111)

```
.text:004010C0  sub_4010C0  proc near        ; CODE XREF: _main + 54↑p
.text:004010C0          var_4 = dword ptr -4
.text:004010C0          arg_0 = dword ptr  8
.text:004010C0                  push    ebp
.text:004010C1                  mov     ebp, esp
.text:004010C3                  push    ecx
.text:004010C4                  mov     [ebp + var_4], ecx
.text:004010C7                  mov     ecx, [ebp + var_4]
```

```
.text:004010CA                  call      sub_4010F0
.text:004010CF                  mov       eax, [ebp + arg_0]
.text:004010D2                  and       eax, 1
.text:004010D5                  jz        short loc_4010E3
.text:004010D7                  mov       ecx, [ebp + var_4]
.text:004010DA                  push      ecx
.text:004010DB                  call      j__free
.text:004010E0                  add       esp, 4
.text:004010E3  loc_4010E3:                          ; CODE XREF: sub_4010C0 + 15↑j
.text:004010E3                  mov       eax, [ebp + var_4]
.text:004010E6                  mov       esp, ebp
.text:004010E8                  pop       ebp
.text:004010E9                  retn      4
.text:004010E9  sub_4010C0  endp
```

First, pay attention to the following two calls in Listing 3.116: sub_4010F0 and j__free. View sub_4010F0, and you'll immediately notice that it simply contains the text that was placed into the destructor (see Listing 3.111). Thus, the sub_4010C0 function is intended for calling procedures required to destroy an object. You have already encountered the j__free function, and you already know that it is simply an implementation of the delete operator. Finally, the value 1 sent to the sub_4010C0 function as a parameter is simply an indication that it is necessary to call the delete operator.

3.2.5. More about Executable Code Investigation

Mathematical Computations

You have encountered mathematical computations many times. Compilers often use different techniques, such as computation at compile time, to reduce the code size or speed up program execution. You also already know about the possibility of using FPU commands. In this section, several other techniques will be covered. First, consider the example program shown in Listing 3.117.

Listing 3.117. Sample program containing a simple numeric computation

```
#include <stdio.h>
#include <windows.h>
void main()
{
        DWORD a, b, c;
        scanf("%d", &a);
        scanf("%d", &b);
        c=((a + b)/8)*(3*a);
        printf("%d\n", c);
};
```

Listing 3.117 provides a program that contains a simple arithmetic computation. Consider how the Microsoft Visual C++ compiler treats this program when
the "create fast code" option was specified at compile time. The disassembled code
of the compiled program is shown in Listing 3.118.

Listing 3.118. Disassembled code of the program shown in Listing 3.117

```
.text:00401000   _main         proc near         ; CODE XREF: start + 16E↓p
.text:00401000           var_8   = dword ptr -8
.text:00401000           var_4   = dword ptr -4
.text:00401000           sub     esp, 8
.text:00401003           lea     eax, [esp + 8 + var_8]
.text:00401006           push    eax
.text:00401007           push    offset unk_408100
.text:0040100C           call    _scanf
.text:00401011           lea     ecx, [esp + 10h + var_4]
.text:00401015           push    ecx
.text:00401016           push    offset unk_408100
.text:0040101B           call    _scanf
.text:00401020           mov     ecx, [esp + 18h + var_8]
.text:00401024           mov     edx, [esp + 18h + var_4]
.text:00401028           lea     eax, [edx + ecx]
.text:0040102B           shr     eax, 3
```

```
.text:0040102E                 imul    eax, ecx

.text:00401031                 lea     eax, [eax + eax*2]

.text:00401034                 push    eax

.text:00401035                 push    offset unk_4080FC

.text:0040103A                 call    _printf

.text:0040103F                 xor     eax, eax

.text:00401041                 add     esp, 20h

.text:00401044                 retn

.text:00401044  _main          endp
```

Note that stack variables in this fragment are addressed using the ESP register. Thus, the var_4 and var_8 stack variables correspond to the a and b variables (see Listing 3.117). Consider the sequence of commands in Listing 3.119.

Listing 3.119. Code pattern using lea for optimization of mathematical computations

```
mov     ecx, [esp + 18h + var_8]

mov     edx, [esp + 18h + var_4]

lea     eax, [edx + ecx]
```

The main issue here is the use of the lea command. Uncommon properties of this command were already covered in *Chapter 1* (see Table 1.2). Now you'll see this command in action. You'll usually encounter this command when it is necessary to optimize arithmetic operations.

Then there is the shr eax, 3 command. You already know that it is simply an integer divided by eight (two raised to the power of three). This command is executed much faster than IDIV. Later, there is the imul eax, ecx command that multiplies the contents of EAX by the contents of ECX. Finally, you encounter the lea command again: lea eax, [eax + eax*2]. This command stands for multiplication of the contents of the EAX register by three.

At this point, the section on mathematical computations has been completed. I hope that you'll easily master on your own other methods of optimizing computations, in particular, using bitwise commands when investigating source code.

Other Constructs

Handling Exceptions

The mechanisms of exception handling at the level of executable code are complicated. Furthermore, details of their implementation might considerably differ for different compilers. A detailed investigation of these mechanisms goes beyond the goals of this book. My goals are more modest: They are to make you acquainted with some basic principles of exception handling and to study how these mechanisms might be reflected in executable code.

Exception handling generated by compilers is based on so-called structured exception handling (SEH). The SEH mechanism is supported at the level of the Windows operating system. The foundation for exception handling is the following: When the operating system of the Windows family runs on an Intel processor, the FS segment register plays a special role. It points to the thread environment block (TEB).[i] This block, in turn, contains several substructures, one of which is the thread information block (TIB). TIB is stored in the beginning of TEB. Finally, the 4-byte value located in the beginning of the TIB structure represents the address of some structure that, first, contains the exception handler address and, second, contains the address of the previous structure of the same type. In reality, the problem is the linked list. This topic will be covered in detail later in this chapter (see the comments that follow Listing 3.121).

The following conclusions can be drawn on the basis of the preceding information:

- Each thread has an individual exception handler.
- Knowing the address, by which the pointer to the exception handler is located, the program can set its own handler procedure.

In essence, these two facts are the foundation for the exception handling mechanisms used by compilers creating executable code intended to run under Windows. Although these are easy to understand, the exception-handling mechanism might be rather complicated.

When describing implementations of the exception handling mechanisms in different compilers, I mean the __try/__except pair of operators implemented

---

[i] Recall that in the protected mode, segment registers store selectors instead of addresses. Selectors are numbers in the descriptors table that define addresses.

in C++.[i] Consider the example program presented in Listing 3.120. This program is trivial. The __try block is used to avoid division by zero when computing the quotient resulting from division of a by b.

Listing 3.120. Sample program illustrating the exception handling mechanism

---

```
#include <stdio.h>
#include <windows.h>

int main()
{
        int a, b;
        scanf("%d", &a);
        scanf("%d", &b);
        __try {
                a = a/b;
                printf("%d\n", a);

                }
        __except(0)
        {
                printf("Error 1! \n");

        };
        return 0;

}
```

The code of this program disassembled by IDA Pro is presented in Listing 3.121. The program was compiled using Microsoft Visual C++ with the "create fast code" option.

Listing 3.121. Disassembled code of the program presented in Listing 3.119

```
.text:00401000 _main           proc near               ; CODE XREF: start + 16E↓p
.text:00401000         var_20 = dword ptr -20h
.text:00401000         var_1C = dword ptr -1Ch
```

---

[i] This is a standard for the C++ programming language; therefore, all C++ compilers support these operators, although implementations might be different.

```
.text:00401000      var_18 = dword ptr -18h
.text:00401000      var_10 = dword ptr -10h
.text:00401000      var_4 = dword ptr -4
.text:00401000              push    ebp
.text:00401001              mov     ebp, esp
.text:00401003              push    0FFFFFFFFh
.text:00401005              push    offset byte_408110
.text:0040100A              push    offset __except_handler3
.text:0040100F              mov     eax, large fs:0
.text:00401015              push    eax
.text:00401016              mov     large fs:0, esp
.text:0040101D              sub     esp, 10h
.text:00401020              push    ebx
.text:00401021              push    esi
.text:00401022              push    edi
.text:00401023              mov     [ebp + var_18], esp
.text:00401026              lea     eax, [ebp + var_1C]
.text:00401029              push    eax
.text:0040102A              push    offset aD_0     ; "%d"
.text:0040102F              call    _scanf
.text:00401034              lea     ecx, [ebp + var_20]
.text:00401037              push    ecx
.text:00401038              push    offset aD_0     ; "%d"
.text:0040103D              call    _scanf
.text:00401042              add     esp, 10h
.text:00401045              mov     [ebp + var_4], 0
.text:0040104C              mov     eax, [ebp + var_1C]
.text:0040104F              cdq
.text:00401050              idiv    [ebp + var_20]
.text:00401053              mov     [ebp + var_1C], eax
.text:00401056              push    eax
.text:00401057              push    offset aD        ; "%d\n"
.text:0040105C              call    _printf
.text:00401061              add     esp, 8
.text:00401064              jmp     short loc_401079
```

```
.text:00401066 ;-----------------------------------------------------------
.text:00401066                 xor     eax, eax
.text:00401068                 retn
.text:00401069 ;-----------------------------------------------------------
.text:00401069                 mov     esp, [ebp - 18h]
.text:0040106C                 push    offset aError1  ; "Error 1! \n"
.text:00401071                 call    _printf
.text:00401076                 add     esp, 4
.text:00401079 loc_401079:                            ; CODE XREF: _main + 64↑j
.text:00401079                 mov     [ebp + var_4], 0FFFFFFFFh
.text:00401080                 xor     eax, eax
.text:00401082                 mov     ecx, [ebp + var_10]
.text:00401085                 mov     large fs:0, ecx
.text:0040108C                 pop     edi
.text:0040108D                 pop     esi
.text:0040108E                 pop     ebx
.text:0040108F                 mov     esp, ebp
.text:00401091                 pop     ebp
.text:00401092                 retn
.text:00401092 _main           endp
```

Pay attention to the presence of the standard function prologue, although in normal conditions standard prologues and epilogues are discarded if compilation was carried out with optimization options. Note that IDA Pro specifies five stack variables even though there were only two of them in the source code of the program. Briefly viewing the code, it is easy to determine (for example, by the calls to scanf) that var_1C corresponds to the a variable and var_20 corresponds to the b variable. Although only part of the function code can be enclosed by the __try block, this block influences the entire function.

The standard prologue is followed by an interesting sequence of commands (Listing 3.122). This code fragment deserves special comments.

Listing 3.122. __try block nesting level and exception handling structures

```
push    0FFFFFFFFh                  ; var_4
push    offset byte_408110          ;
push    offset __except_handler3    ; Address of the new exception handler
```

```
mov      eax, large fs:0          ; Address of the previous
                                  ; handler structure
push     eax                      ; var_10
mov      large fs:0, esp          ; Address of the new handler
```

First, some arbitrary constant is sent into the stack. Later, this value will be changed. This value will determine the nesting level of the __try block. Next, the address of some global memory cell is placed into the stack. The third element is the address of the exception handler formed by the compiler. The last three commands are interesting. The address of the old exception handling structure is placed into the stack, then the address of the entire group composed of 4 double words (this is the new exception handling structure) in the stack is placed into fs:0. This operation adds a new record to a linked list. This list might contain the entire chain of exception handlers. The last structure in the list must contain the value 0FFFFFFFFH in the exception handler address. Also note that the stack contains the old EBP value.

Note the mov [ebp + var_4], 0 instruction. It directly precedes the command that carries out the division operation. This command specifies the nesting level of the __try block. Note that the nesting level is determined by the number of __try blocks in the function, whether one block is nested within another block or not. Trace the content of the var_4 variable because it is the key to the structure of the function's __try blocks.

The value of the ESP register is saved when the stack of the function is formed completely: mov [ebp + var_18], esp. This value is used for restoring the stack in the __except block (see Listing 3.123).

Without diverting to consider standard Assembly commands and calls to the scanf and printf functions, proceed with considering the __except block. You won't encounter any difficulties locating the starting and ending points of this block, because the starting point of this block is always preceded by the customary sequence of commands shown in Listing 3.123.

Listing 3.123. Customary sequence that precedes the start of the __except block

```
jmp      short loc_401079
xor      eax, eax
retn
```

These commands will always be present, no matter which optimization variant of the Microsoft Visual C++ compiler is used. The end of the __except block is defined by the jmp command.

If you resort to the Borland C++ v. 5.0 compiler, the external manifestation of exceptions also will be clear and easily recognizable, even though a slightly different exception handling mechanism is used. The first indication is the presence of the exception setting in the beginning of the block procedure (replacement of the stored value with the FS:0 address). The second indication is the presence of a typical fragment in the center of the procedure. There is no jump to that fragment, and the fragment is bypassed by the JMP command. Finally, in the end of the procedure the command restoring the old FS:0 value must be present.

Identifying the *main* Function and the Start-up Code

Earlier in this chapter, the main function — the function, from which the program starts — was treated as if there were no problems with determining its address. IDA Pro doesn't have any trouble with determining the address of the main function in the executable code of a program compiled using any C++ compiler. However, situations are possible, in which IDA Pro is not close at hand. Furthermore, there are other programming languages, for which the situation is not as simple as for C++.

Any program written in any algorithmic programming language is made up of a certain set of commands. For C++, these are the main or WinMain functions. However, it would be an error to consider that the executable code of the program starts execution exactly from this set of commands. As a rule, the compiler inserts some start-up code before it, which contains the calls to library and API functions. This code carries out some preparations: For instance, it requests the memory from the system, defines the command-line parameters, and obtains the identifier of the executable module. Only after completing this is control passed to the initial commands described before. As I have already mentioned, disassemblers (and debuggers) are not always capable of correctly determining where these commands start.

NOTE

When speaking about the Microsoft Visual C++ compiler, for a console application the start-up codes begin execution from the mainCRTStartup function, which passes control to the main function. For GUI applications, program execution starts from the WinMainCRTStartup function. After execution, the WinMainCRTStartup function passes control to the WinMain function. There also is a technique allowing you to create executable modules that start execution directly from the main or from the `WinMain` function. This allows considerable reduction of the executable module size (the actual size of such a module becomes smaller than the size of standard libraries). However, this is not a common practice, because in this case the programmer would intentionally reject the possibility of using standard C libraries.

To find the start of the user part of the executable code, it is necessary to know how this call is executed. First, consider a console application written in the C++ programming language. In general, the prototype of the `main` function appears as shown in Listing 3.124.

Listing 3.124. Standard prototype of the main function of a console application in C++

```
int main( int argc[ , char *argv[ ] [, char *envp[ ] ] ] );
```

In general, the `main` function has three input parameters. This is an important indication. For example, consider a typical call to the `main` function from the executable code created by the Microsoft Visual C++ compiler (Listing 3.125).

Listing 3.125. Typical main function call from executable code from Microsoft Visual C++

```
mov     eax, dword_40A724
mov     dword_40A728, eax
push    eax
push    dword_40A71C
push    dword_40A718
call    _main
add     esp, 0Ch
```

Note that all three parameters turned out to be global variables. This issue is important. Now, it is necessary to study, which library and API functions are called before and after the call to the `main` function. Armed with this knowledge, you'll be able to easily find the required location within a program. The call to the `GetCommandLine` API function deserves special mention. Using this function, it is possible to obtain the command-line parameters. These parameters are then passed in the second parameter of the `main` function. What would happen if the `main` function doesn't have any parameters or if it has one or two parameters? The answer to this question is as follows: Nothing would be changed, and the call will be carried out in the same way. Thus, search criteria also do not change. However, when dealing with the Borland C++ compiler, the situation is more complicated. The call to the main function is carried out by an indirect call appearing like CALL [ESI + N]. If the disassembler doesn't locate and identify the main function automatically, the code investigator has to use the debugger. However, all previously-mentioned considerations related to the preliminary call to library and API functions (for example, GetCommandLine) are applicable even in this case. Knowing these functions, you'll be able to locate the required code section and then find CALL [ESI + N] or a similar call. In this case, it will also be necessary to use the debugger and breakpoints, because manual analysis of the code aimed at locating the address, by which the call is carried out is a tedious procedure.

Consider the WinMain function. The prototype of this function is provided in Listing 3.126.

Listing 3.126. Prototype of the WinMain function

```
int WinMain(HINSTANCE hInstance,
    HINSTANCE hPrevInstance,
    LPSTR lpCmdLine,
    int nCmdShow
);
```

As you can see, this function has four parameters. This indication is an important search criterion for searching for the start of the program. Listing 3.127 presents a typical fragment demonstrating the call of the WinMain function from the executable module created by the Microsoft Visual C++ compiler.

Listing 3.127. Typical WinMain call from the executable module from Microsoft Visual C++

```
Push    eax
push    dword ptr [ebp - 20h]
push    esi
push    esi                 ; lpModuleName
call    edi                 ; GetModuleHandleA
push    eax
```

```
call    _WinMain@16      ; WinMain(x, x, x, x)
mov     edi, eax
mov     [ebp - 2Ch], edi
cmp     [ebp - 1Ch], esi
jnz     short loc_401508
push    edi              ; int
call    _exit
```

The fragment presented in Listing 3.127 is so typical that it is worth memorizing. This search criterion allows you to find the entry point to the executable code of the program without failure. The call to WinMain function in a module created by the Borland C++ compiler is executed using the CALL [ESI + N] command, as was the case for the main function. Also, the GetModuleHandle API function is called before this call.

In Delphi, the execution starts from the main module of the program (BEGIN...END.); however, before this module there are calls to one or more procedures that initialize start-up. In particular, one such procedure calls the GetModuleHandle API function.

Chapter 4:

THE SOFTICE DEBUGGER

There are different versions of SoftIce for all of Microsoft's operating systems from the Windows family and even for MS-DOS. First, it is necessary to mention that SoftIce is a kernel-mode debugger. This means that it can be used for debugging any programs that run under a specific operating system, including services and drivers running in the protection ring 0. Because SoftIce closely interacts with the operating system, it allows you to obtain lots of internal system information (private information, I'd say) related to the details of the operating system's operation. Therefore, SoftIce is an indispensable tool for everyone who studies the internal mechanisms of Windows operation. Among code diggers, SoftIce is considered the best debugger ever known.

The distribution set, along with the debugger, provides lots of utilities and tools, the most important of which is the *Symbol Loader* (in other words, the loader of the debug information). The Symbol Loader program (loader32.exe) loads the executable module into the memory and calls the SoftIce debugger window. In other words, it sets a breakpoint to the program entry point. If debug information recognizable by the loader is present in the executable module, it also loads this information into the debugger. The debugger allows you to debug executable code not only locally but also remotely. Remote debugging is carried out from a remote computer connected through the COM port to the local computer running the program being debugged.

SoftIce installation deserves separate consideration. Because this debugger operates at the kernel level, developers have to constantly elaborate their product to ensure support for all releases of the Windows operating system. Nevertheless, articles and discussions dedicated to problems related to SoftIce installation and troubleshooting swarm the Internet. I won't provide the installation topics here to economize on space. You can find all required information at the product's support site, **http://www.compuware.com**, where, having registered, you can download the SoftIce Reference Guide. My goal is to provide a brief introduction to application debugging using SoftIce. Therefore, I'll give detailed descriptions of the SoftIce commands most frequently used for debugging standard applications. Also covered will be examples of debugging when the debugging information is present in the modules being debugged, as well as when the debugging information is not available.

All examples provided in this chapter are applicable to Windows XP and Windows Server 2003.

4.1. Basic Information about Working with SoftIce

This section covers the basic information required to start working with this powerful instrument.

4.1.1. Getting Started

Main SoftIce Window

When the SoftIce window pops up, all system functions are "frozen." So, to obtain a screenshot of the SoftIce window, I had to use two computers (Fig. 4.1).

The SoftIce main window appears in the following four cases:

❐ When the user presses the <Ctrl>+<D> keyboard combination. This command pops up the debugger window when executing any program. Thus, you can view the state of the operating system and executed applications at any time.

❐ When loading some application into the memory using the loader32.exe program. In this case, the loading process is interrupted exactly when it encounters the entry point into the executable module. You'll be able to continue application execution in any debugger mode from that point.

❐ When one of the breakpoint conditions is satisfied. You set breakpoint beforehand in the debugger window. The debugger will show exactly the location where the interrupt should be placed. One of the greatest advantages of SoftIce is its capability for working with several applications in parallel. You can set breakpoints to several applications simultaneously.

❐ The SoftIce window can appear in case of a system error or a system crash (Blue Screen of Death, or BSOD).

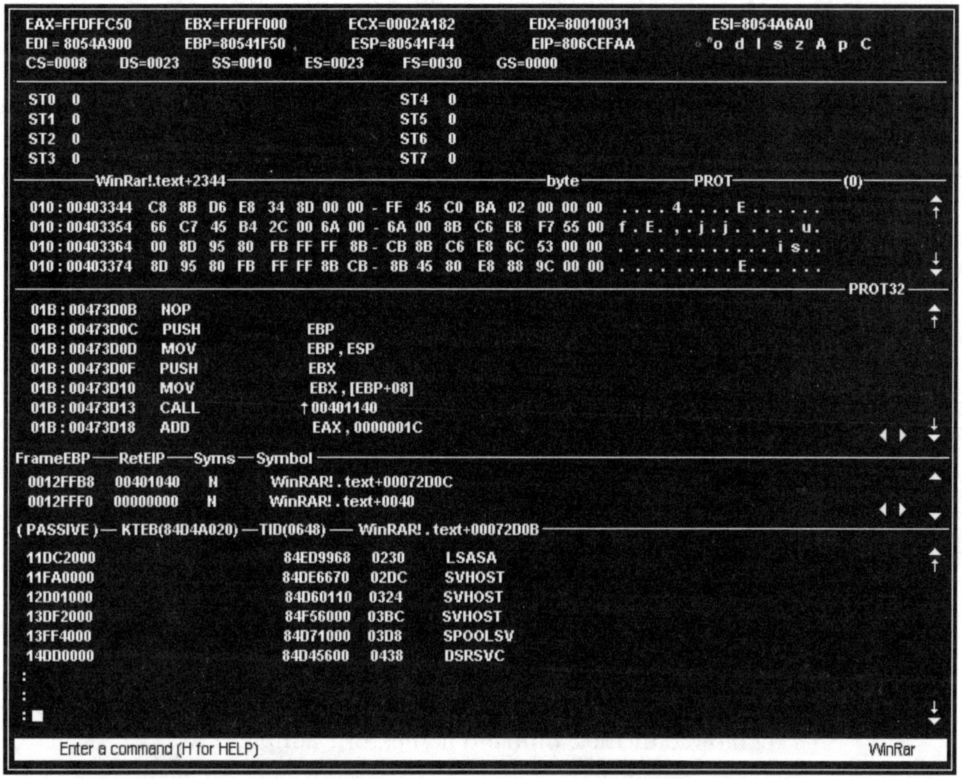

```
EAX=FFDFFC50      EBX=FFDFF000      ECX=0002A182      EDX=80010031      ESI=8054A6A0
EDI = 8054A900    EBP=80541F50 ,    ESP=80541F44      EIP=806CEFAA      ° °o  d  l  s  z  A  p  C
CS=0008    DS=0023    SS=0010    ES=0023    FS=0030    GS=0000

ST0  0                                    ST4  0
ST1  0                                    ST5  0
ST2  0                                    ST6  0
ST3  0                                    ST7  0
──────WinRar!.text+2344───────────────────────────────byte───────PROT─────────(0)──────
010 : 00403344  C8  8B  D6  E8  34  8D  00  00 - FF  45  C0  BA  02  00  00  00    . . . . 4 . . . . E . . . . .    ↑
010 : 00403354  66  C7  45  B4  2C  00  6A  00 - 6A  00  8B  C6  E8  F7  55  00    f . E . , . j . j . . . . . u.
010 : 00403364  00  8D  95  80  FB  FF  FF  8B - CB  8B  C6  E8  6C  53  00  00    . . . . . . . . . . . . i s . .
010 : 00403374  8D  95  80  FB  FF  FF  8B  CB - 8B  45  80  E8  88  9C  00  00    . . . . . . . . . E . . . . . .   ↓
────────────────────────────────────────────────────────────────────────────PROT32──────
01B : 00473D0B    NOP                                                                      ↑
01B : 00473D0C    PUSH          EBP
01B : 00473D0D    MOV           EBP , ESP
01B : 00473D0F    PUSH          EBX
01B : 00473D10    MOV           EBX , [EBP+08]
01B : 00473D13    CALL          ↑ 00401140
01B : 00473D18    ADD           EAX , 0000001C                                      ◄ ►    ↓
FrameEBP────RetEIP────Syms──Symbol
0012FFB8    00401040    N      WinRAR! . text+00072D0C                                    ▲
0012FFF0    00000000    N      WinRAR! . text+0040
                                                                                   ◄ ►
( PASSIVE )─── KTEB(84D4A020) ───TID(0648) ──── WinRAR! . text+00072D0B
11DC2000                    84ED9968    0230      LSASA                                    ▲
11FA0000                    84DE6670    02DC      SVHOST                                   ↑
12D01000                    84D60110    0324      SVHOST
13DF2000                    84F56000    03BC      SVHOST
13FF4000                    84D71000    03D8      SPOOLSV
14DD0000                    84D45600    0438      DSRSVC
:
:
: ■                                                                                       ↓
    Enter a command (H for HELP)                                                  WinRar
```

Fig. 4.1. The Softlce main window

The debugger window is shown in Fig. 4.1. The main window contains several windows that show different information. The number of such windows might vary. For instance, you, at your discretion, can add or remove these windows to or from the main window. The illustration demonstrates the most frequently used windows of the debugger. Note that you not only can view information in these windows but also can change their contents, such as the contents of the processor registers. However, this should be carried out carefully, because changing these registers might result in unpredictable behavior of the application or, perhaps, of the entire system. Thus, consider the debugger windows one by one, from top to bottom (see Fig 4.1):

❏ **Registers window** — This window lists all registers, including the segment registers (except for FPU registers) and their contents. The flags register is also shown, each flag designated by a separate letter. If the flag was changed during the last operation, it is marked by an uppercase letter and highlighted in the different color.

☐ **FPU registers window** — This window shows the contents of the eight FPU registers.

☐ **Data window** — This window is intended for displaying the contents of a specific memory region in both byte format and ASCII format. You can scroll this window, viewing arbitrary memory regions.

☐ **Code window** — This window contains the disassembled code, which also can be scrolled. If the application that you have loaded contains debug information recognizable by SoftIce, then the window would display the program's source code in a high-level programming language.

☐ **Stack window** — The stack window doesn't present the entire stack contents. On the contrary, it displays only the stack frame directly related to the operation of the given application.

☐ **Command window** — In this window, you can enter various SoftIce commands. In particular, from the illustration it is possible to see that by entering the H command you can display the help pane, a list of the debugger commands. To obtain information about an individual command, it is necessary to enter H followed by the command name, for example: H hwnd.

When working in the main (command) window, it is possible to issue commands to control the debugger. Along with the commands issued in the main window, it is possible to use keyboard shortcuts. In addition, provision has been made for using the standard mouse and the context menu.

Also note the lowest window — the help pane. When you issue a command, the help pane can assist you correctly enter that command and its parameters. In particular, the window will list all commands, starting from the characters that you have already entered. Besides, the debugger always displays the current process in the top right corner of the window. Always pay attention to this important issue to avoid confusing applications. This topic will be covered in more detail in *Section 4.1.3.*

In addition to the preceding windows, it is possible to use the **trace window**, where the values of all variables listed in the WATCH command are traced, as well as other windows, including the **MMX registers window** and the **local variables window**.

Operating Modes of the Debugger

After installing the SoftIce debugger, you can choose from the following five methods of start-up:

☐ **Disable** — The debugger doesn't start.

☐ **Manual** — The debugger doesn't start automatically. To start the debugger, issue the `Net start ntice` command. The directory, into which you install SoftIce, contains the ntice.bat file that holds this command. This mode is the safest one; however, it doesn't allow driver debugging at start-up.

☐ **Automatic** — The debugger starts up automatically. However, in this mode you cannot debug kernel-mode drivers.

☐ **System** and **Boot** — In both cases, the debugger starts automatically. The difference between these two modes is the order of loading the system and boot drivers.

4.1.2. The Loader

The main window of the loader32.exe program is shown in Fig. 4.2. As mentioned before, this program is intended for loading executable modules into the debugger. This utility also can retrieve debug information from the modules being debugged (provided that it is present there) and pass this information to SoftIce. When loading the module being debugged, the loader sets a breakpoint to the program entry point.

Loading the Executable Module

To load an executable module into the debugger, it is necessary to proceed as follows:

1. Open the module using the **File | Open...** menu option. You can use the **Open** button on the toolbar for the same purpose.

2. Then, choose the **Module | Load** menu item. It is also possible to use the **Load Symbols** toolbar button. The debugger would first translate the detected symbolic information into the file with the same name as that of the module being loaded and with the NMS file name extension, after which it would load the module, along with the debug information, into SoftIce. If the debugging information is missing, the loader would inform you about this and provide you with the choice whether or not to continue loading the module being investigated into the debugger. Translation of the debug information into the file with the NMS extension can be carried out by a separate command: either use the **Module | Translate** menu or click the **Translate** toolbar button.

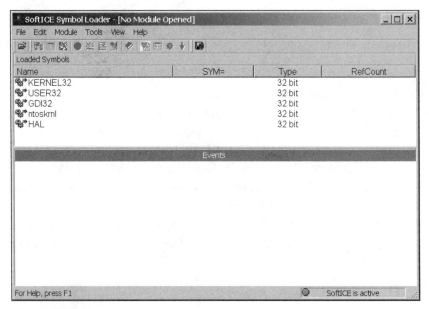

Fig. 4.2. The loader32.exe program window

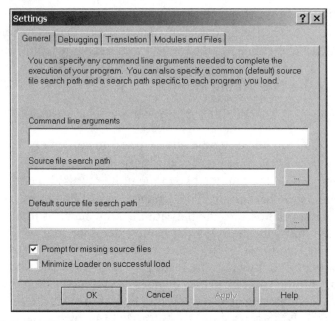

Fig. 4.3. The **Settings** window allows you to set the loading parameters for the modules to be debugged

The **Loaded Symbols** list contains the list of loaded modules. Pay special attention to the **SYM=** column. When loading the executable module, this column contains the size of the loaded symbolic information. Modules that do not contain such information are not displayed in the **Loaded Symbols** list.

Loading Parameters

After loading the module being investigated into SoftIce, it is possible to specify the start-up settings. To achieve this, use the **Module | Settings...** menu. The window, in which you can specify these settings is shown in Fig. 4.3. This window has four tabs, which must be considered in more detail.

❏   The **General** tab contains the following controls:

- The **Command line arguments** field allows you to specify the command-line parameters, with which the program being debugged must be started under the debugger.
- The **Source file search path** field lets you specify the search paths for the files related to the module being debugged.
- The **Default source file search path** field allows you to specify the main search path for the files. The debugger always searches according to the path specified in the **Source file search path** field, and only after that uses this field.
- If the **Prompt for missing source files** flag is set, then the debugger will inform you if all files required for debugging the executable file are not available. In particular, if the debugging information is missing, you'll be prompted to specify whether to continue loading the executable file into the debugger.
- The **Minimize Loader on successful load** flag is used for minimizing the loader size in the memory after the executable program is loaded into the debugger.

❏   The **Debugging** tab allows you to modify some current debugging parameters:

- The **Load symbol information only** and **Load executable** checkboxes allow you to load only debug information into the debugger and to load debug information with the executable module, respectively.
- The **Stop at WinMain, main, DllMain etc.** flag allows you to set a breakpoint to the starting point of the user part of the executable module. If the debug information is not available, the breakpoint is set to the starting point of program execution.

❏ Using the **Translation** tab, you can set the translation parameters of the debug information of the executable module. The switches are as follows:

● **Publics only** — Translate external names only.

● **Type information only** — Translate only information about variable types.

● **Symbols only** — Translate symbolic names only.

● **Symbols and source code** — Translate all debugging information.

● **Package source with symbol table** — Save the translated information in the NMS file.

❏ The **Modules and Files** tab allows you to list all files and their locations. These files will be loaded with the executable module. You can list all files that contain the debug information here. Loading of specific files can be temporarily blocked using a special switch.

4.1.3. Techniques of Working with SoftIce

Getting Started with Processes

Consider the main issues related to working with SoftIce:

❏ You are working in a multitasking operating system. The program that you are going to investigate using SoftIce after loading will become only one of the multiple processes running in the system. You must know exactly, with which process you are working. Do not confuse processes, because this might freeze the entire system. The debugger shows the current process in the bottom right corner of the help window.

❏ When loading an application using the loader32.exe program, the breakpoint is set to the start of program execution. The newly-created process becomes the current one. Thus, you can comfortably trace the newly-loaded application (see *Section 4.2.2*). However, when you close the debugger window by pressing <F5>, and then call it again, the process you were tracing earlier won't be the current process any longer. Each newly-running process has its own virtual address space. This address space is called the *process context*. For example, the D DS:004080AF command will output the memory contents for a specific virtual address space, and that address space will represent the context of the current process. To work with the addresses of an individual process, it is necessary to ensure that this process is the current one. To achieve this, use the ADDR command (a description of this command will be provided in *Section 4.2.2*, see *"Main Informational Commands"*). The following illustrates the use of the ADDR command: : ADDR 058. Here, 058 is the process identifier (PID). The PID value for the current process can be determined by using the ADDR command without parameters.

❑ Breakpoints represent the main tool of investigating executable code. You should clearly understand where the breakpoint is set (in other words, to which process or thread a specific breakpoint relates). In particular, this relates to setting breakpoints to API calls. When you create such a breakpoint, always use conditional constructs to specify, to which process that breakpoint relates. For this purpose, use the PID function that returns the current PID. As relates to the PID value, it can be obtained using the previously-mentioned ADDR command. The following illustrates how to set a breakpoint to the CreateWindowEx API function: : BPX CreateWindowEx if(PID == 0x58). It is necessary to point out again that the PID value for the required process can be determined using the ADDR or PROC commands. To set such a breakpoint, it is not necessary to make the required process the current one.

Breakpoints

When investigating specific executable code, one task always consists of searching for the required location within the program being investigated. When program code written in one of the high-level programming languages is not available (which most often is the case, unless you are debugging your own program), breakpoints are indispensable in research.

Nonpermanent Breakpoints

Nonpermanent (one-shot) breakpoints operate only once. Actually, nonpermanent breakpoint is a line in the code window, to which the cursor (highlighted string) points. To move the cursor, use the U command. The HERE command (or the <F7> shortcut) runs the executable code from the current command to the line of code marked using this method. Bear in mind that the HERE command is issued from the code window; it is necessary to switch to this window by pressing

<F6> before issuing the command. It is also possible to use the G address command, in which case the code will execute to the specified address.

Persistent Breakpoints

A typical example of a persistent (sticky) breakpoint is a breakpoint set to a specific command (a specific virtual address of the process). To set a persistent breakpoint, it is necessary to switch to the code window and use the BPX command without parameters. You can scroll the code and set breakpoints at required addresses. In this case, the lines of code, to which the breakpoints are set, will be highlighted. The same result can be achieved by using the <F9> shortcut. To remove the existing breakpoint, either move the cursor to the existing breakpoint and issue the BPX command, or press <F9>.

The general method of controlling breakpoints is applicable to the following breakpoints: BL to find the numbered list of breakpoints, BC n to delete the breakpoint with the specified number, BC * to delete all breakpoints, and BE n to edit the breakpoint with the specified number. Finally, if you know the address, at which you need to set a breakpoint, you can use that address in the BPX command, for example: BPX 0008:806CEFAB. If you issue the BPX command with the same address again, the breakpoint with the specified address will be deleted. Do not forget that the breakpoint set to the command address is related to a specific address space — in other words, to a specific process.

Conditional Breakpoints

Conditional breakpoints are activated if the conditions specified for them are satisfied. It is impossible to set two different breakpoints to the same address or to the same API function; however, you can use conditional constructs to take into account different variants of calling the same breakpoints. Here are typical examples of using conditional breakpoints.

Example 1

The breakpoint set to a specific address is activated only if the content of the EAX register takes the specified value:

```
: BPX   0008:806CEFAB if(EAX == 406090)
```

Example 2

Consider a small investigation for the breakpoint set to the MessageBox function call (the application under consideration is the WinRar archiving utility). Start the WinRar application, open the SoftIce window, and determine the application identifier using the ADDR command. The identifier turned out to be equal to 0x328. Then, issue the following command to create a conditional breakpoint:

```
: BPX  MessageBoxA  if(PID == 0x328)
```

Issue the BL command to make sure that the breakpoint is set as desired. Note that the A suffix has been specified. This suffix is mandatory, because SoftIce distinguishes API functions by their actual names.

Exit the debugger by pressing <F5>, and execute one of the application's commands that must cause the MessageBox window to appear. The SoftIce window will pop up immediately. The command window will display the message informing you why the SoftIce window has popped up. In this example, this message will appear as follows:

```
Break due to BP 00: USER32!MessageBoxA IF(PID == 0x328) (ET = 2.65 seconds)
```

Now, consider the code window. The first line of the entry into the MessageBox procedure will be highlighted there:

```
USER32!MessageBoxA
001B:77D56471    CMP      DWORD  PTR [77D8C3D0], 0
```

You can easily investigate the stack of the MessageBoxA function call and find the return address and parameter values. Having executed the ? *(ESP + 4) command, you'll obtain the value of the window handle for the window that initialized the MessageBox call (if something is unclear to you, return to *Section 3.2.1, "Stack Structures"*). The HWND value turns out to be equal to 100EC. View the list of windows opened by the WinRar application using the HWND 328 command, and you'll see that such a window exists and that it corresponds to the WinRarWindow class. By the way, in the same table you'll see the address of the window function of this window. Thus, it is possible to dive into studying the operation of this window. However, return to the first line of the MessageBox function call and find the return address. The ESP register points to the return address, Thus, by issuing the ? *(ESP) command, you'll discover that this address is equal to 43C76D.

There is another method of obtaining the return address. To use this method, press <F11>. After the MessageBox window appears, click one of the buttons in this window. The SoftIce window will appear, and you'll find yourself on the line that directly follows the `MessageBox` function call.

NOTE

In general, searching for calls to individual API functions is not a trivial task. To succeed, you must know these functions well and understand that the same result can be achieved using different methods. For example, assume that you need to know where the window is created. At first glance, it seems natural to look for the `CreateWindow` function call. However, this is not so.

First, there is no such function as `CreateWindow`. Even if you call the `CreateWindow` function in your program, the `CreateWindowEx` function is always used.

Second, it is necessary to look for `CreateWindowExA` and `CreateWindowExW` functions instead of `CreateWindowEx`.

Finally, the window might be created by modal dialog functions, such as `DialogBoxIndirect`, `DialogBoxParam`, and `DialogBoxIndirectParam`. Or it might be created by nonmodal functions, such as `CreateDialogParam`, `CreateDialogIndirect`, and `CreateDialogIndirectParam`. Also, do not forget that for all functions it is necessary to take into account the `A` and `W` suffixes.

Example 3

Consider how the register contents can be traced:

```
: BPX EIP IF(EAX == 0x10)
```

The breakpoint specified by this command will be activated when the value of the `EAX` register becomes equal to `0x10`, regardless of in which thread this event takes place.

Breakpoints to Windows Messages

As you know, the main events in GUI applications take place in window functions. Discovering the reaction of the window function to a specific message is the most important goal of program code investigation. Here, breakpoints set to Windows messages are indispensable. An example of the command that sets such a breakpoint is as follows:

```
: BMSG  100EC WM_CREATE
```

The first parameter of this command is the window handle, the function of which must receive the message. By the window handle value, the debugger determines the thread that has created this window, so the investigator doesn't need to care about solving this problem. When the required message arrives, the SoftIce debugger is activated and the code window will display the start of the window function. An interesting point is that the same result can be achieved using a standard BPX command, for example:

```
: BPX  43C76D IF((ESP -> 8) == WM_CREATE)
```

The first parameter is the address of the first command of the window function. Later, the command exploits the fact that the second parameter of the window function is located 8 bytes from the stack top.

Searching for a Window Procedure

How is it possible to locate a window procedure? Here are some helpful and easy tips:

❑ View the list of application windows. This list can be displayed by the HWND n command, where n is the application identifier. As you already know, the application identifier can be obtained using the ADDR command. The list of application windows contains their names, using which it is sometimes easy to locate the required window and, consequently, the window procedure address.

❑ If the list of windows is small, you can easily test all procedures by setting a breakpoint to the start of the window procedure (to be precise, at one of the first commands). If the breakpoint is activated when the window is activated, this means that you have found the required window.

❑ Analyze the window operation to find out, which API function can be called when working with this window (this was method I chose in *Example 2* from the previous section). Set a breakpoint to that function and carry out some operations in that window. In case of an interrupt, determine from which location was that function called. This will be the window function. In addition, bear in mind that most API functions accept the window handle as the first parameter.

Working with Applications that Contain Debug Information

SoftIce is a full-featured debugger, which means that it can load debug information and supply it with the executable code. Thus, when debugging custom applications, SoftIce can be used instead of the standard debugger built into the integrated development environment (IDE). Consider this approach on the example of debugging user applications written in C++ using Visual Studio .NET.

When the "add debug info" option is chosen (for this purpose, the best approach is using the DEBUG project configuration), the debug information database is created with the executable module. This database represents a file that by default has the same name as the executable module and the PDB file name extension (see *Section 1.6.1*). Information stored in that file is enough to represent the structure of the source program, along with the names of local and global variables, and to map this structure to the machine code.

When the loader32.exe program loads the executable module, it also loads the debug information and passes this to the debugger. By default, if the debug information is available for the program, SoftIce presents the program source code without Assembly commands in the source code window. Later, you can use the SRC command to switch to the mixed program representation (the source code of the program and machine code) or to pure machine code. In the first case, step-by-step program execution means that the program is executed one operator at a time. When using mixed representation, one step is equivalent to one machine command. Accordingly, it is possible to set breakpoints both to the operators of a high-level programming language and to machine commands. Listing 4.1 demonstrates several lines from the SoftIce code window when mixed representation was used.

Listing 4.1. Several lines from the SoftIce code window when mixed representation was used

---

```
00006                         a = 10;
001B:00411A2E                 MOV DWORD PTR [EBP - a], 0000000A
00007                         b = 11;
001B:00411A35                 MOV DWORD PTR [EBP - b], 0000000B
00008                         c = 10;
001B:00411A3C                 MOV DWORD PTR [EBP - c], 0000000C
00009                         printf ("%d\n", max(a, b, c));
001B:00411A43                 MOV EAX, [EBP - c]
001B:00411A46                 PUSH EAX

. . .
```

You should understand that in expressions such as [EBP - a] the a value is the address of the a variable in the stack (to be precise, the offset in relation to the address where the old EBP is stored — in other words, simply four).

4.2. Brief SoftIce Reference

This brief SoftIce reference contains most SoftIce commands. These commands are more than enough for investigating executable code.

4.2.1. Hotkeys

Controlling the Screen

- ❑ <Ctrl>+<D> — Open or close the main SoftIce window.
- ❑ <Ctrl>+<Alt> + arrow keys — Move the SoftIce main window over the screen with the increment equal to the character size.
- ❑ <Ctrl>+<Alt>+<Home> — Move the main SoftIce window to the top left corner of the screen.
- ❑ <Ctrl>+<Alt>+<End> — Move the main SoftIce window to the bottom left corner of the screen.
- ❑ <Ctrl>+<Alt>+<PageUp> — Move the main SoftIce window to the top right corner of the screen.
- ❑ <Ctrl>+<Alt>+<PageDn> — Move the main SoftIce window to the bottom right corner of the screen.
- ❑ <Ctrl>+<L> — Refresh the main SoftIce window.
- ❑ <Ctrl>+<Alt>+<C> — Place the main SoftIce window at the center of the screen.

Navigating the Main Window

- ❑ <Alt>+<C> — Switch to the code window from the command window, and vice versa.
- ❑ <Alt>+<D> — Switch to the data window from the command window, and vice versa.
- ❑ <Alt>+<L> — Switch to the local variables window from the command window, and vice versa.
- ❑ <Alt>+<R> — Switch to the registers window from the command window, and vice versa.

❏   <Alt>+<W> — Switch to the watch window from the command window, and vice versa.

❏   <Alt>+<S> — Switch to the stack window from the command window, and vice versa.

It is also possible to switch to any window (except for the FPU window) by clicking the required window with the left mouse button.

Navigating within Windows

❏   <↑> — Move one line back.

❏   <↓> — Move one line forward.

❏   <←> — Move one character left.

❏   <→> — Move one character right.

❏   <PageUp> — Move one page back.

❏   <PageDn> — Move one page forward.

❏   <Home> — Go to the first line of code.

❏   <End> — Go to the last line of code.

Controlling the Command Window

❏   <Enter> — Terminate the command line and execute the command.

SoftIce remembers 32 recently-entered commands. To navigate the list of commands stored in the buffer, use the <↑> and <↓> keys. The prefix that you have already entered into the command line is taken into account. For example, if you have entered the B character, only the commands starting from that character will be displayed. If you are currently in the code window, then to view the commands buffer, use the following shortcuts: <Shift>+<↑> and <Shift>+<↓>.

When editing the command line, use the following commands:

❏   <Home> — Go to the start of the command line.

❏   <End> — Go to the end of the command line.

❏   <Insert> — Toggle the insert/replace modes.

❑ <Delete> — Delete the character to the right of the cursor and move the line fragment to the left.

❑ <Bkspc> — Delete the character to the left of the cursor and move the line fragment to the left.

❑ <←> and <→> — Move the cursor over the line.

The SoftIce debugger has the *command window protocol buffer.* This buffer contains all information previously output into the window. To view the content of this buffer, use <PageDn> and <PageUp>.

Functional Keys

❑ <F1> — Display help (equivalent to the н command).

❑ <F2> — Open/close the registers window.

❑ <F3> — Toggle the source code modes.

❑ <F4> — Display the screen of the application being debugged.

❑ <F5> — Return to the program being debugged.

❑ <F6> — Move the cursor to or from the code window.

❑ <F7> — Execute the application being debugged up to the command pointed to by the cursor.

❑ <F8> — Execute the current command of the application being debugged, stepping into the functions.

❑ <F9> — Set a breakpoint to the current command.

❑ <F10> — Execute the current command, stepping over functions.

❑ <F11> — Go to the calling function of the program being debugged.

❑ <F12> — Execute the function up to the exit to the calling program.

❑ <Shift>+<F3> — Change the output format in the data window.

❑ <Alt>+<F1> — Open/close the registers window.

❑ <Alt>+<F2> — Open/close the data window.

❑ <Alt>+<F3> — Open/close the code window.

❑ <Alt>+<F4> — Open/close the watch window.

❑ <Alt>+<F5> — Clear the content of the command window.

❑ <Alt>+<F11> — Display the data located at the address stored in the first double word of the data window.

❏ <Alt>+<F12> — Display the data located at the address stored in the second double word of the data window.

The complete list of debugger commands that can be obtained by pressing <F1> or by issuing the H command is large; however, it doesn't contain all available commands. The complete list of commands can be found in the SoftIce Command Reference document, which can be downloaded from **http://www.compuware.com** and other Internet sites dedicated to the SoftIce debugger. In this book, I mainly use the list displayed by the debugger when the H command is issued. These commands are more than enough for debugging code and investigating application programs.

4.2.2. SoftIce Commands

SoftIce Macrocommands

The commands described in this section can be combined into macrocommands, or macros. There are two types of macrocommands that can be used in SoftIce. First, consider run-time macros. These commands can exist only within the current debugger session. After you restart the debugger, these commands will disappear. The list of commands that can be used to control these macros is as follows:

❏ MACRO *macro_name* = "*command1;command2;...*" — Create or change a macro. For example, : MACRO _ap "bc *;bpx MessageBox" creates a macro named _ap.

❏ MACRO *macro_name* * — Delete the macro with the specified name. For example, : MACRO _ap * deletes the _ap macro from the list of macros.

❏ MACRO * — Delete all macros from the list.

❏ MACRO *macro_name* — Edit the macro with the specified name.

❏ MACRO — Display the list of macros.

Macros can be defined with parameters. To achieve this, the % character is used. After this character, the parameter number must be specified. The parameter number must belong to the range from one to eight. For example, the MACRO _bpx = "bpx %1;bl" command creates a macro named _bpx that accepts a single parameter. This macro sets a breakpoint to the command specified as a parameter and outputs the list of existing breakpoints. To insert characters such as " or % into the macro name, use the backslash character (\). To insert a backslash, use the (\\) sequence.

To create persistent macrocommands, use the loader32.exe program. To achieve this, use the **Edit | SoftIce Initialization Settings...** menu. After you choose this menu, the SoftIce settings window will appear. In this window, go to the **Macro Definitions** tab (see Fig. 4.4). All further actions should be intuitive. The **Add** and **Edit** buttons are used for adding and editing macros, respectively. To remove an existing macro, use the **Remove** button. Bear in mind that all changes introduced in the SoftIce settings window come into force only after you reload the SoftIce debugger.

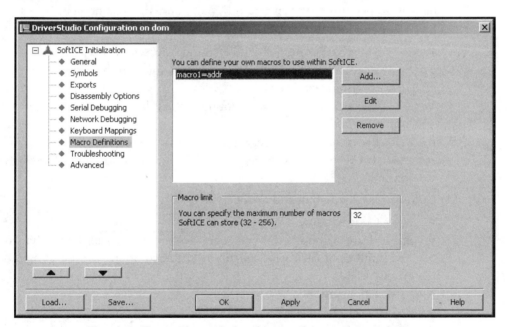

Fig. 4.4. The settings window for creating persistent macros

Commands for Controlling SoftIce Windows

❑ Lines n — This command sets the number of lines in the debugger main window. The value of n can range from 25 to 60.

❑ Width m — This command sets the width of the main window in characters. The value of m can range from 80 to 160.

❏ Set font n — This command sets the size of the font used by the debugger. The n variable can take the values 1, 2, or 3.

❏ Set origin x y — Using this command, it is possible to specify the values of the screen coordinates of the top left window corner.

❏ Set forcepalette [on | off] — If the value of this parameter is set to on, then all changes to the system color palette are blocked.

❏ Color [c1 c2 c3 c4 c5]|[reset] — This command specifies the color palette of the debugger's main window. The color reset command resets the color palette of the debugger's main window to its default state. The c1, c2, c3, c4, and c5 1-byte parameters specify the foreground and background colors for appropriate elements of the debugger's main window. The first half-byte specifies the background color, and the second half-byte sets the foreground color:

- c1 — Main background and foreground colors
- c2 — Background and foreground colors for output of the changed flags (in the registers window)
- c3 — Background and foreground colors for highlighting the current command in the code window
- c4 — Background and foreground colors in the help pane
- c5 — Background and foreground colors for the dividing lines between windows

❏ Commands for opening and closing windows:

- WC — Code window.
- WD — Data window. Several data windows can exist simultaneously. The number of each window can be specified after the separating dot, for example: wd.3.
- WF — FPU window.
- WL — Local variables window.
- WR — Registers window.
- WW — Watch window.
- WS — Stack window.
- WX — MMX registers window.

Each of the preceding commands opens the window of the corresponding type or closes the appropriate window (provided that it has already been opened). The size of the main window doesn't change, so opening a new window or closing an existing one changes the sizes of the existing windows. You can also specify the window size (the number of lines) by putting this parameter in the command. For example, the wd 30 command allocates 30 lines in the data window.

- ❑ EC — This command switches between the command window and the code window (equivalent to the <F6> shortcut).
- ❑ CLS — This command clears the command window (equivalent to the <Ctrl>+<F5> shortcut).
- ❑ RS — Using this command, it is possible to temporarily hide the SoftIce window. When you press any key, the SoftIce window will be restored. The RS command is equivalent to the <F4> shortcut.
- ❑ ALTSCR — This command is intended for redirecting the SoftIce window to an additional monitor. The command format is as follows: ALTSCR [mono|vga|off]. Parameters of this command are as follows:
  - Mono — Monochrome monitor
  - Vga — Monitor supporting video graphics array modes
  - Off — Switch off the alternative monitor (default)
- ❑ FLASH — This command is intended for restoring the screen after the T and P commands. The command format is as follows: FLASH on switches the restore mode on, and FLASH off switches the restore mode off. When executing this command without parameters, the current output mode is used.

Obtaining and Changing Information in SoftIce Windows

- ❑ R — This command is intended for retrieving and modifying information stored in registers. The format is as follows: R [-d|reg_name|reg_name [=] value].
  - The R -d variant outputs the list of registers and their contents into the command window.
  - The R reg_name variant moves the cursor of the registers window to the register specified in the command. You can edit the register content and save the change by pressing <Enter>. It is also possible to switch to the registers window using another method, such as using the mouse, and then proceed in the same way to edit the register content.
  - The R reg_name = value variant (the = character can be omitted) loads the specified value into the specified register.

❏ U — This command outputs the disassembled listing into the command window. The format of the command is as follows: U [address [L length]]. Command parameters are as follows:

- Address — The address, from which to start the listing output. It is possible to specify the register, from which this address should be retrieved.
- Length — The number of bytes in the listing.

When the listing length is specified, the listing will be output into the command window. If the address is specified but the length is missing, then the listing in the code window will start from the specified address. If the command is issued without parameters, the contents in the code window will be scrolled starting from the current address (the one, at which the previous listing was terminated). If the code window is missing, information output will be directed into the command window.

❏ D — This command outputs the memory dump of a specific memory area. The format of this command is as follows: D[size] [address [L length]]. Command parameters are as follows:

- Size — This parameter can take the following values: B to output information in bytes, W to output information in words, D to output information in double words, S to output information in short floating-point numbers (32-bit numbers), L to output information in long floating-point numbers (64-bit numbers), and T to output information in 10-byte blocks.
- address — This parameter specifies the address, from which to start the dump output. It is possible to specify the register, from which this address should be retrieved.
- Length — This parameter specifies the number of bytes for output (the listing length). By default, this value is 128.

The output is directed to the data window. If this window is missing, the dump is output into the command window.

❏ E — This command is intended for editing the memory. The command format is as follows: E[size] [address [data_list]]. Command parameters are as follows:

- Size — The meaning and value of this parameter are the same as for the D command.
- Address — This parameter defines the address of the area to be edited.

- Data_list — If this parameter is missing, the cursor moves to the data window, where you can directly edit a memory cell. Data passed in this parameter are placed into the memory cells starting from the specified address. The data format must correspond to the size parameter. If there are several values, they must be separated by commas.

An example of using this command is as follows: EB EBX 33, 34, 35. This command will place the values 33, 34, and 35, respectively, into three memory cells starting from the address stored in the EBX register.

❏ PEEK — This command reads data directly from the physical memory. The command format is as follows: PEEK[size] address. Command parameters are listed below:

- Size — This parameter specifies the size of the memory cell. It can take the following values: B for byte, W for word, and D for double word.
- Address — This is the address, from which the information is read.

❏ POKE — This command writes the data directly into the physical memory. The command format is as follows: POKE[size] address value. Command parameters are as follows:

- Size — This parameter has the same meaning as the similar parameter for the PEEK command.
- Address — This is the physical address, to which the data must be written.
- Value — This is the value to be written to the physical memory.

❏ PAGEIN — This command loads the missing page into the physical memory. The command format is as follows: PAGEIN address. The command parameter is the virtual page address.

❏ WATCH — This command specifies the expression that will be traced in the watch window, for example: WATCH ds:eax. Thus, the data whose address is stored in the EAX register will be traced.

❏ FORMAT — Using this command, it is possible to change the output format in the data window. This command doesn't accept any parameters. It simply changes the data window format cyclically.

❏ DATA — Using this command, it is possible to create additional windows for viewing data. This command accepts a window number ranging from zero to three as a parameter.

❑ A — This command allows you to enter an Assembly command at the specified address. The command format is as follows: A [address]. The address to which the Assembly command being entered will be placed, is the only parameter of this command. If the address is not specified, the current address from the code segment is used. When executing this command, the help window displays the prompt (address), after which it is possible to enter the required command.

❑ S — This command allows data search. The command format is as follows: S [-acu] [address L length data-list]. Command parameters are as follows:

- c — Case-insensitive search
- u — Search in the Unicode format
- a — Search in the ASCII format
- Address — Starting address for the search range
- Length — Length of the search area
- Data_list — List of data for searching, delimited by commas or blank characters

This command is intended for searching for the required data. If the required data items are found, they will be displayed in the data window, and the command window will display an appropriate message specifying the address, at which they are located. To continue searching, enter this command without parameters. An example of data usage is as follows: S ds:eax L 2000 20. This will search for the 20h byte in the area that has the length 2000h, starting from the address stored in the EAX register.

❑ F — This command is intended for filling the memory area. The command format is as follows: F address L length data_list. Command parameters are as follows:

- Address — Starting address
- Length — Length of the data area to be filled
- Data_list — Data that will be placed starting from the required address (data items must be separated by commas or blank characters)

This command places the data specified by the data_list parameter, starting from the specified address. If the length value is greater than the data length, the data items will be repeated cyclically until they reach the length size. An example of command use is as follows: F ds:eax L 100 "W". Thus, the memory area starting at the DS:EAX address, which has the length of 100H, will be filled with W characters.

- ❏ M — The command for moving data. The command format is as follows: M address1 L length address2. Parameter values are as follows:
  - Address1 — Address, from which the data will be moved
  - Length — Length of the data to be moved
  - Address2 — Address, to which the data will be moved

An example using this command is as follows: M ds: eax L 1000 ds:ebx. With this command, 1000h bytes will be moved from the address pointed at by the EAX register to the area with the address stored in the EBX register.

- ❏ C — This command is intended for comparing two data blocks. The command format is as follows: C address1 L length address2.
  - Address1 — Address of the first data block to be compared
  - Length — Length of the data to be compared
  - Address2 — Address of the second data block

Using this command, it is possible to compare two data blocks. If two data blocks are not equal, then the command window will display the complete addresses of these bytes and their values. An example of command use is as follows: C ds:100 L 10 ds:200. Here, 10h bytes are compared.

- ❏ HS — This command can be used for searching in the command buffer. The command format is as follows: HS [+|-] string. The + or - signs stand for descending (from top to bottom) and ascending (from bottom to top) search orders, respectively. After the sign, the search string is specified. To continue searching, use the command without parameters.
- ❏ . (dot) — If the code window is visible, then this command makes the instruction specified by the CS:EIP visible and highlights it.

Commands for Controlling Breakpoints

Breakpoints are the most important mechanisms for application debugging. SoftIce assigns each breakpoint a number ranging from 0 to 255. Thus, 256 breakpoints can exist simultaneously. Breakpoint numbers can be used for controlling breakpoints: You can remove an existing breakpoint, enable it, or disable it. The total number of breakpoints for accessing memory and input/output ports must not exceed four.

Breakpoint Types

The main types of breakpoints supported by the SoftIce debugger are as follows:

❏ Execution breakpoints — In this case, you can specify the command name, which SoftIce replaces with the INT 3 interrupt. If the name of this command appears in the executable code, code execution is interrupted. In particular, you can set a breakpoint to API calls.

❏ Memory breakpoints — With this breakpoint, the debugger traces access to specific memory addresses.

❏ Interrupt breakpoints — The debugger will trace breakpoints that take place in the operating system by modifying the interrupt descriptor table (IDT) (see *Section 1.2.1*).

❏ Input/output breakpoints — The debugger traces all instructions for INPUT and OUTPUT.

❏ Windows message breakpoints — To set such a breakpoint, it is necessary to know the descriptor of the window, to which a message must arrive.

Capabilities of Breakpoints

When working with breakpoints, it is possible to use conditional constructs. In such cases, the breakpoint will be activated only if the specified condition has been observed. In particular, using conditional constructs it is possible to specify, for which process the given breakpoint would be activated. A typical example of such a condition is as follows: if(pid == 0x058). This condition specifies that the PID must be equal to 0x058. This condition will be used constantly, because you are going to debug specific applications that are running in your operating system.

Using the do operator, it is possible to specify the commands that must be executed if a breakpoint is activated. In general, the format of this command appears as follows: do "command 1; command 2; ...". As a command, it is possible to use both normal commands and macros.

When describing the commands intended for controlling breakpoints, the following designations will be used:

❏ size — This parameter defines the size of the cell, to which the breakpoint will be set. The list of valid values is as follows: B for byte, W for word, and D for double word.

❏ [R|W|RW|X] — This parameter specifies the type of access to the memory cell or input/output port that will be traced. Here, R designates reading from the cell (port), W is for writing to the cell (port), RW is for reading and writing to and from the cell (port), and X is for executing the command that occupies the given memory cell.

❏ Reg_deb — Here, it is possible to specify, which debug register should be used (D0–D3). As a rule, this parameter is skipped, because the debugger chooses the required register on its own.

❏ [IF cond] — Here, it is possible to specify, the condition that must be observed to enable the interrupt at the given breakpoint.

❏ [DO comm] — Using this command, it is possible to specify a command or group of commands that will be executed in case of an interrupt at the given breakpoint.

Commands for Setting Breakpoints

❏ BPM — Using this command, it is possible to set a breakpoint to a specific memory cell. The command format is as follows: BPM[size] addr [R|W|RW|X] [reg_deb] [IF cond] [DO comm]. The addr parameter specifies the cell address. The address can be specified either explicitly or using registers, for example, as follows: ds:eax.

❏ BPIO — This command sets a breakpoint to the input and output to and from a specific port. The command format is as follows: BPIO [R|W|RW] [deb_reg] [IF cond] [DO comm]. The debugger will trace all commands for input and output to and from the specified port.

❏ BPINT — This command is used for setting an interrupt breakpoint. The breakpoint is activated only if the interrupt is activated through the IDT. The command format is as follows: BPINT int_number [IF cond] [DO comm]. Here, int_number is the number of the interrupt being traced. When the breakpoint is activated, the first command will be the first instruction of the interrupt handler.

❑ BPX — This command sets an execution breakpoint, for example, a breakpoint for execution of a specific API function. The command format is as follows: BPX name [IF cond] [DO comm]. Here, name specifies some name, for example, MessageBoxW. The BPX command without parameters sets a breakpoint to the current command. However, to set a breakpoint for the current command, it is necessary to switch to the code window of the debugger.

❑ BMSG — This command is intended for setting a breakpoint to the messages arriving for the specific window in the specific range. The command format is as follows: BMSG hWnd [L] [beg_mes [end_mes]] [IF con] [DO comm]. Parameters of this commands are as follows:

- hWnd — The window handle.
- [L] — When this parameter is set, the message will simply be displayed in the command buffer (the command window); however, the debugger will not be activated.
- [beg_mes] — The first message from the message range. This might be either a numeric or a symbolic designation of the required message.
- [end_mes] — The last message from the message range (when dealing with the message range instead of a single message). If this parameter is missing, only the message specified by the beg_mes parameter will be traced.

If no messages are specified in the command, then the breakpoint is applied to all messages of the given window. The example illustrating the use of this command is as follows: BMSG 01001F WM_PAINT. This command traps the WM_PAINT message for the window with the 01001F handle.

❑ BSTAT — This command outputs statistics on the given breakpoint. As a parameter for this command, specify the breakpoint number. In particular, this command will output the Popups value (the number of times this breakpoint caused the SoftIce window to pop up) and the Breaks value (the number of times the given breakpoint was activated}, among others.

Commands for Manipulating Breakpoints

❑ BPE — This command is intended for editing a given breakpoint. The command accepts the breakpoint number as a parameter.

❑ BPT — This command calls the template for creating a breakpoint with the specified number into the command line. The difference of this command from the previous one is that this command creates a new breakpoint instead of editing the existing one.

❏ BL — This command generates the list of breakpoints, specifying the breakpoint number and the template used for creating the given breakpoint.

❏ BC — This command deletes the specified breakpoint. The parameter of this command is the breakpoint number of the list of breakpoint numbers (separated by commas or blank characters). If the * character is specified as a parameter, then all breakpoints will be deleted.

❏ BD — This command disables all breakpoints specified as parameters. The parameter of this command is a list of all breakpoints to be disabled (breakpoint numbers separated by commas or blank characters). To disable all breakpoints, use the * wildcard character.

❏ BE — This command enables breakpoints. As a parameter, it accepts the list of breakpoints (breakpoint numbers separated by commas or blank characters) or the * wildcard character.

❏ BH — This command outputs the list of breakpoints used in the current and previous debugging sessions. You can navigate this list and can choose the breakpoint that you need by pressing <Insert>. The <Enter> key is used for setting all selected breakpoints. The debugger remembers the last 32 breakpoints.

Tracing Commands

❏ X — This command exits the SoftIce window and returns control to the program whose execution was interrupted by SoftIce. This command is equivalent to the <F5> hotkey or the <Ctrl>+<D> shortcut.

❏ G — This command informs the debugger that it is necessary to execute the application being debugged. The command format is as follows: G [=address1] [address2]. The command accepts the following parameters:

- Address1 — This is the address, from which the execution must start. If this address has not been specified, then execution will start from the current address (CS:EIP).

- Address2 — This is the terminating address for execution. If this address has not been specified, execution will continue until a breakpoint is encountered or until the SoftIce window is called.

The G command without parameters is equivalent to the X command. The G @SS:EBP command is equivalent to pressing <F11> (go to the calling function).

❏ T — This command is intended for step-by-step execution of the code being debugged. The command format is as follows: T [=address] [count]. Command parameters are as follows:

- Address — This is the starting address, from which the tracing must start. If this parameter has not been specified, then execution will start from the current command.

- Count — This parameter specifies the number of instructions to be executed. If this parameter is missing, then only one instruction will be executed.

This command without parameters is equivalent to pressing <F8>. An example of command use is as follows: T CS:EIP - 20 10. Thus, ten instructions will be executed starting from the CS:EIP - 20 address.

❏ P — This command corresponds to execution of the instruction bypassing procedures, interrupts, string commands, and loops. Without parameters, it is equivalent to pressing <F10>. If the RET (P RET) option is present, SoftIce will execute the program until the RETN/RETF instructions are encountered. Execution will stop at the point, to which the jump using these commands is carried out. Thus, this command with a parameter is equivalent to pressing <F12>.

❏ HERE — This command is equivalent to pressing the <F7> hotkey. It instructs the debugger to execute the program starting from the CS:EIP address to the current location of the cursor in the code window.

❏ EXIT — This command is considered obsolete. It is equivalent to the X command. It is recommended that you avoid using this command.

❏ GENINT — This command passes control to the specified interrupt. The command format is as follows: GENINT [nmi|int1|int3|number]. The following parameters are accepted by this command:

- nmi — The call to the nonmaskable interrupt
- Int1 — The call to interrupt number 1
- Int3 — The call to interrupt number 3
- Number — The call to the interrupt with a number ranging from 0 to 5F

This command must be used carefully. When using it, you must be sure that the handler for the specified interrupt exists; otherwise, the command would freeze the entire system.

- ❐ HBOOT — This command resets (reboots) the entire computer system.
- ❐ I1HERE — There are two variants of this command. I1HERE on enables the mode. In this case, the SoftIce window will be called every time the interrupt with the number 1 takes place. I1HERE off disables the mode.
- ❐ I3HERE — This command has two variants: I3HERE on enables the mode. The SoftIce window will be called every time the interrupt with the number 3 takes place. The I3HERE off command disables the mode.
- ❐ ZAP — This command replaces the calls to interrupts 1 and 3 with NOP instructions.

Main Informational Commands

- ❐ GDT — This command displays the global descriptor table (GDT). The command format is as follows: GDT [selector|address]. The list of the command parameters is as follows:
  - Selector — Selector in GDT
  - Address — Segment address

If parameters are not specified, the command would display the entire GDT content.

- ❐ LDT — This command displays the local descriptor table (LDT). The command format is as follows: LDT [selector|table_selector]. Command parameters are as follows:
  - Selector — Selector in LDT
  - Table_selector — LDT selector in GDT

If the command is issued without parameters, the entire LDT will be displayed.

- ❐ IDT — This command displays the contents of the IDT. The command format is as follows: IDT [number|address]. Command parameters are as follows:
  - Number — Number of the interrupt, about which it is necessary to display information
  - Address — Address of the interrupt handler (selector:offset), about which it is necessary to display information

If the command is issued without parameters, the command would display the current content of the entire IDT.

❒ TSS — Using this command, the debugger outputs the contents of the task state segment (TSS) into the command window. The parameter of this command is the selector in GDT, pointing to TSS. If the command is issued without a parameter, then the command will display the contents of the current TSS, whose selector is located in the task register.

❒ CPU — This command displays the complete list of processor registers and their contents.

❒ PCI — This command outputs the information about all PCI devices present in the system into the command window.

❒ MOD — This command outputs the list of all loaded Windows modules. In the command line, it is possible to specify the first characters of the module name, in which case the command will output the list of all modules whose names start with the specified prefix.

❒ HEAP32 — This command outputs the list of memory heaps created by the operating system and applications. The command format is as follows: HEAP32 [hheap|name]. The list of command parameters is as follows:

- hheap — Handle of the heap returned by the CreateHeap function
- Name — Task name

This command outputs the following information: the base address of the heap, the maximum size, the amount of used memory (in kilobytes), the number of segments in the heap, the heap type, and the heap owner. If command parameters are missing, the list of all heaps is displayed.

❒ TASK — When this command is issued, the debugger displays the entire task list and additional information about tasks in the command window. The active heap will be marked by the * character. This command might be useful in a system malfunction, when it is necessary to determine, which task was the cause.

❒ NTCALL — This command lists all system services operating at the kernel level (ring 0).

❒ WMSG — This command displays the list of Windows messages and their numbers in the command window. The command format is as follows: WMSG [partial_name] [number]. Command parameters are as follows:

- Partial_name — Full or partial name of the Windows message
- Number — Number of the Windows message

The command without parameters outputs the list of all Windows messages known to the debugger. If the partial_name parameter is present, the debugger outputs all messages corresponding to the given fragment of the message name. If the message number is specified, then the message number and its name will be displayed.

❑ PAGE — Using this command, the debugger outputs information about memory pages starting from the given virtual address. The displayed information includes virtual and physical addresses, attribute, type, and virtual size. The command format is as follows: PAGE [address] [L length]. Command parameters are as follows:

- Address — Virtual page address
- Length — Number of pages for output

If the command is issued without parameters, the debugger displays the list of all pages.

❑ PHYS — This command displays the list of all virtual addresses corresponding to the given physical address. This command can be used only with the parameter specifying the physical address.

❑ STACK — This command outputs information about the stack structure. The command format is as follows: STACK [thread | frame]. Command parameters are as follows:

- Thread — Either the thread descriptor or the thread identifier
- Frame — Address of the stack frame

If this command is specified without parameters, the debugger outputs information about the current stack on the basis of the SS:EBP address.

❑ XFRAME — This command outputs information about the exception written into the stack (see *Section 3.2.5*). The command parameter is either the thread identifier or the pointer to the stack frame. If the parameter is missing, the debugger uses the current thread.

❑ HWND — This command outputs information about the windows created in the system. The command format is as follows: HWND [-x] [-c] [hwnd|desktop|process|thread|modul|class]. Command parameters are as follows:

- -x — Extended information

- −c — Windows hierarchy
- Hwnd — Window handle or the pointer to the window structure
- Desktop — Desktop descriptor
- Process — PID
- Thread — Thread identifier
- Module — Module name
- Class — Name of the registered window class

If the command is issued without parameters, the debugger outputs information about all windows currently in the system.

❏ CLASS — This command outputs information about window classes. The command format is as follows: CLASS [-x] [process] [thread] [module] [class]. Command parameters are as follows:

- -x — Extended information about window classes
- Process — PID
- Thread — Thread identifier
- Module — Module identifier or name
- Class — Name of the registered window class

If the command is issued without parameters, the debugger will output the list of all registered window classes for the current process.

❏ THREAD — This command is used for obtaining information about threads. The command format is as follows: THREAD [-r|-x-u] [thread] [process]. Command parameters are as follows:

- -r — Information about the thread registers
- -x — Extended information about threads
- -u — Information about user-level thread components
- Thread — Thread identifier
- Process — PID

❏ ADDR — This command is used to output information about existing address contexts (processes) and to establish the current context. To set the current context, it is necessary to supply the command parameter representing the PID, name, or address. Also, it is possible to specify the address of the process environment block (PEB), or kernel process environment block (KPEB). If the command is issued without parameters, the debugger outputs information about all existing address contexts.

- ❑ MAP32 — This command outputs the list of loaded 32-bit modules and additional information about these modules. The command format is as follows: MAP32 [-u|-s] [name|handle|address]. Command parameters are as follows:
  - -u — Display only modules loaded into the user-mode part of available memory
  - -s — Display only modules loaded into the part of the memory allocated for the operating system and the tools that it requires
  - Name — Module name
  - Handle — Base address of a module image
  - Address — Address that falls within the module image

If the command is issued without parameters, the debugger will output the list of all loaded 32-bit modules and additional information about those modules.

- ❑ PROC — This command is intended for obtaining information about the process. The command format is as follows: PROC [-xom] [name]. Command parameters are as follows:
  - -x — Extended information about each branch
  - -o — Extended information about each object
  - -m — Information about the object's memory use
  - Name — Name of the tasks or process, process descriptor, PID, thread name or identifier, or thread descriptor

If the object name has not been specified, then information about all processes will be displayed.

- ❑ QUERY — This command is intended for output of the virtual memory map of the processes. The command format is as follows: QUERY [-x] [address] [name]. Command parameters are as follows:
  - -x — Names of processes (along with information about them) that occupy the specified virtual address
  - address — Virtual address
  - Name — Process name

If the command is issued without parameters, it displays the virtual memory map of the current process.

- ❏ WHAT — This command tries to interpret the parameter specified to it. For example, if the supplied parameter is the PID, the command informs you about this. In other words, you can check the authenticity of the identifier or descriptor on your own.
- ❏ OBJTAB — This command allows you to obtain information about the USER object table.
- ❏ FOBJ — This command outputs information about existing file objects. Such objects are created for each opened file.
- ❏ IRP — This command outputs information about input/output request packets.
- ❏ FIBER — This command outputs the information about the fiber data structure. In particular, this data structure is returned by the CreateFiber() function.

Other Commands

- ❏ PAUSE — This command sets two modes for viewing information in the command window. The PAUSE on mode is the default one, in which the information is displayed in portions, and the next portion of data appears only after the user presses any key. The PAUSE off mode corresponds to continuous information output.
- ❏ ? — This command computes the expression value, for example, ? 34 + 90*2. The debugger simultaneously outputs the result in hex and decimal formats, as well as in the ASCII format.
- ❏ OPINFO — This command allows you to obtain information about a specific processor instruction. For example, if you issue the OPINFO add command, the main information about the ADD processor instruction will be displayed on the screen (Listing 4.2).

Listing 4.2. Information about the ADD processor instruction displayed by the OPINFO command

```
ADD
        Integer addition: DEST <- DEST + SRC
        EFLAGS | OF DF IF SF ZF AF PF CF TF NT RF |
               | M        M  M  M  M  .           |
```

❏ ALTKEY — This command replaces the keyboard combination used for activating the SoftIce debugger. By default, the <Ctrl>+<D> shortcut is used. If this command is issued without parameters, then SoftIce will display the current combination in the command window, for example, ALTKEY Alt P or ALTKEY Ctrl Z. In this case, the SoftIce window will be activated by <Alt>+<P> or <Ctrl>+<Z>, respectively.

Operators

The SoftIce debugger environment allows you to use expressions in commands and breakpoint definitions. Expressions are built using operators. Consider the list of operators used by the debugger.

Addressing Operators

❏ . — If the code window is visible, this command makes the instruction located at CS:EIP visible, and highlights it. The dot operator can be used in expressions.

❏ * — This operator is used for specifying the address, to which the given expression points. For example, *(EAX) designates the contents of the memory pointed to by the EAX register.

❏ -> — Using this operator, as well as using the asterisk operator, it is possible to obtain the memory contents located at the address pointed to by the given expression. For example, if you know the address of the window procedure, which can be obtained using the HWND command, then it is possible to set the following breakpoint at the WM_PAINT message: BPX 6BDFE003 IF (ESP -> 8) == WM_PAINT.

❏ @ — This operator is equivalent to the asterisk operator.

Arithmetic Operators

❏ Unary and binary plus (+) operators, for example, +100 or EBX + ESI
❏ Unary and binary minus (-) operators, for example, -100 or EAX - 8
❏ Binary multiplication (*) operator, for example, EBX*4
❏ Binary division (/) operator, for example, (EAX + EBX)/2
❏ Binary modulo (%) operator, for example, EBX%3
❏ Logical left shift operator (<<)
❏ Logical right shift operator (>>)

Bitwise Operators

❏ Bitwise AND operator (&)

❏ Bitwise OR operator (|)

❏ Bitwise exclusive OR operator (^)

❏ Bitwise negation or NOT operator (~)

Logical Operators

❏ Logical NOT (!), for example, !EBX

❏ Logical AND (&&), for example, EAX && EBX

❏ Logical OR (||), for example, EAX || FF

❏ Equality condition (==)

❏ Inequality condition (!=)

❏ Less than (<)

❏ Greater than (>)

❏ Less than or equal to (<=)

❏ Greater than or equal to (>=)

Built-in SoftIce Functions

The disassembler provides a range of built-in functions. The main built-in functions are briefly outlined here:

❏ Byte — Return the least significant byte of the expression.

❏ Word — Return the least significant word of the expression.

❏ Dword — Return a double word (extend a byte or a word to a double word).

❏ HiByte — Return the most significant byte (or a word or a double word).

❏ HiWord — Return the most significant word.

❏ Sword — Convert a byte into a signed word.

❏ Long — Convert a byte or a word into a long integer.

❏ WSTR — Display the string in the Unicode format.

❏ Flat — Convert the address with a selector (logical address) into the linear address of the flat memory model.

The current contents of the registers can be found using the functions with names corresponding to the names of appropriate registers, for example, EAX, EBX, and EDX.

- ❏ CFL — Return the carry flag's value.
- ❏ PFL — Return the parity flag's value.
- ❏ AFL — Return the auxiliary flag's value.
- ❏ ZFL — Return the zero flag's value.
- ❏ SFL — Return the sign flag's value.
- ❏ OFL — Return the overflow flag's value.
- ❏ RFL — Return the resume flag's value.
- ❏ TFL — Return the trace flag's value.
- ❏ DFL — Return the direction flag's value.
- ❏ IFL — Return the interrupt flag's value.
- ❏ NTFL — Return the nested task flag's value.
- ❏ IOPL — Return the input/output privilege level flag's value.
- ❏ VMFL — Return the virtual machine flag's value.
- ❏ IRQL — Return the interrupt request level flag's value.
- ❏ DataAddr — Return the initial address of the data block displayed in the data window.
- ❏ CodeAddr — Return the address of the first instruction displayed in the code window.
- ❏ Eaddr — Return the effective address of the current instruction, if one is present.
- ❏ Evalue — Return the value located at the current effective address.
- ❏ Process — Return the kernel-mode PEB of the currently active process.
- ❏ Thread — Return the kernel-mode thread environment block of the currently active thread.
- ❏ PID — Return the identifier of the currently active process.
- ❏ TID — Return the identifier of the currently active thread.
- ❏ BPCount — Return the number of times that the breakpoint has been activated, for which the value of the conditional expression was TRUE.
- ❏ BPTotal — Return the total number of times the breakpoint has been evaluated.

- ❏ BPMiss — Return the number of times the breakpoint has been triggered, for which the conditional expression hasn't been satisfied (and the SoftIce window hasn't been activated).

- ❏ BPLog — Silently save into the buffer information about the number of times the breakpoint has been evaluated.

- ❏ BPIndex — Return the number of the current breakpoint in the list of breakpoints.

If the number of any function is preceded by the underscore character, then the disassembler computes the current function value and uses it in further computations: _PID, _TID, _EAX, etc.

Chapter 5:

THE IDA PRO
DISASSEMBLER

I DA Pro is an outstanding instrument for investigating executable code. The foundation for code investigation using IDA Pro is formed by the following features:

☐ The powerful toolset built into the disassembler is designed for investigating the executable code. IDA Pro doesn't draw its own conclusions or assumptions. The privilege of analyzing heuristically is always delegated to human investigators.

☐ Human investigators can participate in heuristic analysis, refine parameters of a specific program's objects, and introduce modifications. In other words, the user of this instrument becomes an active participant in the disassembling process.

☐ The built-in programming language, which is close to the classical C language in its structure, allows for considerable extension of the product's functionality.

This excellent product, characterized by outstanding capabilities, was extensively used throughout this book. The two main goals of this chapter are as follows:

☐ Provide a detailed description of the IDA Pro disassembler.

☐ Provide comprehensive reference information related to the use of this program. Hopefully, you will be able to investigate the executable code (at least when studying the program's capabilities) using the materials of this chapter as a reference, and consulting this book from time to time.

Unfortunately, information about this debugger is scarce. Sources other than the brief information provided in the help file supplied with this debugger are hardly available. Thus, I hope that this chapter will help you master this powerful instrument.

5.1. Introduction to IDA Pro

IDA stands for Interactive Disassembler, although the **About** window displays a beautiful young lady. This instrument is so elegant that its name makes you imagine someone like her.

5.1.1. Getting Started

First, it is necessary to mention that the IDA Pro distribution set includes both console (idaw.exe) and graphical (idag.exe) variants of the program. All further sections will mainly relate to the GUI variant.

General Information about Virtual Memory

If you load some executable module into IDA Pro, two files will be created into the directory, from which you have loaded that module. These will be two auxiliary files with the ID0 and ID1 file name extensions. These are auxiliary virtual memory files used by the IDA Pro debugger for storing intermediate data. After you unload the previously-loaded module (using the **File | Close** menu commands), both files will disappear. The file with the same name as the loaded executable module and with the ID1 file name extension is used for loading the image of that executable module. This image is identical to the image loaded into the 32-bit flat memory model of the Windows operating system. Thus, it becomes possible to ensure that the module being investigated is identical to the module executed by the operating system. This feature makes IDA Pro close to an exclusive debugger. For each address, the file stores a 32-bit characteristic: an 8-bit cell corresponding to the given address and a 24-bit attribute defining various properties of this cell. In particular, this attribute specifies whether the given memory cell relates to an instruction or to the data (and, in the latter case, the type of this data item). Furthermore, this attribute specifies whether there are other objects in the string, such as comments, cross-references, or labels.

Mechanisms of working with the virtual memory used by IDA Pro are identical to the similar mechanisms used by the Windows operating system. When accessing an individual cell, the entire page containing this cell is loaded into the main memory (buffer). If the memory cell is modified, the entire virtual memory page is rewritten. IDA Pro holds part of the memory pages in random access memory.

Modified cells are periodically flushed to the disk. When it is necessary to load a page but the page buffer is full, IDA Pro searches the buffer to find the page that was modified first, flushes it to the disk, and loads the required page into the freed space.

In addition to storing the image of the loadable module, IDA Pro requires memory for information such as labels, function names, and comments. This information is stored in the file with the ID0 file name extension. In official documentation, this memory is called memory for b-tree.

The Program Interface

General Information

In Fig. 5.1, the main IDA Pro window with the loaded executable program is shown. The background analysis of the loaded program has been completed, as designated by the message in the bottom left corner: The initial autoanalysis is finished.

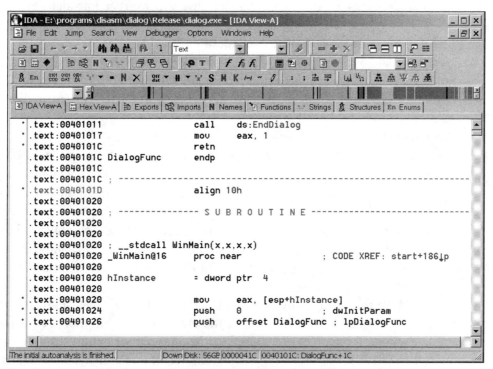

Fig. 5.1. The IDA Pro main window with the loaded executable module

The IDA Pro main window has lots of tabs. By default, there are nine tabs, although in reality there might be more. You can add new tabs using the **Views | Open subviews...** menu. There are two windows that can be duplicates: **IDA View** and **Hex View**. Thus, different sections of code and data can be viewed in different windows. These windows are supplied with suffixes — A, B, C, etc. — so that the user can easily distinguish them.

The main window is **IDA View**. This window displays the main result of executable code analysis. In this window, the user can participate in further analysis of the code.

When working with the IDA Pro debugger, do not forget that there are three main methods of controlling this program: menu commands, toolbar buttons, and hotkeys. Hotkeys do not cover all IDA Pro capabilities; however, there are hotkeys for the most frequently used operations. For example, if some data block raises your suspicion, you can always convert it into code (disassemble) by pressing the <C> key (short for CODE). On the other hand, if some block of Assembly commands seems meaningless, you can always convert it into data by pressing the <D> key (short for DATA).

IDA Pro uses the following configuration files: Ida.cfg is the common configuration file, idatui.cfg is the configuration file for the console variant of the program, and idagui.cfg is the configuration file for the GUI variant of the program. Configuration files must reside in the CFG subdirectory of the IDA Pro main directory.

Loading the Executable Code

After you load an executable module into IDA Pro, you'll see the main IDA Pro window shown in Fig. 5.2. Using this window, you can configure the loading process and the initial analysis. This window provides lots of configuration settings that will be described in the next few sections. In most cases, IDA Pro suggests optimal settings so that the user doesn't need to configure anything. You only need to click the **OK** button and rely on your luck and the disassembler's capabilities. However, because these options are used occasionally, I'll provide brief descriptions.

❐ **Load file directory/name as** contains the list of formats that can be recognized by the current IDA Pro version for the chosen module. In most cases, IDA Pro recognizes the type of file chosen for loading. Other options available in this window are set automatically depending on the chosen type of the loadable module. For example, carry out the following simple experiment. Disassemble the MS-DOS stub of some PE module (see *Section 1.5.1*). To achieve this, choose the **MS-DOS executable** option from the list. To confirm your choice, click the **Set** button. I'd like to point out again that this list corresponds to the choice of the PE module. PE modules can be interpreted both as normal PE modules and as MS-DOS programs, or even as binary files. If you choose a new executable (NE) module, for example, the content of this list will be different.

❑ **Processor type** is a dropdown list that allows you to choose the processor, for which the chosen module was compiled.

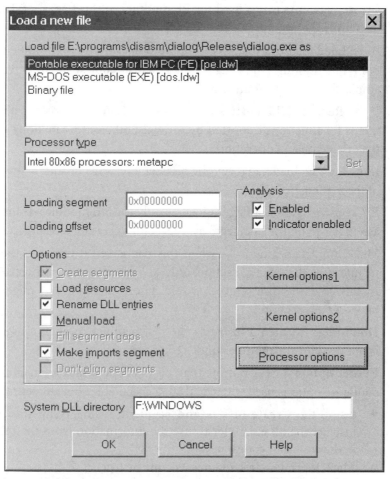

Fig. 5.2. The window controlling executable code loading

❑ **Loading segment** and **Loading offset** are fields that allow you to load the module into a specific segment with a specific offset, which might be useful both for MS-DOS modules and for binary files. These parameters are not used for PE modules.

❑ **Enabled** is a flag from the **Analysis** group that allows you to disable the initial analysis of the executable code. This flag is set by default, which means that the initial analysis will be carried out after loading.

❑ **Indicator enabled** specifies whether the analysis process indication should be carried out. By default, this flag is set.

❑ **Create segments** is not used for PE modules. If this flag is set, IDA Pro creates the required segments.

❑ If the **Load resources** flag is set, the resources of the PE module will be loaded. For binary modules, this flag is called **Load as code segment** and is used, for example, for COM programs.

❑ If the **Rename DLL entries** flag is not set, IDA Pro provides additional comments for functions imported by ordinals; otherwise, functions are renamed at the disassembler's discretion.

❑ If the **Manual load** flag is set, the disassembler will consult the user at every step of the loading process.

❑ **Fill segment gaps** is a flag important only for NE modules. It instructs the disassembler to fill the intersegment space, thus creating one large segment.

❑ **Make imports segment** — when this flag is set, it instructs the disassembler to interpret the `.idata` section only as related to the imported information. In this case, the disassembler would ignore the data that might also be contained in this section.

❑ **Don't align segments** instructs the disassembler to align segments. This flag is not used for the modules under consideration.

❑ **Kernel options1** is a button that displays the window enabling the user to configure options used when analyzing executable code, by setting the flags.

   • Using the **Create offsets and segments using fixup info** flag, you can instruct the disassembler to use the information from the relocations table in the course of code analysis.

   • **Mark typical code sequence as code** instructs the disassembler to use typical processor command sequences in the course of analysis.

- **Delete instructions with no xrefs** allows the disassembler to ignore microprocessor instructions, for which there are no cross-references.
- **Trace execution flow** allows tracing, so that you can discover the processor instructions.
- **Create functions if call is present** instructs the disassembler to recognize functions by calls.
- **Analyze and create all xrefs** is one of the main options that makes the disassembler use cross-references in the main analysis.
- **Use FLIRT signatures** instructs the disassembler to use fast library identification and recognition technology (FLIRT) for recognizing library functions using signatures.
- **Create function if data xref data->code32 exists** instructs the disassembler to check the references to executable code in the data area.
- **Rename jump functions as j_...** allows IDA Pro to rename simple functions containing only the `jmp somewhere` command as `j_somewhere`.
- **Rename empty functions as nullsub_...** allows IDA Pro to rename functions containing one `RET` command as `nullsub_....`
- **Create stack variables** instructs the disassembler to create (define) local variables and parameters of the functions.
- **Trace stack pointer** instructs IDA Pro to trace the value of the `ESP` register.
- **Create ASCII string if data xref exists** instructs the disassembler to consider the data item referenced as ASCII string if its length exceeds a certain value.
- **Convert 32-bit instruction operand to offset** instructs the disassembler to consider a direct data item in the processor instruction as an address, provided that its value falls into the predefined interval.
- **Create offset if data xref to seg32 exists** instructs the disassembler to consider values stored in the data area as addresses, provided that their values fall into the predefined interval.
- **Make final analysis pass** instructs the disassembler to convert all uninvestigated bytes into data or instructions when carrying out the final stage of the analysis.
- ❏ **Kernel options2** is a button that calls another window with another set of flags for the options used in the course of executable code analysis:
  - **Locate and create jump tables** instructs IDA Pro to draw conclusions about the address and size of the jump table.

- If the **Coagulate data in the final pass** flag is off, then only bytes of the code segment are converted at the last stage of analysis (see the **Make final analysis pass** flag).
- **Automatically hide library functions** instructs the disassembler to hide (collapse) library functions detected using FLIRT.
- **Propagate stack argument information** instructs the disassembler to save information about stack parameters of the call in case of future calls (such as a function call from another function).
- **Propagate register argument information** instructs the disassembler to save information about register parameters of the call in case of further calls (such as function calls from another function).
- **Check for Unicode strings** allows the disassembler to check the program for the presence of Unicode strings.
- **Comment anonymous library functions** instructs the disassembler to mark anonymous library functions using the library name and the signature, with which a specific function was detected.
- **Multiple copy library function recognition** allows the disassembler to recognize several copies of the same function within a program.
- **Create function tails** allows you to search for function tails and add them to function definitions.
- ❒ **Processor options** is a button that calls the window with the option flags.
  - **Convert immediate operand of "push" to offset** indicates the possibility of converting the direct operand in the PUSH command to an offset (an address).
  - **Convert db 90h after "jmp" to "nop"** specifies to the disassembler that 90H bytes that follow the JMP command must be interpreted as NOP commands.
  - **Convert immediate operand of "mov reg,..." to offset** indicates the possibility of converting the direct operand in the MOV reg,... command (reg stands for the register) into an offset (an address).
  - **Convert immediate operand of "mov memory,..." to offset** indicates the possibility of converting the direct operand in the MOV mem,... command to an offset (an address).
  - **Disassemble zero opcode instructions** gives the disassembler the following instruction: 00 00 ADD [EAX], AL. By default, this flag is off.
  - **Advanced analysis of Borland's RTTI** (RTTI stands for run-time type information) allows IDA Pro to check and create RTTI structures.

- **Check "unknown_libname" for Borland's RTTI** allows the disassembler to check names marked as `unknown_libname` for the presence of RTTI structures.
- **Advanced analysis of catch/finally block after function** allows the disassembler to search for `catch/finally` exception processing blocks.
- **Allow references with different segment bases** allows the disassembler to specify references to characters even when the value stored by the specified address is not a character (doesn't represent a character code).
- **Don't display redundant instruction prefixes** instructs the disassembler to hide some command prefixes to improve the listing's readability.
- **Interpret int 20 as VxDcall** instructs the disassembler to interpret `INT 20H` as `VxDcall/jump`.
- **Enable FPU emulation instructions** specifies that commands such as `INT 3?H` must be interpreted as emulations of arithmetic coprocessor commands.
- If the **Explicit RIP-addressing** flag is set, it is assumed that relative instruction pointer (RIP) addressing is used in the program. This flag is in force for 64-bit processors.

❑ **System DLL directory** is a field that specifies the directory where IDA Pro would search for DLLs, provided that the file with the .ids file name exception corresponds to the given library.

The Disassembler Window

Because most work with IDA Pro is carried out in the disassembler window, it is expedient to consider this window in detail. It is necessary to point out that the developers of this disassembler have carefully considered representation of the disassembled function and methods of navigating it. Consider some key aspects related to this topic:

❑ *Hiding functions* — Functions in the disassembler window can be shown in a collapsed form (hide) or an expanded form (unhide). In the collapsed form, the function is represented by a single line. This useful feature allows you to considerably improve the disassembled code's readability. To expand and collapse functions, use the <+> and <-> keys on the numeric keypad or the **View | Unhide** and **View | Hide** menu options.

❑ *Indicating jumps* — Fig. 5.3 shows the disassembler window. Pay special attention to the leftmost section of the window. This section is intended for simplifying navigation of the listing. Commands are marked by dots. If the line doesn't contain a dot, this means that the string contains a comment. When the user clicks a dot with the mouse, IDA Pro sets a breakpoint to the respective address. Jumps are designated by continuous or dashed lines. Continuous lines designate unconditional jumps, and dashed lines correspond to conditional jumps.

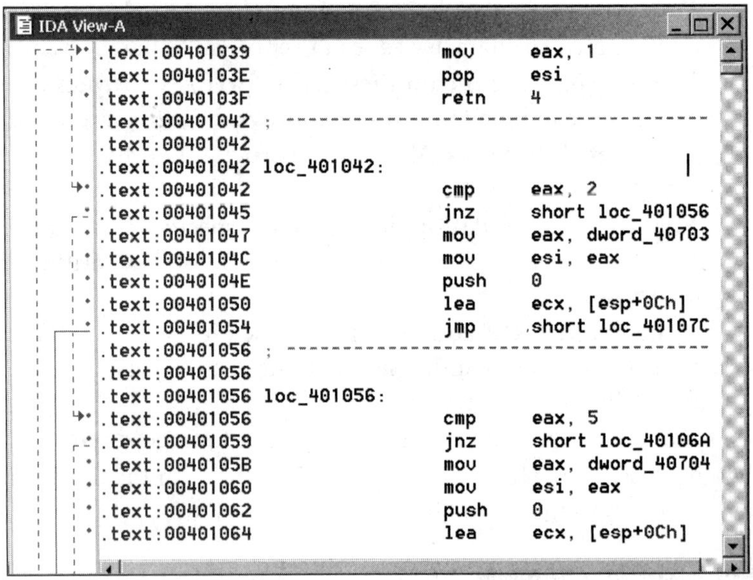

```
 IDA View-A                                                    _ □ ×

 .text:00401039                        mov      eax, 1
 .text:0040103E                        pop      esi
 .text:0040103F                        retn     4
 .text:00401042  ; ----------------------------------------
 .text:00401042
 .text:00401042  loc_401042:                                      |
 .text:00401042                        cmp      eax, 2
 .text:00401045                        jnz      short loc_401056
 .text:00401047                        mov      eax, dword_40703
 .text:0040104C                        mov      esi, eax
 .text:0040104E                        push     0
 .text:00401050                        lea      ecx, [esp+0Ch]
 .text:00401054                        jmp      short loc_40107C
 .text:00401056  ; ----------------------------------------
 .text:00401056
 .text:00401056  loc_401056:
 .text:00401056                        cmp      eax, 5
 .text:00401059                        jnz      short loc_40106A
 .text:0040105B                        mov      eax, dword_40704
 .text:00401060                        mov      esi, eax
 .text:00401062                        push     0
 .text:00401064                        lea      ecx, [esp+0Ch]
```

Fig. 5.3. Indication of jumps in the disassembler window

❏ *Using special comments* — Addresses within a program, to which jumps are carried out (conditional and unconditional jumps or the CALL command) or referenced, contain special comments. The comment starts either from CODE XREF, if the reference has the meaning of jump to the specified address, or from DATA XREF, if this instruction is referenced as data (for example, as follows: MOV EAX, OFFSET L1). These comments are called cross-references because the given address represents the crossing where references from other program locations meet. The cross-reference mark is followed by a colon, which, in turn, is followed by the address counted from the start of the function or section, from which this reference originates. By clicking this address with the mouse, you can call the pop-up window with the code fragment that refers to the given instruction. The address must contain the ↑ and ↓ characters that specify the direction to the line of code that references this instruction. To jump to the line, from which the reference originates, double-click the address with the mouse. If there are fewer than four references to the given line, they are listed; otherwise, the references are designated as dots. In this case, you can right-click one of these addresses and can choose the required item from the **Jump to cross reference** context menu. After that, the window will appear with the list of all addresses. This window will contain the reference to the requested code line. Choose the address you need by clicking it with the mouse (or by clicking the **OK** button after positioning the cursor on the required item), and you'll find yourself at the required position within the listing. The fragment of the disassembler window containing the cross-references is shown in Fig. 5.4.

```
.text:004028F1
.text:004028F1 loc_4028F1:
.text:004028F1                     mov      esp, [ebp-18h]          ; DATA XREF: .rdata:stru_4075F0↓o
.text:004028F4
.text:004028F4 loc_4028F4:                                         ; CODE XREF: sub_4028C0+27↑j
.text:004028F4                                                     ; sub_4028C0+2B↑j
.text:004028F4                     or       dword ptr [ebp-4], 0FFFFFFFFh
.text:004028F8                     add      dword ptr [ebp-1Ch], 4
.text:004028FC                     jmp      short loc_4028D3
.text:004028FE ; ------------------------------------------------------------------------------
.text:004028FE
.text:004028FE loc_4028FE:                                         ; CODE XREF: sub_4028C0+1A↑j
```

Fig. 5.4. Cross-references

❐ *Designating an address* — The listing shown in the disassembler window demonstrates various methods of designating an address. For example, if you are dealing with an API function, the name of that function is explicitly specified. In addition, IDA Pro usually bases the names of references to detected strings on the content of that string. For example, if the string contains the text You are wrong!, then IDA Pro would designate the reference to that string as aYouAreWrong. In this case, the prefix means IDA Pro considers this string an ASCII string. All other names designating function names or data addresses are based on the prefix and an address. For example, you can encounter the following prefixes:

- sub_ — Function
- locret_ — Address of the return instruction
- loc_ — Instruction address
- off_ — Data specifying the address (offset)
- seg_ — Data specifying the segment address

- `asc_` — Address of an ASCII string
- `byte_` — Byte address
- `word_` — Word address
- `dword_` — Double word address
- `qword_` — Address of a 64-bit value
- `flt_` — Address of a 32-bit floating-point number
- `dbl_` — Address of a 64-bit floating-point number
- `tbyte_` — Address of an 80-bit floating-point number
- `stru_` — Structure address
- `algn_` — Alignment directive
- `unk_` — Address of an uninvestigated area

❑ *Using the context menu* — When working with the disassembler window, it is convenient to use the context menu that pops up when you click the right mouse button within a window. Some menu items differ for different parts of the listing, such as function names, instructions, comments, and selected blocks. Some menu items relate to IDA Pro operation as a debugger (**Run to cursor**, **Add breakpoint**, and **Add execution trace**). These items will be described later in this chapter. In particular, pay attention to the **Rename** menu item. This item allows you to edit command contents (operands).

❑ *Navigating a listing* — The most important issue is navigation of the listing. Jumps to locations pointed to by cross-references have been already covered. The same approach (double-clicking the cross-reference with the mouse) can be used for returning (for example, to the conditional jump, to the CALL command, or to the address in a command like MOV EAX, OFFSET address). Note that IDA Pro remembers all of your jumps so that you can always move forward or backward along the chain (as you would follow the links in an Internet browser) using the following toolbar buttons: ← ▼ → ▼.

Other Windows

❑ **Hex View** — This window contains the hex dump of the loaded module, as well as ASCII characters corresponding to this dump. This window is an auxiliary one in relation to the disassembler window and can be easily synchronized with it. To achieve this, it is enough to click the right mouse button somewhere within the window and choose the **Synchronize with | IDA View...** item from the context menu. After switching to the disassembler window, you'll find yourself in the program location that corresponds exactly to the address in the dump window. In addition, IDA Pro tracks the addresses, with which you are working, in the disassembler window. When you switch to the dump, you automatically jump to the required location.

❐ **Exports** — This window contains the list of exported functions. It is helpful for working with DLLs. For normal executable modules, the list is made up of a single element, namely, the `start` function.

❐ **Imports** — This window contains the list of imported functions and the modules, from which they are imported. When you double-click the imported function, you switch to the disassembler window and find yourself in the entry point. Thus, you can easily locate all cross-references to this function within the program.

❐ **Names** — This window contains the list of all imported and library functions, as well as the names of variables and labels recognized by IDA Pro. On the left side of each name is a character that defines the name type:

- **L** — Library function
- **F** — Regular functions and API functions
- **C** — Instruction (label)
- **A** — ASCII string
- **D** — Data
- **I** — Imported function

Double-clicking the name with the mouse jumps you to the program location where that name is used. To create a new name (for example, for the label) and specify the address corresponding to that name, press <Insert>. The entered name will also appear in the disassembler window.

❐ **Functions** — This window contains the entire list of functions recognized by IDA Pro, including library functions and imported user functions.

❐ **Strings** — This window contains all strings found by the disassembler. If you double-click a string, you'll automatically jump to the location within the listing where that string was defined. By default, only C-style strings are presented in this window. If you right-click this window and choose the **Setup** command from the context menu, you can display other types of strings in this window, for example, Unicode strings or Pascal strings.

❑ **Structures** — This window contains all structures found by the disassembler. To add a new structure to the list, press <Insert>.

❑ **Enums** — This window is intended for displaying all enumerations located within the program being investigated.

In addition to the preceding windows, the disassembler can use other windows. In particular, note the libraries window. In the online help system, this window is called the signatures window. This window contains the list of signatures used for recognizing library functions. The signatures window is shown in Fig. 5.5. As you can see, the list specifies the name of the file containing the function signatures, the number of functions found using these signatures, and the name of the library to whose functions these signatures were applied. By pressing <Insert>, you can add the required signature file from the displayed list. The signatures of that file will be immediately used for recognizing new functions.

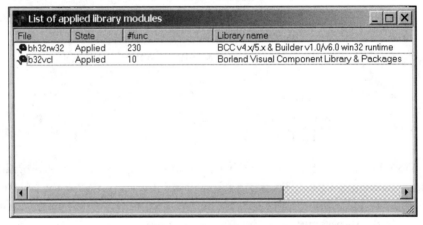

Fig. 5.5. The signatures window

Menus and Toolbars

I am not going to provide a detailed explanation of all IDA Pro menu items and all toolbar buttons. In most cases, you won't encounter any difficulties in studying IDA Pro functional capabilities on your own. It is only necessary to pay special attention to some important functions:

❑ The **File** menu items are as follows:

• **Open** — Load the executable module to be disassembled.

- **Load** — Load different files: **Reload the input file** reloads the disassembled module, **Additional binary file** loads an additional binary file into the database; **IDS file** loads the intrusion-detection system (IDS) file containing the information about the functions of specific import library (all IDS files located within the IDS directory are loaded automatically, **PDB file** loads the PDB file containing debug information, **DBG file** loads the file containing debug information, **FLIRT signature file** loads and applies the signatures file (the same operation is executed in the signatures window, as shown in Fig. 5.5), and **Parse C header file** reads the type definitions from the header file for further declarations of new structures and enumerations (see the description of the **Enums** and **Structures** windows).
- **Produce file** — Create new files of different structures on the basis of the disassembled code: a MAP file that can be used by debuggers, an Assembly file (having the ASM file name extension), an LST file (listing), a listing in the HTML format, etc.
- **IDC file** — Load and execute the script file (see *Section 5.2.1*).
- **IDC command** — Call the window for immediate script execution.
- **Save...** — Save the current disassembling database in the file with the IDB file name extension.
- **Save as...** — Save the current disassembling database under the specified name.
- **Close** — Close the disassembled file, saving the disassembling database.
❑ The **Edit** menu items are as follows:
- **Copy** — Copy the selected fragment into the clipboard.
- **CODE** — Convert the block to the executable code.
- **DATA** — Convert the selected block to data.
- **Struct var...** — Convert the block to the selected structure.
- **Strings** — Convert to a string (string types can be chosen from the submenu).
- **Array** — Convert to the array with the predefined parameters.
- **Undefine** — Mark the selected block as data of an undefined structure.
- **Name** — Rename.
- **Operand type** — Specify the operand type.
- **Comments** — Control comments.
- **Segments** — Control segments.
- **Structs** — Control structures.
- **Functions** — Control functions.

- **Other** — Perform other functional capabilities, such as specifying the alignment directive, entering instructions or data, or highlighting with a color.
- **Plugins** — Use external plug-in modules.

❐ The items of the **Jump** menu are intended for various jumps in the disassembled code, such as jumping to the specified address, jumping to the specified function (which can be chosen from the list), jumping to the program's entry point, marking a code line, and jumping to the specified label.

❐ Items of the **Search** menu are intended for various search operations in the disassembled text, such as searching for text, searching for the next data block, searching for the next Assembly instruction, and searching for the next byte sequence.

❐ Using items of the **View** menu, it is possible to customize the look of the IDA Pro disassembler: Open new windows (**Open Subviews**), create and delete toolbars (**Toolbars**), hide and unhide functions (**Hide** and **Unhide** commands, respectively), open the calculator window, etc.

❐ Commands from the **Debugger** menu allow you to use various IDA Pro debugging capabilities: control breakpoints (**Breakpoints**), control watches (**Watches**), control tracing (**Tracing**); view the contents of various registers (**General registers**, **Segment registers**, and **FPU registers**); etc.

❐ The **Options** menu items allow you to change various IDA Pro settings, some of which were covered earlier when I described the loading control window.

❐ Using items of the **Windows** menu, you can control IDA Pro windows.

❐ The **Help** menu items allow you to display help topics and obtain technical support.

Program Start-Up Keys

When starting IDA Pro, you can use the following start-up keys:

❐ -a — Disable automatic analysis.

❐ -A — Start IDA Pro and automatically load the last database.

❐ -b#### — Specify the address for loading a module.

❐ -B — Start IDA Pro and automatically generate IDB and ASM files.

❐ -c — Remove the old disassembling database.

❑   -ddirective — Start IDA Pro and specify the loading directive for the first-pass analysis.

❑   -Ddirective — Start IDA Pro and specify the loading directive for the second-pass analysis.

❑   -f — Exclude FPU instructions.

❑   -h — Open the IDA Pro help window.

❑   -i — Specify the address of the program's entry point.

❑   -M — Disable the mouse (for the console variant of loading).

❑   -O#### — Pass options for the plug-in module, -Oplug1:opt1:opt2:opt3, where plug1 is the name of the plug-in module and opt1, opt2, and opt3 are module options.

❑   -o#### — Specify the database name (used in combination with the -c key).

❑   -p — Specify the processor type.

❑   -P+ — Pack the database.

❑   -P- — Do not pack the database.

❑   -R — Load resources from the executable file.

❑   -S#### — Execute the specified IDC file.

❑   -W#### — Specify the Windows directory.

❑   -x — Do not create segments.

❑   -? — Display help about IDA Pro start-up keys.

5.1.2. Simple Examples of Code Investigation

In this section, I'll return to the examples written in Assembly language considered in *Section 1.6.* The reason I decided to do so is straightforward. Using Assembly, it is easy to model the required situation to demonstrate specific patterns of code investigation in IDA Pro.

About IDA Pro Capabilities

Easy Examples

In the preceding chapters, lots of examples were considered that illustrate the capabilities of IDA Pro in analyzing executable code. Consider the program shown in Listing 5.1.

Listing 5.1. Easy Assembly program (see Listing 1.43)

```
.586P
.MODEL FLAT, STDCALL
includelib e:\masm32\lib\user32.lib
EXTERN          MessageBoxA@16:NEAR
; Data segment
_DATA SEGMENT
TEXT1 DB 'No problem!', 0
TEXT2 DB 'Message', 0
_DATA ENDS
; Code segment
_TEXT SEGMENT
START:
        PUSH OFFSET 0
        PUSH OFFSET TEXT2
        PUSH OFFSET TEXT1
        PUSH 0
        CALL MessageBoxA@16
        MOV  ESI, 3
        ADD  ESI, OFFSET L2
L2:
        CALL ESI
        RETN
L1:
        XOR  EAX, EAX
        RETN
_TEXT ENDS
END START
```

You should immediately notice the small trick hidden behind the code fragment, shown in Listing 5.2.

Listing 5.2. Fragment of the program in Listing 5.1 that hides a small trick

```
    MOV  ESI, 3
    ADD  ESI, OFFSET L2
L2:
    CALL ESI
    RETN
L1:
```

The CALL ESI command jumps to the L1 label. How would IDA Pro react to this situation? Consider the disassembled code produced by IDA Pro (Listing 5.3).

Listing 5.3. Disassembled listing of the program in Listing 5.1, produced by IDA Pro

```
.text:00401000 _text                        segment para public 'CODE' use32
.text:00401000                              assume cs:_text
.text:00401000                              ; org 401000h
.text:00401000 assume es:nothing, ss:nothing, ds:_data, fs:nothing, gs:nothing
.text:00401000 ; ------- S U B R O U T I N E ---------------------------
.text:00401000                 public start
.text:00401000 start           proc near
.text:00401000                 push    0                  ; uType
.text:00401002                 push    offset Caption   ; lpCaption
.text:00401007                 push    offset Text      ; lpText
.text:0040100C                 push    0                  ; hWnd
.text:0040100E                 call    MessageBoxA
.text:00401013                 mov     esi, 3
.text:00401018                 add     esi, offset loc_40101E
.text:0040101E loc_40101E:                               ; DATA XREF:
start+18↑o
.text:0040101E                 call    esi                ; sub_401021
.text:00401020                 retn
.text:00401020 start           endp
.text:00401021 ; ------- S U B R O U T I N E ---------------------------
```

```
.text:00401021
.text:00401021 sub_401021      proc near     ; CODE XREF: start:loc_40101E↑p
.text:00401021                 xor      eax, eax
.text:00401023                 retn
.text:00401023 sub_401021      endp
.text:00401023
.text:00401024 ; [00000006 BYTES: COLLAPSED FUNCTION MessageBoxA.
.text:00401024 ; PRESS KEYPAD "+" TO EXPAND]
.text:0040102A                 align 200h
.text:0040102A _text           ends
```

From Listing 5.3, it is evident that IDA Pro clearly traces the value of the ESI register and, thus, determines the start of the sub_401021 procedure. The arithmetic here is easy. It is only necessary to add three to the address of the loc_40101E procedure to obtain the exact address of the called procedure. Having located the start of the procedure, it is easy to determine its end. In this case, the end of procedure is defined by the RETN command nearest the start.

Now, modify the program from Listing 5.1. The modified code is shown in Listing 5.4. As it turns out, even the slightest modification produces some difficulties with code disassembling.

Listing 5.4. Modified code of the program shown in Listing 5.1

```
.586P
.MODEL FLAT,STDCALL
includelib e:\masm32\lib\user32.lib
EXTERN          MessageBoxA@16:NEAR
; Data segment
_DATA SEGMENT
TEXT1 DB 'No problem!', 0
TEXT2 DB 'Message', 0
_DATA ENDS
; Code segment
_TEXT SEGMENT
```

```
START:

        PUSH OFFSET 0

        PUSH OFFSET TEXT2

        PUSH OFFSET TEXT1

        PUSH 0

        CALL MessageBoxA@16

        MOV  ESI, 3

        ADD  ESI, OFFSET L2

        PUSH ESI

        POP  EDI

L2:

        CALL EDI

        RETN

L1:

        XOR  EAX, EAX

        RETN

_TEXT ENDS

END START
```

Consider the listing of the disassembled code produced by IDA Pro — after analysis of the executable code created by the Assembly translator from the program shown in Listing 5.4. The disassembled result is provided in Listing 5.5.

Listing 5.5. Disassembled text of the program shown in Listing 5.4

```
.text:00401000 _text              segment para public 'CODE' use32

.text:00401000                     assume cs:_text

.text:00401000                     ; org 401000h

.text:00401000 assume es:nothing, ss:nothing, ds:_data, fs:nothing, gs:nothing

.text:00401000 ; ------- S U B R O U T I N E ---------------------------

.text:00401000                     public start

.text:00401000 start               proc near

.text:00401000                     push    0               ; uType

.text:00401002                     push    offset Caption  ; lpCaption
```

```
.text:00401007                 push    offset Text      ; lpText
.text:0040100C                 push    0                ; hWnd
.text:0040100E                 call    MessageBoxA
.text:00401013                 mov     esi, 3
.text:00401018                 add     esi, offset loc_401020
.text:0040101E                 push    esi
.text:0040101F                 pop     edi
.text:00401020 loc_401020:                               ; DATA XREF: start+18↑o
.text:00401020                 call    edi
.text:00401022                 retn
.text:00401022 start           endp
.text:00401023 ; ------- S U B R O U T I N E ---------------------------
.text:00401023                 xor     eax, eax
.text:00401025                 retn
.text:00401026 ; [00000006 BYTES: COLLAPSED FUNCTION MessageBoxA.
.text:00401026 ; PRESS KEYPAD "+" TO EXPAND]
.text:0040102C                 align 200h
.text:0040102C _text           ends
```

Consider Listing 5.5, which presents the analysis carried out by the IDA Pro disassembler. As you can see, as a result of slight modifications of the program's source code the procedure located at the 00401023 address can no longer be recognized by the disassembler. To understand how the analysis was carried out, it is necessary to consider the algorithm used by IDA Pro. However, some conclusions can be drawn even without viewing the algorithm. As I already mentioned, IDA Pro is a careful program. It avoids drawing premature conclusions. In this case, there is a certain probability that some jump (an indirect one) will be made to the loc_401020 label. This jump originates from some different location within a program, in which case it is probable that the procedure address will be different. This is hard to assess and evaluate; however, to be on the safe side it is possible to take such a possibility into account and rely on the interactive work with the user. Nevertheless, consider the code fragment shown in Listing 5.6.

Listing 5.6. Code example, for which IDA Pro correctly identifies the procedure address

---

```
    PUSH ESI
    POP  ESI
L2:
    CALL ESI
```

In this example, IDA Pro doesn't encounter any difficulties and correctly identifies the procedure address.

Interactive Work with IDA Pro

Consider examples of interactive work of the code investigator with IDA Pro.

The example shown in Listing 5.7 contains a simple Assembly program. As can be easily seen, the CALL EDI command is executed by the address corresponding to the L1 label.

Listing 5.7. Simple Assembly program illustrating interactive work of the code investigator and IDA Pro

---

```
.586P
.MODEL FLAT, STDCALL
includelib e:\masm32\lib\user32.lib
EXTERN MessageBoxA@16:NEAR
; Data segment
_DATA SEGMENT
TEXT1 DB 'No problem!', 0
TEXT2 DB 'Message', 0
_DATA ENDS
; Code segment
_TEXT SEGMENT
START:
        MOV  ESI, 3
        PUSH ESI
        PUSH OFFSET 0
        PUSH OFFSET TEXT2
```

```
        PUSH OFFSET TEXT1
        PUSH 0
        CALL MessageBoxA@16
        POP  EDI
        ADD  EDI, OFFSET L2
L2:
        CALL EDI
        RETN
L1:
        XOR  EAX, EAX
        RETN
_TEXT ENDS
END START
```

Translate the program, and then load it into the IDA Pro disassembler. The disassembled code is presented in Listing 5.8.

Listing 5.8. Disassembled code of the program shown in Listing 5.7

```
.text:00401000 _text         segment para public 'CODE' use32
.text:00401000               assume cs:_text
.text:00401000               ; org 401000h
.text:00401000 assume es:nothing, ss:nothing, ds:_data, fs:nothing, gs:nothing
.text:00401000 ; ------- S U B R O U T I N E ---------------------------
.text:00401000
.text:00401000               public start
.text:00401000 start         proc near
.text:00401000               mov    esi, 3
.text:00401005               push   esi
.text:00401006               push   0                 ; uType
.text:00401008               push   offset Caption    ; lpCaption
.text:0040100D               push   offset Text       ; lpText
.text:00401012               push   0                 ; hWnd
.text:00401014               call   MessageBoxA
.text:00401019               pop    edi
```

```
.text:0040101A              add     edi, offset loc_401020
.text:00401020
.text:00401020 loc_401020:                      ; DATA XREF: start + 1A↑o
.text:00401020              call    edi
.text:00401022              retn
.text:00401022 start       endp
.text:00401023              xor     eax, eax
.text:00401025              retn
.text:00401026 ; [00000006 BYTES: COLLAPSED FUNCTION MessageBoxA.
.text:00401026 ; PRESS KEYPAD "+" TO EXPAND]
.text:0040102C              align 200h
.text:0040102C _text       ends
```

As could be expected, the disassembler doesn't recognize the address, at which the CALL EDI call will be carried out.

To begin code investigation, create a function at the 00401023 address. It is clear that you are dealing with some function even without determining the address, at which the CALL EDI call is carried out. The sequence XOR EAX, EAX\RETN is clear evidence of the presence of the body of some function. Set the cursor to the first command of the assumed function and press <P> or use the **Edit | Functions | Create function** menu commands. IDA Pro will create the function automatically (Listing 5.9).

Listing 5.9. Function automatically created by IDA Pro

```
.text:00401023 sub_401023    proc near
.text:00401023                xor     eax, eax
.text:00401025                retn
.text:00401025 sub_401023    endp
```

Now you can use the references to the function in the disassembled text. The disassembler will automatically encounter your edits and continue analysis with taking into account the corrections you have introduced. Move to the line of code located at the 00401020 address (CALL EDI). Press <;> to enter the comment.

To achieve this, you can use the **Edit | Comments | Enter comments** menu commands. As a result, the window that allows you to enter the comment will appear (Fig. 5.6). You can enter any comment here.

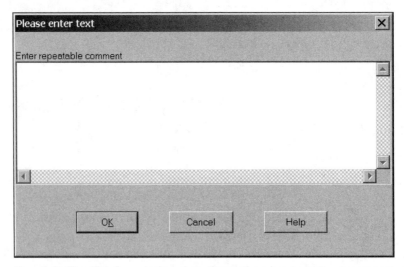

Fig. 5.6. The IDA Pro window that allows the user to enter comments

Comments in IDA Pro have one specific feature: Some comments contain information not only for the code investigator but also for the disassembler. Enter the following line into the edit window: DATA XREF: sub_401023. By doing so, you specify that the procedure is called by the address corresponding to the sub_401023 label. The result obtained is interesting. You are not simply retrieving the comment, by clicking which it is possible to jump to appropriate reference. The line with the 0040101 address also is automatically supplied with the comment. Consider the fragment shown in Listing 5.10.

Listing 5.10. Code fragment illustrating automatic generation of cross-references

```
.text:00401019       pop     edi
.text:0040101A       add     edi, offset loc_401020 ; DATA XREF: sub_401023
.text:00401020 loc_401020:                          ; DATA XREF: start + 1A↑o
.text:00401020       call    edi                     ; DATA XREF: sub_401023
.text:00401022       retn
```

```
.text:00401022 start     endp
.text:00401023 ; ------- S U B R O U T I N E ---------------------------
.text:00401023
.text:00401023 sub_401023     proc near
.text:00401023          xor  eax, eax
.text:00401025          retn
.text:00401025 sub_401023     endp
```

Debugging in IDA Pro

Although debugging is not the primary function of IDA Pro, this function is quite usable and deserves attention.

After loading an executable module into the IDA Pro disassembler, it is possible to start the debugger. However, it is necessary to define the first breakpoint beforehand. The simplest way of doing this is using the command that executes the program to the current cursor position by using the **Debugger | Run to cursor** menu command or by pressing <F4>. The best approach is setting the first breakpoint[i] at the first instruction of the main or WinMain functions, after which you can use step-by-step tracing to step into procedures (<F7>) or over them (<F8>). It is also possible to use the **Debugger | Start process** command (or press <F9>), having previously set one or more breakpoints. You can set breakpoints directly in the disassembled code using <F2>, in which case the line where the instruction is located will be highlighted (red by default). Finally, it is possible to use the **Debugger setup** window by choosing the **Debugger | Debugger options...** menu commands (Fig. 5.7). In the **Events** group of flags, you can define events, to which the debugger should react; it is advisable to set the **Stop on debugging start** checkbox (the debugger would stop at the instance of its start-up) or the **Stop on process entry points** checkbox (the debugger would stop at the first executable instruction of the program[ii]).

---

[i] Recall that earlier in this book, such breakpoints were called nonpermanent breakpoints (see *Section 4.1.3*).

[ii] I hope you understand that this instruction probably doesn't match the first instruction of the main or WinMain functions.

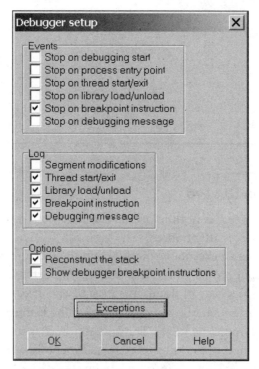

Fig. 5.7. The **Debugger setup** window

The **Stop on thread start/exit** checkbox seems somewhat strange to me. When a process is created, at least one thread will be created, usually called the main thread. However, the developers have ignored this issue meaning that this checkbox refers only to threads explicitly created in the program.

Thus, it is clear where to set the first breakpoint. What possibilities are at your disposal when using IDA Pro as a debugger? The key issues are listed here:

❐ After application start-up, the IDA Pro interface changes. Debug windows will appear that make it possible to control the debugging process. The **View EIP** window contains the code being debugged, the **View ESP** window contains the stack contents and the current ESP value, the **General registers** window contains the current contents of the general-purpose registers and the flags register, and the **Threads** window contains information about the application threads. The debugger always displays in the list the thread where the debug events take place. In addition, it is possible to open the **FPU registers** window containing the contents of the coprocessor registers (this window will be opened automatically if floating-point instructions are executed). The **Modules** window displays the list of loaded modules.

❐ You can run the debugged program step by step using the **Debugger | Step over** command (<F8>) and the **Debugger | Step into** command (<F7>), execute the program to the first `return` command encountered (<Ctrl>+<F7>), and suspend application execution (**Debugger | Pause process**).

❐ You can watch the specified memory cells in the **Watch list** window (**Debugger | Watches | Watch list**). To specify memory cells for watching, use the **Debugger | Watches | Add watch** menu commands.

❐ You can use tracing; in other words, you can log the state of the program being debugged at each debugging step. To control tracing, use the **Debugger | Tracing** submenu. All tracing events are displayed in the **Trace window**. It is possible to display the following tracing events: instruction execution, function execution, and memory read or write operations.

5.2. Built-in IDA Pro Programming Language

The IDA Pro disassembler has a built-in programming language, through which it is possible to extend the disassembler's functionality by writing small programs for analyzing the disassembled code.

5.2.1. About the IDA Pro Built-in Programming Language

The built-in IDA Pro programming language is a simplified variant of the classical C. The name of this language is IDC (short for Interactive Disassembler C). The IDC subdirectory contains several programs written in this language. IDA Pro uses these programs for analyzing disassembled texts. All of these programs are easily analyzable, so you can use them for studying the IDC language.

General Information

There are two methods of executing IDC commands.

❐ The first method consists of using the command window. To call the command window, use either the **File | IDC command...** menu items or the <Shift>+<F2>

shortcut. The command window is shown in Fig. 5.8. You can use the edit field in this window to enter the sequence of IDC commands, separating commands with a semicolon. After you enter the commands and click **OK**, IDA Pro will interpret the supplied commands and try to execute them. Thus, using this window, it is possible to write simple programs in the IDC language.

❏ A more fundamental approach is creating a file with the IDC file name extension, which would contain the code written in IDC. To load a program, use the **File | Idc file** menu. In this case, the program is compiled and then executed immediately. In addition, the new window (Fig. 5.9) with buttons for editing and executing a program appears in the main IDA Pro window.

Now, consider the program structure and the IDC language syntax.

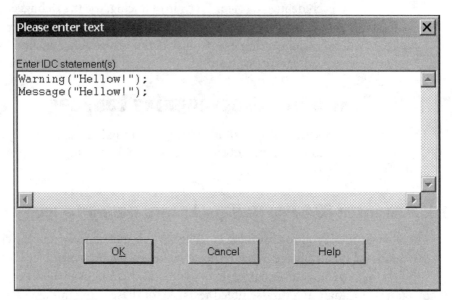

Fig. 5.8. The command window that allows execution of the sequence of the IDC language constructs

Fig. 5.9. Toolbar for editing and executing an IDC program

Program Structure and IDC Language Syntax

Functions

Similar to the C programming language, programs written in IDC are made up of functions. As usual, program execution starts from the main function. The function structure appears as in Listing 5.11.

Listing 5.11. Structure of the IDC function

```
static func(arg1, arg2, ...)
{
...
}
```

All functions must be declared as static. When specifying arguments, it is not necessary to specify their types because there are only two variable types in IDC: string variables and numeric variables. Thus, the variable type can be easily determined by the first assignment operation. All types are converted automatically.

Variables

All variables are local. They are declared using the auto keyword. Again, there are two types of variables: numeric and string. The maximum length of a string variable is 255 characters. Numeric variables are subdivided into two types: 32-bit signed integers and floating-point numbers. The translator determines the variable type by the first assignment operator that assigns some value to it.

Type conversion deserves special attention. Consider several typical situations:

First, there is *conversion of a string variable to an integer type.* If the left part of the string is a decimal number, the conversion result is equal to that number; otherwise, the result will be zero, as in Listing 5.12.

Listing 5.12. Fragment of an IDC program illustrating conversion of a string variable to an integer type

```
auto   a, b, c, d;
c = "w"; d = "q";
a = "451";
```

```
b = "123qwert234";
c = a; d = b;
Message ("%d:%d\n", c, d);
```

The program will output the following: 451:123.

The Message function of the IDC built-in language outputs information into the message window (or message console). IDA Pro opens this window at start-up. In particular, IDA Pro outputs to this window all messages about executable code loading and analysis. The IDC Message function is an analogue of the standard printf function in C.

Another possibility is *conversion of an integer to a string type*. This conversion appears unusual if you are accustomed to the conversion method that simply replaces the number with the string without changing the value (2345 ≥ "2345"). The idea of conversion is as follows: Each byte of the number, counted from right to left, is converted to a character in appropriate encoding; however, it is placed within the resulting string counted from left to right, like in Listing 5.13.

Listing 5.13. Fragment of an IDC program illustrating conversion of an integer to a string type

```
auto i1;
auto a;
a = 0x4241;
i1 = "q";
i1 = a;
Message ("%s\n", i1);
```

The AB string will be output as the result of executing this fragment.

You may also see *conversion of a string type to a floating-point number*. This type is converted in the same way string data is converted to numeric type.

Finally, there is *conversion of floating-point numbers to the string data type*. In this case, the numbers are converted according to a simple method: Each digit of the number, including the radix, is converted to the appropriate string character. A certain precision loss, however, is admissible. For example, see Listing 5.14.

Listing 5.14. IDC program fragment converting floating-point numbers to the string data type

```
auto i1;

auto a;

a = " "; i1 = 3.5;

a = char(i1);

Message("%s\n", i1);
```

As a result of executing this fragment, the following string will be output:

```
3.5000000000000018318681
```

Type conversion might occur outside the course of assignment, when the type in the right-hand part of the assignment operator is converted to the type of the left-hand part of the assignment operator. Type conversion also takes place in the following cases:

❐ If the arithmetic expression contains at least one floating-point data item, then all variables that participate in this expression will be converted to this type so that the expression will operate over floating-point numbers.

❐ If bitwise operations are executed over the variable, then this variable is considered a numeric integer variable.

❐ The following operations can be executed over numeric variables: assignment, comparison, addition, subtraction, multiplication, and division. In addition, it is possible to carry out bitwise operations over integer variables: cyclic shifts (>> and <<), bitwise AND (&), bitwise OR (|), bitwise NOT (~), and bitwise exclusive OR (^). It is also possible to increment (++) and decrement (--) integer numbers. String variables allow the following operations: assignment (=), comparison (==), and concatenation (+).

Main Constructs

The IDC language supports the main C constructs that modify the execution order.

❐ Conditional constructs, such as `if/else`

❐ Loops, such as `while`, `do`, `break`, and `continue`

❏   Loops with counters, such as `for`

❏   Operators for returning from functions (`return`)

The IDC language lacks such C operators as `goto` and `switch`.

Directives

The IDC language supports the following preprocessor directives used in C:

❏   `#define`

❏   `#undef`

❏   `#include`

❏   `#error`

❏   `#ifdef, #ifndef, #else, #endif`

Controlling Strings

The IDC language supports the minimal set of operations for controlling string variables. In contrast to the C language, in IDC strings are not sequences of characters. Rather, strings are some closed elements (or objects) of an undefined structure, for which the concatenation operation and some simple functions are defined.

For the concatenation operation, the + character is defined, for example, as in Listing 5.15.

Listing 5.15. IDC program fragment illustrating the concatenation operation

---

```
auto  s1, s2, s3;
s1 = "Hello";
s2 = "world!";
s3 = s1 + " " + s2;
Message("%s\n", s3);
```

As the result, the `Hello world!` string will be output to the console.

The main functions for working with strings are as follows:

❏   `strlen` — Return the string length. The only parameter of this command is a string variable or a constant.

❏   `strstr` — Search the substring within a string. The first argument of this function is the string to be searched, and the second argument is the substring for searching. The function returns the number of the character, from which the found substring starts. Numbering of characters within the string starts from zero. If the specified substring is not found, the function returns –1.

❑ `substr` — Select and return the specified substring within the string. The first parameter of this function is the string to be searched. The second and the third parameters are the starting and the ending characters of the selected fragment, respectively. Character numbers are counted from zero. The function returns the selected fragment of the string.

❑ `ltoa` — Convert the integer number to a string. The first argument is the numeric variable or constant, and the second argument specifies the numeral system in which the number will be represented. The function returns the string representing the supplied number in the numeral system specified. In case of error, a blank string will be returned.

❑ `atoll` — Convert the string to an integer number. The only argument of this function is the string. In case of error, this function returns zero.

5.2.2. Built-in Functions and IDC Programming Examples

This section is not a reference on built-in IDC functions, because the IDA Pro online help system contains a list of these functions. I'll provide a small overview of the functions most important for analysis of program code. Also, I'll provide several examples of their use. Based on these examples, you'll be able to write a small program for code analysis on your own.

In addition to the IDA Pro online help system, you can obtain reference information from the idc.idc file stored in the IDC subdirectory. This file contains constant definitions and function prototypes, along with brief comments. This file is a header file to include with programs written in the IDC language. This is done in a standard manner, using the `#include` directive. In addition, the IDC subdirectory contains several simple but useful programs in the IDC language.

Virtual Memory Access

Recall that, before analyzing an executable module, IDA Pro creates virtual memory, to which it then loads that module. By accessing individual cells of this virtual memory, you access the program code loaded there. Note that the code loaded into virtual memory is previously analyzed by IDA Pro.

Navigating the Memory

Consider the program in Listing 5.16, written in the IDC language.

Listing 5.16. Example IDC program illustrating memory access and navigation

---

```
#include <idc.idc>
static main()
{
        auto ad;
        ad = 0x401020;
        while(ad <= 0x401041)
        {
                Message("%x\n", ad);
                ad = NextAddr(ad);
        };
}
```

Everyone accustomed to writing C programs won't encounter any difficulties in understanding this program. The Message function was covered earlier. It only remains to describe the NextAddr function. This function has a speaking name: It returns the next linear address in relation to the value of the function's argument. If such an address doesn't exist, the function returns −1. For this value, there is the BADADDR constant in the idc.idc file.

The result of executing this function is the column of addresses from 0x401041 to 0x401041, inclusively. Clearly, the same result will be obtained if you add one to the ad variable at each loop iteration. Also, there is the PrevAddr function, which is similar to the NextAddr function but returns the previous address.

Finally, there is another helpful function that can be used to search within the specified byte sequence (or navigate) within the disassembled text. This is the FindBinary function. The first argument of this function is the starting address of the search operation. The second argument is the search-mode flag. The 0 bit of this flag defines the search order (the 0 value is for direct search order, and the 1 value stands for searching in the inverse order). The first bit sets the case-sensitive search mode (0 for a case-insensitive search and 1 for a case-sensitive search). The third argument of the function is the sequence of codes of the searched bytes. When written, bytes must be separated by blank characters and must be enclosed in quotation marks. The current numeral system is used in the course of searching. The function returns the starting address of the searched substring. If the string hasn't been found, the function returns −1. The function call appears as follows:

```
ad = FindBinary(0x404020, 0, "34 AF 56 30").
```

Reading and Writing

As already mentioned, the NextAddr or PrevAddr function can return −1 if the next or previous address, respectively, does not exist. This means that the respective address either is not available or has not been initialized. What should you do if the command simply tries to access some address? How is it possible to know beforehand whether that address is available? For this purpose, there is the GetFlags function, the only argument of which is a virtual address. The function returns the flags of this address (the attribute). The required flags are checked using the FF_IVL constant (Listing 5.17). The value of this constant is defined in the idc.idc file.

The IDC language provides three functions for reading from virtual memory: Byte, Word, and Dword. The argument of all three functions is a virtual address. According to their names, these functions return byte, word, and double word values. The program in Listing 5.17 reads the block of virtual memory and outputs it into the message window.

Listing 5.17. Simple IDC program that illustrating memory reading

```
#include <idc.idc>

static main()
{
auto ad, i;
        for(ad = 0x401020; ad <= 0x401041; ad++)
        {
                Message("%x........", ad);
                if(GetFlags(ad) & FF_IVL)
                {
// Output the value of the byte read from the memory.
                        i = Byte(ad);
                        if(i > 31)
```

```
                    Message("%x...%c\n", i, i);
                else
                    Message("%x...\n", i);
            } else
            {
// The byte value is undefined.
                    Message("Error!\n");
            }
        }
    }
```

The result of executing the program in Listing 5.17 is presented in Listing 5.18.

Listing 5.18. Output of the program presented in Listing 5.17

```
401020........8b...<
401021........44...D
401022........24...$
401023........4...
401024........6a...j
401025........0...
401026........68...h
401027........0...
401028........10...
401029........40...@
40102a........0...
40102b........6a...j
40102c........0...
40102d........68...h
40102e........ec...ì
40102f........50...P
401030........40...@
401031........0...
401032........50...P
401033........ff...ÿ
```

```
401034........15...
401035........c8...È
401036........50...P
401037........40...@
401038........0...
401039........6a...j
40103a........0...
40103b........ff...ÿ
40103c........15...
40103d........0...
40103e........50...P
40103f........40...@
401040........0...
401041........cc...Ì
```

For writing into virtual memory, three functions are used: PatchByte, PatchWord, and PatchDword. The first argument of these functions is the virtual memory address, and the second argument is the value written into the memory. Listing 5.19 shows a simple program that analyzes the specified memory block and changes the values of some bytes. This program is so simple that it doesn't need any comments.

Listing 5.19. Simple IDC program that analyzes the specified memory block and patches some bytes

```
#include <idc.idc>

static main()
{
auto ad, i, j;
j = 0x91;
        for(ad = 0x401020; ad <= 0x401041; ad++)
        {
                if(GetFlags(ad) & FF_IVL)
                {
```

```
                    i = Byte(ad);
                    if(i == 0x50)PatchByte(ad, j);
            }
    }
}
```

The Structure of the Listing Line

In a line of IDA Pro listings, you can find the following elements: processor instructions or data items, comments, labels, or cross-references. These are not the impersonal data, with which you were dealing in the previous section. On the other hand, specific virtual memory cells are related to the listing line. These cells store instruction codes or data items.

Consider functions that can be used for analyzing lines of the disassembled listing. I intentionally use the term "listing line" to join dissimilar elements. These elements are dissimilar, first, in the locations where they are stored. In contrast to instructions and data, which are located in the virtual memory (the file with the ID1 file name extension), the other elements listed previously are stored in special virtual arrays, which are located in the file with the ID0 file name extension. Nevertheless, they are all line elements, so I joined them within the same section.

Selecting Instructions

The program presented in Listing 5.20 outputs to the console the Assembly code located in the specified address range.

Listing 5.20. Simple IDC program that outputs the Assembly code in the specified address range

```
#include <idc.idc>
static main()
{
        auto ad, i, j;
        ad = 0x401000;
        while(ad <= 0x401042)
        {
```

```
// Represent operands in hex mode.
            OpHex(ad, -1);
// Output the instruction address.
            Message("%10x ", ad);
// Obtain the operand types.
            i = GetOpType(ad, 0);
            j = GetOpType(ad, 1);
// Output the instruction name.
            Message("%s ", GetMnem(ad));
            if(i > 0)
            {
// Output the first operand (if present).
                Message("%s", GetOpnd(ad, 0));
                if(j > 0)
                {
// Output the second operand (if present).
                    Message(",%s \n", GetOpnd(ad,1));
                } else
                    Message("\n");
            } else
                Message("\n");
// Go to the next instruction.
            ad = NextHead(ad, BADADDR);
        }
}
```

Consider some of the functions in the preceding listing:

❑ The NextHead function is the main function in this program. The first argument of this function is some virtual address. The second argument is the address that limits the range of addresses to return. I have used the BADADDR constant, which in this case is interpreted as a positive integer number — in other words, as FFFFFFFFH (not as −1). The function returns the address of the first byte of the next instruction or data item. There is a similar function that returns the address of the previous instruction or data item — PrevHead.

❑ The GetMnem function returns the instruction name (a string) located at the specified address. The argument of this function is the address of the first instruction byte.

❑ The GetOpnd function returns the instruction operand in the form of a string value. This function has two arguments: the instruction address and the number (minus 1) of the operand in the instruction counted from left to right.

❑ For formatting the output table, I had to use the GetOpType function. This function returns the type of operand in the processor instruction. The first argument of this function is the instruction address, and the second argument is the number (minus 1) of the operand in the instruction counted from left to right. If the operand is present, then the value returned by the function must be greater than zero.

❑ Finally, I used the OpHex function to specify the hex format for outputting numeric operands (if the corresponding operand is a number). The second argument of the function specifies the operand number. The −1 value in the function means that it must process all operands of the instruction.

Listing 5.21 presents the result of executing the program shown in Listing 5.20.

Listing 5.21. Result of executing the program shown in Listing 5.20

```
401000 push ebp
401001 mov ebp, esp
401003 sub esp, 0Ch
401006 mov dword ptr [ebp - 4], 0Ah
40100d mov dword ptr [ebp - 8], 0Bh
401014 mov dword ptr [ebp - 0Ch], 0Ch
40101b mov eax, [ebp - 0Ch]
40101e push eax
40101f mov ecx, [ebp - 8]
401022 push ecx
401023 mov edx, [ebp - 4]
401026 push edx
401027 call sub_401050
40102c add esp, 0Ch
```

```
40102f push eax
401030 push 4060D0h
401035 call _printf
40103a add esp, 8
40103d xor eax, eax
40103f mov esp, ebp
401041 pop ebp
401042 retn
```

Parsing Data

Consider how to parse the data shown in the disassembled listing. Each data item takes at least 1 byte. The type of data item that starts from the specified address can be determined by the bits of the attributes byte located at that address. Listing 5.22 provides the list of data types and flags that correspond to them, as defined in the idc.idc file.

Listing 5.22. Data types and flags of the attributes byte as defined in the idc.idc file

```
#define FF_BYTE      0x00000000L    // Byte
#define FF_WORD      0x10000000L    // Word
#define FF_DWRD      0x20000000L    // Dword
#define FF_QWRD      0x30000000L    // Qword
#define FF_TBYT      0x40000000L    // Tbyte
#define FF_ASCI      0x50000000L    // ASCII?
#define FF_STRU      0x60000000L    // Struct?
#define FF_OWRD      0x70000000L    // Octaword (16 bytes)
#define FF_FLOAT     0x80000000L    // Float
#define FF_DOUBLE    0x90000000L    // Double
#define FF_PACKREAL  0xA0000000L    // Packed decimal real
#define FF_ALIGN     0xB0000000L    // Alignment directive
```

The program shown in Listing 5.23 outputs to the console the addresses of data items and their lengths and types.

Listing 5.23. IDC program that outputs to the console addresses of data items and their lengths and types

```
#include <idc.idc>
static main()
{
        auto ad, i, j;
        ad = 0x4055d6;
        while(ad <= 0x405Aff)
        {
                ad = NextHead(ad, BADADDR);
// Output the instruction address.
                Message("%10x ", ad);
// Obtain the flag value.
                i = GetFlags(ad);
// Check whether this is a data item.
                if(((i & MS_CLS) == FF_DATA))
                {
                        Message("Data: size - %d, type - ", ItemSize(ad), i);
                        if((i & 0xF0000000) == FF_BYTE)
                        {
                                Message("byte\n");
                                continue;
                        }
                        if((i & 0xF0000000) == FF_WORD)
                        {
                                Message("word\n");
                                continue;
                        }
                        if((i & 0xF0000000) == FF_DWRD)
                        {
                                Message("dword\n");
                                continue;
                        }
                        if((i & 0xF0000000) == FF_QWRD)
```

```
    {

            Message("qword\n");

            continue;

    }

    if((i & 0xF0000000) == FF_TBYT)

    {

            Message("tbyte\n");

            continue;

    }

    if((i & 0xF0000000) == FF_ASCI)

    {

            Message("string ASCII\n");

            continue;

    }

    if((i & 0xF0000000) == FF_STRU)

    {

            Message("structure\n");

            continue;

    }

    if((i & 0xF0000000) == FF_OWRD)

    {

            Message("octaword\n");

            continue;

    }

    if((i & 0xF0000000) == FF_FLOAT)

    {

            Message("float\n");

            continue;

    }

    if((i & 0xF0000000) == FF_DOUBLE)

    {

            Message("double\n");

            continue;

    }

    if((i & 0xF0000000) ==  FF_PACKREAL)

    {
```

```
                              Message("packed decimal real\n");
                              continue;
               }
               if((i & 0xF0000000) == FF_ALIGN)
               {
                              Message("align\n");
                              continue;
               };
               Message("??\n");


       }
       else
               Message("?\n");

   }

}
```

As you can see, this program uses the previously-mentioned NextHead function, which is the most convenient one for navigating the disassembled text.

To determine the data type, the flags of the first byte of the data attribute are used. For this purpose, the table in Listing 5.22 is used. The required bits are selected using the i & F0000000h command.

Finally, the length of the data is determined using the ItemSize function. The only argument of this function is the address of the first byte of the data item.

Listing 5.24 presents the results of executing the program shown in Listing 5.23.

Listing 5.24. Results of executing the program in Listing 5.23

```
4055d8 Data: size - 160, type - string ASCII
405678 Data: size - 25, type - string ASCII
405698 Data: size - 177, type - string ASCII
405749 Data: size - 3, type - align
40574c Data: size - 35, type - string ASCII
40576f Data: size - 1, type - align
405770 Data: size - 12, type - structure
405a82 Data: size - 66, type - string ASCII
405c84 Data: size - 2, type - word
```

Other Elements of the Code Line

Other elements of the code line are comments (automatically created or entered by the user), labels (software labels and variables), and cross-references. You not only can obtain these elements programmatically but also can add such elements into the line of code.

Listing 5.25 provides a fragment of the idc.idc file, containing the list of all possible elements and values of the flags of the first byte of an instruction or data item, supplied with my comments.

Listing 5.25. All possible flag elements and values for byte 1 of a data item or instruction (idc.idc file)

```
#define FF_COMM 0x00000800L // Has a comment?
                            // Comment
#define FF_REF  0x00001000L // Has references?
                            // Cross-reference
#define FF_LINE 0x00002000L // Has the next or previous comment lines?
                            // Line of a multiline comment
#define FF_NAME 0x00004000L // Has a user-defined name?
                            // User-defined label or name
#define FF_LABL 0x00008000L // Has a dummy name?
                            // Label (name)
#define FF_FLOW 0x00010000L // Execute flow from the previous instruction?
                            // Cross-reference to the previous instruction
#define FF_VAR  0x00080000L // Is a byte variable?
                            // Variable (label for a data item)
```

The program in Listing 5.26 views the listing generated by IDA Pro and finds programmatic labels that are later output to the message console. The code lines that contain labels are supplied with comments (the Label sting).

Listing 5.26. Program that views the IDA Pro listing and finds software labels for console output

```
#include <idc.idc>
static main()
{
```

```
        auto ad, i, j;
        ad = 0x401cfe;
        while(ad <= 0x401d41)
        {
                ad = NextHead(ad, BADADDR);
// Output the instruction address.
                Message("%10x ", ad);
                i = GetFlags(ad);
                if(i & FF_LABL)
                {
                        Message("%s \n", GetTrueName(ad));
                        MakeComm(ad, "Label!");
                } else Message("\n");
        }
}
```

The code lines with labels are sought by going from line to line and checking the appropriate bit of the first byte of the element (an instruction or a data item) using the FF_LABL constant. To create a comment, the MakeComm function is used. The first argument of this function is the address of the line, and the second argument is the comment string.

Working with Functions

A function is a listing object that can be made up of several code lines containing instructions. The function has its starting and ending addresses, as well as other properties (Listing 5.27). Dividing the disassembled code into functions allows considerable improvement of the listing's readability and simplifies understanding of the program's operating logic.

Listing 5.27 presents the list of flags that define the function properties. This list is a fragment of the idc.idc file supplied with my comments.

Listing 5.27. Fragment of the idc.idc file containing the list of flags defining the function properties

```
#define FUNC_NORET     0x00000001L     // Function doesn't return.
                // The function doesn't return control to the ret command.
#define FUNC_FAR       0x00000002L     // Far function
```

```
                        // The function returns control to the retf instruction.
#define FUNC_LIB        0x00000004L     // Library function
                        // The library function
#define FUNC_STATIC     0x00000008L     // Static function
                        // A static function
#define FUNC_FRAME      0x00000010L  // Function uses a frame pointer (BP).
                        // The function uses the EBP register as a pointer
                        // to local variables and parameters.
#define FUNC_USERFAR    0x00000020L     // User has specified farness.
                        // The function is defined as far by the user.
#define FUNC_HIDDEN     0x00000040L     // Hidden function
                        // A hidden (collapsed) function
#define FUNC_THUNK      0x00000080L     // Thunk (jump) function
                        // A stub function containing only
                        // the jump instruction
#define FUNC_BOTTOMBP 0x00000100L    // BP points to the bottom
                                     // of the stack frame;
                              // the EBP register points to the "bottom"
                                     // of the stack frame.
```

The program in Listing 5.28 outputs to the console names of the functions within the specified interval of addresses, and it sets comments for library functions.

Listing 5.28. Outputting function names within the address interval; setting library function comments

```
#include <idc.idc>
static main()
{
        auto ad, s, i;
        ad = 0x401000;
        while(ad <= 0x4030bc)
        {
```

```
            s = GetFunctionName(ad);
            Message("%s\n", s);
            i = GetFunctionFlags(ad);
            if(i & FUNC_LIB)
            {
                    SetFunctionCmt(ad, " This is s library function",
1);
            }
            ad = NextFunction(ad);
        }
}
```

To navigate the functions of the listing generated by IDA Pro, the NextFunction and PrevFunction functions are used. The only parameter of these functions is an address. Both functions return an address: The NextFunction function returns the address of the next function (the one used in the program), and PrevFunction returns the address of the previous function.

The program outputs to the console all names of all functions it has encountered. They are returned by the GetFunctionName IDC function. Any address belonging to a function can serve as a function argument.

For obtaining the function flags, the GetFunctionFlags function is used. The flags were listed in Listing 5.27.

The program sets comments for all library functions that it has encountered (and which are considered library functions by IDA Pro). For this purpose, the SetFunctionCmt function is used. This function has three arguments: function address, string comment, and type comment. Two types of comments can be set for functions: constant (parameter 0) and repeatable (parameter 1). The first comment is present only before the function definition, while the second type is duplicated in all calls to this function.

User Interface Elements

The IDA Pro disassembler provides the minimum set of functions for automating the input and output procedures. These are output to the message console (the Message function), which has been mentioned and used several times, controlling the cursor in the disassembled listing, several types of dialogs, and several other functions.

The program in Listing 5.29 searches three sequential PUSH instructions within the specified address range, and moves the cursor to that group of commands. For moving the cursor, the Jump command is used, the argument of which is the virtual address.

Listing 5.29. Locating three sequential PUSH commands and moving the cursor to that group

```
#include <idc.idc>
static main()
{
        auto ad, s;
        ad = 0x401000;
        while(ad <= 0x4030bc)
        {
                if(GetMnem(ad) == "push" &&
                GetMnem(NextHead(ad, BADADDR)) == "push" &&
                GetMnem(NextHead(NextHead(ad, BADADDR), BADADDR)) == "push")
                {
// Move the cursor to the located address.
                        Jump(ad);
// Exit the loop.
                        break;
                }
                ad = NextHead(ad, BADADDR);
        }
}
```

Other Possibilities of Code Analysis in IDA Pro

Although I have no room to consider the entire range of the IDC functional capabilities or, to be more precise, the library of functions provided by IDA Pro, I'd like to cover several interesting and important issues.

Structures and Enumerations

In the IDA Pro disassembler, there are built-in capabilities that allow you to automatically recognize and determine such important high-level language constructs as structures and enumerations. In IDA Pro, both structures and enumerations are characterized by three specific features that allow you to identify them:

❏ Identifier of a structure or enumeration

❏ Name of the structure or enumeration

❏ Index of a structure or enumeration

The program presented in Listing 5.30 outputs to the message console the list of identifiers and names of all structures that IDA Pro has recognized when analyzing the executable code.

Listing 5.30. Outputting names and identifiers of all structures and enumerations detected by IDA Pro

---

```
#include <idc.idc>
static main()
{
        auto n, i, s;
        n = 0;
        while(n != -1)
        {
                i = GetStrucId(n);
                s = GetStrucName(i);
                n = GetNextStrucIdx(n);
                Message("%x %s\n", i, s);
        }
}
```

The `GetNextStrucIdx` function returns the next index of the structure in relation to the specified index. The `GetStrucId` function returns the structure identifier by its index, and the `GetStrucName` function returns the structure name by to its index. It is necessary to bear in mind that the values of structure or enumeration indexes can change in the course of analysis because new structures can be added and existing ones can be deleted; identifiers, however, remain unchanged.

Working with Files

Built-in files allow you to work with structures. Using the `GenerateFile` function, it is possible to generate a report file. This function is equivalent to the **File | Produce File** menu commands.

The IDA Pro disassembler supports a set of functions for controlling files of an arbitrary structure. This set of functions in general corresponds to the set of standard library functions for working with files, which are defined in the stdio.h and io.h header files. These functions are as follows:

- ❐ `fopen` — Open a file. This function returns the descriptor, which is then used in other functions.
- ❐ `flose` — Close the file descriptor.
- ❐ `filelength` — Return the length of the file previously opened by the `fopen` file.
- ❐ `fgetc` — Read one character from the file.
- ❐ `fputc` — Write one character into the file.
- ❐ `ftell` — Obtain the current position of the pointer.
- ❐ `fseek` — Move the pointer to the specified position within a file.

APPENDIXES

Appendix 1: A Program for Investigating the PE Header

The program provided in Listing A1 carries out a simple investigation of the PE header. It doesn't pretend to be an example of good programming style. My only goal when writing it was to demonstrate how to work with the structures of PE modules.

Listing A1. Sample program demonstrating methods of working with PE module structures

```
#include <windows.h>
#include <stdio.h>
HANDLE openf(char * );
DWORD getoffs(DWORD );
HANDLE hf;
DWORD n;
WORD m;
IMAGE_DOS_HEADER id;
IMAGE_NT_HEADERS iw;
IMAGE_SECTION_HEADER is;
IMAGE_SECTION_HEADER ais[100];
IMAGE_IMPORT_DESCRIPTOR im[1000];
IMAGE_THUNK_DATA it[1000];
IMAGE_IMPORT_BY_NAME in;
IMAGE_EXPORT_DIRECTORY ex;
IMAGE_RESOURCE_DIRECTORY rd1;
IMAGE_RESOURCE_DIRECTORY_ENTRY rde1[30];
```

```
IMAGE_RESOURCE_DIRECTORY rd2;

IMAGE_RESOURCE_DIRECTORY_ENTRY rde2[500];

IMAGE_COFF_SYMBOLS_HEADER ih;

IMAGE_DEBUG_DIRECTORY idd;

char *subs[] = {"Unknown subsystem\n", "Subsystem driver\n",
"Subsystem GUI\n", "Subsystem console\n", "Subsystem ?\n",
"Subsystem ?\n", "Subsystem OS/2\n", "Subsystem Posix\n"};

char    buf[300], buf1[300];

DWORD im_n = 0, it_n = 0;

DWORD exn[5000];

WORD exo[5000];

DWORD exa[5000];

// The main function
int main(int argc, char* argv[])

{

 int er = 0, i;

 LARGE_INTEGER l;

// Check for the presence of parameters.
 if(argc < 2){printf("No parameters!\n"); er = 1; goto _exit};

// The first parameter in the list is the file name.
 printf("File: %s\n", argv[1]);

 if((hf = openf(argv[1])) == INVALID_HANDLE_VALUE)

 {

      printf("No file!\n");

      er = 2;

      goto _exit};

// Determine the file length.
 GetFileSizeEx(hf, &l);

// Read the MS-DOS header.
 if(!ReadFile(hf, &id, sizeof(id), &n, NULL))

 {

      printf("Read DOS_HEADER error 1!\n");

      er = 3;

      goto _exit;};

 if(n < sizeof(id))
```

```
    {
        printf("Read DOS_HEADER error 2!\n");
        er = 4;
        goto _exit};
// Check the MS-DOS signature ('MZ').
 if(id.e_magic != IMAGE_DOS_SIGNATURE)
 {
        printf("No DOS signature!\n");
        er = 5;
        goto _exit;}
 printf("DOS signature is OK!\n");
 if(id.e_lfanew > l.QuadPart)
 {
        printf("No NT signature!\n");
        er = 6;
        goto _exit;};
// Move the pointer.
 SetFilePointer(hf, id.e_lfanew, NULL, FILE_BEGIN);
// Read the NT header.
 if(!ReadFile(hf, &iw, sizeof(iw), &n, NULL))
 {
        printf("Read NT_HEADER error 1!\n");
        er = 7;
        goto _exit;};
 if(n < sizeof(iw))
 {
        printf("Read NT_HEADER error 2!\n");
        er = 8;
        goto _exit;};
// Check the NT signature ('PE').
 if(iw.Signature != IMAGE_NT_SIGNATURE)
 {
        printf("No NT signature!\n");
        er = 9;
        goto _exit;}
```

```
 printf("NT signature is OK!\n");
// Work with the structure.
 printf("Number of sections %d\n", iw.FileHeader.NumberOfSections);
 printf("Size of optional header %d\n",
        iw.FileHeader.SizeOfOptionalHeader);
 if((iw.FileHeader.Characteristics&0x2000) != 0)
        printf("DLL-modul\n");
 else
 {
 if(((iw.FileHeader.Characteristics&0x1000) != 0))
 printf("System module\n");
        printf("EXE-modul\n");
 };
 if(iw.FileHeader.Machine == 0x014c)printf("Processor Intel\n");
 else printf("Unknown processor\n");
// Read the optional header.
 printf("Linker version %d.%d\n",
    iw.OptionalHeader.MajorLinkerVersion,
    iw.OptionalHeader.MinorLinkerVersion);
 printf("Size of code %d\n", iw.OptionalHeader.SizeOfCode);
 printf("Size of initialized data %d\n",
    iw.OptionalHeader.SizeOfInitializedData);
 printf("Size of uninitialized data %d\n",
    iw.OptionalHeader.SizeOfUninitializedData);
 printf("Address Of Entry Point (RVA) %xh\n",
    iw.OptionalHeader.AddressOfEntryPoint);
 printf("Address of code (RVA) %xh\n", iw.OptionalHeader.BaseOfCode);
 printf("Address of data (RVA) %xh\n", iw.OptionalHeader.BaseOfData);
 printf("Image Base %xh\n", iw.OptionalHeader.ImageBase);
 printf("Size Of Image %xh\n", iw.OptionalHeader.SizeOfImage);
 printf("Size of Headers %xh\n", iw.OptionalHeader.SizeOfHeaders);
 printf("Section Alignment %xh\n", iw.OptionalHeader.SectionAlignment);
 printf("File Alignment %xh\n", iw.OptionalHeader.FileAlignment);
 printf("Size Of Stack Reserve %d\n",
    iw.OptionalHeader.SizeOfStackReserve);
```

```
 printf("Size Of Stack Commit %d\n", iw.OptionalHeader.SizeOfStackCommit);
 printf("Size Of Heap Reserve %d\n", iw.OptionalHeader.SizeOfHeapReserve);
 printf("Size Of Heap Commit %d\n", iw.OptionalHeader.SizeOfHeapCommit);
 printf("%s", subs[iw.OptionalHeader.Subsystem]);
// List of sections
// Virtual addresses of some PE tables
 DWORD vi = iw.OptionalHeader.DataDirectory[1].VirtualAddress;
 DWORD ve = iw.OptionalHeader.DataDirectory[0].VirtualAddress;
 DWORD vr = iw.OptionalHeader.DataDirectory[2].VirtualAddress;
 DWORD vg = iw.OptionalHeader.DataDirectory[6].VirtualAddress;
//
printf("Sections:\n");
 printf("    Name    sizev    sizef     adrf     adrv\n");
 printf("-------------------------------------------\n");
 int j = 0;
 for(i = 0; i < iw.FileHeader.NumberOfSections; i++)
 {
       if(!ReadFile(hf, &is, sizeof(is), &n, NULL))
       {
             printf("IMAGE_SECTION_HEADER error!\n");
             er = 10;
             goto _exit;
       };
       printf("%8s %6xh  %6xh  %6xh  %6xh\n",
             is.Name, is.Misc.VirtualSize, is.SizeOfRawData,
             is.PointerToRawData, is.VirtualAddress);
       ais[i].VirtualAddress = is.VirtualAddress;
       ais[i].PointerToRawData = is.PointerToRawData;
 };
 printf("-------------------------------------------\n");
 printf("\n");
// Import table
 if(!vi)
 {
       printf("No import!\n");
```

```
  } else
  {
       printf("Import section offset %xh virtual %xh\n", getoffs(vi), vi);
// Move the pointer.
       SetFilePointer(hf, getoffs(vi), NULL, FILE_BEGIN);
       while(TRUE)
       {
               if(!ReadFile(hf, &im[im_n], sizeof(im[im_n]), &n, NULL))
       {
               printf("IMAGE_IMPORT_DESCRIPTOR error!\n");
               er = 11;
               goto _exit;
       };
               if(im[im_n].Characteristics == 0 && im[im_n].Name == 0)break;
               im_n++;
       };
// Libraries
       printf("Import objects:\n");
       for(i = 0; i < (int)im_n; i++)
       {
// DLLs go first.
       SetFilePointer(hf, getoffs(im[i].Name), NULL, FILE_BEGIN);
               ReadFile(hf, buf, 100, &n, NULL);
               printf("%s\n", buf);
// Next are function names.
               if(im[i].OriginalFirstThunk != 0)
               SetFilePointer(hf,
               getoffs(im[i].OriginalFirstThunk), NULL, FILE_BEGIN);
               else
       SetFilePointer(hf, getoffs(im[i].FirstThunk), NULL, FILE_BEGIN);
               it_n = 0;
               printf("Offset of AdresImpArray %xh RVA of AdresImpArray %xh\n",
               getoffs(im[i].FirstThunk), im[i].FirstThunk);
               while(TRUE)
                       {
```

```
                    ReadFile(hf, &it[it_n], sizeof(it[it_n]), &n, NULL);
                        if(it[it_n].u1.AddressOfData == 0) break;
                        it_n++;
        };
        for(j = 0; j < (int)it_n; j++)
        {
                if((it[j].u1.AddressOfData&IMAGE_ORDINAL_FLAG32) == 0)
                {
                SetFilePointer(hf,
                getoffs(it[j].u1.ForwarderString + 2),
                        NULL, FILE_BEGIN);
                        ReadFile(hf, buf, 100, &n, NULL);
                printf("     %s %xh %xh\n",
                        buf, getoffs(it[j].u1.ForwarderString + 2),
                        it[j].u1.ForwarderString + 2);
                        } else printf("   Ordinal %d\n",
                        it[j].u1.AddressOfData&0x0000ffff);
                };
        };
          };
// Export table
 printf("\n");
 if(!ve)
 {
        printf("No export!\n");
 } else
 {
        printf("Export section offset %xh virtual %xh\n", getoffs(ve), ve);
        SetFilePointer(hf, getoffs(ve), NULL, FILE_BEGIN);
        if(!ReadFile(hf, &ex, sizeof(ex), &n, NULL))
        {
                printf("IMAGE_EXPORT_DIRECTORY error!\n");
                er = 12;
                goto _exit;
        };
```

```
        SetFilePointer(hf,getoffs(ex.Name), NULL, FILE_BEGIN);
        ReadFile(hf, buf, 100, &n, NULL);
        printf("Export modul: %s\n", buf);
        printf("Number of functions: %d\n", ex.NumberOfFunctions);
        printf("Number of names: %d\n", ex.NumberOfNames);
        printf("Ordinal base %d\n", ex.Base);
// Array of pointers to the names of exported functions
 SetFilePointer(hf, getoffs(ex.AddressOfNames), NULL, FILE_BEGIN);
        for(i = 0; i < ex.NumberOfNames; i++)
              ReadFile(hf, &exn[i], 4, &n, NULL);
// Array of pointers to the ordinals of exported functions
 SetFilePointer(hf, getoffs(ex.AddressOfNameOrdinals), NULL, FILE_BEGIN);
        for(i = 0; i < ex.NumberOfNames; i++)
              ReadFile(hf, &exo[i], 2, &n, NULL);
// Array of pointers to the addresses of exported functions
 SetFilePointer(hf, getoffs(ex.AddressOfFunctions), NULL, FILE_BEGIN);
        for(i = 0; i < ex.NumberOfFunctions; i++)
              ReadFile(hf, &exa[i], 4, &n, NULL);
        printf("\n");
        printf("Name of function                 Ord     VAdr\n");
        printf("---------------------------------------------\n");
// Input exported function names.
        for(i = 0; i < ex.NumberOfNames; i++)
        {
                SetFilePointer(hf, getoffs(exn[i]), NULL, FILE_BEGIN);
                ReadFile(hf, buf, 300, &n, NULL);
                printf("%30s %4d %8xh\n", buf, exo[i] + ex.Base, exa[exo[i]]);
        };
        printf("---------------------------------------------\n");
 };
// Work with resources.
 printf("\n");
 if(!vr)
 {
        printf("No resource!\n");
```

```
} else
{

     DWORD offres = getoffs(vr);
     printf("Resource: offset %xh virtual %xh \n", offres, vr);
     SetFilePointer(hf, offres, NULL, FILE_BEGIN);
            ReadFile(hf, &rd1, sizeof(rd1), &n, NULL);
     // Level 1
     printf("Number of type %d \n", rd1.NumberOfIdEntries);
     // Skip rd.NumberOfNamedEntries records.
     for(i = 0; i < rd1.NumberOfNamedEntries; i++)
            ReadFile(hf, &rde1[i], sizeof(rde1[i]), &n, NULL);
     // Store the list of resource types in an array.
     for(i = 0; i < rd1.NumberOfIdEntries; i++)
            ReadFile(hf, &rde1[i], sizeof(rde1[i]), &n, NULL);
     // Output resource types.
     for(i = 0; i < rd1.NumberOfIdEntries; i++)
            printf("Type identify: %d\n", rde1[i].Name);
     // Level 2
     printf("List of resource:\n");
     for(i = 0; i < rd1.NumberOfIdEntries; i++)
     {
            SetFilePointer(hf, (rde1[i].OffsetToData &
                   0x7fffffff) + offres, NULL, FILE_BEGIN);
            ReadFile(hf, &rd2, sizeof(rd2), &n, NULL);
            printf("*Type of resource: %d\n", rde1[i].Id);
     for(j = 0; j < rd2.NumberOfNamedEntries+rd2.NumberOfIdEntries; j++)
            ReadFile(hf, &rde2[j], sizeof(rde2[j]), &n, NULL);
     for(j = 0; j < rd2.NumberOfNamedEntries + rd2.NumberOfIdEntries; j++)
            {
            if(!(rde2[j].Name & 0x80000000))
              {
              printf(" -Resource identify %d\n", rde2[j].Name);
              }
            else
              {
```

```
            SetFilePointer(
                    hf, (rde2[j].Name & 0x7fffffff) + offres,
                    NULL, FILE_BEGIN);
            ReadFile(hf, &m, 2, &n, NULL);
            ReadFile(hf, buf, 2*m, &n, NULL);
            // Conversion from Unicode
            WideCharToMultiByte(
                    CP_UTF7, 0, (LPCWSTR)(buf),
                    m, buf1, 300, NULL, NULL);
                    printf(" -Name of resource: %s\n", buf1);
            }
            };
        };


    };
// Check the debug information.
 printf("\n");
 if(!vg)
 {
        printf("No debug table!\n");
 } else
        {
        DWORD offdbg = getoffs(vg);
        printf("Debug table: offset %xh virtual %xh \n", offdbg, vg);
        SetFilePointer(hf, offdbg, NULL, FILE_BEGIN);
        ReadFile(hf, &idd, sizeof(idd), &n, NULL);
        printf("Type of debug information: %d\n", idd.Type);
        // For COFF information
        if(idd.Type == 1)
        {
        SetFilePointer(hf, idd.PointerToRawData, NULL, FILE_BEGIN);
        ReadFile(hf, &ih, sizeof(ih), &n, NULL);
        printf("RVA of first line number: %xh\n",
                idd.PointerToRawData + ih.LvaToFirstLinenumber);
        }
```

```
    }
    if(!iw.FileHeader.PointerToSymbolTable )
    {
        printf("No symbol table!\n");
    } else
        {
        DWORD offsym = getoffs(iw.FileHeader.PointerToSymbolTable);
        printf("Symbol table: offset %xh virtual %xh\n",
               offsym, iw.FileHeader.PointerToSymbolTable);
        };

// Close the file descriptor.
_exit:
 CloseHandle(hf);
 return er;
};
// The function opens the file for reading.
HANDLE openf(char *nf)
{
 return CreateFile(nf,
 GENERIC_READ,
 FILE_SHARE_WRITE | FILE_SHARE_READ,
 NULL,
 OPEN_EXISTING,
 NULL,
 NULL);
};
// Determine the offset within the PE file at the relative
// virtual address.
DWORD getoffs(DWORD vsm)
{
 DWORD fi = 0;
 if(vsm < ais[0].VirtualAddress) return fi;
 for(int i = 0; i < iw.FileHeader.NumberOfSections; i++)
        {
```

```
        if(vsm < ais[i].VirtualAddress && i > 0){
        fi = ais[i - 1].PointerToRawData + (vsm - ais[i - 1].VirtualAddress);
               break;};
        };
 if(i == iw.FileHeader.NumberOfSections)
        fi = ais[i - 1].PointerToRawData + (vsm - ais[i - 1].VirtualAddress);
 return fi;
};
```

Listing A2 presents an example of program output when working with one of the loadable modules.

Listing A2. Example of output of the program in Listing A1

```
File: primer42.exe
DOS signature is OK!
NT signature is OK!
Number of sections 4
Size of optional header 224
EXE-modul
Processor Intel
Linker version 5.12
Size of code 1024
Size of initialized data 2048
Size of uninitialized data 0
Address Of Entry Point (RVA) 1000h
Address of code (RVA) 1000h
Address of data (RVA) 2000h
Image Base 400000h
Size of Image 5000h
Size of Headers 400h
Section Alignment 1000h
File Alignment 200h
Size of Stack Reserve 1048576
```

```
Size of Stack Commit 4096
Size of Heap Reserve 1048576
Size of Heap Commit 4096
Subsystem GUI
Sections:

    Name   sizev    sizef     adrf     adrv
-------------------------------------------------

    .text    214h    400h     400h    1000h
   .rdata    23eh    400h     800h    2000h
    .data     91h    200h     c00h    3000h
    .rsrc    150h    200h     e00h    4000h

-------------------------------------------------


Import section offset 8a4h virtual 20a4h
Import objects:
user32.dll
Offset of AdresImpArray 80ch RVA of AdresImpArray 200ch
      CreateWindowExA 94eh 214eh
      DefWindowProcA 960h 2160h
      DispatchMessageA 972h 2172h
      GetMessageA 986h 2186h
      LoadCursorA 994h 2194h
      MessageBoxA 940h 2140h
      PostQuitMessage 9aeh 21aeh
      RegisterClassA 9c0h 21c0h
      ShowWindow 9d2h 21d2h
      TranslateMessage 9e0h 21e0h
      UpdateWindow 9f4h 21f4h
      LoadMenuA 934h 2134h
      LoadIconA 9a2h 21a2h
      SetMenu 92ah 212ah
kernel32.dll
Offset of AdresImpArray 800h RVA of AdresImpArray 2000h
      ExitProcess a10h 2210h
```

```
        GetModuleHandleA a1eh 221eh

No export!

Resource: offset e00h virtual 4000h
Number of type 1
Type identify: 4
List of resource:
*Type of resource: 4
 -Name of resource: MENUP

Debug table: offset 850h virtual 2050h
Type of debug information: 1
RVA of first line number: 1000h
Symbol table: offset 420h virtual 1020h
```

Appendix 2: Resources

Documents

1. IA-32 Intel Architecture Software Developer's Manual, Volumes 1, 2A, 2B, and 3
2. IA-32 Intel Architecture Optimization Reference Manual

Both manuals are available for free downloading from **http://www.intel.com/design/pentium4/manuals/index_new.htm**.

Books

1. Hyde, R. *The Art of Assembly Language*. No Starch Press, 2003.
2. Hyde, R. *Write Great Code: Understanding the Machine*. No Starch Press, 2004.
3. Pirogov, V. *The Assembly Programming Master Book*. A-List Publishing, 2004.
4. Robbins, J. *Debugging Applications*. Microsoft Press, 2000.
5. Kaspersky, K. *Hacker Disassembling Uncovered*. A-List Publishing, 2003.
6. Kaspersky, K. *Hacker Debugging Uncovered*. A-List Publishing, 2005.

Internet Resources

1. The Art of Disassembly from Reversing Engineering Network (**http://www.reverse-engineering.net/**) — the Bible of the disassembly.
2. Open Reverse Code Engineering Community Web site (**http://www.openrce.org**).

3. Introduction to Reverse Engineering Software by Mike Perry and Nasko Oskov (**http://www.acm.uiuc.edu/sigmil/RevEng/**)

4. Reverse Engineering Team Web site (**http://www.reteam.org/**)

5. **www.phrack.org** — the best e-zine available, contains lots of articles, including the ones focusing on stack overflow.

6. Revenge — a site dedicated to reverse engineering and decompiling (**http://revenge.berlios.de/**)

7. Journal for Software Engineering, Virus-Research, Software-Protection, and Reverse Code Engineering (**http://www.codebreakers-journal.com/**)

Appendix 3: CD Contents

The CD contents are divided into directories, with each directory corresponding to the appropriate chapter or application. Each directory, in turn, is divided into subdirectories that store the source code of all practical examplex provided in this book.

Listings providing the source code of programs are stored as full projects so that they can be immediately loaded and compiled in an appropriate programming environment (for example, Visual C++ or Borland C++). For each program, there also is a ready-to-use executable module. This relates to the Assembly programs, for which the MASM32 translator is used. Other listings are ASCII files.

Each subdirectory also contains a read.me file in the ASCII format that provides a brief description of the listing included and a reference to the corresponding listing inside the book.

Index